Contents

Contents

Contents

REAL ESTATE DEVELOPMENT

URBAN PLANNING

Contents

Contents

The Future of the Architect
Mark Wigley, dean

Education is all about trust. The best teachers embrace the future by trusting the student, supporting the growth of something that cannot be seen yet, an emergent sensibility that cannot be judged by contemporary standards. A school dedicated to the unique life and impact of the thoughtful architect must foster a way of thinking that draws on everything that is known in order to jump into the unknown, trusting the formulations of the next generation that by definition defy the logic of the present. Education becomes a form of optimism that gives our field a future by trusting the students to see, think and do things we cannot.

This kind of optimism is crucial at a school like the GSAPP at Columbia. The students arrive in New York City from around 55 different countries armed with an endless thirst for experimentation. It is not enough for us to give each of them expertise in the current state-of-the-art in architecture so that they can decisively assert themselves around the world by producing remarkable buildings, plans and policies. We also have to give them the capacity to change the field itself, to completely redefine the state-of-the-art. More than simply training architects how to design brilliantly, we redesign the figure of the architect. Columbia's leadership role is to act as a laboratory for testing new ideas about the possible roles of designers in a global society. The goal is not a certain kind of architecture but a certain evolution in architectural intelligence.

Architecture is a set of endlessly absorbing questions for our society rather than a set of clearly defined objects with particular effects. Architects are public intellectuals, crafting forms that allow others to see the world differently and perhaps to live differently. The real gift of the best architects is to produce a kind of hesitation in the routines of contemporary life, an opening in which new potentials are offered—new patterns, rhythms, moods, sensations, pleasures, connections and perceptions. The architect's buildings are placed in the city like the books of a thoughtful novelist might be placed in a newsstand in a railway station, embedding the possibility of a rewarding detour amongst all the routines, a seemingly minor detour that might ultimately change the meaning of everything else. The architect crafts an invitation to think and act differently.

GSAPP likewise cultivates an invitation for all the disciplines devoted to the built environment to think differently. Its unique mission is to move beyond the highest level of professional training to open a creative space within which the disciplines can rethink themselves, a space of speculation, experimentation and analysis that allows the field to detour away from its default settings in order to find new settings, new forms of professional, scholarly, technical and ethical practice.

The heart of this open-ended laboratory is the design studios. All the overlapping and interacting programs at the school—Architecture, Urban Design, Historic Preservation, Urban Planning and Real Estate Development—teach design and are united in their commitment to the global evolution of the 21st century city. Every semester, the school launches more than 35 explorative studio projects that head off in different directions before reporting back their findings in juries, exhibitions and publications that stimulate an intense debate and trigger a new round of experiments. With a biodiversity of continually evolving research trajectories, the school operates as a multi-disciplinary think tank, an intelligent organism thinking its way through the uncertain future of the discipline and the global society it serves.

As in any other architecture school, the real work is done in the middle of the night. Avery Hall, the school's neo-classical home since 1912—with its starkly defined symmetrical proportions communicating to the world the old belief that the secret of architectural quality is known, universal and endlessly repeatable—now acts as the late night incubator of a diversity of possible futures. At its base is Avery Library, the most celebrated architectural collection in the world, a remarkable container of everything architects have been thinking about in the past, neatly gathered within the traditional quiet space of a well organized archive. Up above are the dense and chaotic studio spaces bristling with electronics and new ideas. Somewhere between the carefully catalogued past and the buzz of the as yet unclassifiable future, the discipline evolves while everyone else sleeps. Having been continuously radiated by an overwhelming array of classes and waves of visiting speakers, symposia, workshops, exhibitions and debates, the students artfully rework the expectations of their discipline.

The pervasive atmosphere at GSAPP, the magic in the air from the espresso bar to the pin-up walls to the front steps to the back corner of the big lecture hall, is the feeling of being on the cutting edge, straddling the moving border between the known and the unknown in our field. It is hopefully an open questioning atmosphere in which students are able to do work that teaches their teachers. In the end, a school's most precious gift is its generosity towards the thoughts that the next generation has yet to have.

Editor's Statement
Scott Marble, editor

The legacy of schools like the GSAPP are defined by the people who step in for a given period of time to lead and establish a direction that inspires faculty and students to do their best work. This can result in a lasting imprint on the future of the school, on architectural education and on the many professions that address the built environment. This edition of Abstract marks an important juncture in the evolution of the GSAPP. After ten years of leading the school, Mark Wigley announced he would step down as Dean following the 2013/2014 academic year.

In the first issue of Abstract under Mark's leadership, he wrote a Dean's Statement in the form of a short manifesto, "The Future of the Architect," that outlined a new direction for the school. When preparing the content for subsequent each issue of Abstract, we would discuss whether the statement should change, but he never waivered from this initial vision. In a school that was growing and expanding in its ambitions each year often in seemingly uncontrollable ways, this statement served as a point of reference to measure the progress of the school each year.

The sheer increase in size and content of Abstract from the first issue to the current is a reflection of the growth of the school under Mark's leadership. The development of initiatives like the Global StudioX network, the Critical, Curatorial + Conceptual Practices program, the many Research Labs and Centers and the Industry Sponsored Flagship Projects have added entirely new areas of study and resources to the school. The Global StudioX network has become a vital part of the school giving faculty and students a home base for conferences, exhibitions, lectures and classes in cities around the world. This is unique among architecture schools and has firmly established the GSAPP as a leader in a type of global outreach that deeply engages with host cities to benefit both the school and the local culture. The research labs have given faculty members a framework to conduct specialized projects that extends the work from studios and seminars into ongoing inquiries. These labs have also served as a link between the professional practice of many faculty members and their academic work. With the addition of the Critical, Curatorial + Conceptual Practices program, the GSAPP added to its already comprehensive programs of study. The CCCP program developed from an expanded definition of architectural practice and the non-traditional career paths around criticism, publishing, curating and

exhibiting that many GSAPP students pursue. Through the
Flagship Projects, unprecedented partnerships were created
with the DESTE Foundation for Contemporary Art, Oldcas-
tle Building Envelop and Audi of America, among others.
These partnerships gave students direct access to outside
institutions and industry innovators that resulted in local
and international conferences and exhibitions, numerous
publications and sustained research projects at the school.

 These are just some of the accomplishments of the
school that we have tracked in the pages of Abstract over
the past decade. What is only indirectly apparent in these
pages is the generous support and encouragement that Mark
gave to each individual faculty member, and the amount
of optimism and confidence that he had in the students to
propose ideas and create designs that far exceeded our
expectations. It is our hope that this final Abstract during
Mark's tenure as Dean captures the results of the wide-open
experiment that was envisioned, cultivated and realized at
the GSAPP under his leadership. On behalf of Mark, we hope
that it also helps to set the stage for the next Dean to build
on this experiment and take the school to a new place.

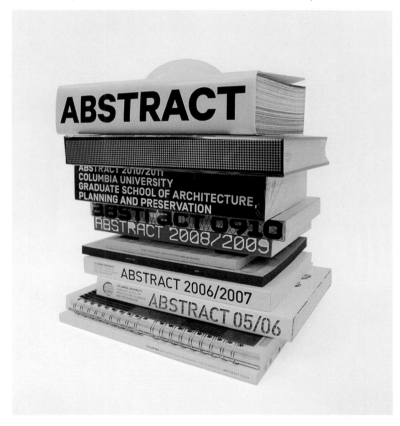

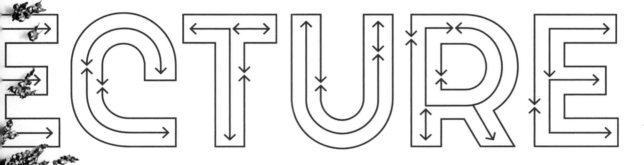

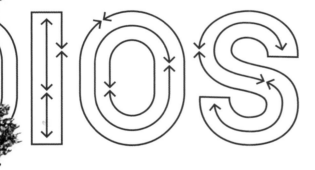

Core Architecture Studios
Michael Bell, director

The three-semester Core Studio sequence develops a capacity to work with skill and invention at all levels of architectural design. Studio methods vary with each of the design critics, but there is a common desire to re-think architectural and urban problems at each phase of developing a project. Explorations include new organizations of building processes, new systems of manufacturing and construction and new considerations of use and programming. In recent years, the programming aspects of the studios have become a focus of invention, and this year both Core 1 and 2 focused on complex program intensive projects — addressing highly defined programs in Core 1 and giving specificity to what was termed "generic" programs in the Core 2.

The Core Studios are taught by a group of faculty who collectively guide each of the twenty studio sections that constitute the three semesters of the Core Studio sequence. Each semester the Core Studios were coordinated by an individual faculty member who leads the group of six to eight design studios.

Students and faculty work within emergent forms of contemporary and historic New York urban life. Focused on sites in the city, the studios seek to understand the texture and public nature of their work and to understand and respond to the complexity and diversity of New York constituencies. Employing an array of both local and global data sets; an analysis of historic urban form, and projecting the potentials of new programming and redevelopment issues that are re-shaping the city, the studios also aggressively coordinate work in new means of fabrication, tectonics and structure. Each faculty member offers a unique form of exploring these issues as a network of design potentials that are understood to be sustaining, but also re-defining the role of the architect.

As a whole, the Core is coordinated to give parallel structure to the studios. The first two semesters consider the conceptual implications of architectural space as a form of speculative research. Core 1 and Core 2 consist of a semester-long project divided into distinct phases and exercises that fold into the development of an architectural proposal for an urban site. With each phase of the project, emphasis is placed on synthetic design processes that rigorously address issues of site and program on both conceptual and practical levels. The third and final semester of the Core Studio sequence is focused on the design of urban housing. Students work in teams of two to carry each project to a high level of resolution in terms of materials, details and ultimately in response to social needs and political realities. While the studio sites are within metropolitan New York, the studio is equally based on a renewed analysis of the history of housing policies both in the New York and in the wider United States. Students are asked to bring the analytical expertise of the first two semesters to these issues and to create a project that addresses a full spectrum of concerns from the immediate detail to the larger urban and political consequences of design.

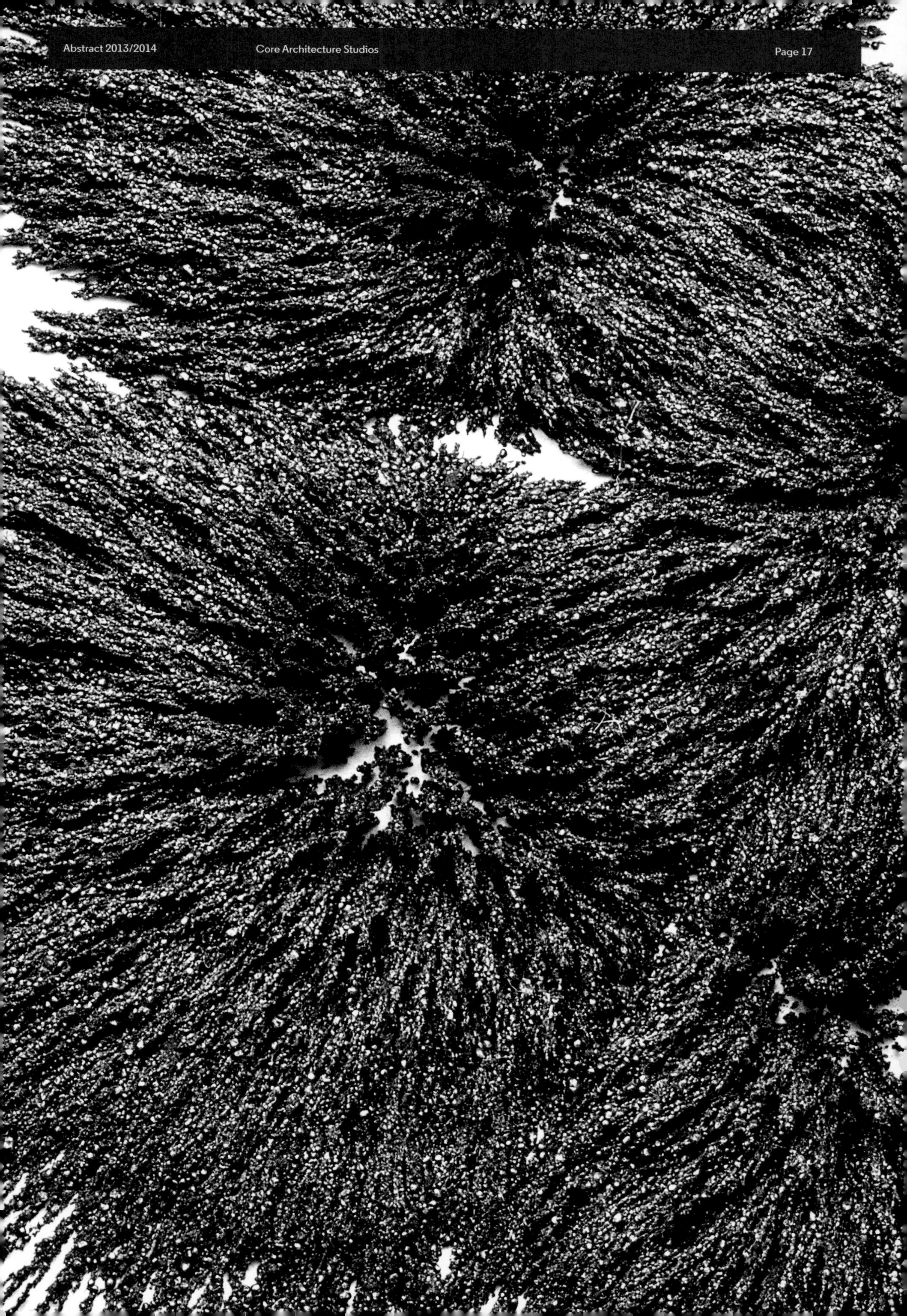

HYDROLOGIC
Core Architecture Studio 1
Fall 2013
*Galia Solomonoff, coordinator +
critic, Pep Aviles, Marta Cal-
deira, Janette Kim, Cristoph A.
Kumpusch, Mark Rakatansky,
Paula Tomisaki + Joshua Uhl,
critics, with Juan Pablo Azares*

Core 1 consisted of three interrelated briefs. Each brief asked for action, control, measurement and representation while challenging relationships between objects, bodies, space and the city.

Brief I – Shell: The brief asked students to observe, scan, draw and measure a seashell as geometric organism and in terms of its performance as shelter for the slug. Color, shape and geometry were seen as resultants of processes rather than mere forms. (1 week)

Brief II – Public Bathroom: The brief called for the design of a bathroom in a public park and considered how it would work and signal use to the public through form. The interdependence of form and performance were crucial and understood as universal in the case of the public bathroom. (2 weeks)

Brief III – Natatorium + Auditorium: The brief called for the design of a swimming pool and an auditorium in a public housing building and for public use. Water, community, street and city were intricately linked. The site was the New York City Housing Authority superblock – 100 to 104 Streets and Manhattan to Columbus Avenues. In resolving the natatorium and changing rooms as

well as auditorium and café, the categories of public-private and individual-collective were thoroughly discussed. (9 weeks)

The studio's desire was to expand the common language of architectural thought, understand its research and propositional modes and convey a clear sense of massing properties through various modes of representation. Through drawing, a shared architectural language emerged, which allowed students to formulate individual expressions of shape and thought. The aim was to transform ideas into elements present in the physical world, to explore findings, to resist preconceived notions and to structure relationships of space, content and form.

A

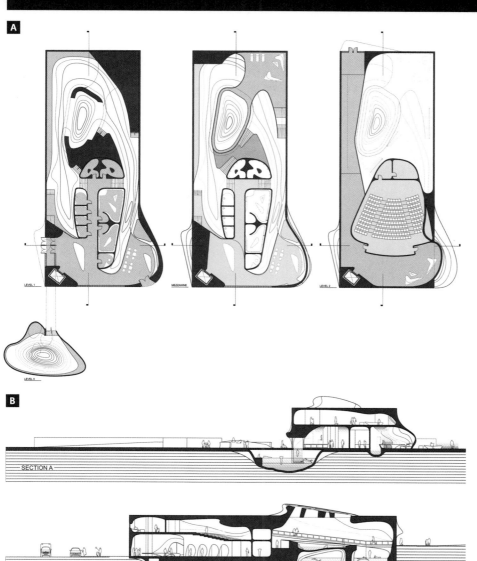

LEVEL 1   MEZZANINE   LEVEL 2

LEVEL B

HYDROLOGIC
Core Architecture Studio 1
Fall 2013
*Galia Solomonoff,
coordinator + critic*

Jesse Catalano **A/B**
Ren Wang **C/D**
Christopher James Botham **E**
Andrea Tonc **F/G**

B

SECTION A

SECTION B

C

D

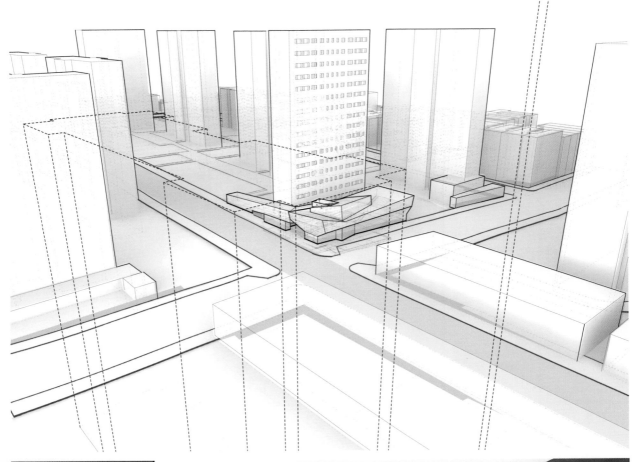

E

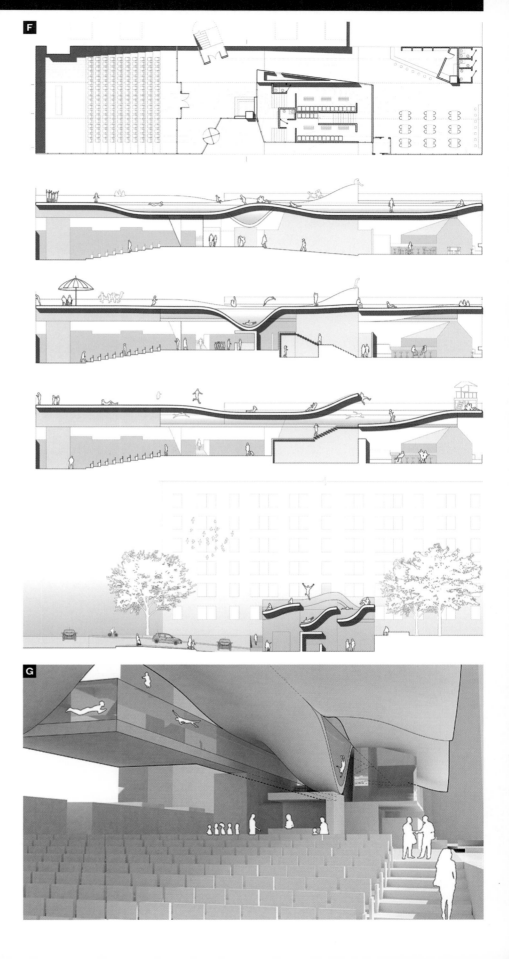

HYDROLOGIC
Core Architecture Studio 1
Fall 2013
Pep Aviles, critic

Emily E. Mohr A/B
Harrison Ratcliff C/D
Sharon Leung E/F

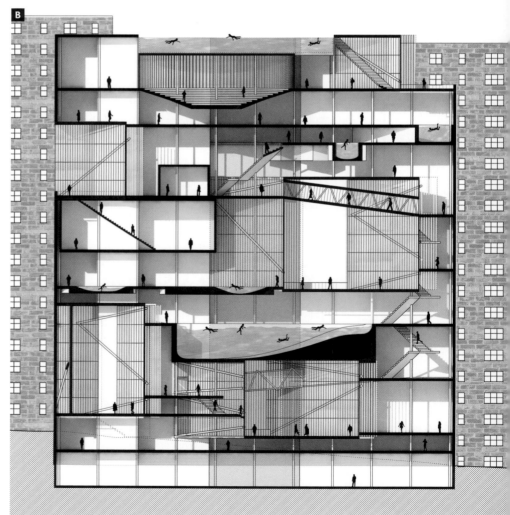

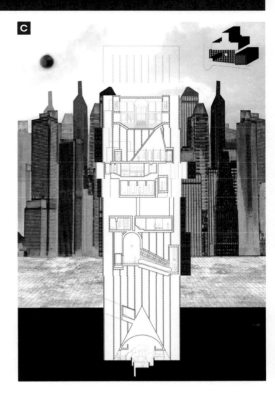

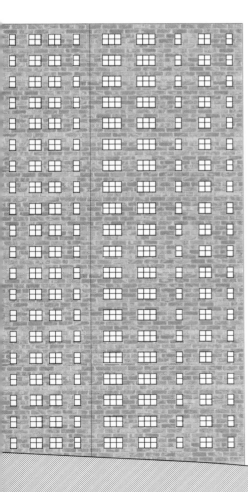

D

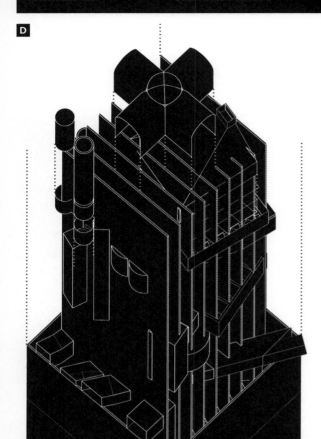

E

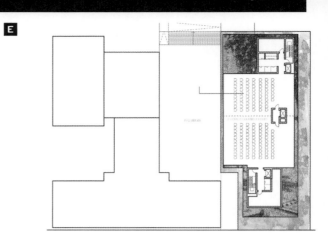

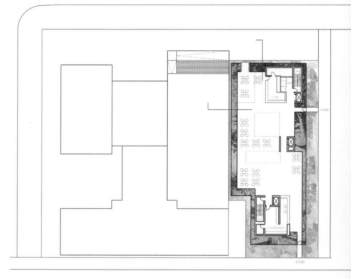

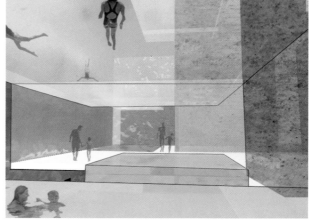

HYDROLOGIC
Core Architecture Studio 1
Fall 2013
Marta Caldeira, critic

Alessandra Calaguire **A/F**
Joann Feng **B/C**
Benjamin Hochberg **D/E**

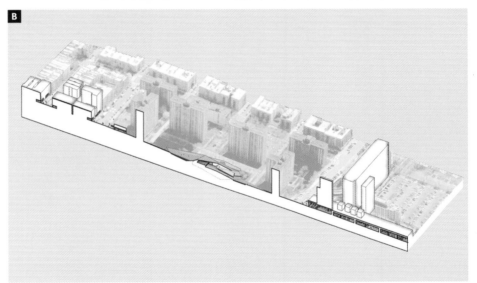

C

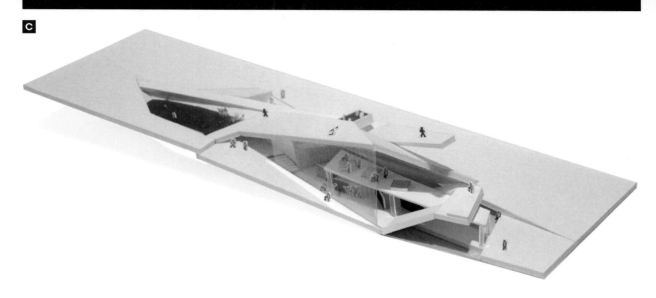

D

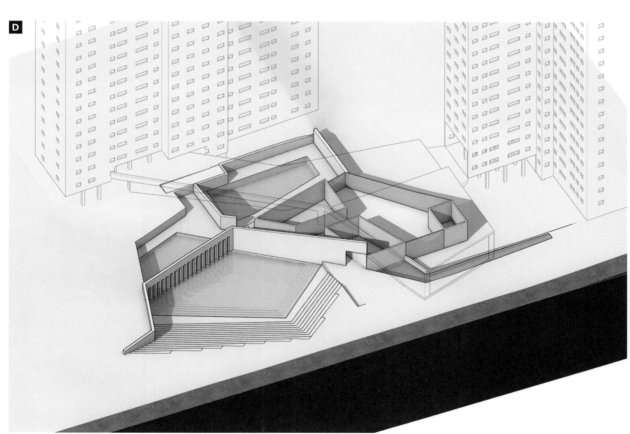

E

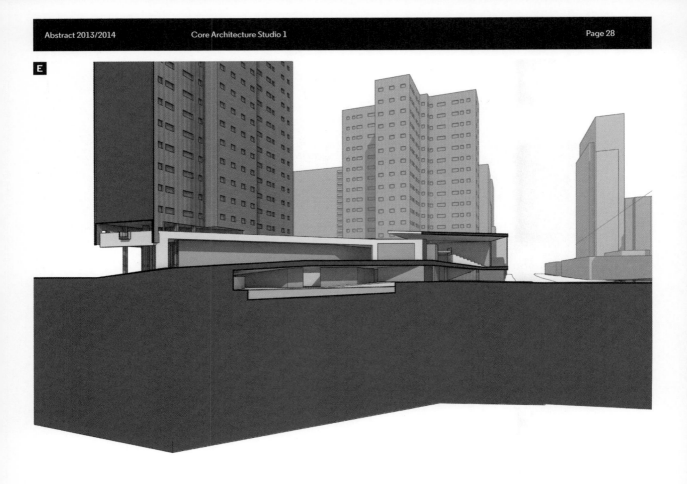

HYDROLOGIC
Core Architecture Studio 1
Fall 2013
Janette Kim, critic

Boyuan Jiang **A/B**
Jason Danforth **C/D/E/F**

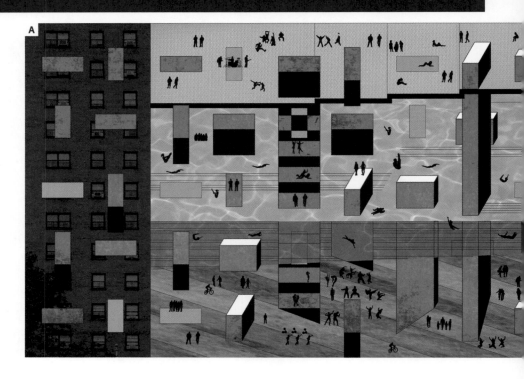

section BB   0   2   6   14 m

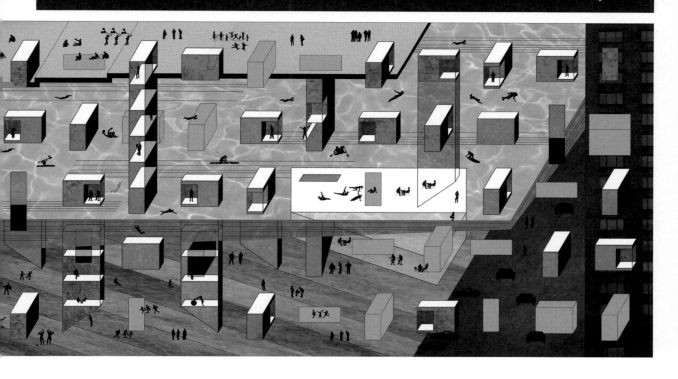

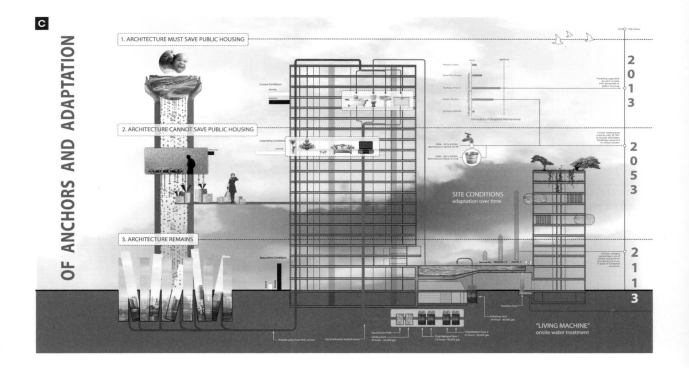

OF ANCHORS AND ADAPTATION

1. ARCHITECTURE MUST SAVE PUBLIC HOUSING

2. ARCHITECTURE CANNOT SAVE PUBLIC HOUSING

3. ARCHITECTURE REMAINS

SITE CONDITIONS
adaptation over time

"LIVING MACHINE"
onsite water treatment

2013

2053

2113
3

D

section : A
climate : ZONE 1

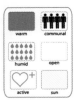

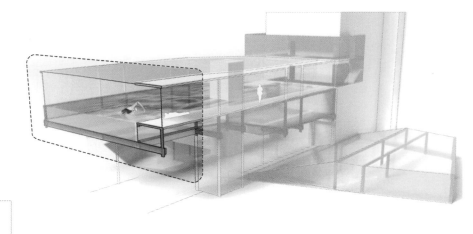

2053

90% Amenity : 10% Necessity　　　　program:　PRIVATE POOL

E

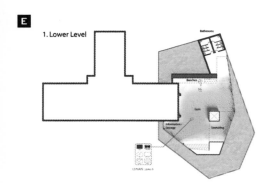

1. Lower Level

2. Site Level

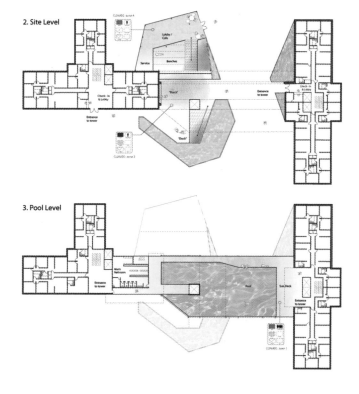

4. Top Level

3. Pool Level

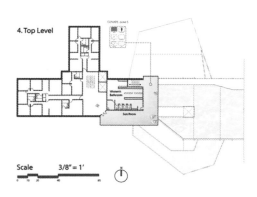

Scale　　3/8" = 1'

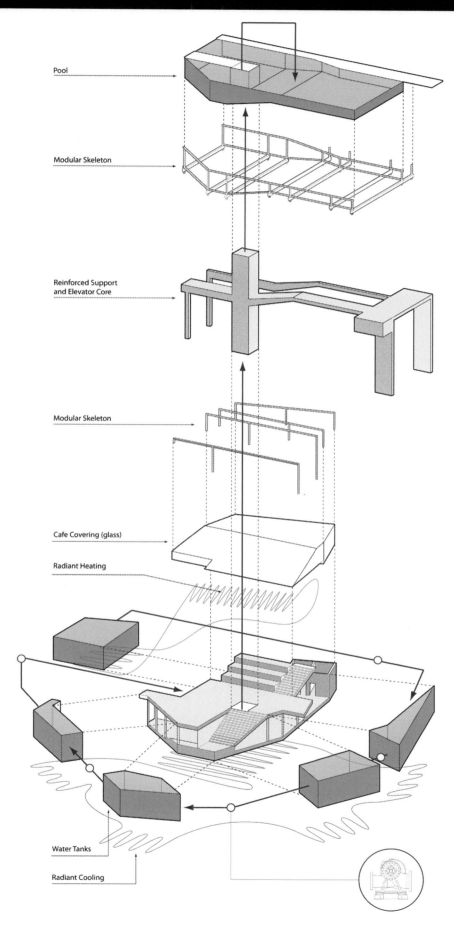

Pool

Modular Skeleton

Reinforced Support and Elevator Core

Modular Skeleton

Cafe Covering (glass)

Radiant Heating

Water Tanks

Radiant Cooling

HYDROLOGIC
Core Architecture Studio 1
Fall 2013
Cristoph A. Kumpusch, critic

Andras Balla **A/B/C**
Yuhong Du **D/E**
Ryan Day **F/G**

A

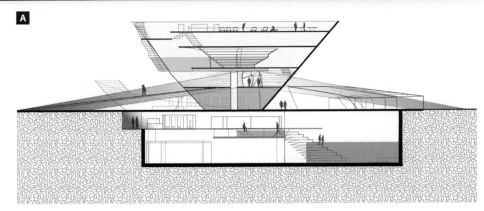

B

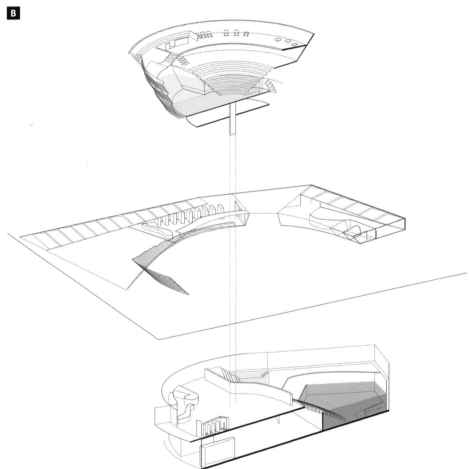

C

D

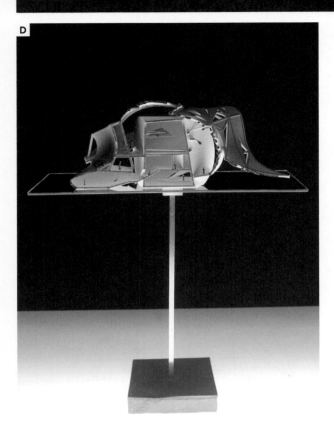

E

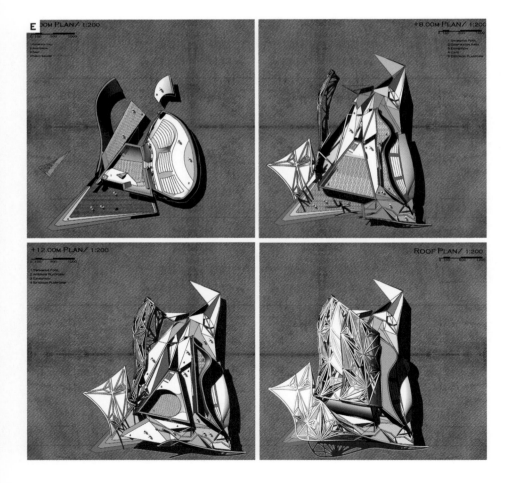

F

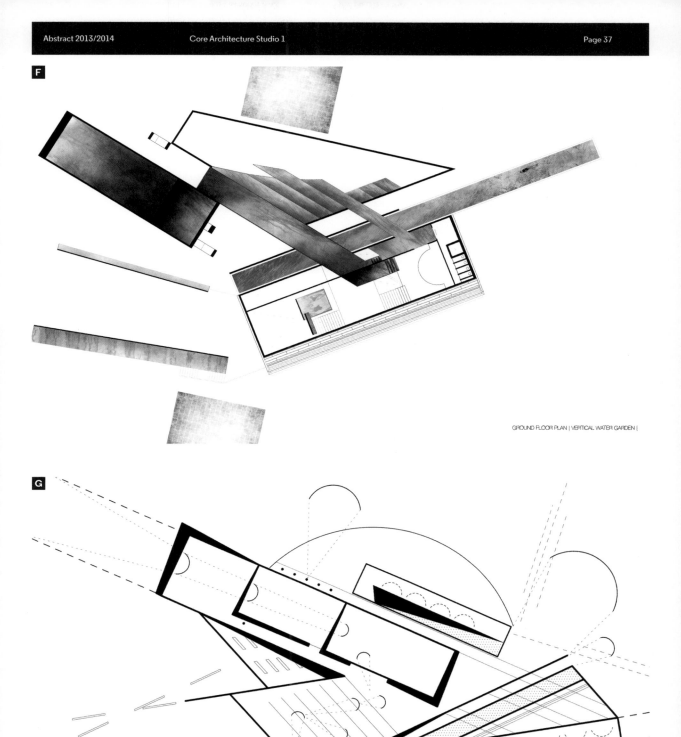

GROUND FLOOR PLAN | VERTICAL WATER GARDEN |

G

HYDROLOGIC
Core Architecture Studio 1
Fall 2013
Mark Rakatansky, critic

Seth Turner **A/B/C**
Jean Gu **D/E**
Nile Greenberg **F**

A

B

C

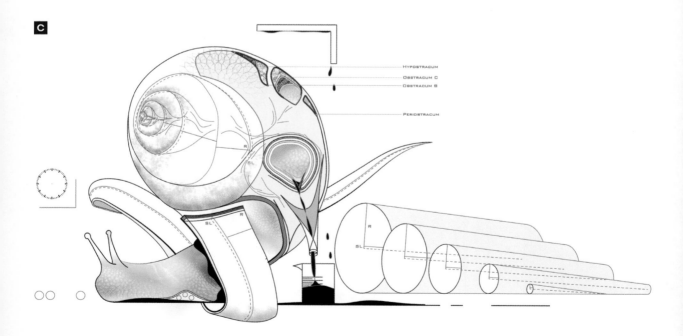

D

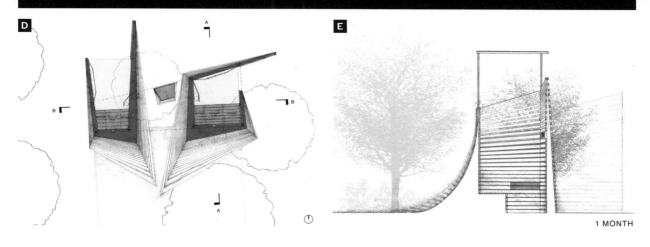

E

1 MONTH

2 YEARS

F

HYDROLOGIC
Core Architecture Studio 1
Fall 2013
Paula Tomisaki, critic

Alexandros Darsinos **A/B**
Bingyu Guan **C/D**
Yuchen Guo **E/F**

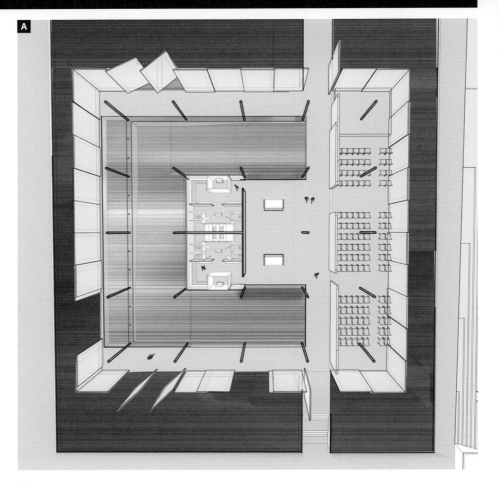

C

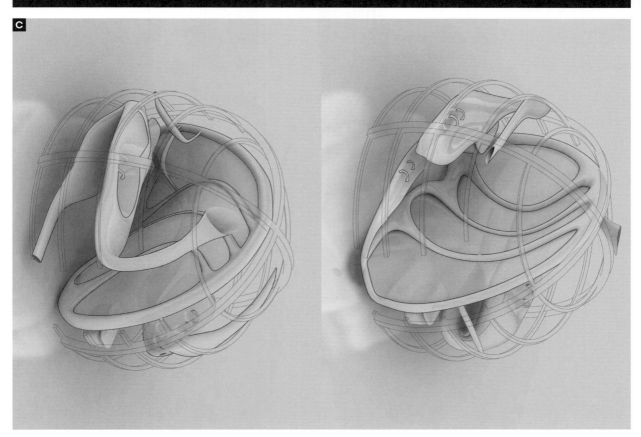

D

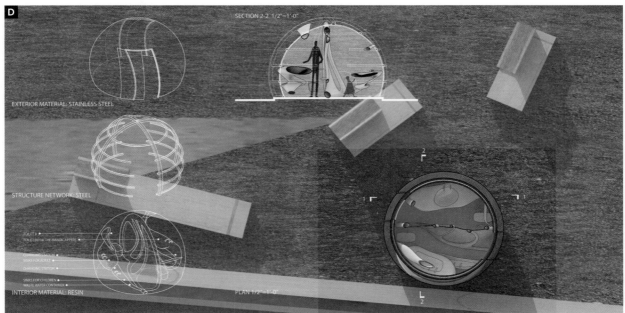

SECTION 2-2 1/2"=1'-0"

EXTERIOR MATERIAL: STAINLESS STEEL

STRUCTURE NETWORK: STEEL

TOILET A
TOILET FOR THE HANDICAPPED
CHANGING STATION
SINKS FOR ADULT
CHANGING STATION
SINKS FOR CHILDREN
WASTE WATER CONTAINER
INTERIOR MATERIAL: RESIN

PLAN 1/2"=1'-0"

E

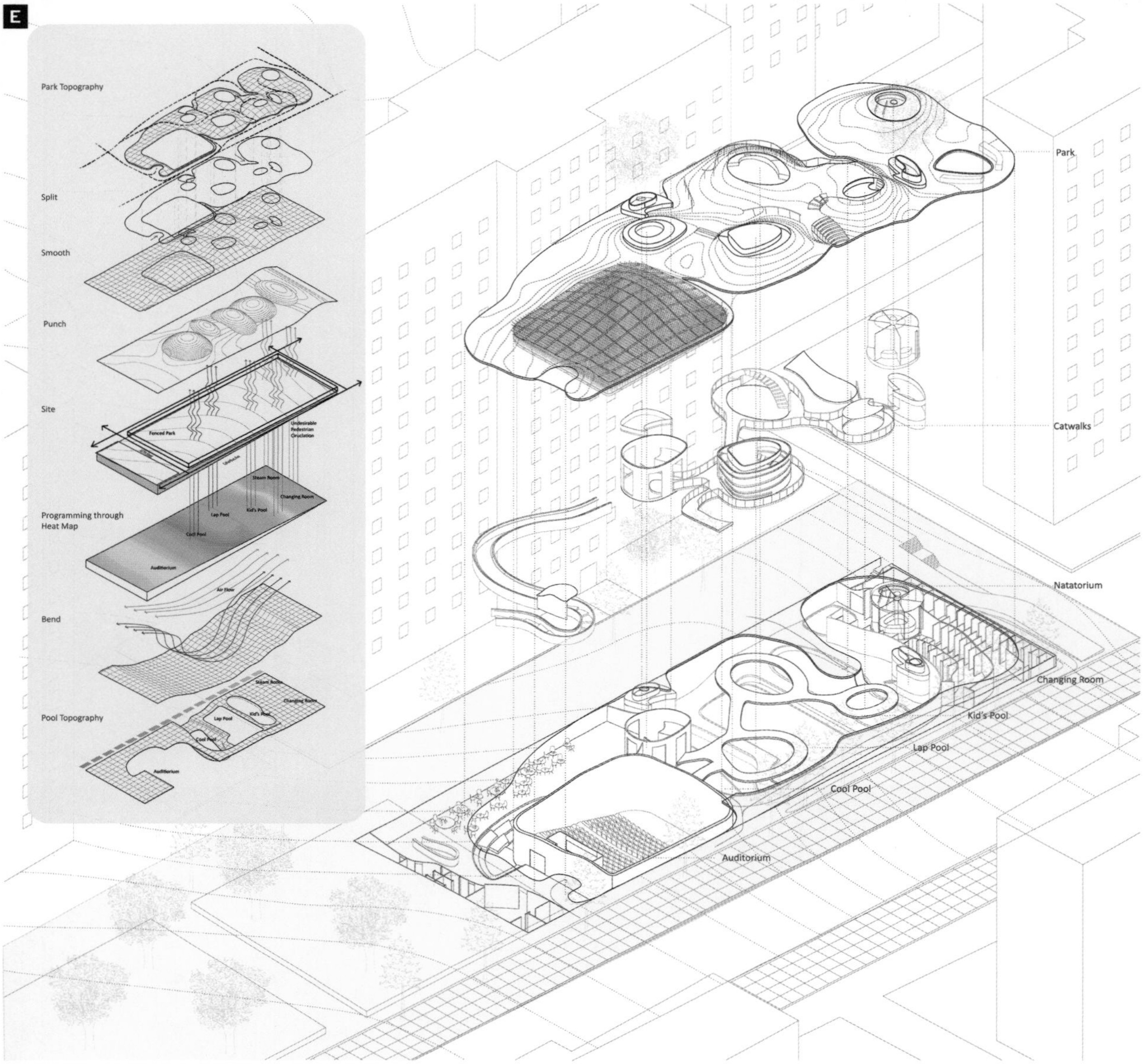

Park Topography

Split

Smooth

Punch

Site

Programming through
Heat Map

Bend

Pool Topography

Park

Catwalks

Natatorium

Changing Room

Kid's Pool

Lap Pool

Cool Pool

Auditorium

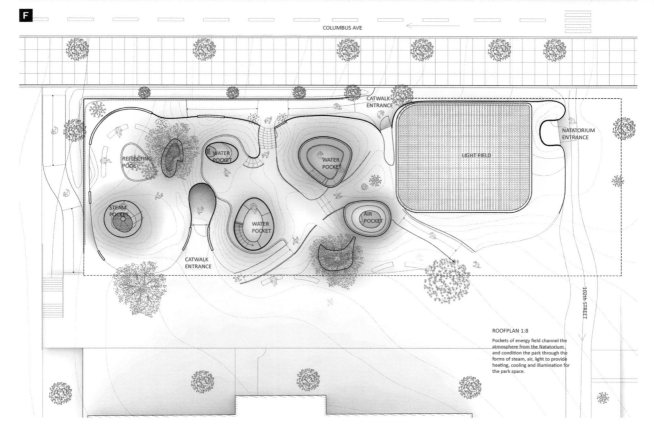

COLUMBUS AVE

CATWALK
ENTRANCE

NATATORIUM
ENTRANCE

REFLECTING
POOL

WATER
POCKET

WATER
POCKET

LIGHT FIELD

STEAM
POCKET

WATER
POCKET

AIR
POCKET

CATWALK
ENTRANCE

102th STREET

ROOFPLAN 1:8

Pockets of energy field channel the
atmosphere from the Natatorium
and condition the park through the
forms of steam, air, light to provide
heating, cooling and illumination for
the park space.

HYDROLOGIC
Core Architecture Studio 1
Fall 2013
Joshua Uhl, critic

Amanda Ortland **A/B**
Rachel Watson **C/D/E**
Eugene Chang **F**
Xiaoyu Wang **G**

B

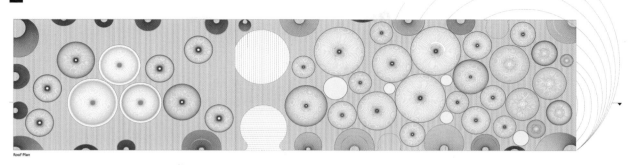

Roof Plan

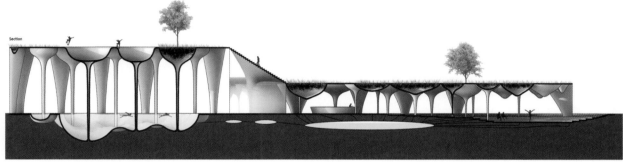

Section

C

D

E

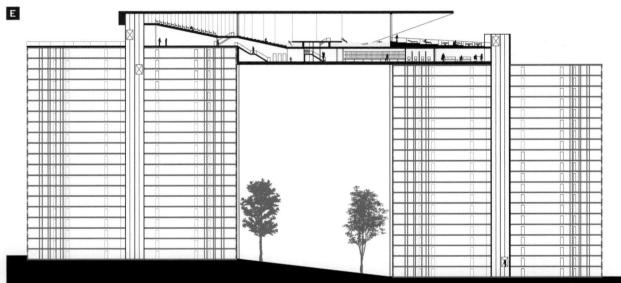

F

G

X Bank: The Bank +
the Workplace
Core Architecture Studio 2
Spring 2014
Amale Andraos,
coordinator + critic, with
Margaux Young

For this iteration of the X Bank, the studio moved beyond traditional representations of banks – as secure or transparent, awe-inspiring or accessible, elitist or populist, DIY or technological – to reveal the 'behind the scenes:' the work environments – whether physical or virtual – that constitute most of the banking space. As a type, headquarter bank buildings are office buildings with an expanded public lobby where most transactions occur. The space of representation is intensely focused on the ground floor lobby, art-filled public plaza and structure and surface of the façade. Inside, a thick crust of call-center type open offices, screens, conference rooms and glass clad executive offices become the 'true' representation of financial flows and transactions. It is this generic, banal everyday space that the studio re-examined, to turn the bank inside out. The studio questioned how the history of work environments parallels that of banks, and how technology continues to reshape physical spaces of interaction.

Located in the heart of the Brooklyn Tech Triangle, the studio built on current trends in the Tech industry and asked what the future of the work environment could hold and how this might impact the image of banking.

Boyuan Jiang **A**
Justin Lui **B/C**
Yuchen Guo **D/E/F**

section AA

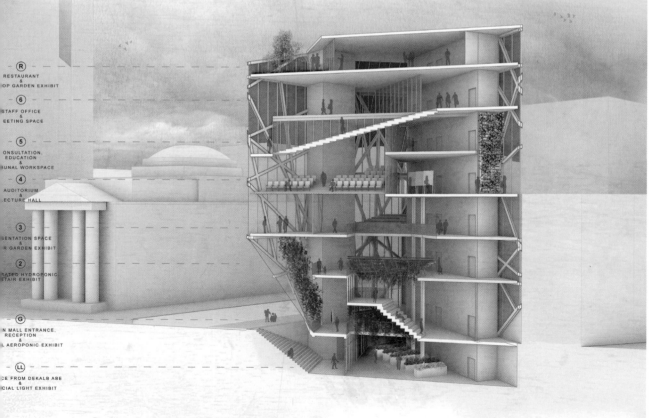

(R)
RESTAURANT
&
OP GARDEN EXHIBIT

(6)
STAFF OFFICE
&
EETING SPACE

(5)
ONSULTATION,
EDUCATION
&
IUNAL WORKSPACE

(4)
AUDITORIUM
&
ECTURE HALL

(3)
ENTATION SPACE
R GARDEN EXHIBIT

(2)
RATED HYDROPONIC
STAIR EXHIBIT

(G)
N MALL ENTRANCE,
RECEPTION
&
L AEROPONIC EXHIBIT

(LL)
CE FROM DEKALB ABE
CIAL LIGHT EXHIBIT

D

SECTION 1
CENTER
1:1/4

E

F

X Bank: "Capital (It Fails Us Now)"
Core Architecture Studio 2
Spring 2014
William A. Arbizu, critic

The twentieth century saw a shift in the perception of banks from stability to instability—bank retail outlets now appear and disappear as frequently as any endeavor subject to market pressures. Using images of "happy lifestyles," banks sugarcoat harsh mechanisms of self-interest that have brought them to the brink of insolvency.

Considering that the function of a bank at its most basic level is the aggregation and preservation of "something of value"—in order to leverage and increase said value—our 'X' Bank went beyond monies and currencies to explore architecture's role in the creation of space for disparate communities to coalesce around the services that a newly civic-minded bank might provide.

Our studio process conceived architecture as a way of imagining possible futures, a "bringing forth" as Martin Heidegger would put it. Prevailing social conditions can either be reified or challenged, making architecture a prime site for the proposition of new ideas. As Robert Hughes observed, "[t]he home of the utopian impulse was architecture rather than painting or sculpture...[B]uilding is the art we live in; it is the social art par excellence...It is also the one art nobody can escape."

For our studio, architecture was a verb, it does not symbolize, it creates, it "brings forth."

Christopher James Botham **A/B**
I-Hsuan Wang **C**
Jean Gu **D**
Maxwell Miller **E/F**

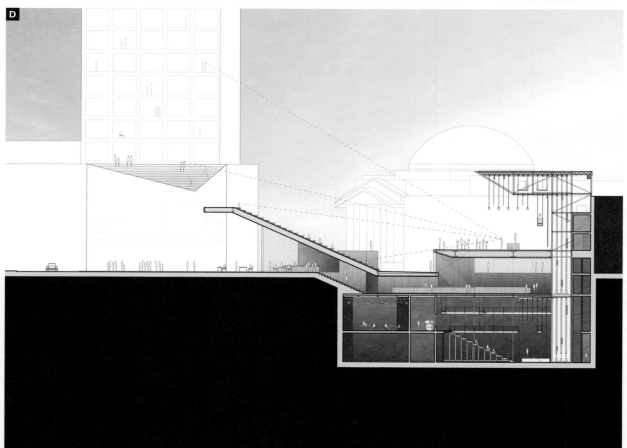

E

F

The Bank as Mining Colony
Core Architecture Studio 2
Spring 2014
Karel Klein, critic

This studio designed buildings for trading, storing and, most importantly, mining Bitcoins. There are many strange things about Bitcoin, but one thing in particular stands out: like gold, a Bitcoin has to be mined. However, we are not talking about digging for metals in the ground, but about server farms, sometimes vast server farms, decrypting numbers. Even though there is no central authority, once a Bitcoin is mined, a Bitcoin needs to be stored and sometimes traded. It was not that long ago when the globalization of money was celebrated as the culmination of civilization's push for universal exchange—something even better than a universal language. However, currencies still depend on centralized financial institutions to regulate and authenticate transactions. Questioning the necessity and the legitimacy of third party institutions, peer-to-peer currencies such as Bitcoin have now emerged posing difficult questions regarding the future of banks. Are banks losing their role as an institutionalized authority? Are there other reasons for banks to exist? Is it possible to have financial transactions without financial institutions? And if banks are mostly virtual, how are we to define their architectural counterparts? This studio explored the possibilities that these questions provoke.

Joann Feng **A/B**
Nile Greenberg **C/D**
Travis Heim **E/F**

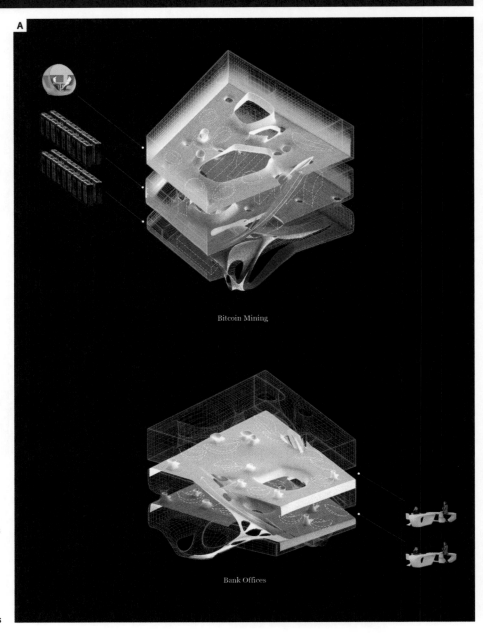

Bitcoin Mining

Bank Offices

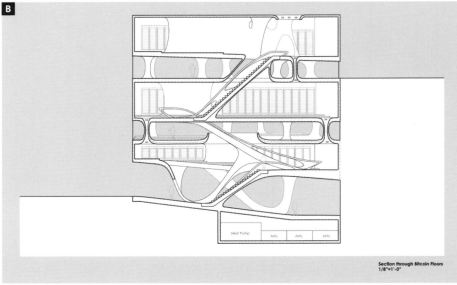

Section through Bitcoin Floors
1/8"=1'-0"

C

D

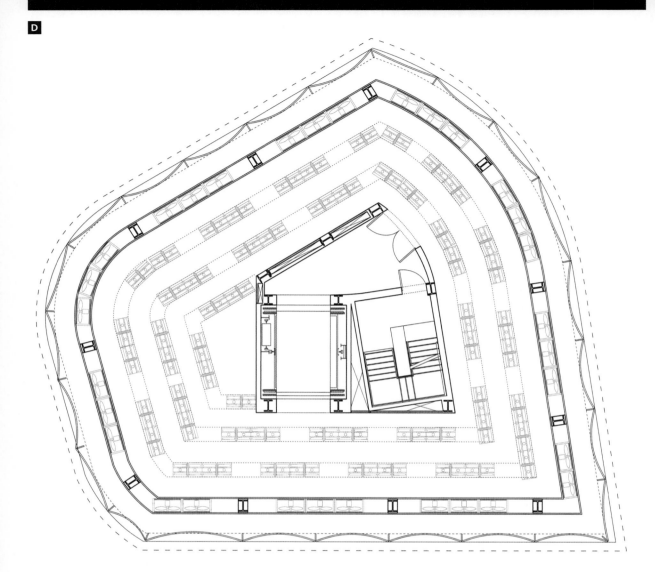

E

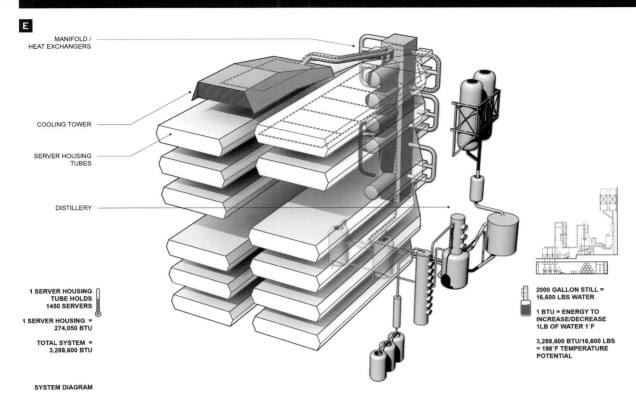

MANIFOLD /
HEAT EXCHANGERS

COOLING TOWER

SERVER HOUSING
TUBES

DISTILLERY

1 SERVER HOUSING
TUBE HOLDS
1450 SERVERS

1 SERVER HOUSING =
274,050 BTU

TOTAL SYSTEM =
3,288,600 BTU

2000 GALLON STILL =
16,600 LBS WATER

1 BTU = ENERGY TO
INCREASE/DECREASE
1LB OF WATER 1˚F

3,288,600 BTU/16,600 LBS
= 198˚F TEMPERATURE
POTENTIAL

SYSTEM DIAGRAM

F

BANKS - RE:invent the Type or the World?
Core Architecture Studio 2
Spring 2014
Cristoph A. Kumpusch, critic

From tech stocks to high gas prices, banks have engineered every major market manipulation since the Great Depression --- and they are about to do it again. The first thing you need to know about banks is that they are everywhere. The world's most powerful investment bank is a great vampire squid wrapped around the face of humanity, relentlessly jamming its blood funnel into anything that smells like money. In fact, the history of the recent financial crisis, which doubles as a history of the rapid decline and fall of the suddenly swindled dry American empire, reads like a Who's Who of investment bank graduates.

The bank's unprecedented reach and power have enabled it to turn all of America, and Europe, into a giant pump-and-dump scam, manipulating whole economic sectors for years at a time, moving the dice game as this or that market collapses and all the time gorging itself on the unseen costs that are breaking families everywhere: high gas prices, rising consumer credit rates, half-eaten pension funds, mass layoffs, future taxes to pay off bailouts. All that money that you are losing is going somewhere, and, in both a literal and a figurative sense, Banks are where it is going.

Alessandra Calaguire **A**
Guangbin Zhen **B/C**
Bingyu Guan **D/E**

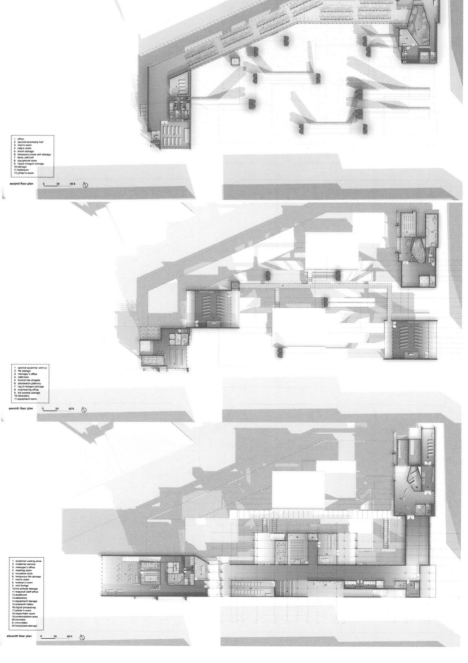

C

D

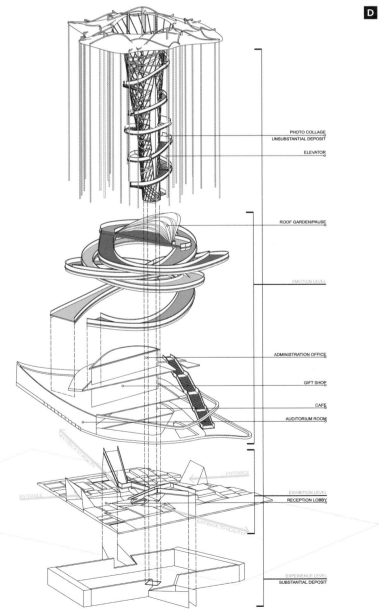

PHOTO COLLAGE
UNSUBSTANTIAL DEPOSIT

ELEVATOR

ROOF GARDEN/PAUSE

EMOTION LEVEL

ADMINISTRATION OFFICE

GIFT SHOP

CAFE

AUDITORIUM ROOM

ENTRANCE

EXHIBITION LEVEL
RECEPTION LOBBY

EXPERIENCE LEVEL
SUBSTANTIAL DEPOSIT

E

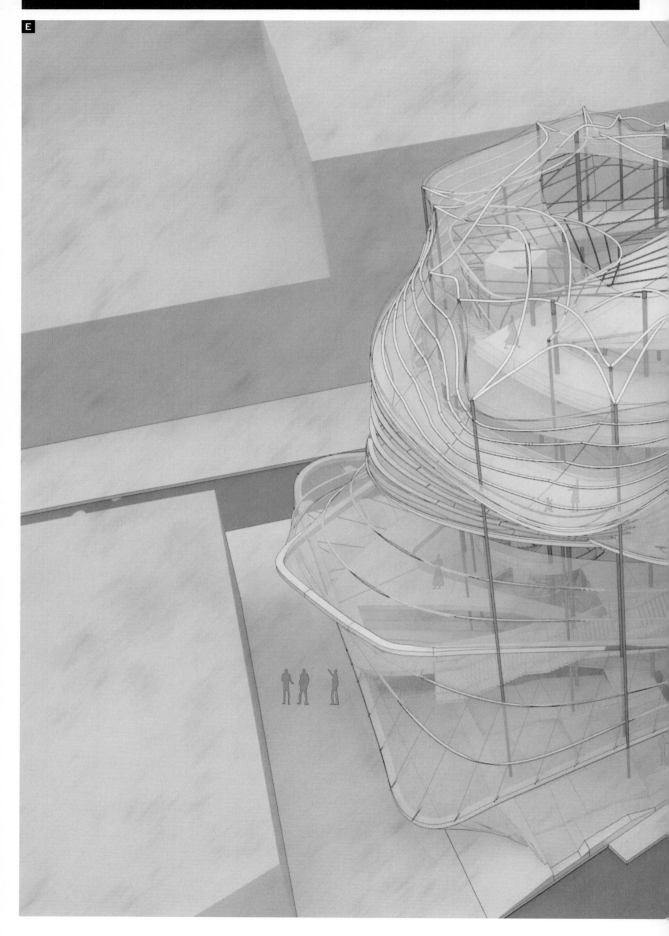

X-Ray Bank
Core Architecture Studio 2
Spring 2014
Mark Rakatansky, critic

Beyond simple transparency, X-rays and MRIs and CAT scans and PET scans are used to figure out and make figural the workings of the body, as well as those aspects that are not working well, those blockages and pathological parts and diseased areas. Imagine "scanning" the body of the bank to figure out its formal organization and make figural its workings and its not-workings. As architects we are supposed to have extra-human x-ray vision; like Superman, it seems we are able to leap up and look over and into buildings — in plan and in section and in perspective section and in 3-D modeling — in order to see how the interior programmatic, structural and infrastructure networks all work in relation to each other. This studio imagined providing that vision to everyone, so they too could see manifest in the building the structured and socialized spatial networks of the institutions with which we all engage everyday.

Andrea Tonc **A**
Mathew Dolan **B/C**
Zaw Lin Myat **D/E**

Perpetual Memory Bank
Core Architecture Studio 2
Spring 2014
*Karla Maria Rothstein,
critic, with Aya Maceda*

The archive is a form of banking, a system of recording and sorting, a method of deposit and retrieval and a place of occasional alchemic transformation.

Both memory and finance slip between material and immaterial significance—physical, worldly substances and ephemeral, shifting impressions of value. A Perpetual Memory Bank is a public repository, reflecting and projecting personal and civic consequence. It is an inconstant, non-denominational space of temporary storage, exchange and collective commemoration, where investments deal with traces and legacy.

Embedded in the public flux of the metropolis, projects navigated and re-shaped the present with an awareness of remembered pasts and a persistent drive for anticipated futures. Grounded in both conceptual and urban arguments, the proposals were tangible, spatial and material places, whose experience, like human memory, is fragmentary, incomplete and continually being re-written. The holdings of these banks act as a barometer, measuring and celebrating urban life, projecting forward and glancing backward at the same time.

Brendan Paul Vogt **A/B**
Harrison Nesbitt **C/D**
Rachel Watson **E/F**

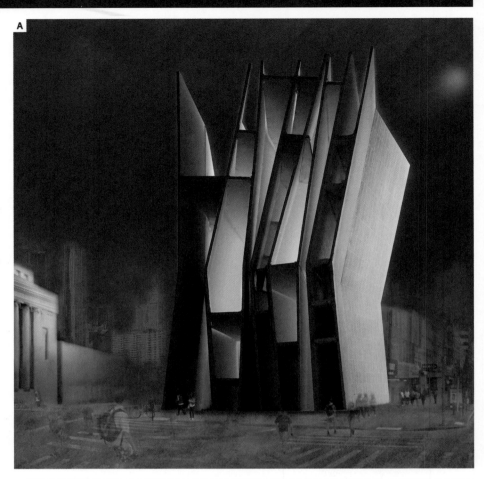

C

D

E

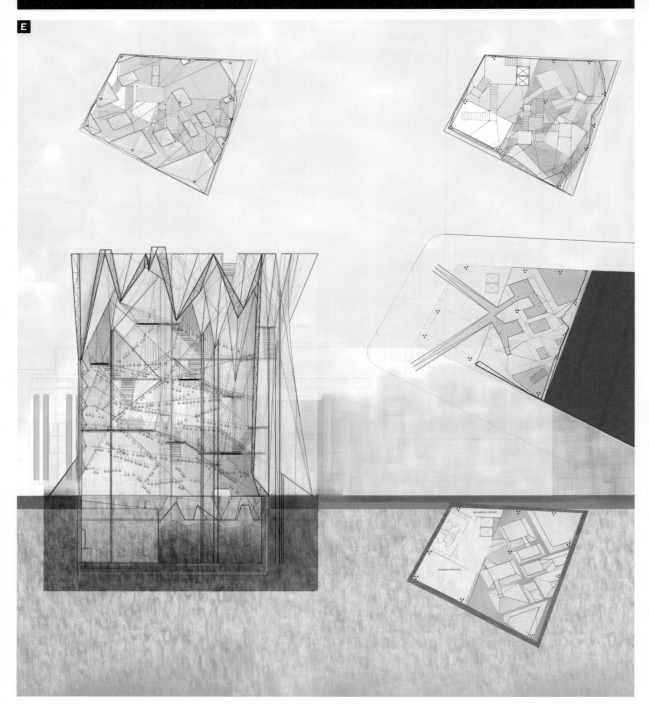

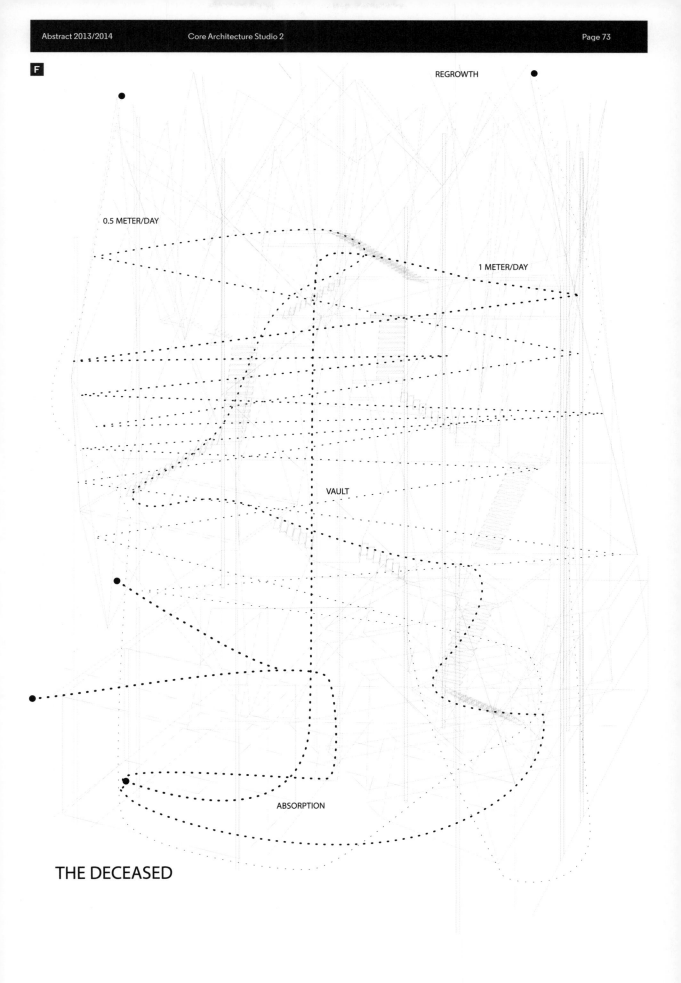

REGROWTH

0.5 METER/DAY

1 METER/DAY

VAULT

ABSORPTION

THE DECEASED

Non Profit Architecture
Core Architecture Studio 2
Spring 2014
Rafi Segal, critic

The studio called to explore the urban potential of this strategically located Brooklyn site. Before asking what a bank needs or what it could be, we asked: what can benefit the city? What does this part of the city desire? How can the urban context inform our project, and how can our project transform the site? In this studio, architecture was valued by its contribution to the city, as the architect gave expression to an idea of public good.

Angela Yang A
Britt Johnson B/C
Jesse Catalano D
Yu Wu E/F

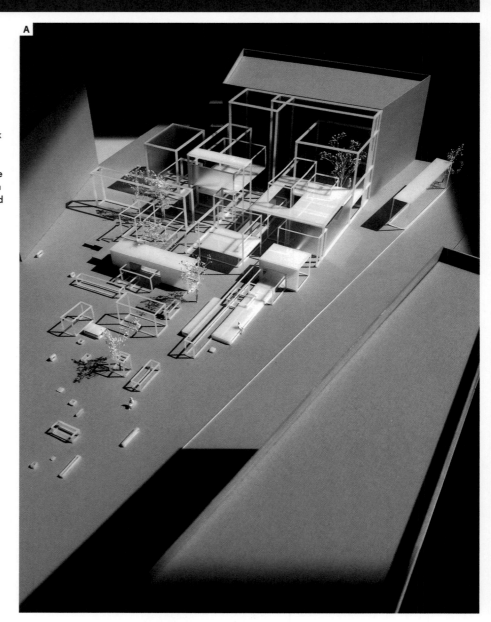

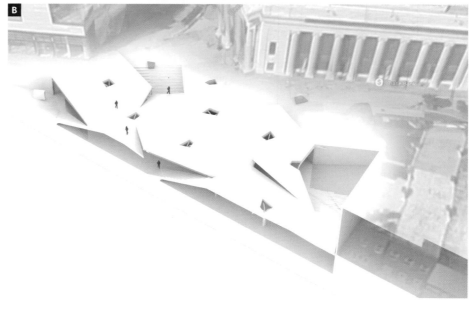

Vendor Storage

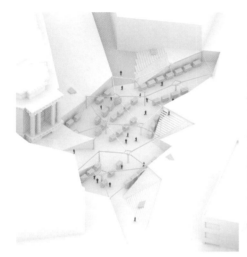

Market Place

Community Space

dataBANK
Core Architecture Studio 2
Spring 2014
*Mabel Wilson +
Brigette Borders, critics*

We no longer find ourselves dealing with the mass/individual pair. Individuals have become "dividuals," and masses, samples, data, markets, or "banks." Gilles Deleuze, Postscript on Societies of Control

The computerization of all facets of everyday life means that we produce large quantities of information. We create a trail of data through our most mundane acts—swiping our Metrocard, posting photographs on Facebook, searching Google, shopping with a credit card, filing our tax forms, giving blood at a lab, providing finger scans at the border and so on. The same terminology that was once reserved for banks—vaults, walls, breaches, master keys—is now common parlance for securing our virtual transactions and identities. In the United States most of us no longer manufacture goods; instead we produce data. And for some—businesses, investors, researchers and hackers—our data holds value. A new paradigm of banking—the dataBANK—creates an innovative institution that stores our biometric data and information, which include our personal memories, histories and other traces of our daily existence. If banks increasingly store more data, the studio investigated the new physical spaces that will need to be created that engender meaningful and productive social relations between banks and customers, information and users, the institution and its urban community.

Brian Galyean **A/B/C**
Lindsey Wikstrom **D/E**

A STRUCTURAL DIAGRAM_001

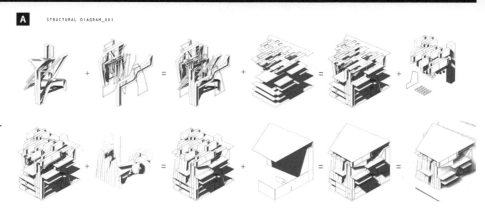

B SECTION_001 3/16"=1'

C PLAN_004 1/8"=1' N¨

09_MEMORY/DATA SUPPORT
13_FLOATING PODS

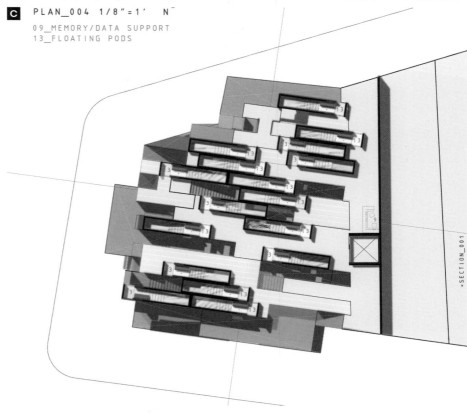

D

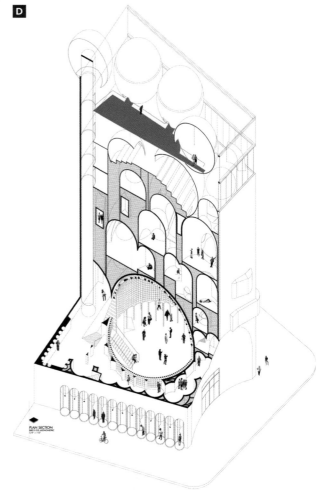

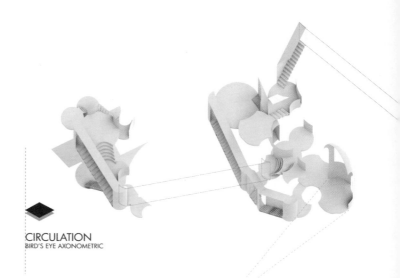

CIRCULATION
BIRD'S EYE AXONOMETRIC

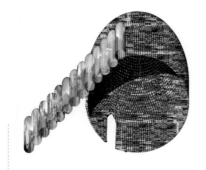

IMAGE
WORMS EYE AXONOMETRIC
INTERIORS

FRESH

TRENDING

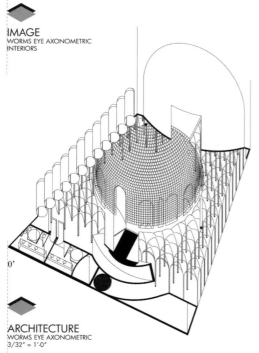

0'

ARCHITECTURE
WORMS EYE AXONOMETRIC
3/32" = 1'-0"

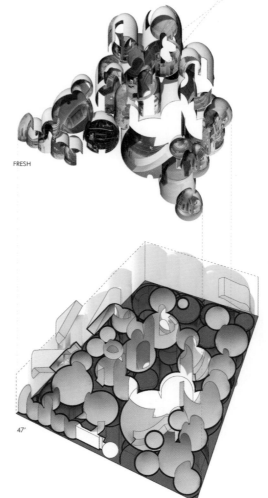

47'

64'

GALLERY

IMMERSIVE

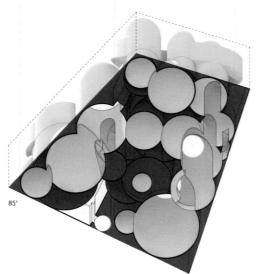

85'

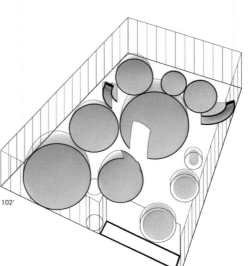

102'

**The Housing Studio:
Different States of Housing
Social through Form**
*Hilary Sample, coordinator +
critic, Eric Bunge, Ammr
Vandal, Charles Eldred,
Douglas Gauthier, Mario
Gooden, Robert Marino,
Rafi Segal, Ada Tolla +
Giuseppe Lignano, critics*

This year's studio focused on
the many different states of
housing that we, as architects,
typically encounter in practice.
Throughout the term, each
student examined the many
different states of housing-both
past and present-that are found
in the city, and, through team
projects, speculated on the
rich potential for contemporary
housing types in the city. The
focus of the studio was twofold:
research & analysis and design.
The first part of the studio
was framed around methods
of research and a preliminary
understanding of the context.
Each studio was introduced to
housing typologies, followed
by the site and program. The
studio project was to design a
high-density perimeter block.
Each of these projects was built
upon the other over the term.
In response to the precedent
assignment and urban site
study and program analysis,
the studio looked at the many
different states of housing in
the development of the main
studio site. The studio acted as
a laboratory for exploring new
urban possibilities for living
within East Harlem. Though the
brief put forward the perimeter
block housing type for the
given site, no type of housing
was off limits for exploration.

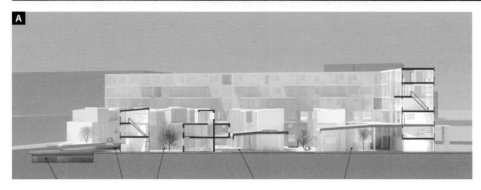

Stress + Wellness in Housing: Rethinking Social through Form
Core Architecture Studio 3
Fall 2013
Hilary Sample, coordinator + critic, with Richard Duff

This semester focused on the relationship between urban health and housing through the subject of stress. New York City has been at the forefront of new formal types of housing and new strategies for promoting public health. The studio consisted of three parts: acts, forms and ends. Acts meant that each student proactively questioned architecture's performance through structures and technologies. Forms indicated a straightforward demonstration of knowledge and understanding concepts of forms under different types of stress. Ends required that these studies produced end results that were critiqued and evaluated within a collective setting. In response to different forms of stress from the housing shortage in New York City urban social stress, the city's infrastructure becomes stressed including roads, bridges, highways, sewers, railroads, waterways and maintenance systems, which are all being stretched thinly to the point of failure. G. Robert LeRicolais, 1894-1977, examined the "beauty of failures" in structures. The studio began with the most basic and bodily, examining stress through structures and physics. Exploring everything from O.M. Ungers's IBA housing in Berlin to writings such as Alison Smithson's "Byelaws of Mental Health" set the framework for exploring "stress free zones."

Kyong Kim + Joan Kim **A/B/C**
Wade Cotton + Isabelle Kirkham-Lewitt **D/E/F**

C

D

E

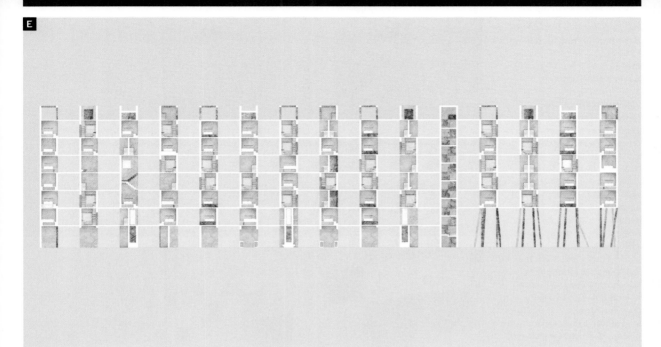

F

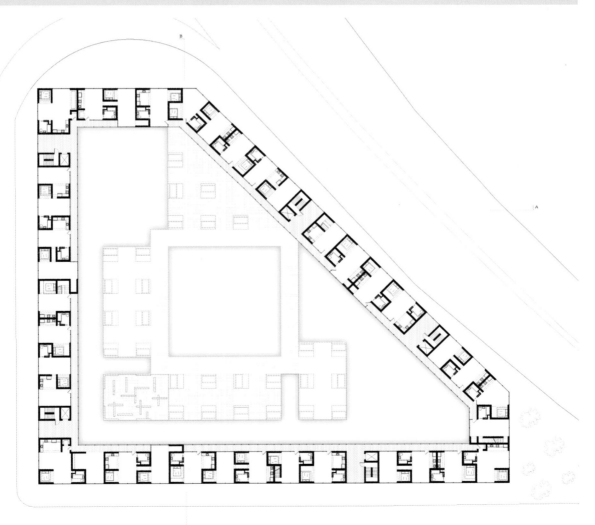

HOUSING co-DETERMINANTS
Core Architecture Studio 3
Fall 2013
Eric Bunge +
Ammr Vandal, critics

In housing design, performance, innovation and experience are constrained, or one could even say determined, by a series of decision-making frameworks. These emerge from a wide spectrum of considerations, including organization of circulation and distribution of services. As a result, housing design for many architects is a sort of combinatorial game or datascape.

Our studio section critically acknowledged housing design's game-like aspect, pursuing typological and formal innovation through an extreme prioritization of determinants. Each group selected one or two determinants that reframed other decision-making contexts. These included systems or elements that, through exaggeration, suppression or re-contextualization, have the capacity to provoke radical reformulations of housing design. In the spirit of the studio-wide emphasis on working at a spectrum of scales, these co-determinants connected the domestic scale of the unit to that of the collective.

Beyond serving merely as pedagogical framework, we consistently asked the question as to which determinants are relevant today and should, therefore, be exerting such unequal influence. To this end we considered broader philosophical and cultural goals that resonate with a healthier and more sustainable contemporary society – attuned to the needs of future demographics and to new possibilities for urban life.

Gawon Shin + Qiuli Qu **A/B/C**
Sukwon Lee + Cecil
Barnes **D/E/F**

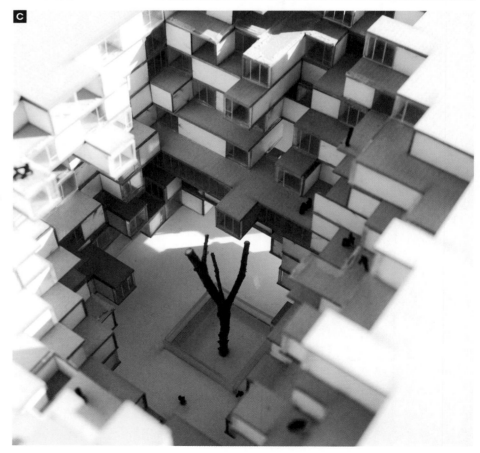

D

E

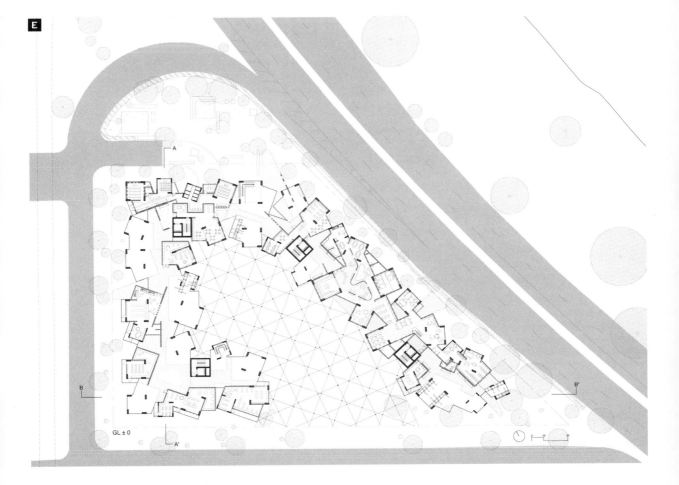

Where Does Value Live?
Core Architecture Studio 3
Fall 2013
Charles Eldred, critic

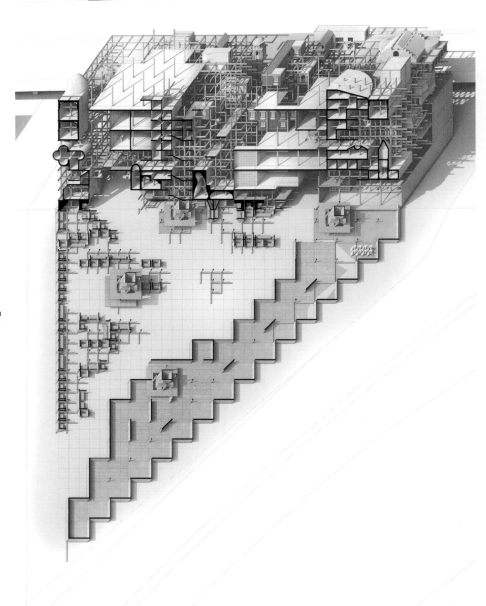

In his 1962 treatise "Supports: An Alternative to Mass Housing," John Habraken suggests that value might arise through the act of making your mark on your place and aligning your place with your person. He states, "Possession is inextricably connected with action. To possess something we have to take possession. We have to make it part of ourselves... Something becomes our possession because we make a sign on it, because we give it our name, or defile it, because it shows traces of our existence." For Habraken, possession would inscribe human agency into inhabitation in the face of mass housing. Habraken was reacting to the depersonalized, anti-urban housing projects of the 1905s and 1960s. Perhaps this formula remains equally valid in the context of the contemporary city, which grew out of the brutal, sometimes dehumanizing, competitions of a market economy.

Situated at the intersection of value and values, architecture participates in the intertwined negotiation between the desire for possession and the willingness – or ability – to pay for it. When one thing is chosen, what is left behind? What do we want as citizens, as consumers and as inhabitants? How can we be sure?

Carlo Bailey +
Lorenzo Villaggi **A/B**
Lily Wong + Michelle Tse **C/D**
Ricardo A. Leon +
Sucheta Nadig **E/F**

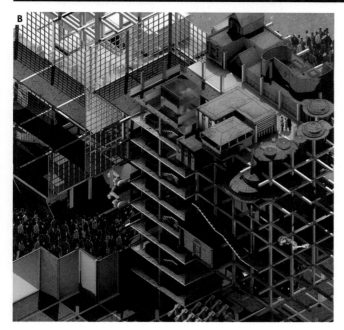

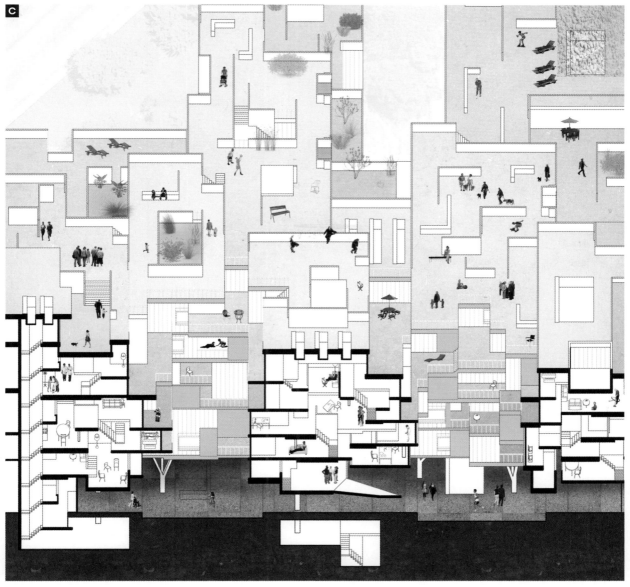

F

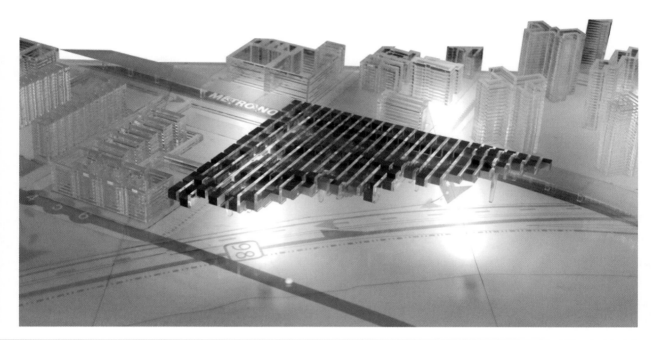

Housing
Core Architecture Studio 3
Fall 2013
Douglas Gauthier, critic

Housing in the near future will need to address changes in population; there will be more people, meaning denser urban neighborhoods, and broader age range as we start to live longer. Cities will need new housing types designed to support a variety of abilities and help urban residents not only maintain their independence but also participate in their communities. To support well being and longevity, the home environment will need to be programmed for exercise, accessibility and healthy levels of light, air quality, sound and temperature – ideally, with activity as part of the building's circulation.

Modernist utopias are easily editorialized into caricatures of efficiency of a minimalist ideal of low-income families consisting of thirty-year-old tri-athletes. Such a lifestyle of discipline and rigor, which caters and celebrates the material order and clarity of architecture, may add up to a luxury demanded by fashion in which form and circumstance relieve the burden of everyday decision-making. If decision fatigue is a measurable condition supported by data sets of entwined health and insurance industries, is not design's ability to define concepts of universality an opportunity to redefine housing for Claireece Precious Jones — a real public with greater need for choice and accessibility? The studio questioned the research value of addressing these oversimplified extremes as well as the potential of design to serve, refine and experiment with concepts and constituents of Universal Housing through spatial proposals distilled from non-intuitive efficiencies of both life and lifestyle.

Albert Franco +
Gear Puekpaiboon **A/B**
Ho-gyum Kim, Mimi Ho +
Louis Jin **C/D/E**

C

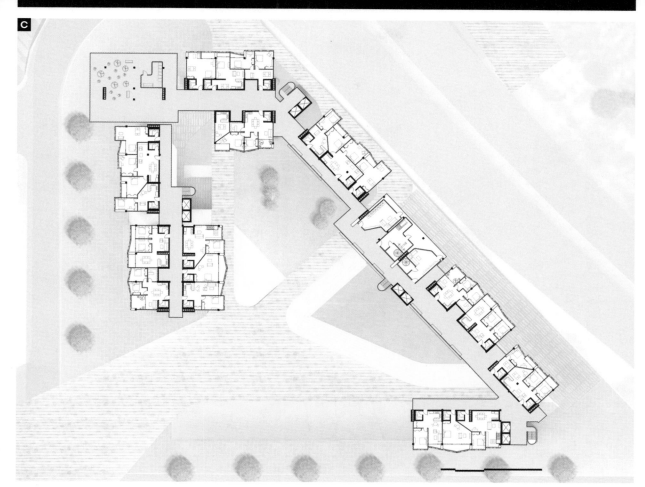

D

E

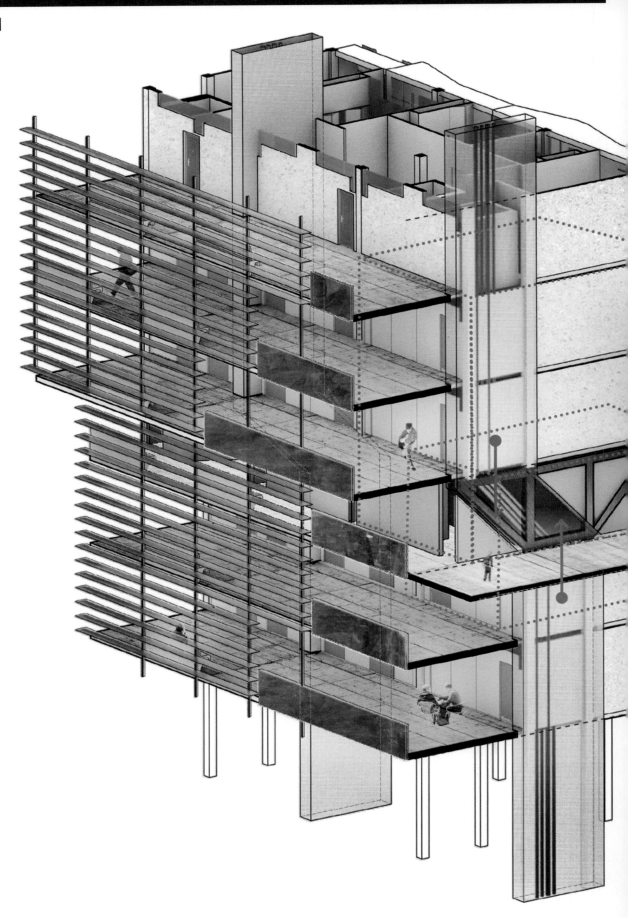

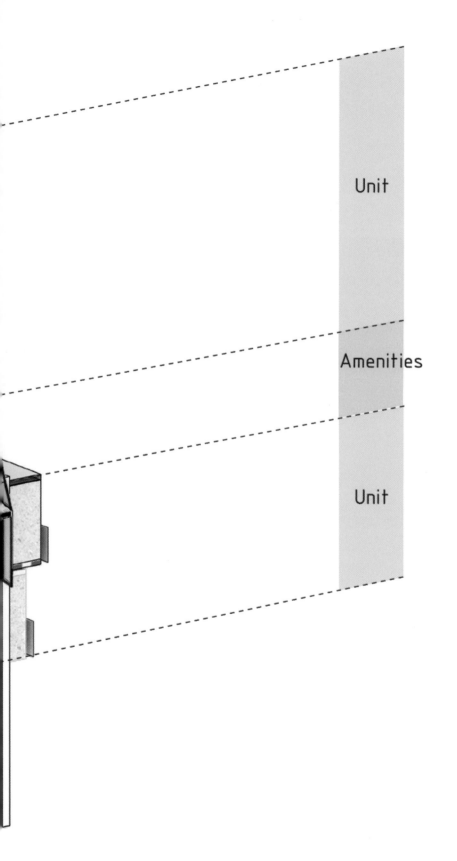

Housing
Core Architecture Studio 3
Fall 2013
*Mario Gooden, critic,
with Carson Smuts*

As Foucault illustrates in "Discipline and Punish: The Birth of the Prison," each process of modernization entails disturbing effects with regard to the power of the individual and the control of government. Foucault examines the ways that government claims control and enforcement of ever more private aspects of our lives. Recent controversies surrounding the National Security Administration data mining and collection attest to this claim, and the New York City Police Department's policy of Stop, Question and Frisk – predominantly among men of color and mostly in Harlem and East Harlem – is another example of the exertion of power by the government over private bodies. Additionally, Mayor Michael Bloomberg suggested that all 620,000 residents of New York City's public housing should be fingerprinted as a way of keeping criminals out of the buildings.

While walking in the city, the body is not simply surveyed, but the consuming eye engages an unconscious relationship between seeing and being watched. Within the domestic realm, the private body not only gazes toward the city or is affronted by the public eye through the window of the computer screen, but also, in the extreme, the public eye of government and police crash the physical threshold that separates privacy and publicity.

Hence, the studio questioned how the conditions of surveillance, space and power inform the discourse of housing and the body.

Ivy Hume + Xiaoxi
Chen Laurent **A/B/C**
Jeffrey Montes + Damaskene
Danae Vokolos **D**

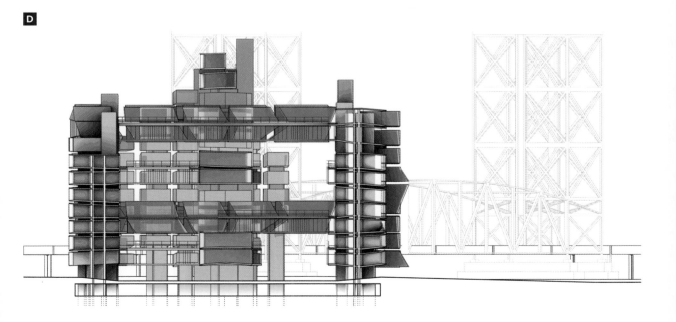

The Module vs. the Unit
Core Architecture Studio 3
Fall 2013
Robert Marino, critic

Prefabrication immediately forces the designer into confronting one of the most aesthetically powerful theoretical topics in the creation of housing. The pedagogical focal point for the semester was the result of organizing housing into two mutually exclusive systems: the module derived from the exigencies of factory production and the unit derived from the habits and necessities of living in an urban area.

The module was investigated as a result of careful calculation as to what can be efficiently made in a factory setting, what can be transported and what can be erected quickly. Material choice and technique of assembly played a major role in this investigation. The module was also subject to architectural control through digital means with a direct correlation between three-dimensional drawing techniques and virtual assembly of modules. One field trip was made to Arup & Partners to learn about SHoP Architects' prefab project B2, understood to be the most progressive prefabricated tall building project under construction.

The unit acted as the traditional architectural encapsulation of private life in the city. We simultaneously understood that the unit in which one would live would be adjacent to many other such units, with all the advantages and disadvantages implicit in this arrangement. The resulting three-dimensional bulk had another profound effect: to create urban space and to enter the realm of urban design. To be an urban dweller at once meant accommodating the necessities of both unit life and the urban life of the street.

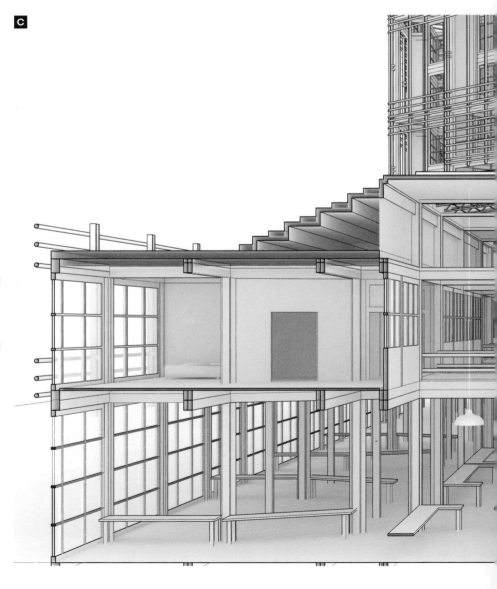

Chido Chuma +
Julien Gonzalez **A**
Serena Li + Ernest Pang **B**
Daniel Watson de
Roux + Lisa West **C**
Sabrina Barker + Rebecca Riss **D**
Sigmund Lerner +
Chenyu Pu **E/F/G**

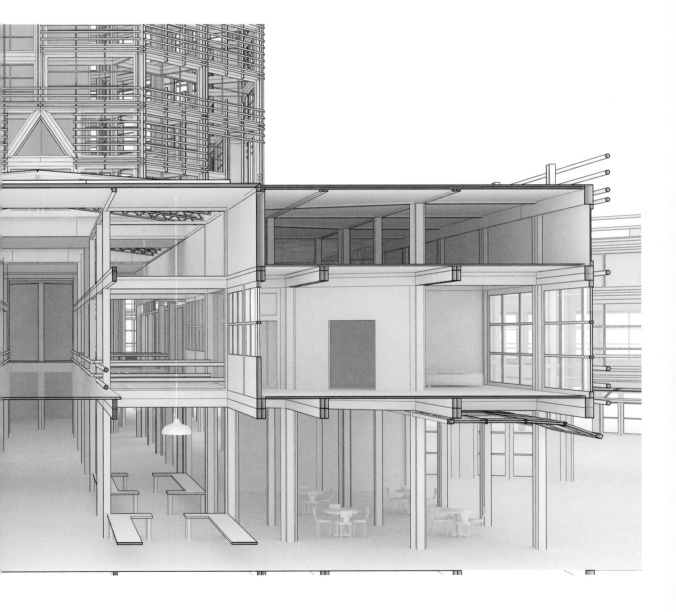

D

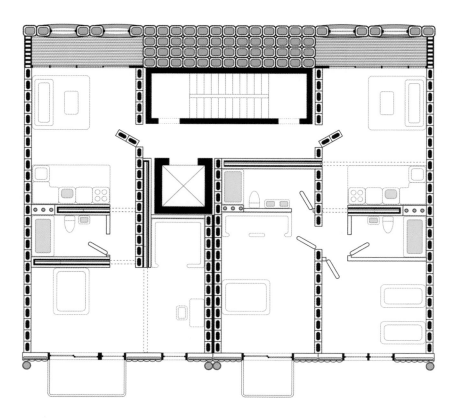

1 and 2 Bedroom Unit Plans
1/4" = 1'-0"

E

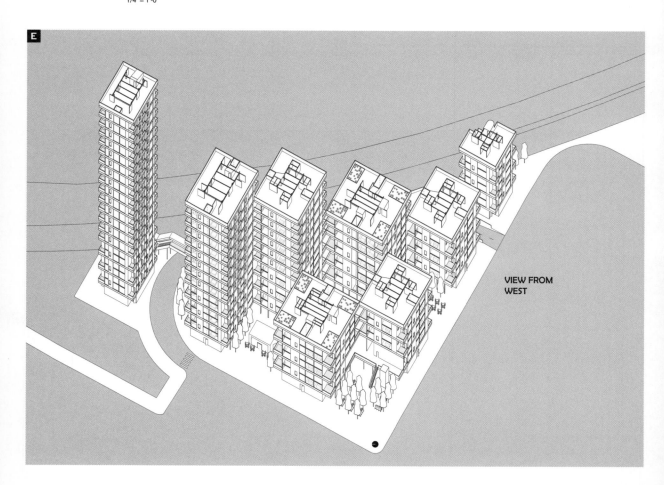

VIEW FROM
WEST

F

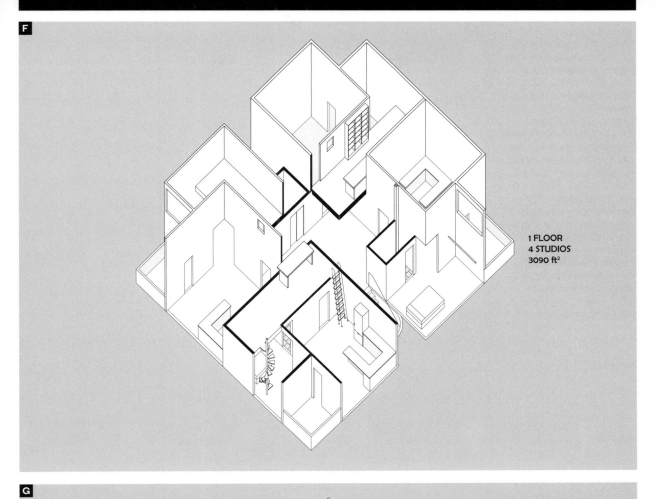

1 FLOOR
4 STUDIOS
3090 ft^2

G

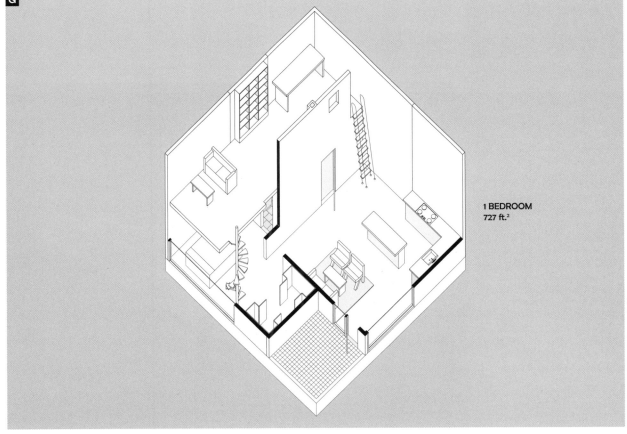

1 BEDROOM
727 ft.^{2}

Housing
Core Architecture Studio 3
Fall 2013
Rafi Segal, critic

The studio explored different
typologies of housing for East
Harlem, while considering a
variety of states and programs
that could allow a better integration of housing on a problematic edge site into the city.

Chelsea Hyduk +
Stephanie Jones **A**
Lucas Lind +
Jack Schonewolf **B**
Seuk Hoon Kim +
Myung Jae Lee **C/D**
Steve Chappell +
Skylar Bisom-Rapp **E/F/G**

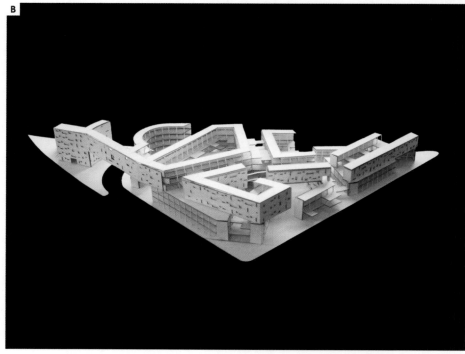

0　　5　　10　　20 (m)

D

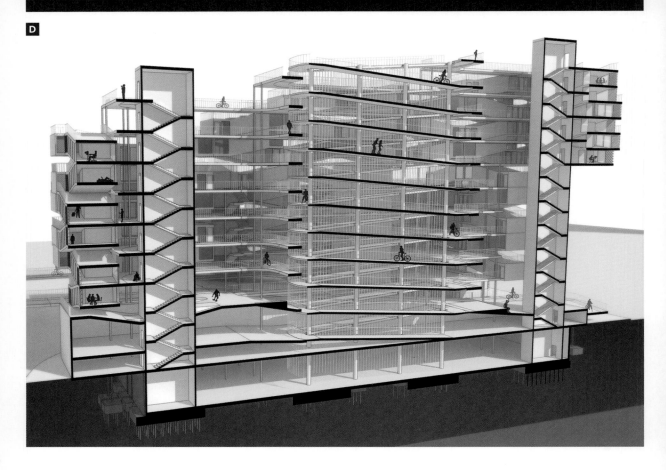

E

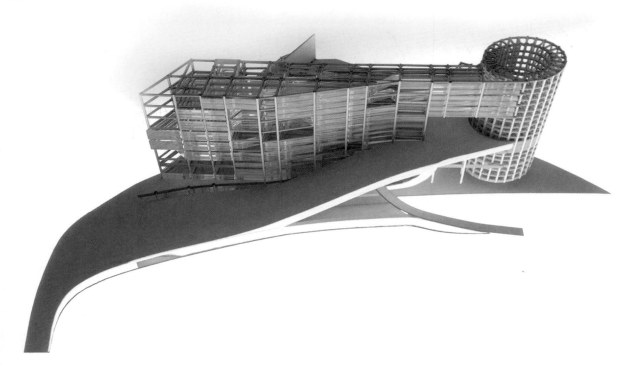

F

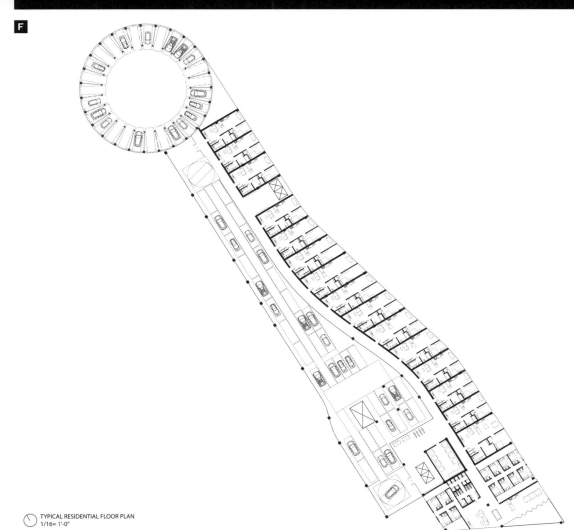

TYPICAL RESIDENTIAL FLOOR PLAN
1/16= 1'-0"

G

**LOT-EK Housing / Food
versus Shelter**
Core Architecture Studio 3
Fall 2013
*LOT-EK, Ada Tolla +
Giuseppe Lignano, critics,
with Thomas de Monchaux*

In Food versus Shelter, our approach to housing began with our longstanding interest in infrastructural technology and building systems. We observed that assertions about economies of scale and concentrations of mechanical services are deployed to justify both large-scale rural agribusiness monocultures and large-scale urban housing developments. We also considered the social injustice and health crisis of the urban food desert as well as studied local and slow food cultures — in all their problematic fashionability. We observed that both the calorie and the watt are units of the rate of expenditure of energy, and that these rates can be mutually dependent.

Each team in our section was assigned a food group from the semi-obsolete USDA food pyramid and was required to support production of food commodities from this group in intimate collaboration with the structure and infrastructure required for collective domestic life. Rather than the good old vertical farm, we sought to establish new architectural typologies and topologies in which the production, processing and consumption of commodities is radically localized, urbanized and mechanized – with domestic routines and infrastructure deeply and critically interwoven. This year, we brought special attention to upstream and downstream waste cycles and the behavior of radically closed-loop or open-ended systems.

Casey McLaughlin +
Keonwoo Kim **A/B/C/D**
Lingyuan Jiang + You Zhou **E/F**

C

D

E

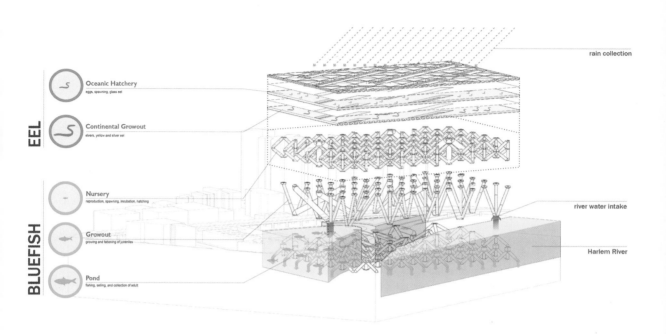

EEL

Oceanic Hatchery
eggs, spawning, glass eel

Continental Growout
elvers, yellow and silver eel

BLUEFISH

Nursery
reproduction, spawning, incubation, hatching

Growout
growing and fattening of juveniles

Pond
fishing, selling, and collection of adult

rain collection

river water intake

Harlem River

F

Advanced Architecture Studios
Mabel Wilson, director

The Advanced Studio sequence fosters an experimental design culture sensitive to the many different roles played by architects in contemporary society.

Beginning in Studio 4, students have the additional option of selecting the Columbia Building Intelligence Project's Integrated Design Studio. This studio offers a new working environment and a goal of preparing the next generation of architects to lead in the development of new modes of design and practice. The C-BIP semester focuses on the themes of energy and adaptation in the context of existing urban structures and the urgent need of cities to change in response to what is increasingly defined as a global climate crisis. The studio explores radical new forms of interdisciplinary and collective workflow through design and communication software and works with a team of consultants and advisors who greatly expand the learning capacity of the studio.

In Studios 5 and 6, students continue to take on specialized individual design trajectories with sites and programs often dispersed globally. Studios travel to sites supporting their studio research topics and travel is funded by GSAPP in the form of Kinne Travel Grants. Students from both the Master of Architecture and AAD programs join together where the diversity of backgrounds, experiences and specialties they bring forges a collective energy. Students are exposed to a greater number of studio critics and consultants and assume greater autonomy in structuring their goals. The complexity of conceptual issues, small scale as well as broad urban programs and sites, builds upon the basic skills gained in the Core Studio and summer AAD sequence.

Emergent Technologies + Sensory Architectures
Advanced Architecture Studio 4
Spring 2014
Michelle Fornabai, critic

Do buildings dream...?
of neon sheep?
with concrete feet?
people who don't sleep?
that they can leap?

The studio explored dreams in architecture through the design of 30,000 square feet.

Insubstantial, intangible, ethereal, dreams are incorporeal experiences that are paradoxically manifest using the same sensory pathways that provide access to the "real." Dreams are material--manifest by bodies by the matter of its nerves, fluids, muscles and sense organs--yet such corporeal experience is understood as unreality even as dreaming maintains many constraints which correlate with the empirical. While dreaming, the conscious subject is displaced by an unconscious presence, directed experience, intentional and, coincidentally, is subsumed by involuntary perceptions, physical laws changed and material properties shifting. Provocatively, dreaming may structure a critical reconsideration the apparent truth of sensory experience by problematizing a latent essentialism in the construction of presence, place and properties.

Students critically explored dreams, dreaming and the subjectivity of the dreamer by producing drawings and design work while inducing a series of hypnagogic states. Hypnagogic experiences make use of a neurological "default network" which is activated while resting, doing nothing, in the recollection of memories, in dreaming of the future, in social cognition and in counterfactual processing. A "threshold consciousness" experienced while falling asleep or waking and common to daydreaming, working reveries and lucid dreaming, hypnagogia manifests as a diffuse attention, a cognitive state which is suggestible, illogical and fluid in the association of ideas.

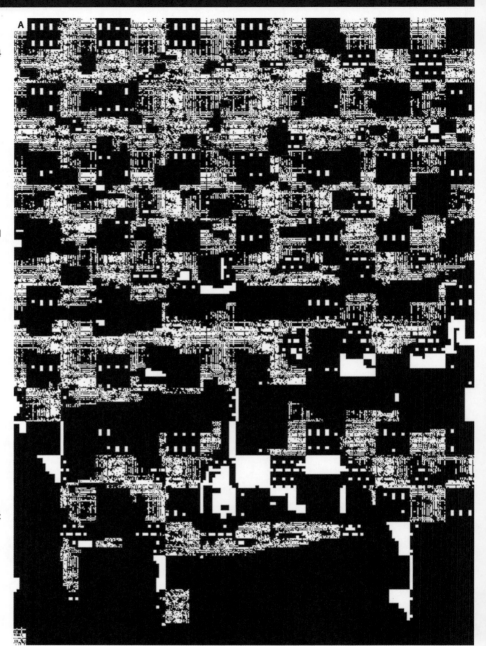

A

Danae Vokolos **A/B**
Michelle Tse **C/D**
Dream Studio Panorama **E**
Ricardo Leon **F**

B

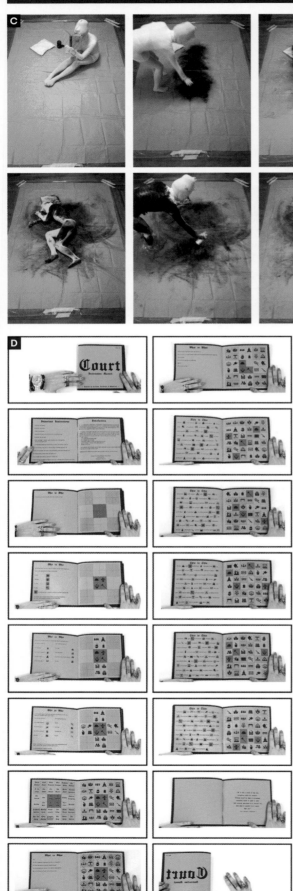

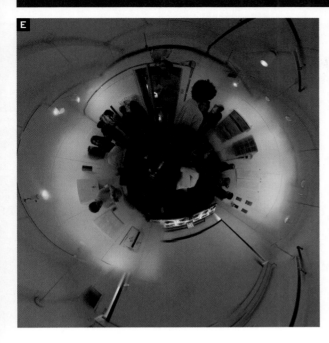

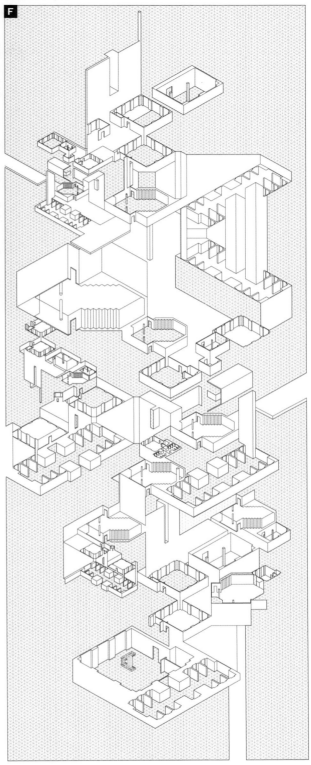

Brain Hacking 4: Future Factory, New Manufacturing Typologies for Tokyo
Advanced Architecture Studio 4
Spring 2014
Toru Hasegawa +
Mark Collins, critics

Steve Jobs said that "the boundary between soft and hard is really grey. Software is something that didn't get implemented into the hardware." The same is true for cities, where tangible structures embody the pulsating rhythms of urban life. New infrastructures are emerging to serve this twenty first century city and its evolving needs. This semester our studio examined the reflexivity between the physical and the digital by proposing new manufacturing typologies for the city of Tokyo. By studying the different manufacturing/fulfillment strategies of Toyota, Amazon.com and Shapeways we proposed a major consumer infrastructure integrated into Tokyo's urban core. By turning the manufacturing and fulfillment center inside-out, each project came to terms with material consumption patterns in an exponentially accelerating society.

The studio used programming alongside conventional modeling and rendering tools. Programming literacy was a core issue for us. Computing was used as a powerful way to understand our surroundings. We wanted to externalize as much of our design thinking into these codes as possible to find what is inextricably human. We approached coding from the ground up, with specially designed workshops and tools for first time programmers.

Our studio traveled to Tokyo Japan as part of the William Kinne fellowship. As part of this travel we visited research labs developing the next generation of communications and sensing technologies. We directly engaged with roboticists, bio-medical engineers and neuroscientists to gain unique insights into rapid technological development.

Myung Jae Lee **A/B**
Pari Agarwal **C/D/E/F**

A

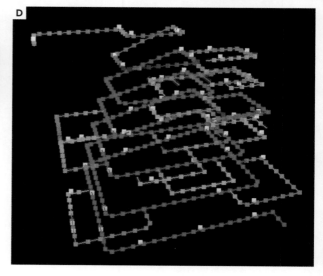

E   more curated
        products

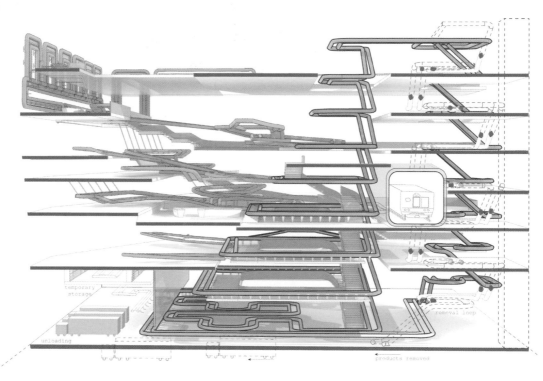

temporary
storage

removal loop

unloading

products removed

less curated
products

F

Known Unknowns
Advanced Architecture Studio 4
Spring 2014
Janette Kim, critic

The idea of a risk society expands existing discourse about environmentalism—often focused on preservation, conservation and restraint—to include broader questions about an economy of contested and common resources. Swelling oceans, extreme temperatures, food scarcity and disease outbreaks, among other climate-related hazards, spread collateral damages of modern marvels to new, greater collectives.

Using the double-barrel strategies of mitigation and adaptation, architects build efficient buildings, transform consumption patterns, alter settlement patterns, reinforce public service networks and reform shorelines. Yet, the known unknowns prevail and are compounded by the volatility of markets and political will. Attempts to alleviate some problems only precipitate new ones. Consensus remains elusive, as events devastating to some open up great opportunity for exploitation by others. Ultimately, the challenges of climate change call for architects to grapple not only with the design of envelopes and arrangements of urban life, but also for techniques for managing uncertainty.

Known Unknowns investigated the political ecology of climate change through the lens of risk management in architecture and urbanism. We used scenario planning techniques to prompt speculation, evaluate the implications of our designs and to illuminate political dynamics of climate change that often go unexamined.

Sareeta Patel **A/B/C**
Skylar Bisom-Rapp **D/E/F**

CBIP
Advanced Architecture Studio 4
Spring 2014
*Scott Marble + Laura Kurgan,
critics, with Adam Modesitt,
John Cerone (software
consultants); Jason Roberts +
Dan Taeyoung Lee
(teaching assistants)*

Manufacturing 2.0
New York City has historically
been a center of manufacturing
due to its abundant waterfront
ports, railroad infrastructure
and a large diverse population.
After a steady decline that
accelerated over the past 50
years, manufacturing is return-
ing to New York in a new form.
Unlike the large scale operations that were once a dominate
economic driver and significant
source of jobs, the new version
is made up of smaller, specialized technology-driven firms
that respond to local demands
more than mass market appeal.
Building on the many initiatives
currently under way to address
local manufacturing as essential
to both economic diversity and
sustainability in NYC, this studio developed scalable design
strategies for design and manufacturing incubators to redefine
an industry historically defined
by large, dominant companies
into a stable network of smaller,
more specialized entities.

Data 2.0
Over the course of just one
generation, there has been a
radical shift in the overall ways
in which we inhabit, navigate,
use, communicate and build
urban spaces. While we used
to replicate the physical world
within computational space,
now we use computational
space to guide us through physical space. These spaces have
physical location but are only
visible as ecologies, systems
and networks by finding them
in dataspace, then examining,
processing and understanding
the information that makes
them visible. There is traceable
evidence of these urban phenomena through information
and data, but they only become
coherent within a context of
spatial information and social
media that allows us to 'see'
their architectural presence,
sometime in unrecognizable
forms. Our task for this studio
was to consider information
space and urban infrastructures
as catalysts for the invention of
new programs and uses beyond
conventional categories.

Albert Franco, Sukwon Lee +
Timmie Tsang **A/B/C/D**
Carlo Bailey + Lorenzo Villaggi **E**
Scott Overall **F**

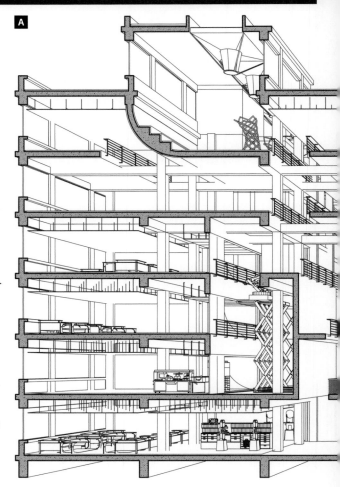

A

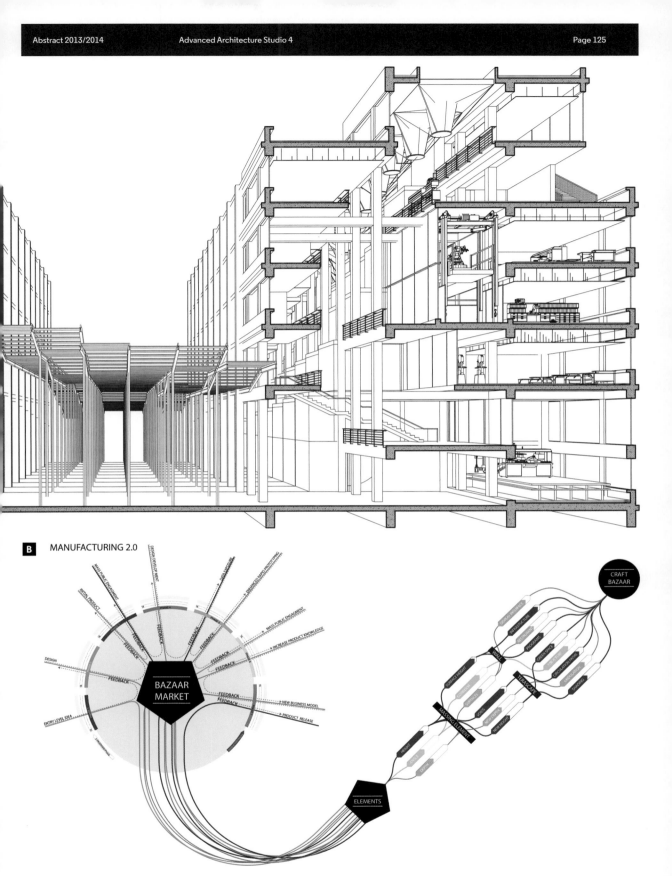

B MANUFACTURING 2.0

C   *BAZAAR TYPES_CATALOG*

What programs of bazaar do you want? and what types of geometrical articulation do you want? Here, we have the catalog of different programmatic distribution and geometrical inputs and outputs. Depending on your demands, you can choose and free to apply these schemes to the masterplan. If you want more customized version other than thses, please contact SAT (sl3531@columbia.edu). They will provide client-oriented solutions quickly.

CROSS SECTION   LONGITUDINAL SECTION

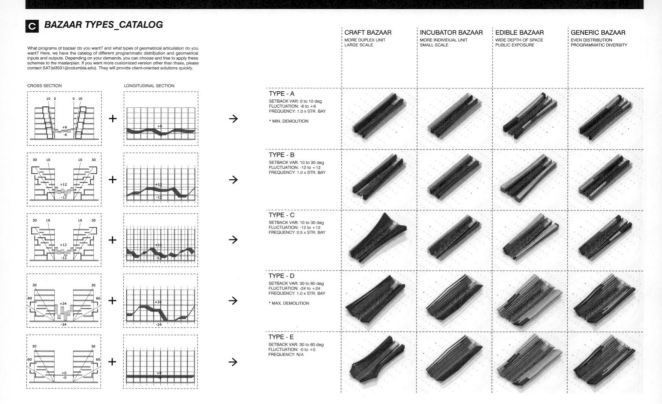

CRAFT BAZAAR
MORE DUPLEX UNIT
LARGE SCALE

INCUBATOR BAZAAR
MORE INDIVIDUAL UNIT
SMALL SCALE

EDIBLE BAZAAR
WIDE DEPTH OF SPACE
PUBLIC EXPOSURE

GENERIC BAZAAR
EVEN DISTRIBUTION
PROGRAMMATIC DIVERSITY

TYPE - A
SETBACK VAR: 0 to 10 deg
FLUCTUATION: -6 to +6
FREQUENCY: 1.0 x STR. BAY

* MIN. DEMOLITION

TYPE - B
SETBACK VAR: 10 to 30 deg
FLUCTUATION: -12 to +12
FREQUENCY: 1.0 x STR. BAY

TYPE - C
SETBACK VAR: 10 to 30 deg
FLUCTUATION: -12 to +12
FREQUENCY: 0.5 x STR. BAY

TYPE - D
SETBACK VAR: 30 to 60 deg
FLUCTUATION: -24 to +24
FREQUENCY: 1.0 x STR. BAY

* MAX. DEMOLITION

TYPE - E
SETBACK VAR: 30 to 60 deg
FLUCTUATION: -0 to +0
FREQUENCY: N/A

D   *GENERATIVE SURFACE DESIGN*

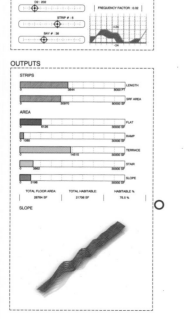

INPUTS

D1 : 503   VERTICAL FACTOR : 0.25
D2 : 202   FREQUENCY FACTOR : 0.02
STRIP # : 6
BAY # : 36

OUTPUTS

STRIPS
LENGTH   0   3644   8000 FT
SRF AREA   0   30970   80000 SF

AREA
FLAT   0   6126   30000 SF
RAMP   0   1068   30000 SF
TERRACE   0   14515   30000 SF
STAIR   0   3862   30000 SF
SLOPE   0   3196   30000 SF

TOTAL FLOOR AREA: 28784 SF
TOTAL HABITABLE: 21706 SF
HABITABLE %:   75.5 %

SLOPE

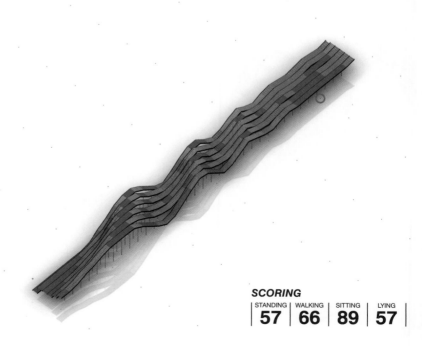

SCORING

STANDING	WALKING	SITTING	LYING
57	66	89	57

E

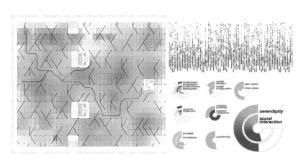

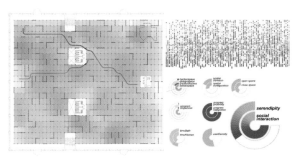

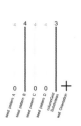
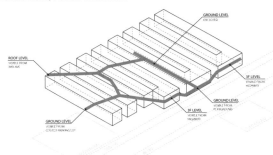
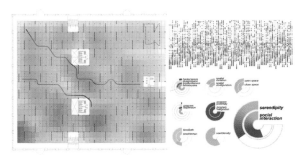

F **STRATEGY**

PUBLIC PATH / PUBLIC INTERFACE

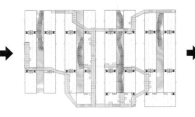

PROCESS

FREEHAND SKETCH (INPUT)   PARAMETRICALLY GENERATED PATH   CATIA WIREFRAME (OUTPUT)

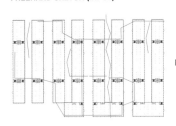
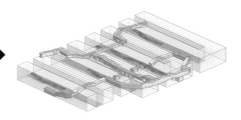

Dance Vessel
Advanced Architecture Studio 4
Spring 2014
Robert Marino, critic

To say that matter is material and spirit is spiritual is not false, but it is more true to say that matter is spiritual and spirit, material. Pessoa

Vessels are commonly thought to be boats or ships upon the sea, or closed forms to hold liquids. In this studio, we considered the potential for the vessel to define architectural space, keeping in mind that the vessel also is the beautiful method of transport to a different place, perhaps allowing a transcendent change in our lives. As a holder of people, the vessel brings us together in unpredictable ways.

The easternmost end of Long Island has only recently become a popular recreational adjunct of New York City. As was the case everywhere in the new world, it was initially a place to gain a foothold, a place for survival. Through most of its history it was a seafaring territory, most easily gotten to from Boston Harbor, Nantucket, Martha's Vineyard or Cape Cod. It was land surrounded by the sea, yet blessed with very fertile alluvial soil. Its inhabitants were just as apt to be of the seafaring as well as the farming type, able to gain their livelihood as their Native American forbears did, through a balance of fishing and farming.

Things have changed. It is now a place primarily appreciated as being one of the last remaining natural environments within a 2-3 hour drive of New York City, and as such it is primarily a place of recreation. The tensions generated by change are evident. One of the most interesting current political discussions involves the theories of land use and preservation: How should the natural environment be used? How much of, and of what type of business establishments should be supported? Are there alternate uses of public land that are more in keeping with open space preservation?

Janice Leong **A/B/C**
Kate Reggev **D/E/F**
Tanya Lucia Griffiths **G**

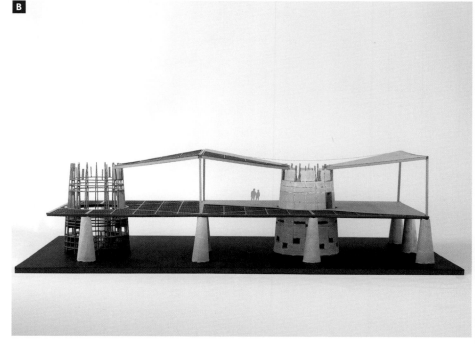

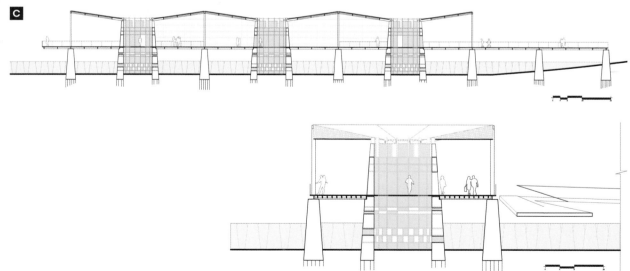

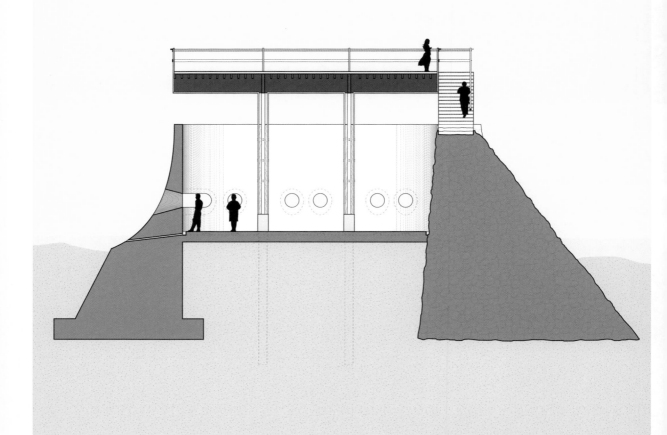

F

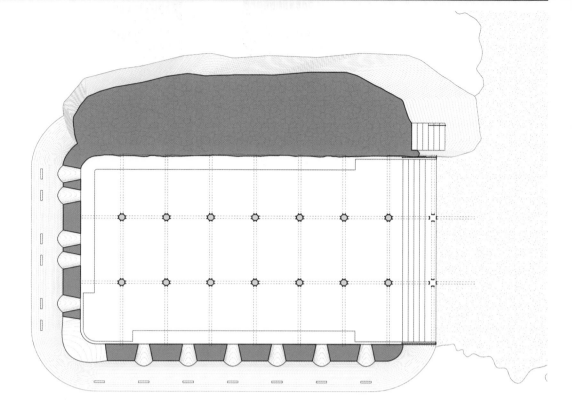

G

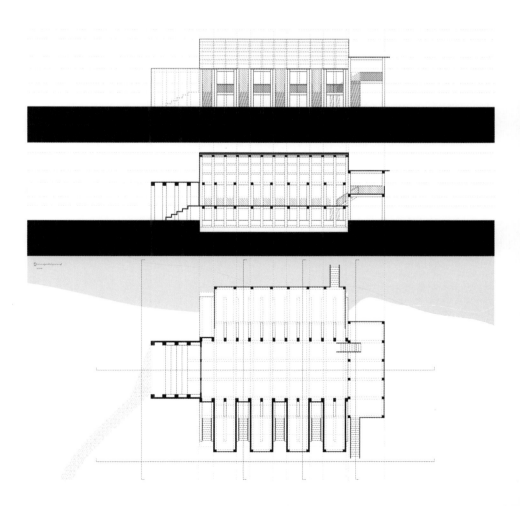

Space Studio 13 - Lunar Health Stations

Advanced Architecture Studio 4
Spring 2014
Michael Morris, Kelsey Lents + Christina Ciardullo, critics, with Melodie Yashar

Humans live short lives, but as a species we have always thought and planned for the distant future...Our ability for abstract thought that can reach beyond the horizons of space and time-is perhaps our most remarkable trait...If anything will enable us to endure past the limited lifetime of planets, it will have to be our ability to think.
Dimitar Sasselov, *Life of Super-Earths*, 2012

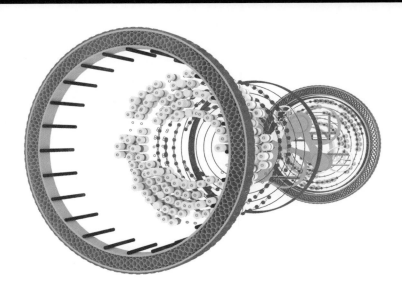

A

Drawing from Sasselov's concept that the future of astronomy is biology, Lunar Health Stations is the second semester to have focused on architecture that supports human health as part of Space Studio's ongoing series investigating future long-duration manned space missions and outposts far beyond Earth's atmosphere.

Sited near the Moon's south pole at Shakleton Crater or, conversely, in lunar orbit, each project synthetically explored means and methods of construction in response to conditions of the extreme environment(s) to establish a sanitarium / sanatorium that would serve as a transitional galactic hub, a restorative health center, and could become the foundational infrastructure for pioneering lunar communities. Examining the science and art of preventing and treating disease so as to imagine how architecture could promote health and sustain and prolong human life was vital to the projects' programming and design. Focused research into previous space missions as well as conversations with scientists at NASA's Johnson Space Center, Houston and with expert guest critics and international lecturers provided key information regarding the safety

requirements, procedures and protocols currently associated with living in the microgravity environments such as on the ISS (International Space Station). Understanding the existing successes and challenges of building and living in these environments today laid the groundwork for the students' redefinition of space architecture and its effect on what life beyond Earth could one day be.

Gawon Shin **A/B/C**
Jeffrey Montes **D/E**

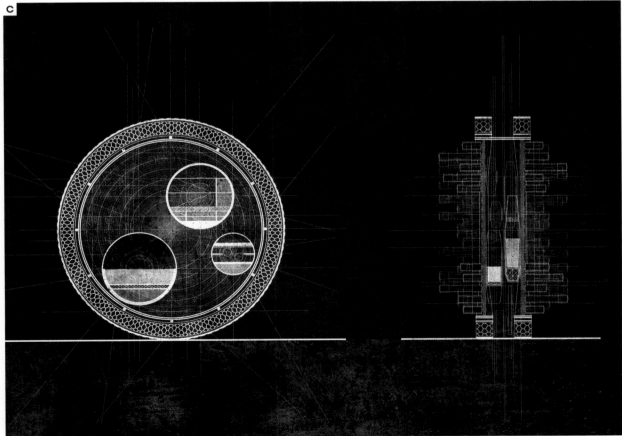

D

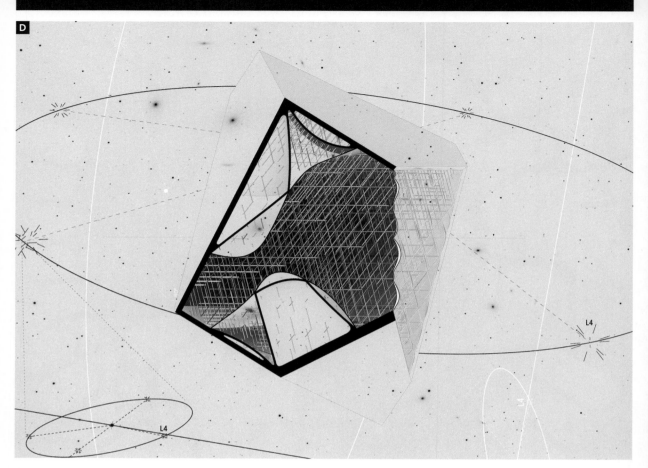

E

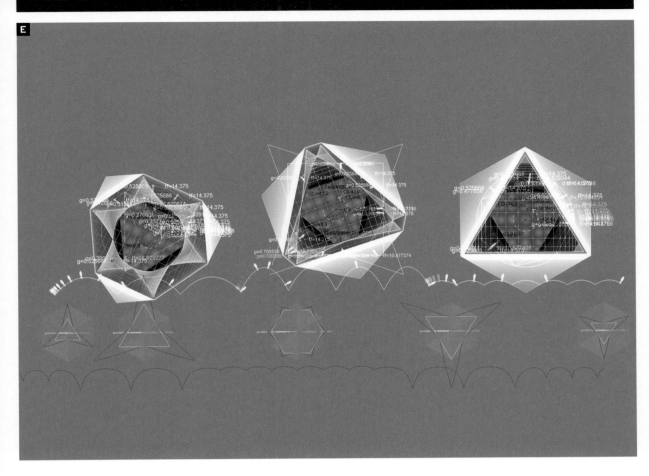

Uneven Growth:
Hong Kong 2047
Advanced Architecture Studio 4
Spring 2014
*Kazys Varnelis, critic, with
Jochen Hartmann*

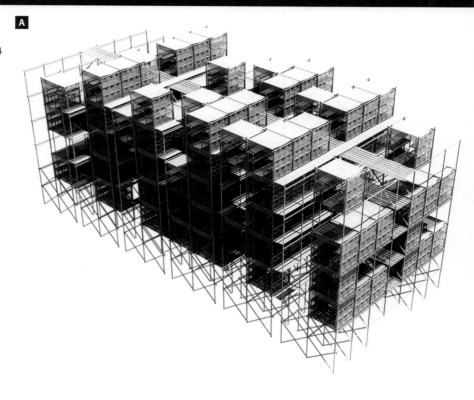

A

This studio paralleled and informed the Uneven Growth exhibition opening at the Museum of Modern Art in November 2014. The intent of both studio and exhibition was to tackle the complex condition of the megacity and the growing economic and social inequality within it.

As in the exhibition, the Network Architecture Lab's physical site was Hong Kong and the temporal site was the year 2047. At this point the "One Country, Two Systems," doctrine that began in 1997 as the former British colony was handed over to the People's Republic of China is scheduled to run out, and the city is scheduled to lose its status as an exceptional zone within China. We hypothesized that Hong Kong will not disappear, but that instead China will.

We set out to ask how architecture can address uneven growth in Hong Kong and other megacities. We maintained that buildings could be constructions of thought in addition to material, conceptual machines that produce arguments and state positions. This studio's central task was the invention of an ethics of design appropriate to a diminished future.

Casey McLaughlin **A/B/C**
Qiuli Qu **D**
Steve Chappell **E**
Seuk Hoon Kim **F**

B

C

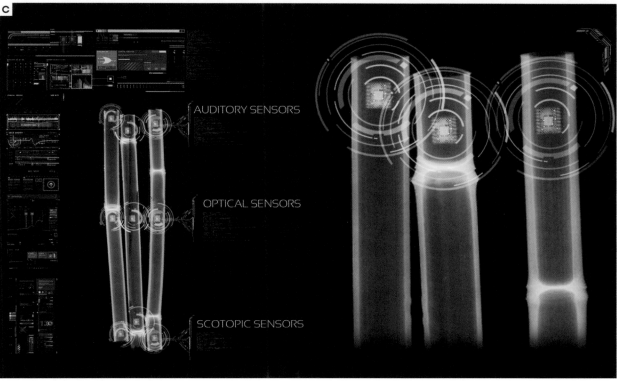

AUDITORY SENSORS

OPTICAL SENSORS

SCOTOPIC SENSORS

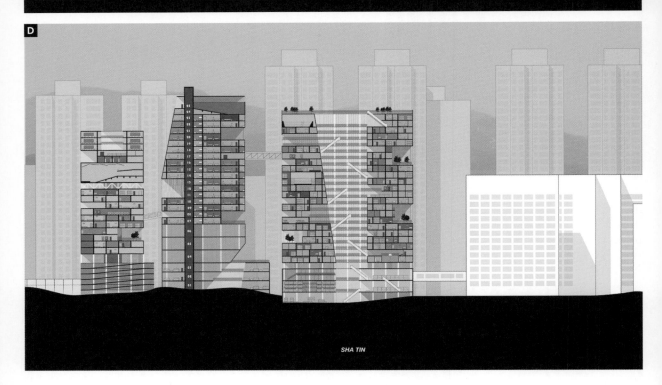

SHA TIN

The New University
Advanced Architecture Studio 5
Fall 2013
*Laurie Hawkinson +
Jordan Carver, critics*

This experimental studio formally linked to a seminar, speculated ways in which the new university will possess a new architecture in every sense of the term. Together with the seminar, the intention was to explore and reimagine that architecture, and its role in shaping knowledge now and in the future.

Both the studio and the seminar were primarily aimed at informed speculation and conceptual risk-taking at a moment in history that already witnessed vast changes in the educational, institutional and intellectual landscape. This unique form of integrated teaching and learning used the frame of architecture to both re-conceptualize and re-invent The New University.

This New University, with its new concepts for programs and departments, assumed new forms of learning, new technologies, new cross-disciplinary forms of knowledge, learning and research.

What would be the form of this new university?

What would be housed in the buildings / building? How would these buildings perform to suit the new endeavors?

Architecture and the campus plan are thought of as leading the organization of key universities; could architecture galvanize new programs of knowledge into new configurations?

Would these new alliances and relationships of cross-disciplinary working form new configurations and form a completely new modality?

Would this new university produce architecture of alternative concepts and spatial configurations?

Karl Issara Roarty **A**
Laura Buck + Hajeong Lim **B/C/D**
Tiffany Rattray **E/F/G**

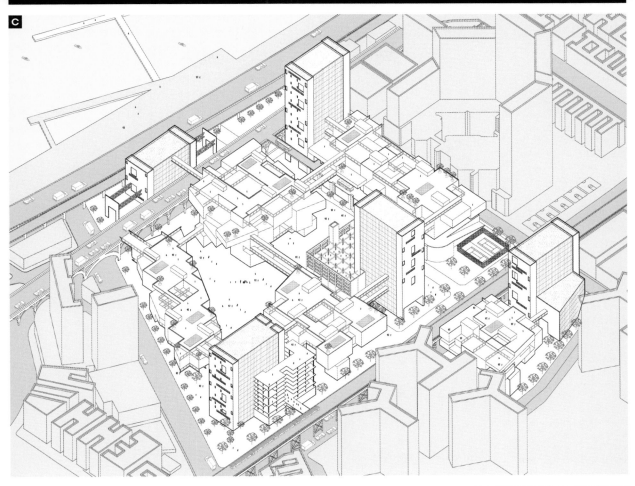

E

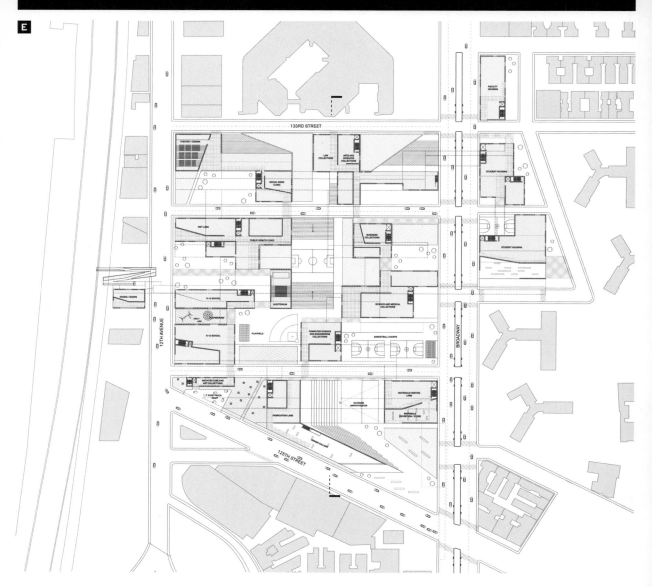

F

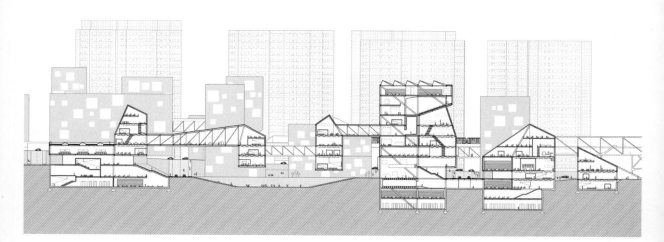

G

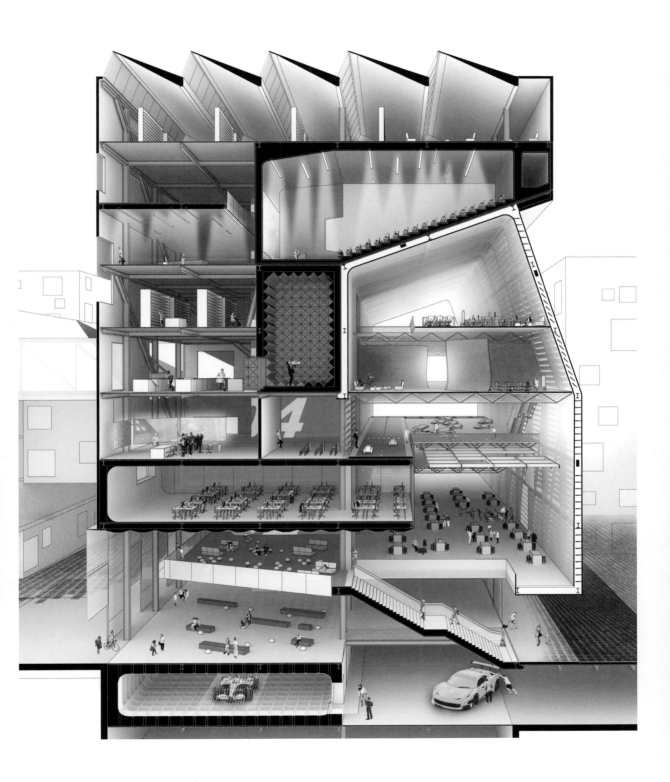

Architecture + Representation: The Lens of Diplomacy
Advanced Architecture Studio 5
Fall 2013
Amale Andraos, critic,
with Alfie Koetter

This studio aimed at re-thinking the relationship between Architecture and Representation by proposing a new American Embassy in Amman. Building on the long history of enlisting Architecture to serve America's image abroad, students were asked to go beyond the resurgence of orientalist trends seen in recent iconic projects–whether at the scales of architecture or urbanism– and find instead more complex and critical ways to represent the difficult meeting of local context and US power. In particular, students embraced the State Department's official security and design guidelines, working within their constraints while searching for new ways to promote exchange and rede-fine the spaces of diplomacy.

Jenny Y Lin **A/B**
Margaux Young **C**
Rong Zhao **D/E**
Maya Porath **F/G**

A

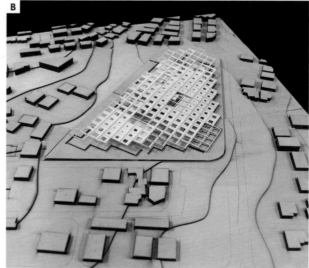

B

C

D

E

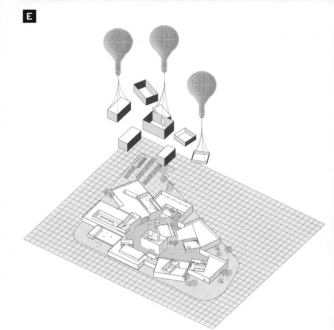

F

G

What is Plastic Architecture Today?
Advanced Architecture Studio 5
Fall 2013
Michael Bell + Zachary Kostura, critics, with Brian Lee + Hyon Woo Chung

The Materials-Based Design Studio focused on meanings of the term plastic and the role of plastics in architecture. We explored the historical term plastics and its spatial themes not only in the context of plastics in commodity items but also as an economy themselves. The studio explored plastics as a building element that needs to be un-covered and indeed re-seen as a zone of material innovation.

   Architecture studios generally accept materials as givens or as organized by industry and by materials science, as is true for glass, concrete and metals as well as plastics. In seeking to improve the building industry we generally focus on putting known elements together better; knowing that the commodity practices that underlie development and building in the United States have standardized building materials and means, we accept materials as a given. Working with a roster of known materials and practices allows us to manage risk and assure safety, but often curtails innovation in ways by which the auto or electronics industry seem to be less limited. Looking closely at materials and bringing students to the mechanics and chemistry of materials projects like Permanent Change aimed to break that threshold. Vinyl and other polymers become uniquely fascinating because they are fully engineered but even more embedded in industry–jobs, production and economy. Our studio work sought to address a case study of relatively small scale by exploring how a new model of housing for an American suburb could be more closely linked to the materials and industries of which it is made.

Andrew Maier III **A/B**
Jinglu Huang **C**
Munyoung Lee **D/E**
Ying Chen Lin **F/G**

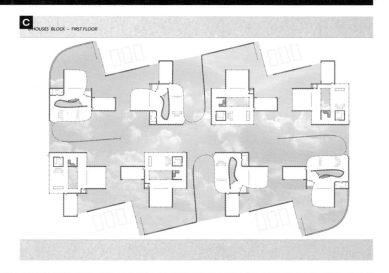

C — 9 HOUSES BLOCK – FIRST FLOOR

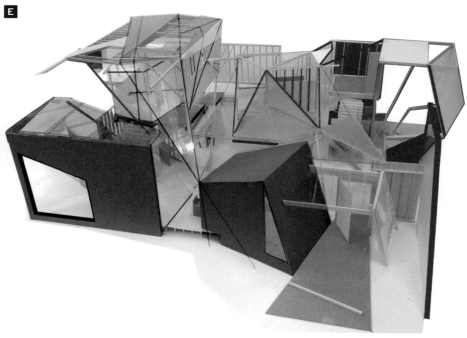

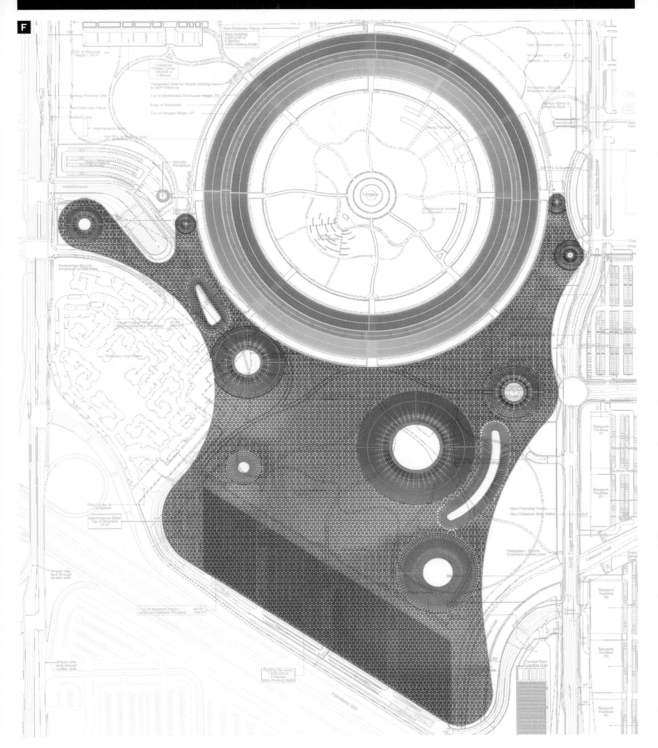

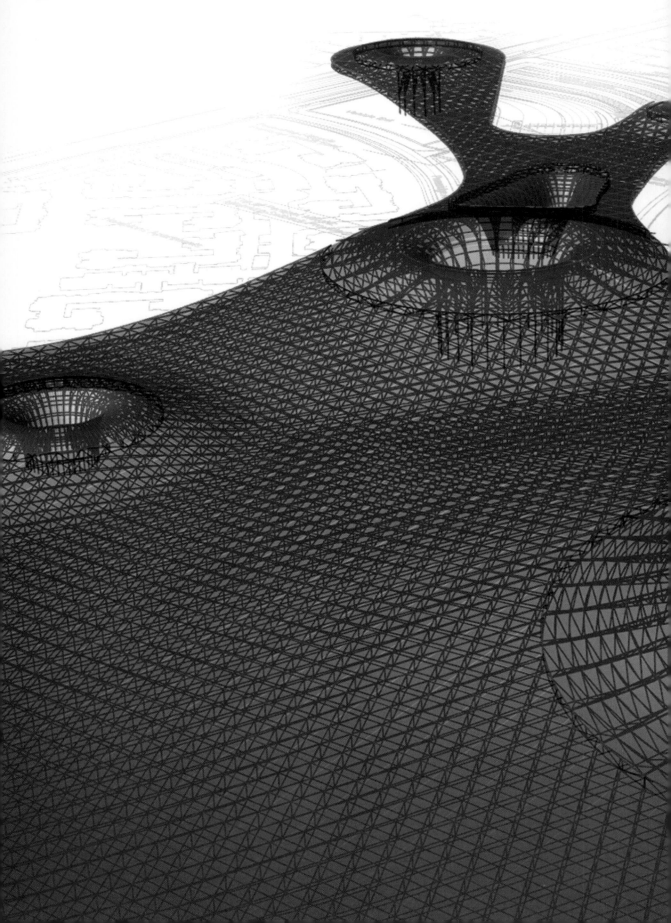

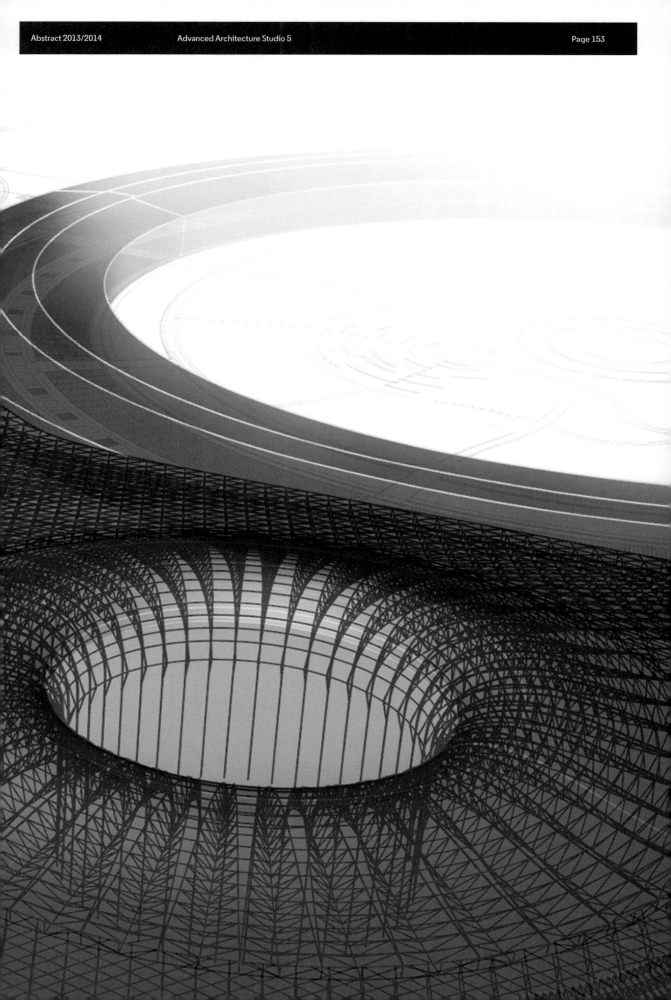

Regenerative Architecture
Advanced Architecture Studio 5
Fall 2013
David Benjamin + Ali Brivanlou,
critics, with Danil Nagy +
Jesse Blankenship,
software consultants

Biological growth has fasci-
nated architects for centuries,
but recent developments in our
understanding of biological systems—and our ability to gather
data from them, model them in
the computer, and directly ma-
nipulate them—have opened
up startling possibilities to
actively integrate biology and
design. This unique advanced
architecture studio leapt to the
forefront of new collaborations
between architecture and biology and aimed to produce novel examples of how they may
affect buildings of the future.

In this studio, we proposed
to bring human architec-
tural designs to life as dynamic
systems through the logic of
embryonic pattern formation
and the rules of morphogen-
esis. Foreshadowing a new
generation of bio architects,
students used the logic of cell
growth, differentiation and
morphogenetic movements to
program dynamic architecture.

This studio explored a design
ecosystem where humans and
biological cells cooperate to
generate designs that a human
alone—or nature alone—could
never produce. This involved
collaborating with biology
rather than imitating it.

This new design process
involved designing with unknowable forces and designing
dynamic relationships rather
than designing fixed forms.
These transformations from
the typical design process are
fitting for the dynamic and
unstable world in which we live.
This human-cell cooperation
represents a new paradigm
for the Century of Biology and
the future of architecture.

David Isaac Hecht +
Marc Mascarello **A**
James Stoddart +
Ray Wang **B/C/D/E**
Junhee Cho **F/G**

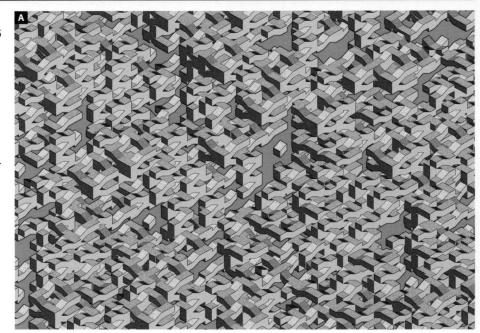

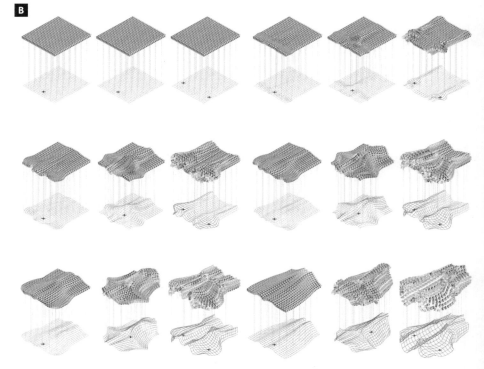

C

D

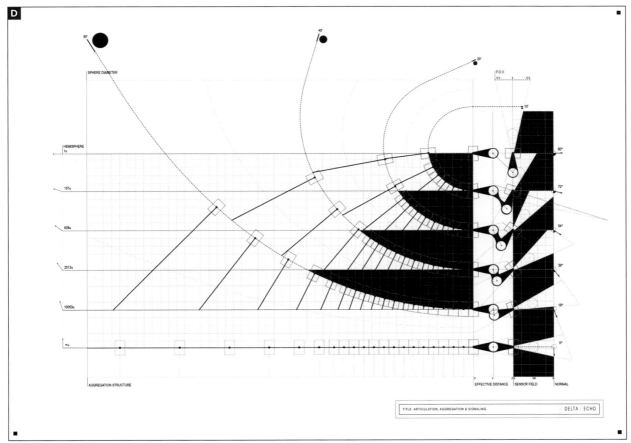

TITLE: ARTICULATION, AGGREGATION & SIGNALING   DELTA : ECHO

E

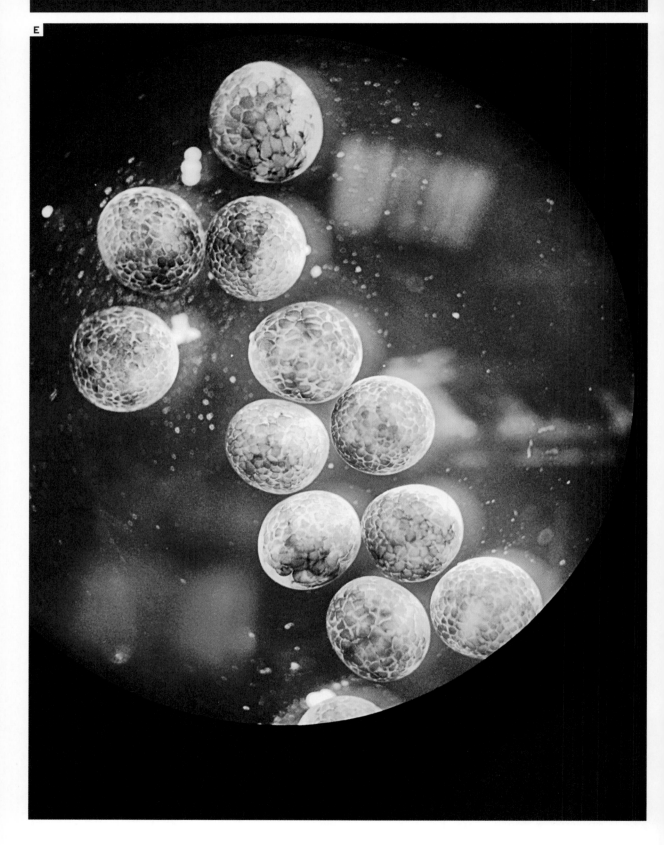

F

EXISTING BUILDING LIFECYCLE

G

SPECULATION : ADDITIONAL INVAGINATION

Hypothetical growing model: multiple inviginaltion

Multiple invagination introduce multiple void inside embryo, compose layered structure repeating their life cycle : emergence · expanding · stacking · balancing · contracting · aging · extinction

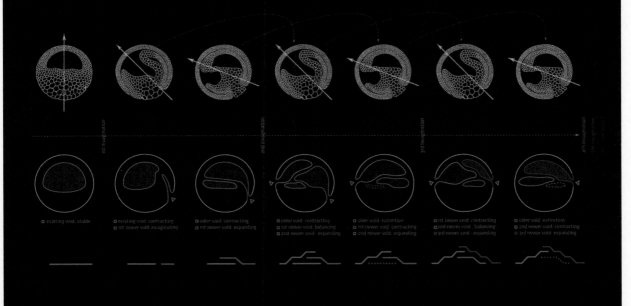

Memory, Memorial + Memorialization
Advanced Architecture Studio 5
Fall 2013
*Lynne Breslin + Kunio Kudo,
critics, with Esteban Reichberg*

Though the country was devastated, still mountains and rivers remain. On Spring coming, the City was filled with trees and grasses. Toho

On 3.11.2011, a magnitude 9 earthquake and the resulting 40-meter-high tsunami struck Northeastern Japan. Some 20,000 people were killed or reported missing; over 4,000 houses were lost. The enormous loss was compounded as hundreds of square miles of land disappeared under ocean water. Fields were salted and entire cities ravaged.

Our studio carefully examined the nature of memory, how architecture treats loss and how to best accommodate the needs of individuals, whose loss is personal, along with the collective memories of community members, the region and nation. Visiting the Kesennuma and Sendai, students determined the course of events through the traces of debris, fragments and altered lives. We designed a repository for these memories and artifacts on a site now sacred to a community.

Memory, Memorial and Memorialization re-imagined a basic, fundamental motivation of architecture—to accommodate the ephemeral, eternal and spiritual. The spirit of "moving on" and economic stimulus were essential to programming the memorial for Kesennuma.

Arkadiusz Piegdon **A**
Natasha Amladi **B/C/D**
David Hui **E**
Mark Pothier **F**

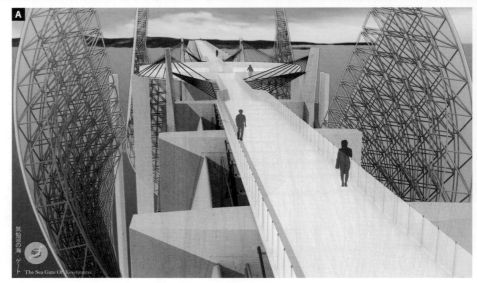

気仙沼の海・ゲート
The Sea Gate Of Kesennuma

S.02
HATCHED LOBSTERS TRANSFERRED TO PRELIMINARY AQUAHIVES

C

S.03
**TRANSFER OF LOBSTERS TO SECONDARY AQUAHIVES
EDUCATION CENTRE AND CAFE**

D

S.04
**LOBSTER CRATES PLACED IN SEAWATER
EMERGING AT SEA LEVEL AMONGST THE MEMORIAL POOLS**

E

F

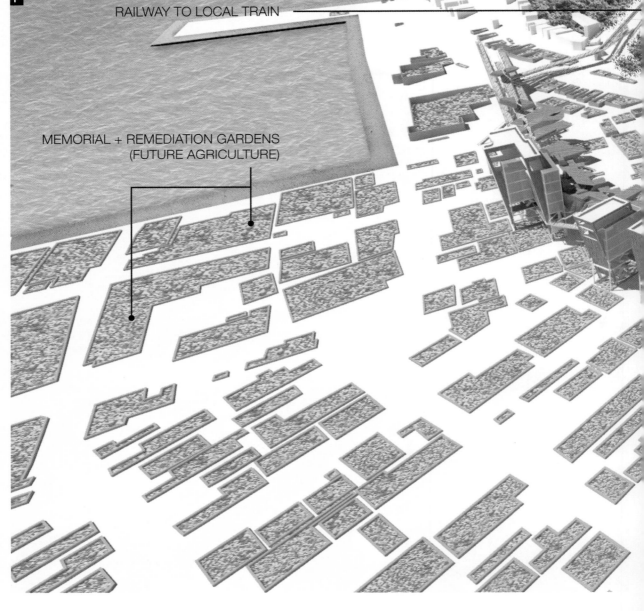

RAILWAY TO LOCAL TRAIN

MEMORIAL + REMEDIATION GARDENS
(FUTURE AGRICULTURE)

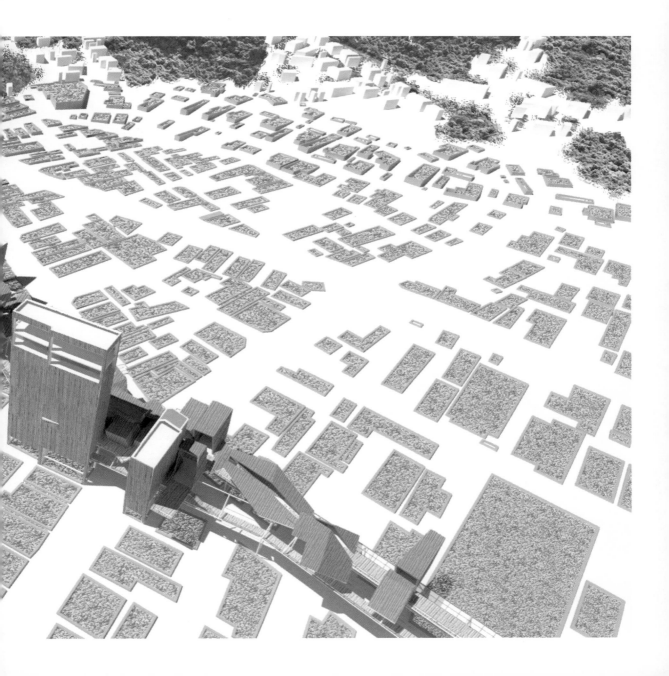

The Architecture of Liquid Cities

Advanced Architecture Studio 5
Fall 2013
Lise Anne Couture, critic, with Liam Lowry + Robert Eleazor

As cities continue to evolve, what are the new possibilities or, perhaps, imperatives for creating new types of urban architectural and infrastructural assemblies? Within these, how can new technological, political, social, economic and environmental prerogatives be addressed?

Hyper-densification makes cities victims of their own success. Transferrable air rights in desirable locations are depleted or stratospherically expensive. An ensuing space race for developable air rights urgently requires urban expansion into untapped territory. In order for supply to meet demand the space above the rivers and waterways that meander through or around the city is recouped as the site for new urban development. The City benefits from leasing air rights to private entities, or the City uses the new development for public amenities for which there is no longer any urban site available.

In this studio, we created and invented new habitable structures to span across waterways and colonize this new airspace. Neither conventional bridges nor mega buildings, these interventions are intended to be a 'somewhere' between a 'here' and a there,' to connect rather than separate, to be places of production and occupancy, as well as spaces of mobility. The studio explored what might be the outcome of an infrastructural condition that is entwined with a rich assortment of programs, functions and public amenities. The studio searched for ways in which technologies and characteristics associated with infrastructure such as the integration of sensors, robotics and automation, redundancies, modularity, flexibility and adaptability could create an architecture of pliability and resilience.

Blair Denhart Dargusch + Michael Bosbous **A/B/C**
Minjin Kim **D/E**
Seo Hyun Lee **F/G**

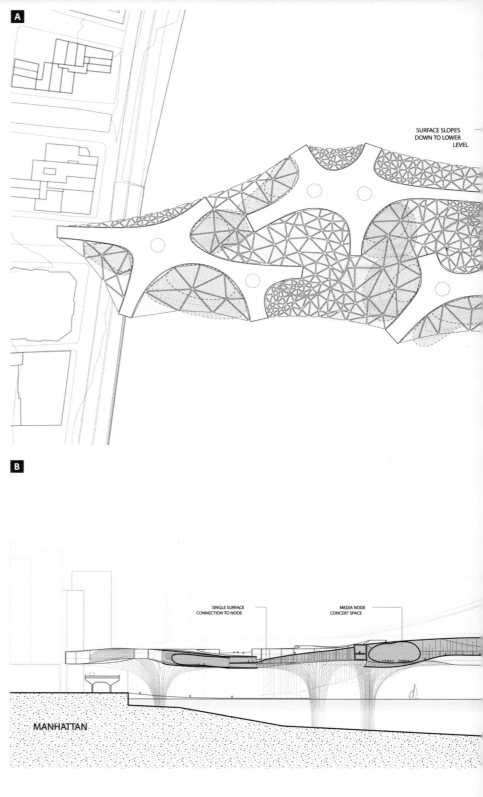

SURFACE SLOPES
DOWN TO LOWER
LEVEL

SINGLE SURFACE
CONNECTION TO NODE

MEDIA NODE
CONCERT SPACE

MANHATTAN

0   250'   5000

P+

PNEUMATIC NESTED
WITHIN NODE

BREAK IN UPPER TESSLE
SURFACE

BREAK IN UPPER TESSLE
SURFACE

BREAK IN UPPER TESSLE
SURFACE

SINGLE SURFACE
ACCESS TO
SPACE BEYOND

SLOPED CONNECTION TO
BKB PARK

BROOKLYN

KEY PLAN

C

SURFACE STATE CHANGES

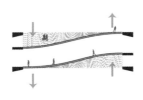
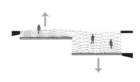

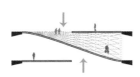
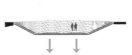

CLOSED   BRIDGE   SPLIT   FLAT

D

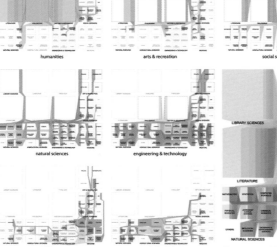

E

humanities   arts & recreation   social sciences

natural sciences   engineering & technology

medicine   agricultural sciences

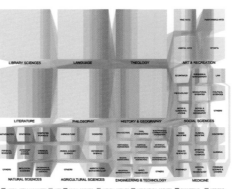

Mega-cityfication/Syncretism: A New Island in the Caspian Sea for Baku, Azerbaijan

Advanced Architecture Studio 5
Fall 2013
Markus Dochantschi,
critic, with Carolina Ihle

Baku is ambitiously taking its place within the global family of modern mega cities, and like China, is establishing itself with the world of international mega buildings.

In this context of accelerated development the studio tackled the potential problems and consequences that these developments hold. Can neoliberalism and globalization promote a new form of architecture and social fabric? Will architecture have the power and tools to express a political agenda? Can architects and urban planners invent a new political agenda and form urban systems rather than solitary objects?

The studio established a new idealized philosophy for living. Rather than designing an architectural object, the students designed an island embracing the complex ecosystem of actors involved. The design was a reflection of the research and the student's specially curated narrative to promote a new socio-political model. Each manifesto became the basis for a master planning methodology, which guided the design of a new high-density development on the coast of Baku.

During the trip to Baku the studio collected data and interviewed urban planners, architects, designers, city officials and residents. The data became the basis for the design of both the master planning methodology and the environment for the new neighborhoods establishing a symbiotic or mutualistic relationship between multiple socio-economic cultures.

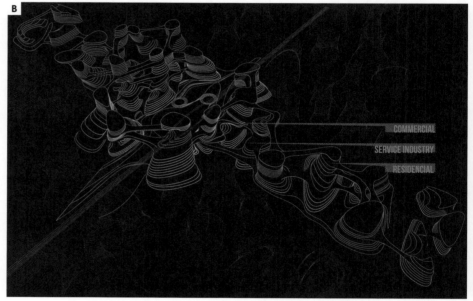

COMMERCIAL
SERVICE INDUSTRY
RESIDENCIAL

Astry Duarte, Harsha Nalwaya + Reece Tucker **A/B**
Juan Pablo Azares + Tina Yao Xu + Miao Wei **C/D**
Tengxiao Gao **E/F**

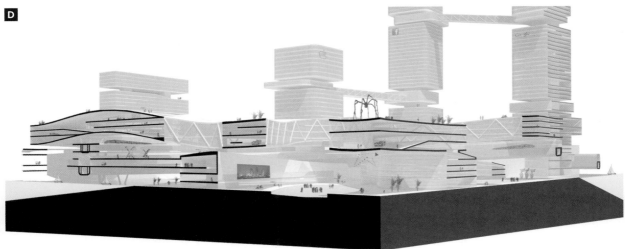

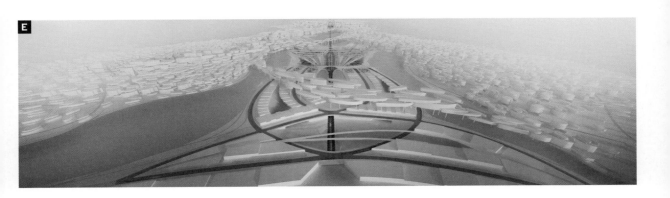

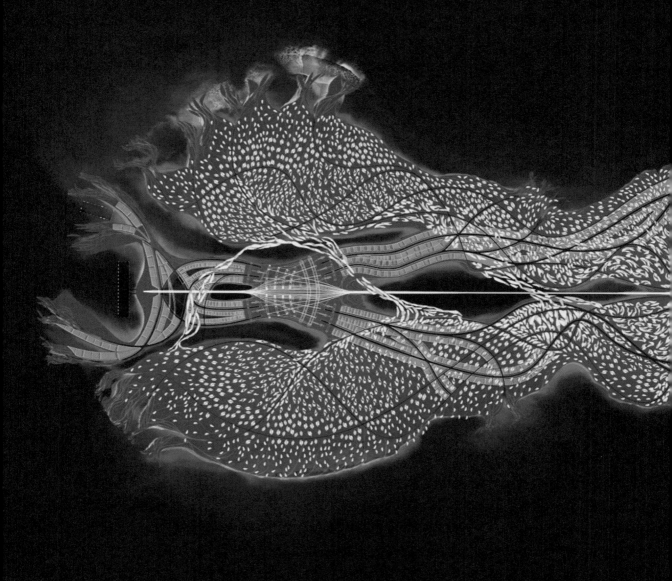

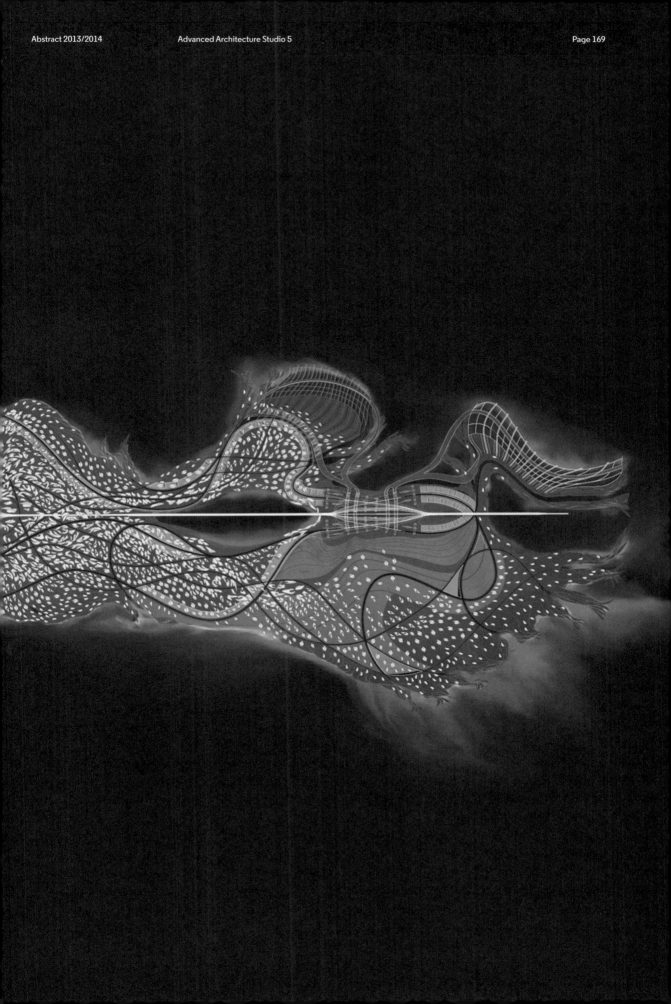

The Urban Imaginary Project: Medellin a Narco Post-War Imaginary

Advanced Architecture Studio 5
Fall 2013
*Cristina Goberna, critic,
with Diana Cristobal*

This class was the first installment of a series of studios that investigate the construction of Urban Imaginaries—or the desired idea that cities and their inhabitants consciously produce—through the vindication of the role of the architect as a Public Intellectual, that is, a designer that participates in public debates, risking his or her own position by questioning the general status quo. Medellin is still popularly associated with the idea of narco-trafficking, the drug lord Pablo Escobar, and extremely high murder rate suffered in the city from the 1970s through the 1990s. However, in 2013, Medellin has been awarded The Most Innovative City of the Year in a competition organized by the Wall Street Journal, beating contenders such as New York City and Tel Aviv. This studio operated as an international urban consulting agency, a group of experts able to deliver current diagnoses and potential Urban Imaginaries for cities, based in programmatic strategies and architectural operations. We travelled to Medellin to participated in an intensive workshop hosted by URBAM (EAFIT University), a prestigious research center of urban and environmental studies. The students were trained to develop their independent critical skills taking radical positions, learning to construct strong arguments and defend them graphically and orally. Approximately once a week pedagogical sessions were organized with guest lecturers, along with debates, acting workshops and a wide range of time constrained games.

Andres Macera, Marco Salazar + Ignacio Urquiza **A/B/C/D**
Eileen Chen + Li Li **E/F**

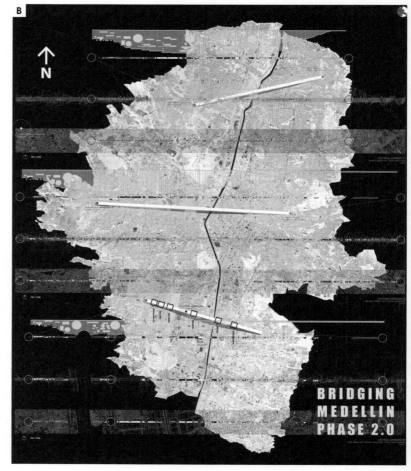

BRIDGING
MEDELLIN
PHASE 2.0

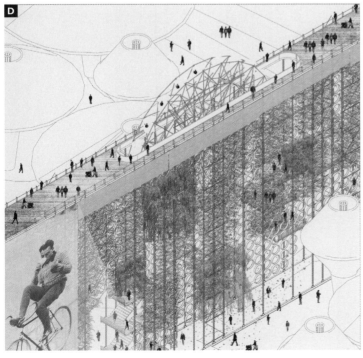

E

Sweet Home Urbanism
Advanced Architecture Studio 5
Fall 2013
Andrés Jaque, critic,
with Ernesto Silva

In the past, the concept of the 'home' has been seen in opposition to the urban, the social and the disputed: as the sweet realm of familiarity. A direct account of how the 'home' is daily performed clearly probes things to be slightly more complex and therefore further more interesting. The unpacking of this misunderstanding provides an opportunity to calibrate the notions of the role material devices play in the production of the way that architectural discipline defines its competences.

"Sweet Home Urbanism" focused on detecting, describing and versioning urban networks in which 'home' is collectively produced and made available. Starting with the accounting of New York based architectural devices— such as Manhattan Storage buildings, gay oriented bars, phone apps and the cheapest apartment rentals in town—we mapped the expanded network dimensions and their political tensions along with possible scenarios of evolution.

Jose Brunner **A**
Mintra Maneepairoj **B**
Patrick Craine **C/D/E/F**

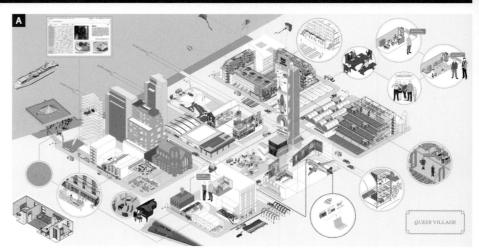

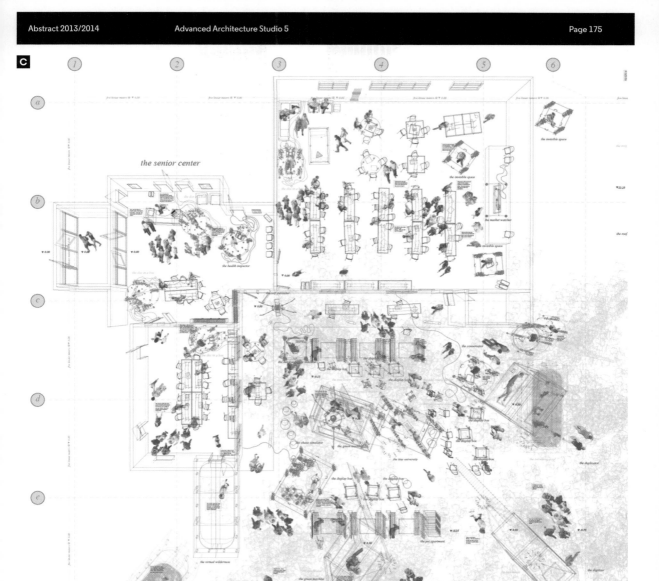

the senior center

the health inspector

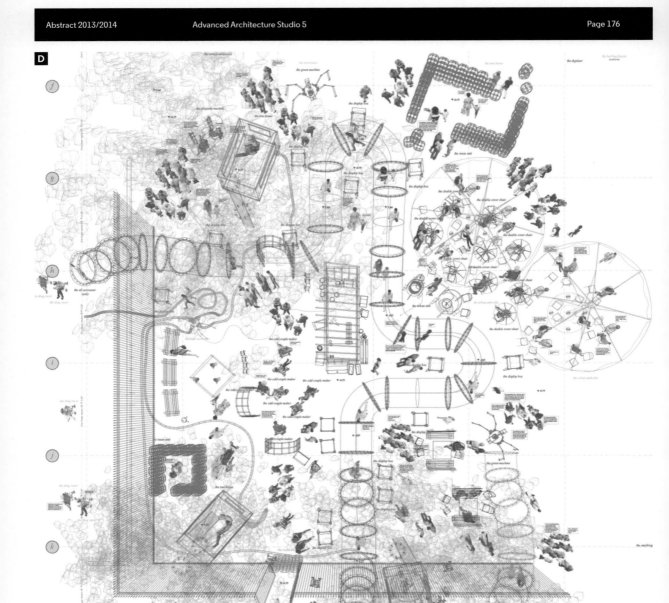

E

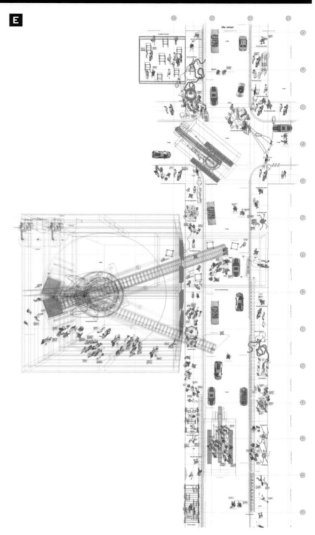

F

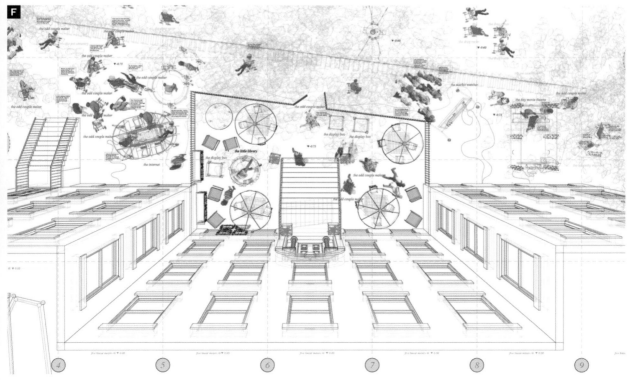

Recommissioning Saarinen: Reconsidering the Former US Embassy in Oslo Norway
Advanced Architecture Studio 5
Fall 2013
*Jorge Otero-Pailos +
Craig Konyk, critics*

The United States Embassy in Oslo Norway was designed by Eero Saarinen and completed in 1959. A black labradorite-clad triangular form, it is architecturally the older cousin of Saarinen's 1965 CBS Headquarters Building in New York—nicknamed "The Black Rock"—as well as the limestone clad US Embassy in London, designed by Saarinen in 1960. Sited across from the Royal Palace in Oslo's central Vika District, its fortress-like quality was reinforced post-9/11 to include bollards, barricades and a 3-meter high perimeter fence. Saarinen's Oslo Embassy is being decommissioned, with a replacement Embassy being planned. The Oslo replacement Embassy is being designed by EYP Architects and is to be located in the Huseby residential district. Ground was broken for this new building in May of 2012, with a completion expected in 2015. Meanwhile discussions have begun as to what is the most suitable new purpose for the existing Saarinen Embassy Building, with ideas ranging from a new Police Headquarters to a US Cultural Center. The task of the studio was to propose alternative uses for the existing Saarinen Embassy that consider the multitude of issues that it exposes. For purposes of the studio it was assumed that the United States will maintain ownership of the building. The Studio traveled to Oslo the third week of October, holding the Midterm Review at the AHO School of Architecture in Oslo, and attended lectures given by Saarinen scholars on his embassies and other notable works.

Whitney Starbuck Boykin **A/B**
Susan Bopp **C/D**
Saovanee Sethiwan **E/F**

A

B

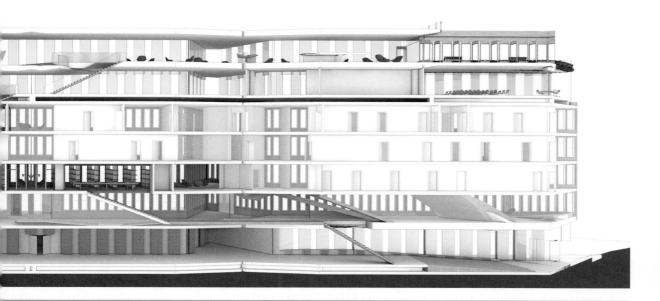

C

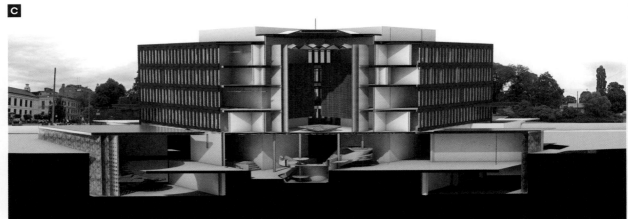

D

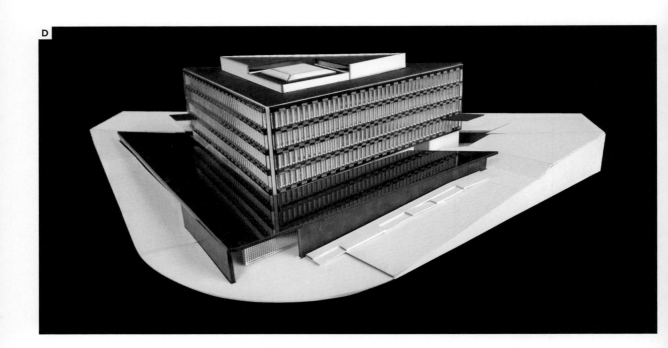

E

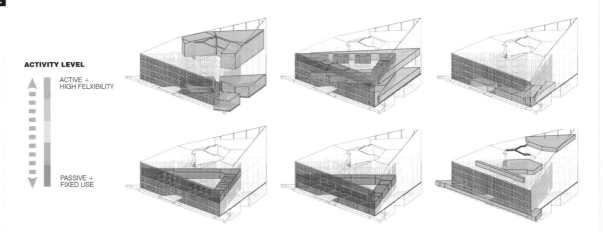

ACTIVITY LEVEL

ACTIVE +
HIGH FELXIBILITY

PASSIVE +
FIXED USE

F

Event City–Madison Square Garden Arena
Advanced Architecture Studio 5
Fall 2013
Frederic Levrat, critic,
with Angie Jeawon

The Manhattan Arena will need to relocate, or be redesigned within a new masterplan for Penn Station. The entire neighborhood is going through a major change, with the gigantic Hudson Yard development, the redesign of Penn Station and phase three of the High Line.

The opportunity to redesign Madison Square Garden allows us to rethink what is a major arena in the twenty-first century. MSG is one of the most well known performance spaces in the United State and currently hosts music entertainment, NBA Basketball, NHL Hokey and political conventions.

Formerly considered as "containers," arenas are now more interactive, where the distinction between the inside event and the city outside becomes permeable. The relationship between live events and mediated events is quite complex. Nevertheless, the actual "presence" of the event is also the essence of the city. The feeling that one can actually participate in the information generated by being present at a specific place at a specific time is essential and raises the question of "presence" in regard to Architecture. The city and the arena are both event generators and their relationship/synergy was investigated through this studio.

Jeongin Kim **A/B**
Soyae Baek **C/D/E/F**

C

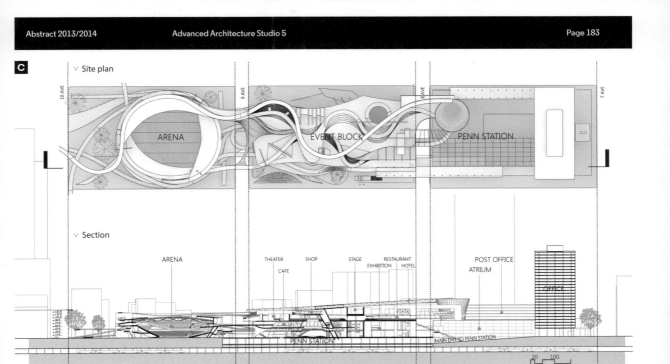

∨ Site plan

10 AVE   9 AVE   8 AVE   7 AVE

ARENA   EVENT BLOCK   PENN STATION

∨ Section

ARENA   THEATER   SHOP   STAGE   RESTAURANT   POST OFFICE
         CAFE   EXHIBITION   HOTEL   ATRIUM

OFFICE

PENN STATION   MAIN ENT TO PENN STATION

20   100
0   60   150 ft

D

E

GATE 13

GATE 8   GATE 9

F

Jamaica Bay 2050
Advanced Architecture Studio 5
Fall 2013
Kate Orff + Kate Ascher,
critics, with Johannes
Pointl + Gena Wirth

This studio looked at design
scenarios for "living with
water" and the latent urban and
ecological potential of Jamaica
Bay as a place of resiliency and
renewed economic vitality.
The Bay, currently in a state
of neglect, could become a
harbinger of a new relationship between water, urban
development and park space
in New York City. Our goal
was to transform the conceptions of urban waterfront to
include an emphasis on coastal
protection, soft infrastructure,
robust marine habitat and new
forms of post-Sandy housing,
commercial development,
recreational programming and
energy generation relative
to the twenty-first century
city. Together with MSRED
students, we explored the
past, present and future of the
Bay alongside projections for
growth in the NYC region and
the fact that tens of thousands
of people living and working
in this area are threatened by
sea level rise and continued
storm surge events. What are
currently peripheral lands and
waters became a laboratory for
innovation and experimentation. Emphasis was placed on
developing a science-driven
design methodology that spans
many scales, from macro-
level hydrological studies at
the scale of the outer Harbor
to small settlement clusters, to
targeted material prototypes.

Emily Koustae +
Marissa Nava **A/B**
Katie Zaeh **C/D/E/F/G/H/I**

A

B

C

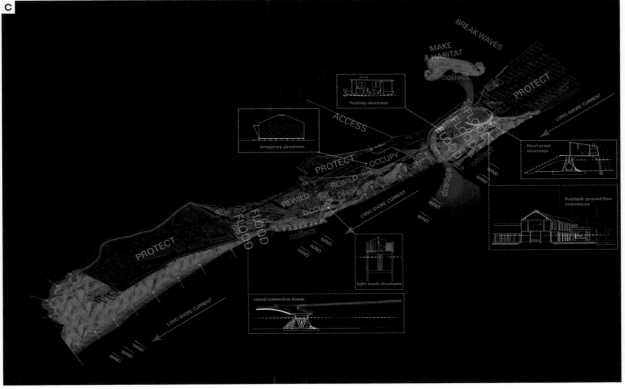

D

F

I

H

I

New Edge City

Advanced Architecture Studio 5
Fall 2013
*Richard Plunz + Patrica
Culligan, critics, with
Vanessa Espaillat, Robert
Elliott + Martin Hojny*

The 2013 Urban Ecology
studio was a collaboration
between GSAPP, the Columbia
University School of Engineering and Applied Sciences and
the City of New Rochelle. It
was also made in coordination
with the GSAPP Urban Design
Studio 2 and the Urban Design
Lab in the Earth Institute. The
challenge of this studio was
to work between the limits of
the disciplines of architecture,
urban planning and urban
engineering, through exploring
a new field in which to create
urban situations in space and
time. The studio emphasized
collaborative multi-disciplinary
thinking about the future
of urban environments.

The studio was sponsored by
the New Rochelle Department
of Development (DOD). Our
general topic engaged the New
York City region and ecological considerations related to
urban development for its water
edges. The outcome would be
a new realization that we must
now treat our urban waterfronts
differently than in the past.
The studio test case for this
question was the Long Island
Sound and its most urbanized
edge along the waterfront of
New Rochelle. In particular the
studio envisioned new development for David's Island, which
is located just off the coast and
is presently unoccupied and
recently devoid of building.

Brian Kim + Julia Green **A/B/C**
Geoffrey Bell, Brittany
Wright + Adam Atia **D/E**
Hannah Marcus, Siobhan
Watson + Sarah LeNet **F**

A

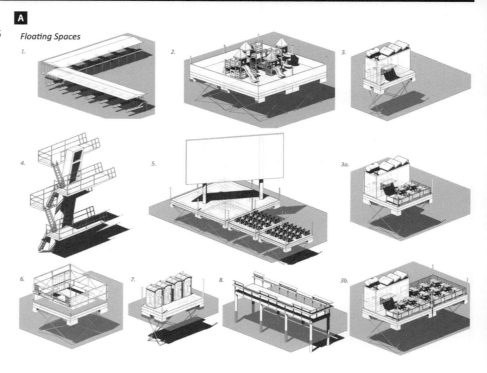

Floating Spaces

B

D

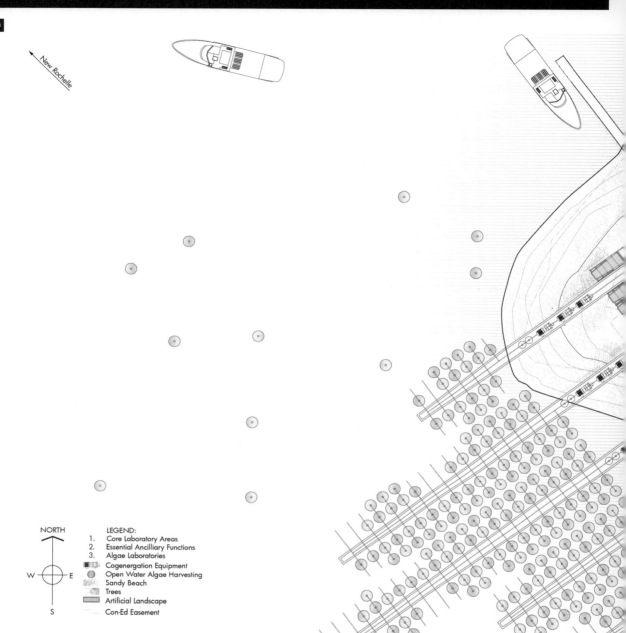

New Rochelle

NORTH

W   E

S

LEGEND:
1.   Core Laboratory Areas
2.   Essential Ancilliary Functions
3.   Algae Laboratories
    Cogenergation Equipment
    Open Water Algae Harvesting
    Sandy Beach
    Trees
    Artificial Landscape
    Con-Ed Easement

E

F

(n)certainties

Advanced Architecture Studio 5
Fall 2013
*Francois Roche + Ezio Blasetti,
critics, with Luis Felipe Paris*

The studio was in pursuit of the previous Opus – including materiality of the construction by ''computation and robotic process'' developed more precisely in this following text and integrating a notion of "life span," as a protocol of death and life, of "Eros and Thanatos", The new Opus developed scenarii from two novels, High-Rise by J G Ballard and ZOO by James Patterson and Michael Ledwidge, and a design process which stuttered between the pathology of an architecture including the multiple disorder of its inhabitants and the anarchic behavior of the other species from the nature. This antagonism, the dilemma, the confrontation – sympathy, empathy, antipathy – between human and animal was located in Bangkok, at the place of an existing ZOO.

Carlos Garcia, Allen Ghaida + Bian Lin **A/B/C**
Nikolaos Vlavianos + Hamid Reza Malhooz **D/E/F**

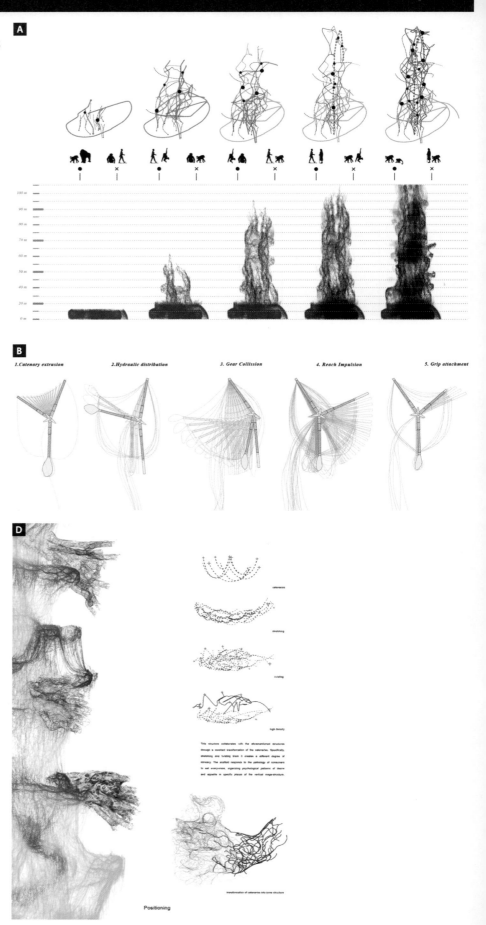

B
1. Catenary extrusion
2. Hydraulic distribution
3. Gear Collission
4. Reach Impulsion
5. Grip attachment

Positioning

C

E

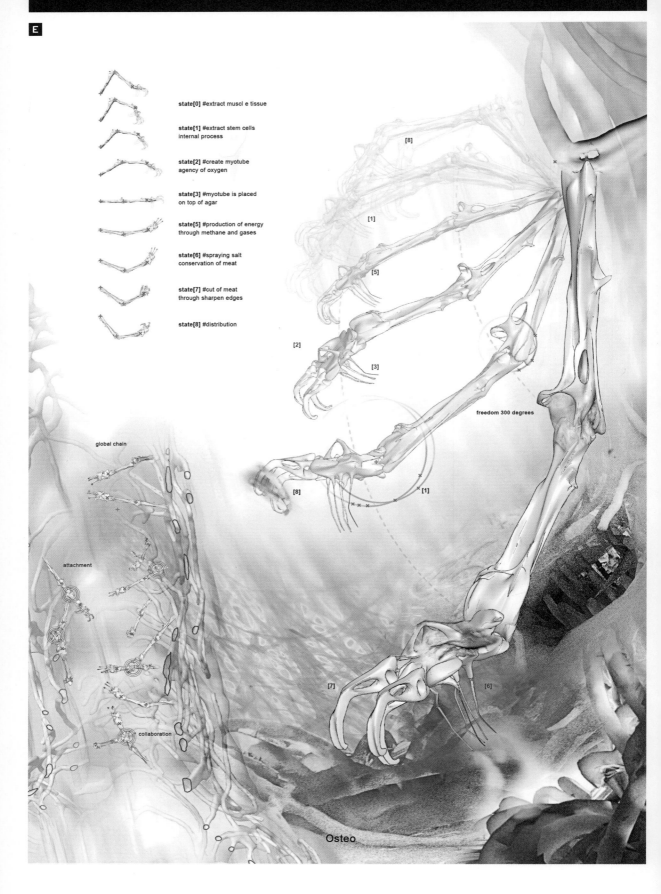

state[0] #extract muscl e tissue

state[1] #extract stem cells
internal process

state[2] #create myotube
agency of oxygen

state[3] #myotube is placed
on top of agar

state[5] #production of energy
through methane and gases

state[6] #spraying salt
conservation of meat

state[7] #cut of meat
through sharpen edges

state[8] #distribution

global chain

attachment

collaboration

freedom 300 degrees

Osteo

[8]
[1]
[5]
[2]
[3]
[1]
[8]
[7]
[6]

F

Exploring vertigo

Transience
Advanced Architecture Studio 5
Fall 2013
Karla Maria Rothstein, critic,
with Aya Maceda + David Zhai

The metropolis embodies a mortal palimpsest—accumulations and traces of humanity and temporality. This studio was about revolutionizing how we live with death in the city, and how progressive architecture may couple with urban infrastructure—in this iteration: ferry, farm, skyscraper, edge, billboard and waste—to radically re-qualify public space.

   In the dislocated contexts of our increasingly placeless-timeless-mediated existence—life is both profoundly ethereal and palpably real. Projects defined agile boundaries and intersections of life, death, transience, finitude and urbanity; exploring the precise moments where design meets life, where the manifestation of our intellectual position shapes space and material, reframing phenomena and human relations.

   Traditional funerary procedures and their associated structures are fraught with logistic, spatial and environmental burdens, incommensurate with the social actualities of our urban existence. Proposals engaged emergent forms of corpse disposition which more sensibly accelerate natural biological decomposition, enabling innovative models of civic space and new modalities of intimate remembrance, while questioning the need for permanent repositories and markers of our dead.

   We no longer live in an epoch of solidity with a steady belief in the eternal. Thus unconstrained by scriptures of all definitions, we are dedicated to necessary, innovative and plausible possibility.

Chi Feng Wu + Kuan I Ho **A/B/C**
Kangsan Danny Kim +
Ruoyu Wei **D/E**
Zhao Gao + Li Ling Lin **F/G/H**

A

D

E

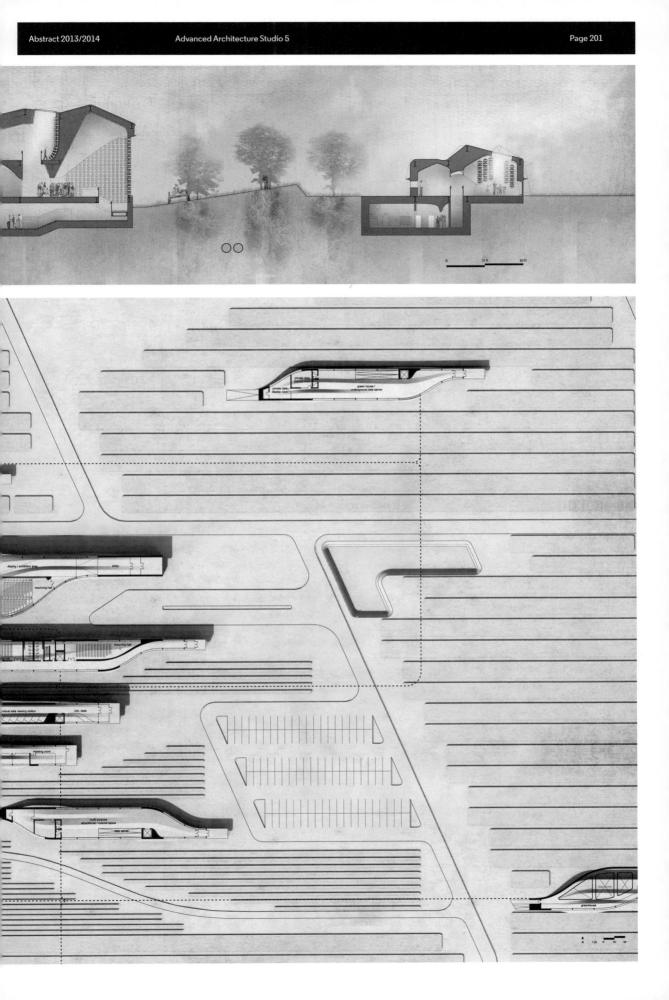

F

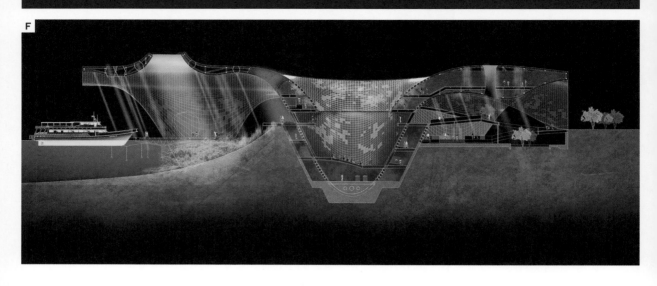

G

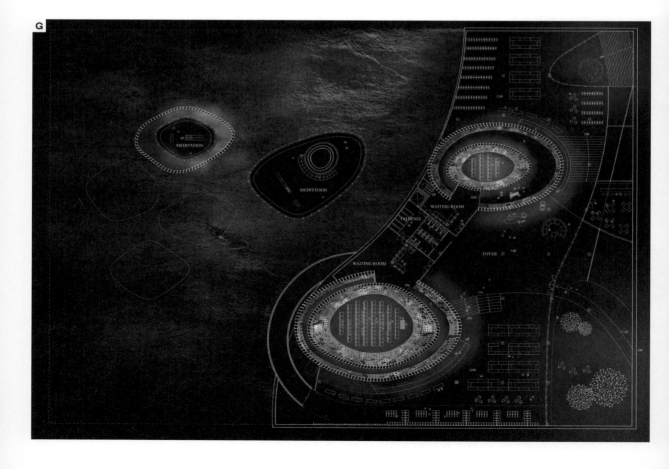

H

Pandora, Pandora, Pandora
Advanced Architecture Studio 5
Fall 2013
Yehuda Safran, critic,
with Silvia Perea

This advanced studio embraced Le Corbusier's understanding that architecture is the practice of a gift above all. Not only in the potlatch sense of North American Indians who were prepared to sacrifice all for the sake of rank and posterity, but as the way to fulfill one's vocation, one's love of architecture.

Our site was Alphabet City. Writers, poets, artists and Jazz musicians together with drug addicts and homeless made this part of Manhattan an island within. We proposed the Pandora House as a place of hedonistic cult. We developed a new typology to provide a social condenser, not in the Constructivist sense that was still in the shadow of production and utilitarian view of mankind, but in an expanded sense of George Bataille's earlier, pre-World War II writings, as a vision of excess, the notion of expenditure.

We examined a great number of prototypes illustrating a so-called hedonistic program in order to invent and shape an unprecedented prototype for the future, engaging all our inalienable gifts; the gift of pain and pleasure, the gift of language, the gift of rational insight, the gift of color, among many other gifts.

Estebande Backer **A/B/C**
Fernando Ceña **D**
Rodrigo Valenzuela Jerez **E/F**

D

E

F

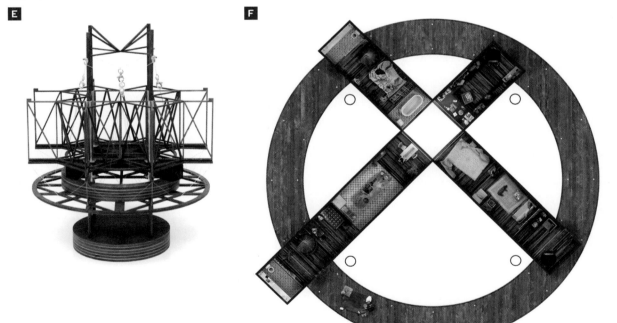

Concept + Notation

Advanced Architecture Studio 5
Fall 2013
*Bernard Tschumi, critic, with
Bart-Jan Polman, Jerome
Haferd, Maria Esnaola
Cano + Jake Matatyaou*

Our Fall Studio 2013 explored 'Concept + Notation.' It was entitled "Armory Generator Notation." Its aim was to invent a new type of urban generator for the twenty-first century.

As an urban generator, the students had to design a place that could foster and encourage new modes of living unknown until today—i.e. loft living or multipurpose airports that didn't exist until the 1970s and then changed urban lifestyles on small and large scales. Today, with virtual reality and social networks altering urban perceptions, how will these phenomena generate a new architecture?

By 'Armory', we meant a space that replaced a now obsolete type. A potent urban example existed in the once military-turn-civic space found within the Armories of Manhattan and surrounds. Still present in every city in the US, its typology can be open to every interpretation.

By notation we meant that in order to avoid falling into the trap of "hyperrealist" cliché representation and renderings, we asked the students to invent new modes of notation, that described space, time, activity, processes, body, light, private, public, etc., in a novel way.

Maria Lozano + Wen Zhu **A/B**
Mengfan Fu +
Theodora Felekou **C/D**
Pedro Figueiredo +
Sudarshan Venkatraman **E/F/G**

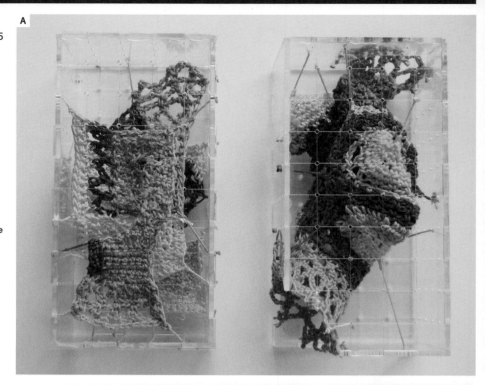

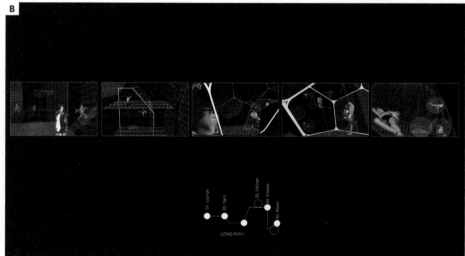

D

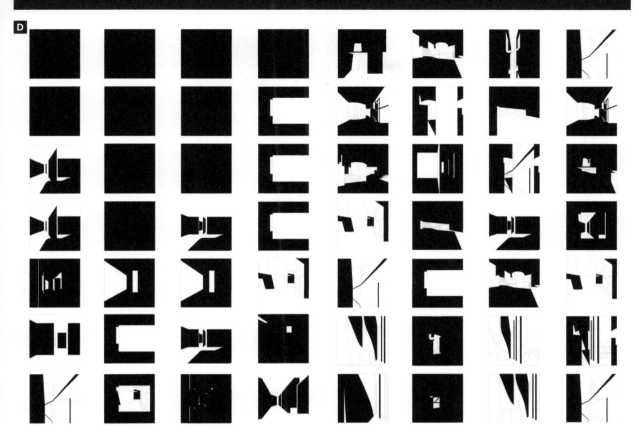

How will the fragmented paths be connected?

E

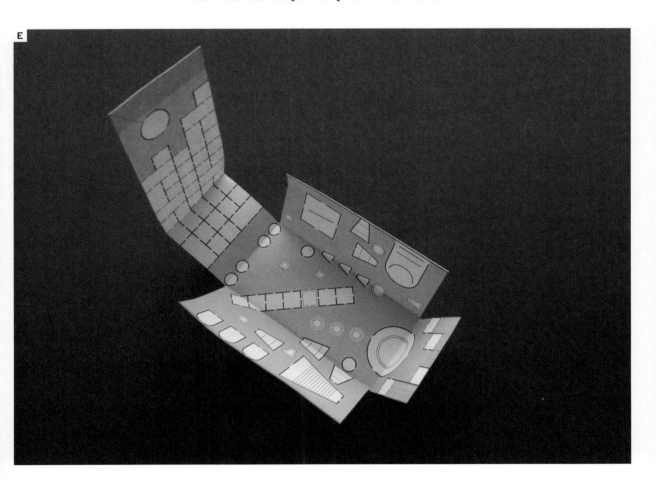

F

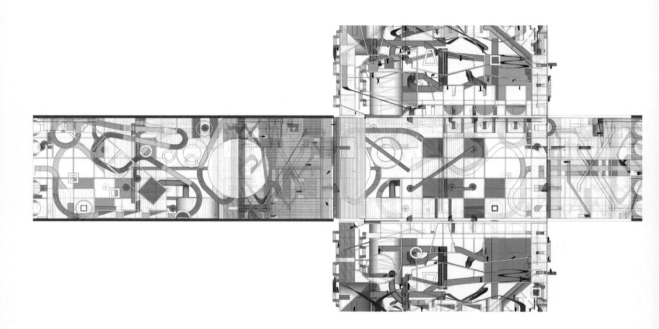

G

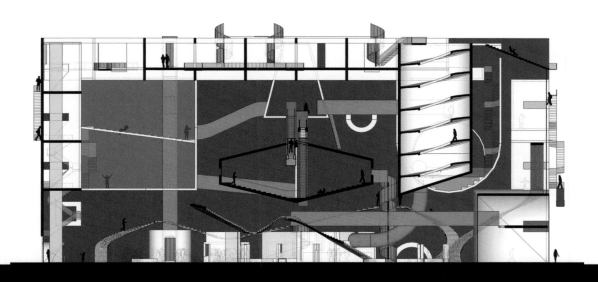

Institute of Spatial Perception–Subjectivity, Neuroscience + Spatial Praxis
Advanced Architecture Studio 5
Fall 2013
Marc Tsurumaki, critic,
with John Morrison

Today, when virtual stimuli and technological interfaces impinge more and more on unmediated experience, questions of how we perceive our environment and architecture's role in locating the subject among competing inputs have become increasingly vital. Siting our research in the fluid territory between spatial form and human cognition, the studio engaged both emerging research in the neurosciences and artistic practices grounded in sensory phenomena to address the politics of perception in contemporary culture and the agency of architecture in a hyper-saturated sensory environment.

Examining the intersection between architectural, artistic and neurobiological paradigms of human perception through the design of a cross-disciplinary research institute in New York City – the project attempted to liberate new potentials within timeworn debates over space as both a cognitive and cultural construct. Seeking a more nuanced and polyvalent understanding of spatial perception at the convergence point of science, technology and art, architecture's inevitable dialogue with optic, haptic, auditory and tactile conditions acted as the source of new propositions that engaged the entanglement of embodied perception, temporal extension and material form. The studio questioned how architecture itself—as a powerful medium for orchestrating both individual and collective subjectivities might generate new potentials within dominant perceptual modalities.

Ebberly Strathairn **A/B/C/D**
Jeremy Kim **E/F/G**

B

D

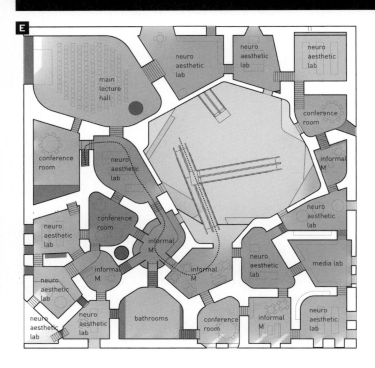

E

Labels within plan:
- main lecture hall
- neuro aesthetic lab
- neuro aesthetic lab
- neuro aesthetic lab
- conference room
- conference room
- neuro aesthetic lab
- informal M
- neuro aesthetic lab
- neuro aesthetic lab
- conference room
- informal M
- neuro aesthetic lab
- media lab
- neuro aesthetic lab
- informal M
- informal M
- neuro aesthetic lab
- neuro aesthetic lab
- bathrooms
- conference room
- informal M
- neuro aesthetic lab

F

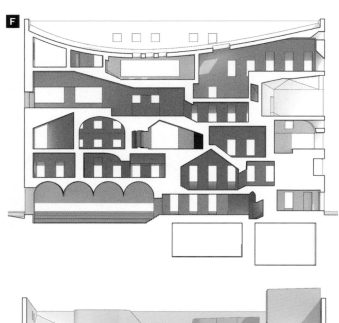

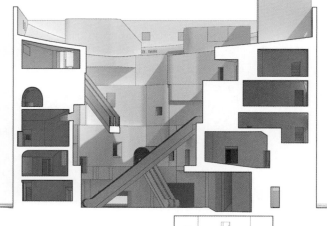

G

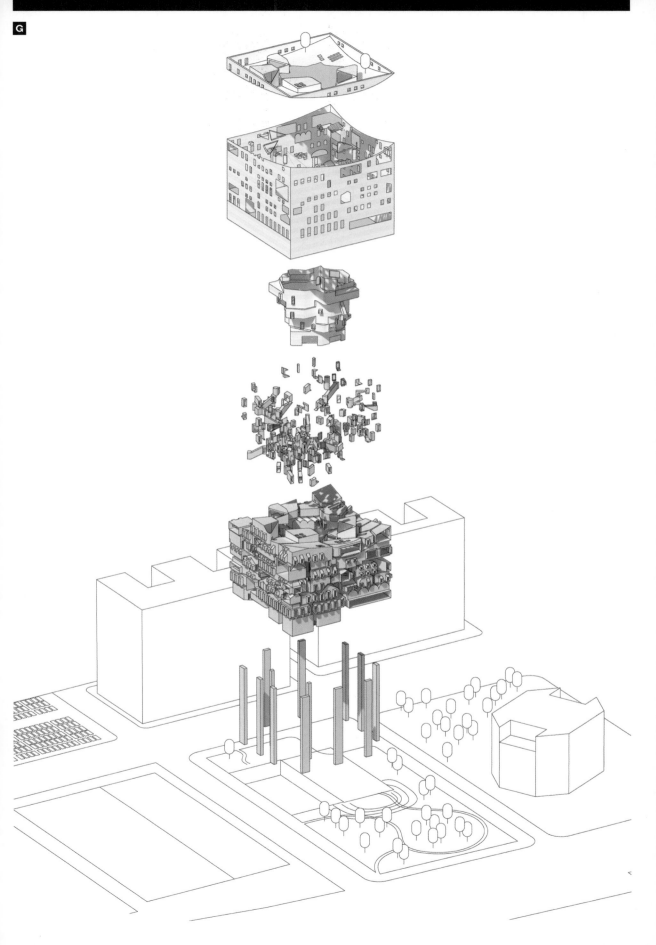

Urban Futures/Future Architectures Africa 5.0—Tracking Topologies of Global Trade

Advanced Architecture Studio 5
Fall 2013
Mabel Wilson, critic, with Mokena Makeka, Brigette Borders + Carson Smuts

Acts of trading produce the vapor trails of globalization's expansive reach. Various forms of trading circulate goods, services, ideas, data, waste and those people engaged in it across borders, continents and oceans. Tracking Topologies of Global Trade examined networks of trade that link people, institutions and places in the vibrant global hub of Johannesburg, South Africa. During the first four weeks of the studio, students attended workshops introducing techniques of data mining and parametric modeling that allowed these systems and phenomena to be studied in magnitude from the global to the local along with how they change over time. These animated models (chronoscapes) and conventional mappings captured the dynamic temporal and spatial dimensions of these systems and networks. The studio made a weeklong visit to Johannesburg in the first half of the semester for reviews, research and workshops at Studio X. Drawing on this rich body of research, the studio developed propositions for the African Trade Zone Observatory whose mission is to monitor, collect, research and publicize data on trading as it occurs in real-time across the continent. Students developed theses on the utopian or dystopian possibilities of global trade as the studio made evident its links to the rise of Neo-Liberalism, informality, surveillance, exploitation of resources and despoiling of land.

Che-Wei Yeh **A**
Chisom Ezekwo **B/C/D**
Darius Somers **E/F**

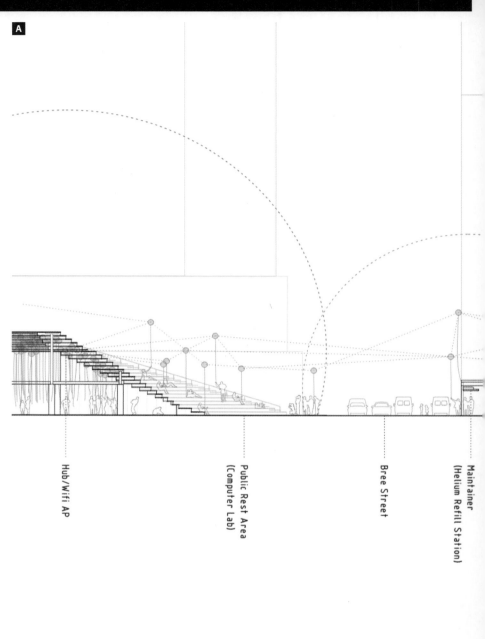

A

Hub/Wifi AP

Public Rest Area
(Computer Lab)

Bree Street

Maintainer
(Helium Refill Station)

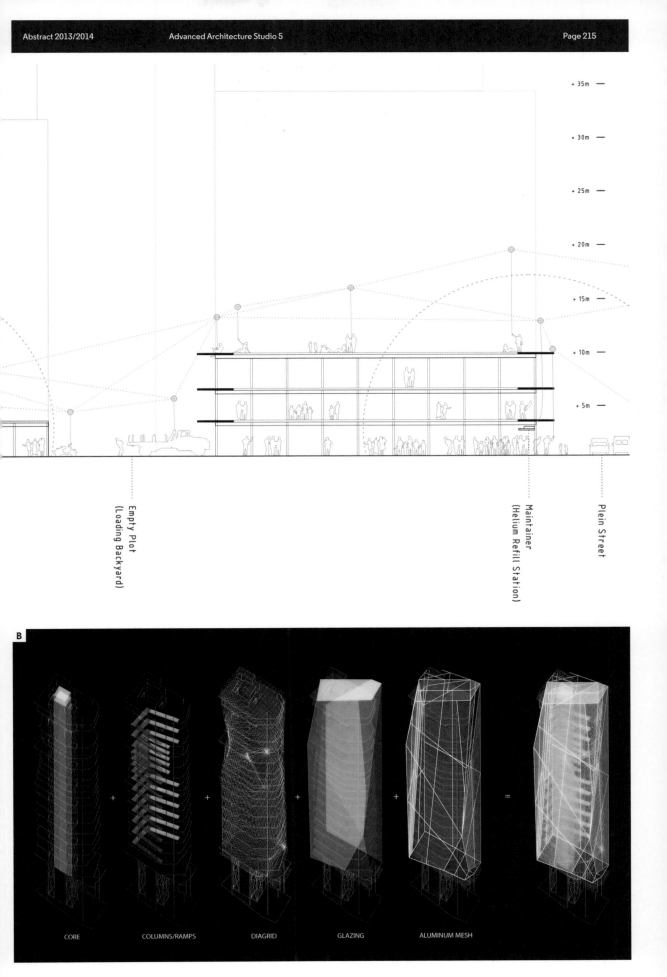

+ 35m

+ 30m

+ 25m

+ 20m

+ 15m

+ 10m

+ 5m

Empty Plot
(Loading Backyard)

Maintainer
(Helium Refill Station)

Plein Street

B

CORE   +   COLUMNS/RAMPS   +   DIAGRID   +   GLAZING   +   ALUMINUM MESH   =

E

F

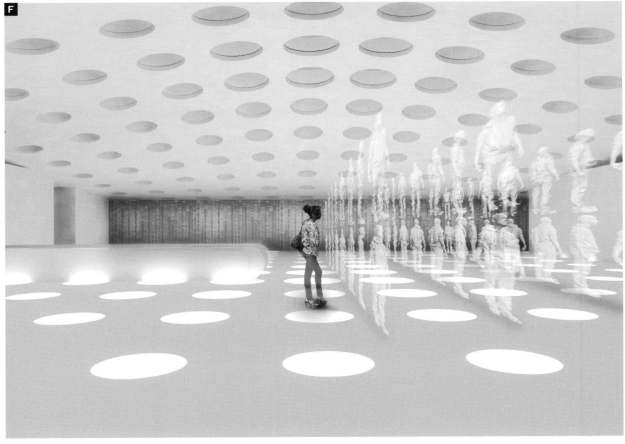

40,000 Houses / 347 Apartments - Area 5: A New Unité
Advanced Architecture Studio 6
Spring 2014
Michael Bell + Zachary Kostura, critics

On a redevelopment site in Fort Lee, New Jersey the studio explored a reinvention of Le Corbusier's Unité d'Habitation. The project followed a contemporary analysis of the building and its programming as well as its materials, thermal and structural goals and its overall scale and architectural qualities. The studio was not overtly a call to work in the manner of Le Corbusier, but it focused on the fusion of programming, material and social goals in architecture as a unified structure.

On an economic level the studio was set against a backdrop of the tremendous investment in single-family houses made en masse by equity groups since the housing market collapse of 2008. Our particular study focused on the Blackstone Groups whose purchase of approximately 40,000 houses from foreclosure turned formerly individually owned houses into a single massive rental property to create an investment portfolio that unifies the houses as a single investment within securities.

A central question was how do architectural models such as the Unité d'Habitation, a 347 unit apartment building and kindergarten with retail provisions, sustain and compel re-evaluation when seen as ultimately small in scale against emerging forms of mass housing today?

Heeyun Kim + Sam Yul Huh **A/B/C**
Minglu Zheng **D/E**

A

C

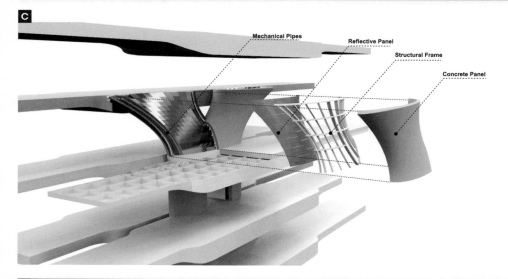

Mechanical Pipes

Reflective Panel

Structural Frame

Concrete Panel

D

E

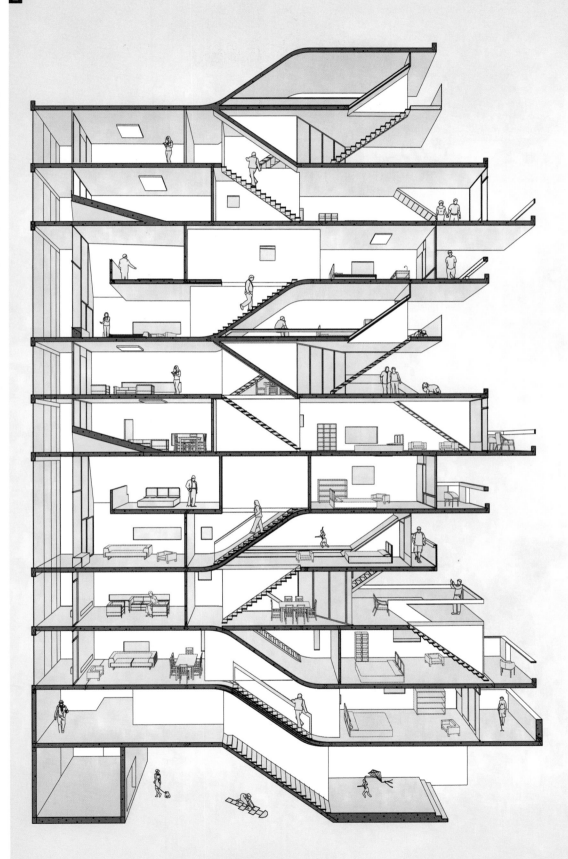

CBIP 2014: AUTOMATION 2.0
Advanced Architecture Studio 6
Spring 2014
David Benjamin, critic, Adam Modesitt, John Cerone + Jason Roberts, software consultants

In this section of the CBIP studio, we considered how architecture might be defined by an ecology of numbers—an ebb and flood of input numbers and output numbers. To start, we engaged input numbers as a technique to grow geometry. We used parametric modeling software to create adaptive three-dimensional models that are defined by precise inputs. Then we wrote scripts that generate complex forms based on changes in the inputs. This general approach reflected a relatively new paradigm in artificial intelligence: rather than program machines to follow fixed and known rules, set up an emergent system to evolve new and unexpected results.

But applying scripting to generate geometry was only the beginning. The heart of our research involved the study of how specific input numbers correspond to specific output numbers. After a set of inputs generates a precise form, how do we measure its performance?

For performance analysis, we used a variety of digital simulation packages to test the performance of possible designs under various conditions. We also considered how to quantify objectives such as program and aesthetics in order to measure each design.

We used software to investigate data, to explore a very wide potential design space, to minimize our preconceptions, to avoid relying on old rules of thumb, to derive unexpected high-performing results and to enhance our creativity. Most importantly, we used software to collaborate and to develop designs that are not fixed singular, but instead are adaptive and re-usable.

Automation 2.0 was one unit of the CBIP collaborative studio, and we shared a common workflow with the other two units.

Che-Wei Yeh **A/B**
Li-Ling Lin **C/D**
Ying-Chen Lin **E/F**

A

"CONTRACTORS' TEMPLATE"
EFFICIENCY

"LAWYERS' TEMPLATE"
EFFICIENCY

"ENGINEERS' TEMPLATE"
EFFICIENCY

"ARCHITECTS' TEMPLATE"
EFFICIENCY

"CONTRACTORS' TEMPLATE"
ANXIETY

"LAWYERS' TEMPLATE"
ANXIETY

"ENGINEERS' TEMPLATE"
ANXIETY

"ARCHITECTS' TEMPLATE"
ANXIETY

"CONTRACTORS' TEMPLATE"
RELIABILITY

"LAWYERS' TEMPLATE"
RELIABILITY

"ENGINEERS' TEMPLATE"
RELIABILITY

"ARCHITECTS' TEMPLATE"
RELIABILITY

B

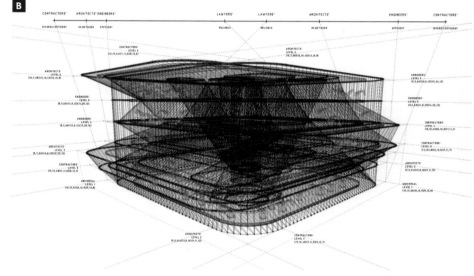

C

40   55   52   51

retangular grid(only one row of robots overlay) get higher efficiency.

A diagonal Tube gets lower scores but more spatial experiences.

OPTIMAL MODE

INPUT : #001

- Robot type
- Robot autonomy   =2X2

- Opening
- Opening location
- Chanel ratio

OUTPUT :

- Robot efficiency
  4.4
- Robot capacity
  0.66(44/66)
- Human territory
  0.61(224.34m2/362.5m2)
- Energy generation =120W
- Chanel volume   =48.665m3

INPUT : #002

- Robot type
- Robot autonomy   =5X5

- Opening
- Opening location
- Chanel ratio

OUTPUT :

- Robot efficiency
  6.0
- Robot capacity
  0.66(6/9)
- Human territory
  0.94(343.66m2/362.5m2)
- Energy generation =120W
- Chanel volume   =48.665m3

INPUT : #003

- Robot type
- Robot autonomy   =5X2

- Opening
- Opening location
- Chanel ratio

OUTPUT :

- Robot efficiency
  7.8
- Robot capacity
  0.625(15/24)
- Human territory
  0.87(315.4m2/362.5m2)
- Energy generation =120W
- Chanel volume   =48.6d5m3

INPUT : #004

- Robot type
- Robot autonomy

- Opening
- Opening location   A(15.362,1.881) B(6.395,2.926)
- Chanel ratio

OUTPUT :

- Robot efficiency
  7.6
- Robot capacity
  0.6(14/24)
- Human territory
  0.87(318.54m2/362.5m2)
- Energy generation =120W
- Chanel volume   =48.6d5m3

D

E

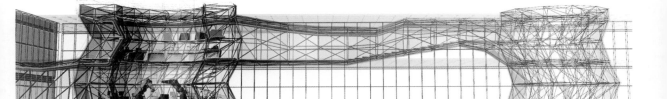

F

Plastic + Elastic: The Museum
Advanced Architecture Studio 6
Spring 2014
Lise Anne Couture, critic

This studio resided at the intersection of the urban realm and the space of culture. As the interface between architecture and the city, and between the public realm and the private interior, occur within the thickness and across the surface of enclosure, the studio explored the architectural possibilities of a hybrid condition that stretches between a taut two dimensional envelope and a sculptural three dimensional articulated mass… plastic and elastic were not intended to be taken literally as an aesthetic or physical quality but rather describe a terrain that enabled multiple kinds of exchanges and experiences through shared and overlapping territory. The studio was driven by three intertwined areas of investigations: form and surface, urbanism and program.

Lindsey Barker **A**
Munyoung Lee + Soojin Kim **B/C**
Ricardo Vega **D/E/F**
Zhao Gao **G/H/I**

D

E

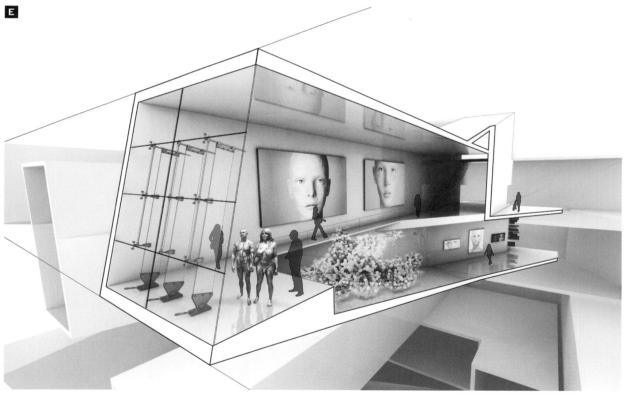

F

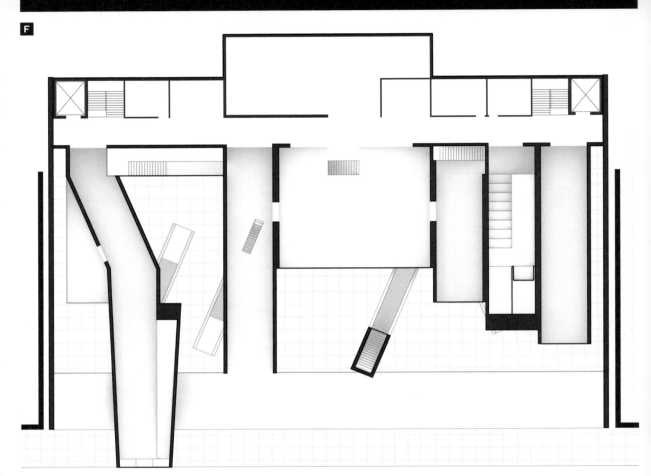

G

H

I

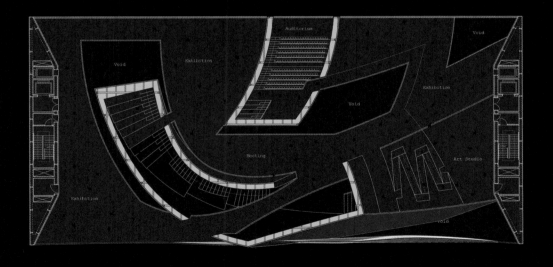

TAHRIR AS BREAK |
Between a City + a
Square--Spaces of Power
Advanced Architecture Studio 6
Spring 2014
Shahira Fahmy, critic,
with Emanuel Admassu

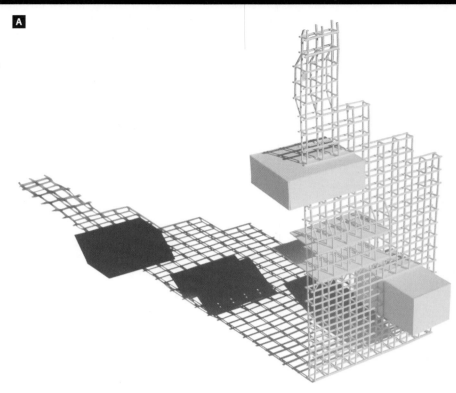

This design studio aimed to examine the current conditions of fluidity and volatility in Istanbul and Cairo as possible sites for architectural invention. By investigating the emerging patterns of power, the research moved beyond the boundaries of Tahrir Square and Gezi Park to examine the micro, spatial contestations that are shaping these cities. Identifying echoes between 'sites of contestation' in Cairo and Istanbul, the studio proposed strategies that would empower a specific network of stakeholders while maintaining their access to the city. Devising specific means of representation, the proposals dissected the complexity behind the construction or reconstruction of urban infrastructure to facilitate resistance. Each project analyzed strategies—organizational, representational and material—that are defining our contemporary understanding of boundaries within the city. The discoveries from this analysis were used to develop site(s) of contestation with varying scales and scope, based on the conflicts framed by the research of each city. The projects revealed or camouflaged pre-existing socio-political conditions that contribute to the constructed identity of the present moment: tactically oscillating between a city, Cairo / Istanbul, and a square, Tahrir / Gezi.

Fernando Ceña **A/B/C**
Qi Shan **D/E**
Karl Issara Roarty **F/G**

C

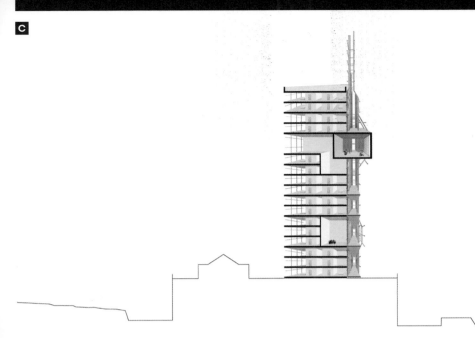

D

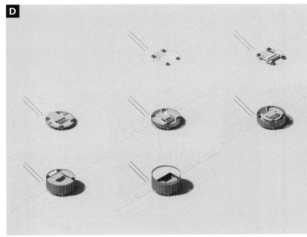

E

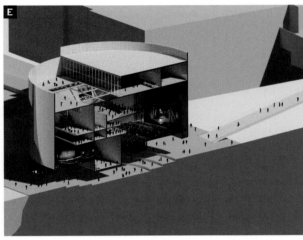

F

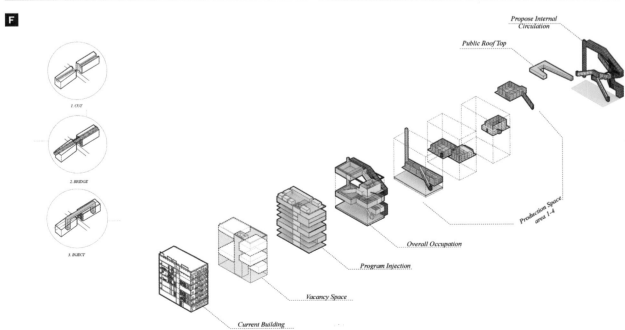

1. CUT

2. BRIDGE

3. INJECT

Propose Internal Circulation

Public Roof Top

Production Space area 1-4

Overall Occupation

Program Injection

Vacancy Space

Current Building

G

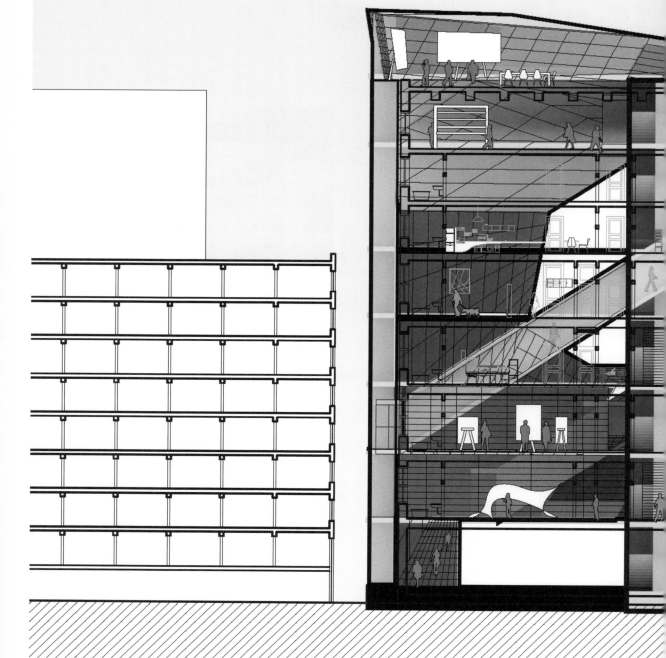

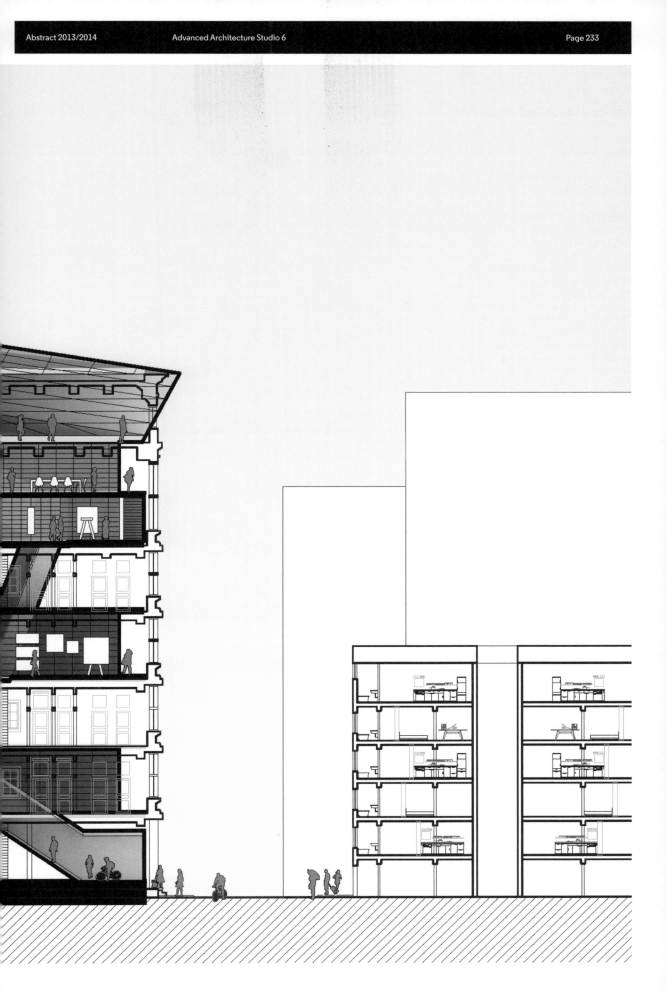

Color Studio
Advanced Architecture Studio 6
Spring 2014
Leslie Gill + Mike Jacobs, critics

Color exists in itself.
Henry Matisse

Color cannot stand alone.
Wassily Kandinsky

Color is suited to simple races, peasants and savages.
Le Corbusier

Color is a concrete expression of a maximum difference within identity. Adrian Stokes

The study of color is a tricky endeavor that breeds contradictory and didactic opinions. Yet, color has maintained a central role in cultural discourse, continuously evolving, understood through new technologies, altered by production capabilities and responding to pertinent questions of the day. David Batchelor has argued that the Western world is currently chromophobic: "it manifests itself in the many and varied attempts to purge color from culture, to devalue color, to diminish its significance, to deny its complexity."

This studio investigated three parallel trajectories of color; the symbolic, the measurable and the perceptual, in order to initiate strategies to design. These strategies were, in turn, situated, developed and tested within the tangible constraints of three monochromatic landscapes of the Arctic: the boreal forest (green), fresh and salt water (blue) and the cryosphere (white).

Students were asked to design two structures in two sites: The first, an Arctic-based data collection outpost, designed to support the research of our increasingly fragile ecosystem; the second, a local "Habitat Preserve," an Archive and Museum designed with the mandate to preserve in miniature, increasingly threatened Artic landscapes. Part scientific archive, part visual spectacle, the Habitat Preserve considered all key stakeholders—Human, Animal, Mineral and Plant—in an effort to effectively lobby for, and protect the biodiversity of this globally significant eco-region for future generations.

Andrew Maier **A/B/C**
Blair Denhart Dargusch **D/E/F**
Hajeong Lim + James Stoddart **G**

A

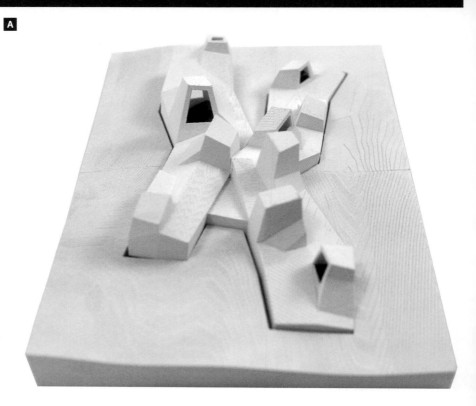

B

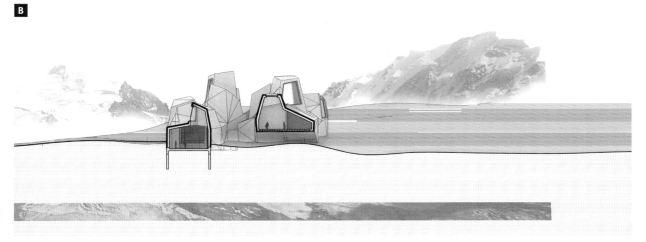

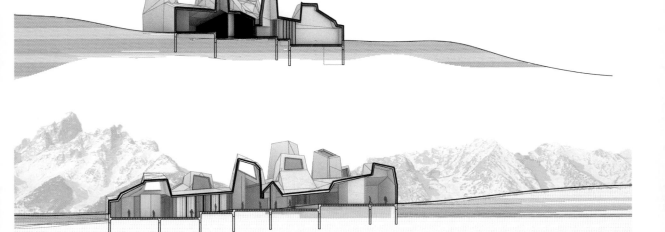

C

D

E

GROUND LEVEL PLAN

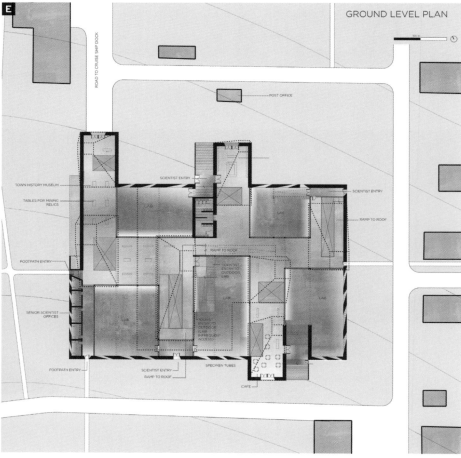

F

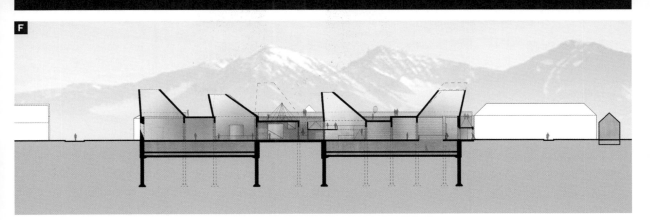

G

Image Cities Circus
Advanced Architecture Studio 6
Spring 2014
Mario Gooden, critic,
with Carson Smuts +
Mokena Makeka

In the age of globalization the image of the city exists in the imaginary of its media images proliferated by the Internet, global media conglomerates and social media. In line with globalization and urban entrepreneurialism, the meanings of cultural elements are produced and circulated to symbolically represent values and the identity of the city itself. No longer is the image of the city defined by its environment, but rather, the image of the city is defined by its "image dimension" and its ability to construct itself as a brand in order to seek international attention and to market itself to global investment. That Johannesburg has re-branded itself as "A World Class African City" signifies the international attention the city received in recent years and the expected global investments, as the igniting forces of globalization transition from China and Southeast Asia, to Brazil and South America and now to the African continent.

The studio used advanced computational methods and parametric modeling to research, analyze and translate the reflexive flows and topological conditions image city Johannesburg. The preliminary research engaged the new types of relations and exchanges via time-sharing social practices, social media and social networks that collapse virtual topology upon urban topography and physical construct in order to allow for adaptive responses to create an increasingly complex heterogeneous and mutable landscape.

The studio traveled to Johannesburg and Cape Town, South Africa for a week in March for fieldwork and site reconnaissance and to visit Studio-X Johannesburg.

Junhee Cho **A/B/C**
Marlin Torres **D/E**

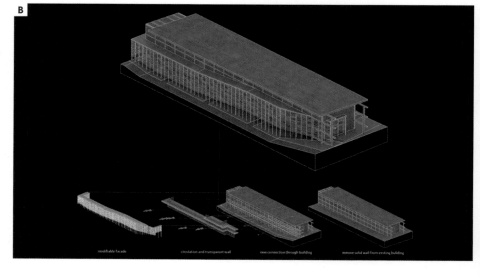

modifiable facade   circulation and transparent wall   new connection through building   remove solid wall from existing building

C

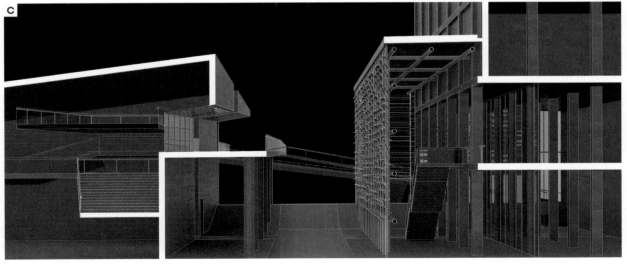

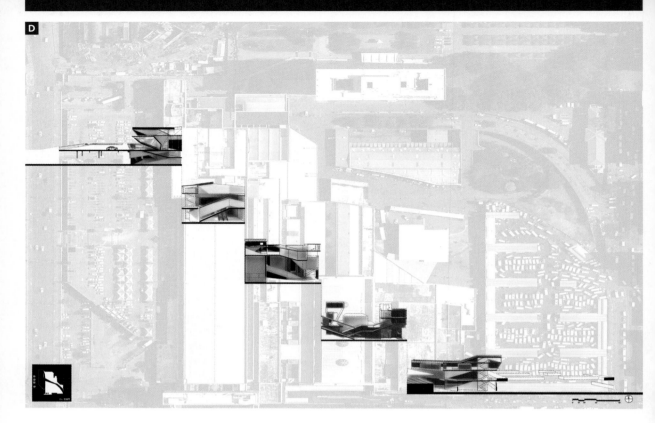

Chapter 4: Mumbai, Hybrid Residential Infrastructures in the Central City
Advanced Architecture Studio 6
Spring 2014
Juan Herreros, critic,
with María Esnaola +
Diana Cristóbal

Typological Correction: Mumbai, as a laboratory of centers that have lost their ideal conditions for living but offer a physical fabric full of architectural interest, is asking for a second chance to find a pertinent role in the urban scene. The analysis of the starting conditions and the connections between architecture and the social, economic and political coordinates become fundamental to the discussions.

Conceptual Representation: Analyzing, describing, testing and communicating our work is intimately linked with the instruments we use to quantify. Election, implementation and even invention of new systems of representation are a pertinent object of study in CAD-times.

Global Practice: Everyone is involved today in a global practice. Hence, it is important to develop a critical sense when acting in contexts where neither mimesis nor imposition is an alternative. Allowing the foreign gaze to discover new equations and to re-set the context with a different lexicon gives the locals the opportunity to build new affections for what they have, while re-contextualizing them into global culture.

Re-programming, re-presenting, re-densifying, re-living, etc. To recycle urban fragments by converting them into pieces of sufficient scale that alters the system of centers of gravity of the city.

Chi Feng Wu **A/B**
Marco Salazar **C**
Michael Schissel **D/E/F**

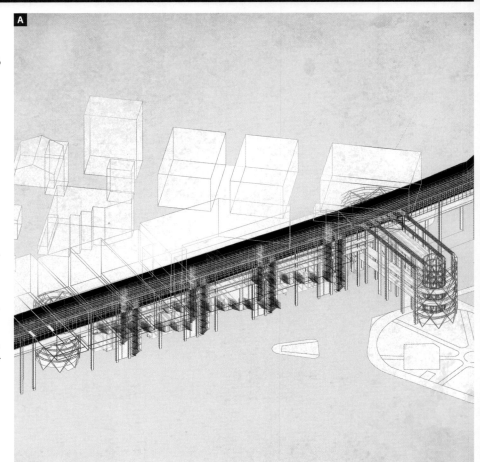

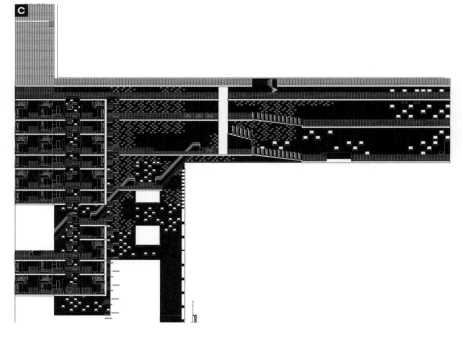

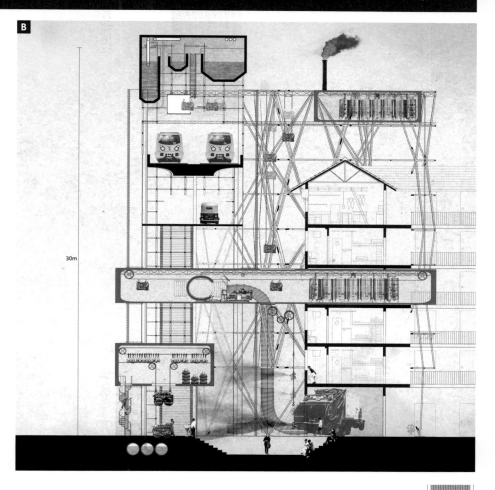

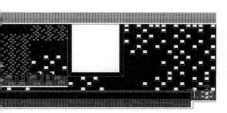

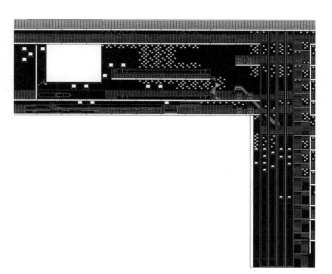

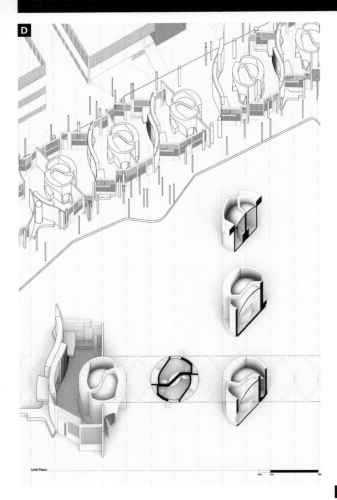

Unit Plans

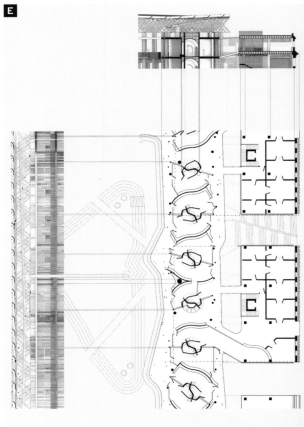

Unit Plans

Language: Structure + Light
Advanced Architecture Studio 6
Spring 2014
*Steven Holl + Dimitra
Tsachrelia,critics*

*Why are there any languages?
Why are there so many?*

Is the Man Who is Tall Happy?
Noam Chomsky

As an experimental test in three parts, this studio focused on Language: Structure and Light. The first part was an analysis of particular historical works of a clear language: Linear, Planar and Volumetric. This exercise was based on analytical drawings and model studies as "language fragments". For part two the students created a synthesis of structure and light in actual materials. They were challenged to construct a physical model within 16x16x16 inches and make a three minute video focused on passages through space in light. For part three the students explored art, poetry and sound space. The site was located in the center of Colombia's capital city, within the campus of the National University established in 1937 and designed by Leopold Rother. The campus was envisioned as an experimental infrastructure, a laboratory of architecture and urbanism, manifesting the balance between science and art. The 50,000 square foot new facility for Art/ Poetry/ Sound space aimed at being a catalyst and social bridge connecting the University with local communities. The inventions of its flexible programs were integral to a new architecture and central to the studio problem.

Dimitrios Spyropoulos +
Gemma Gene **A/B**
Ruoyu Wei + Haochen Yu **C/D**
Zachary Maurer + Vahe
Markosian **E/F/G**

C

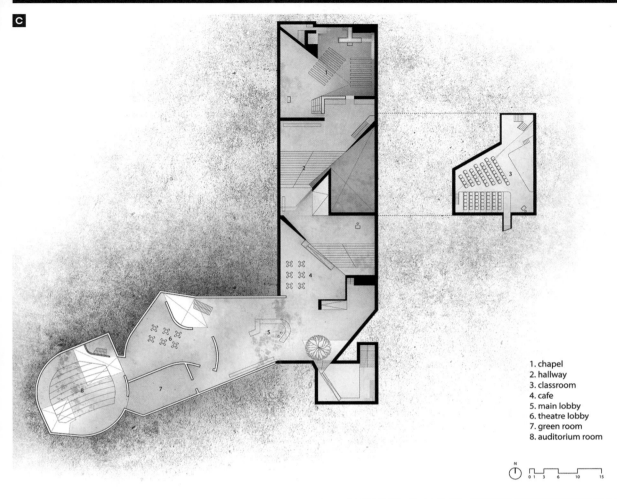

1. chapel
2. hallway
3. classroom
4. cafe
5. main lobby
6. theatre lobby
7. green room
8. auditorium room

N
0 1 3   6   10   15

D

0 1 3   6   10   15 m

E

Machines for Architecture to be Lived in
Advanced Architecture Studio 6
Spring 2014
Jeffrey Inaba + Benedict Clouette, critics

Architecture relies on a range of technologies to make the structures of our cities livable. In their absence, buildings would lack basic services like water and power. There would be no heating, cooling, lighting, fire safety or elevators. Repairs and maintenance would be impossible, digital and communication technology also out of the question. The capacity to support life would be severely diminished. Architecture would be reduced to basic shelter.

C-Lab's studio considered the environmental and mechanical performance of a building as an active input of the design process. Machines are vital to the life of buildings and it would be undesirable to have architecture without them, but it would be better if architecture were itself conceived of as a machine whose forms, spaces and technology collectively condition the interior. Certainly, this technological aspect does not have to be seen in the experience of the architecture, just as buildings today and, for that matter, building machinery do not look like the technologies housed within them. Instead, the form the technology takes on could be in the service of the architect's preoccupation, laying the groundwork for an inquiry about space, figuration or urbanism. In other words, deepening the dialogue about climate technology can circulate novel strategies for how to integrate buildings and machines, as well as give architecture a breath of fresh air.

Dichen Ding **A/B**
Ebberly Strathairn + Rich Duff **c**
Zhonghan Huang + Li Li **D/E/F**

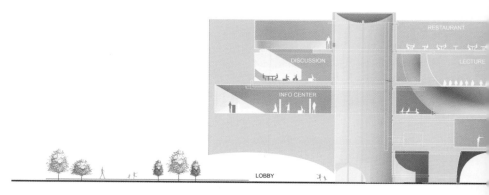

SECTION
scale 1' = 1/16"

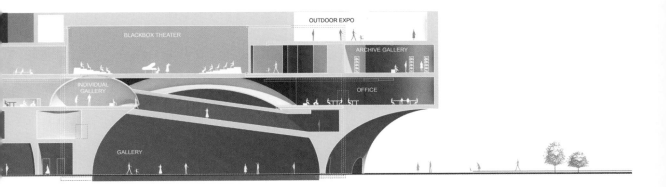

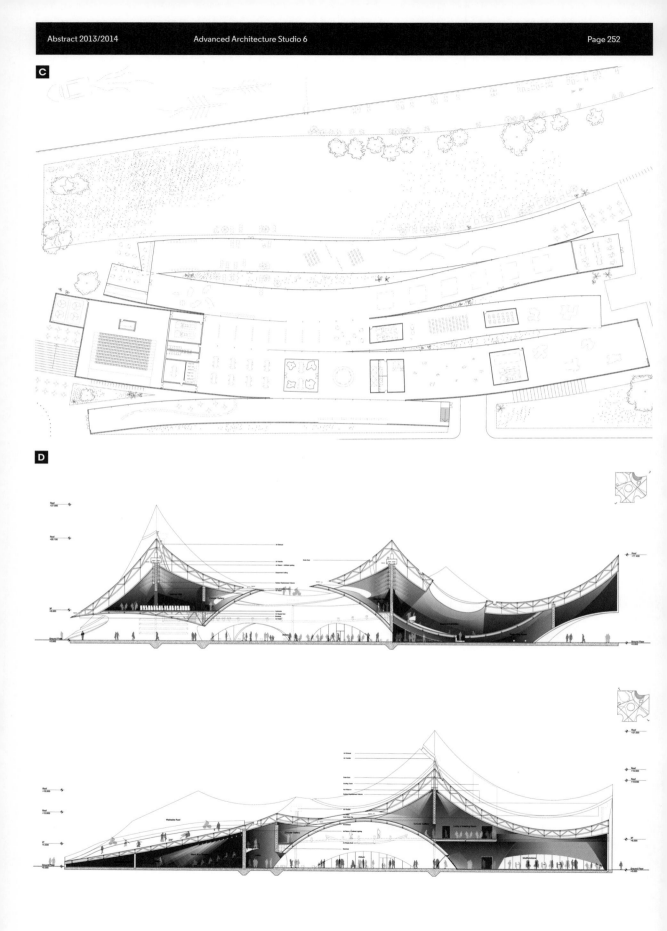

E

F

Beyond the Museum
Advanced Architecture Studio 6
Spring 2014
*Jeffrey Johnson + Pei Zhu,
critics, with Zoe Florence*

The studio was the second of a series that takes as its starting point the China Megacities Lab research on the Future of the Museum in China. The research provided a number of suppositions that were tested through the design of a project in the studio. The research defined the general context, while the studio offered a design speculation. As a possible alternative model of the museum of the future, the studio designed a multi-functional cultural facility in Dali, Yunnan Province, China.

The studio reasserted the importance of nature and the natural setting of the site into the project. The relationship between building and nature has throughout China's history been of primary importance. How can this be interpreted today in contemporary China when much of this relationship has been lost? Additionally, to assist in defining a primary architectural condition, the studio studied and adapted two contrasting archetypes that are analogous with historical approaches to architecture in China – the Cave and the Nest.

Astry Duarte **A/B/C**
Paul Chan **D/E**

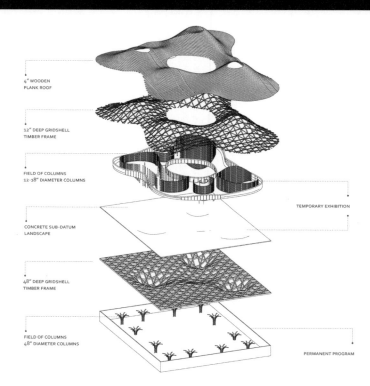

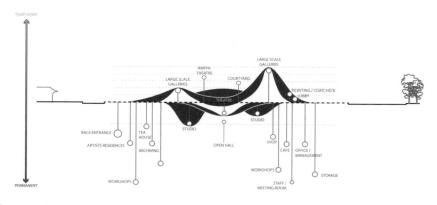

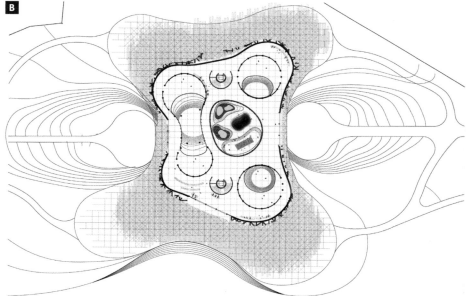

C

D

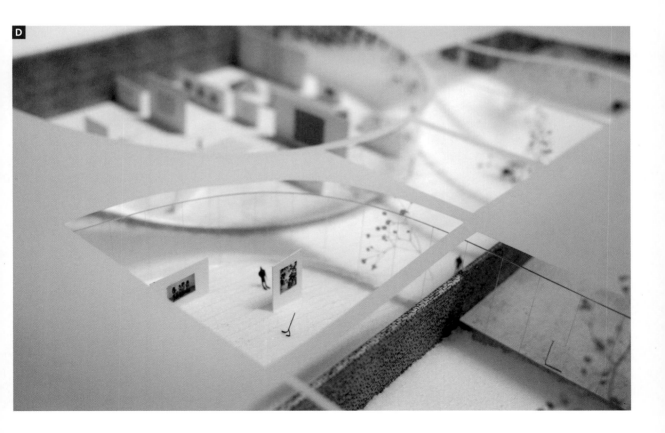

E

Studio Sangue Bom 6:
Rio das Pedras

Advanced Architecture Studio 6
Spring 2014
*Keith Kaseman + Raul Corrêa
Smith, critics, with Noah Z. Levy*

Rio das Pedras is an astonishing place. A relatively autonomous city within the city of Rio, its distinctive configuration has evolved into a super dense and incredibly diverse fabric loaded with myriad lessons for anyone intrigued by innovative forms of urban occupation and charge. Horizontally expansive and couched at the edge of Lagoa da Tijuca, Rio das Pedras is on the one hand imbued with an extensive set of socio-spatial complexities, environmental challenges and public health concerns and, on the other, uniquely charged by the vibrant radiance of its residents.

Studio Sangue Bom 6 engaged Rio das Pedras on multiple, privileged fronts throughout the semester. As this studio was just one component of a much larger GSAPP and Columbia University endeavor that is set to focus on Rio das Pedras over the next two years, our ambition was to project spatial questions for a currently unoccupied and supercharged site. Explorations centered on notions of new market armatures that may support or be infused by recreational, environmental and/or social bonuses. Immeasurable insight was gained through our mid-review mixer at CAIC, a municipal school in the heart of Rio das Pedras, where thirty stellar high school students radically informed the work.

Dina Mahmoud **A/B**
Tianhui Shen **C/D**
Tiffany Rattray **E/F**

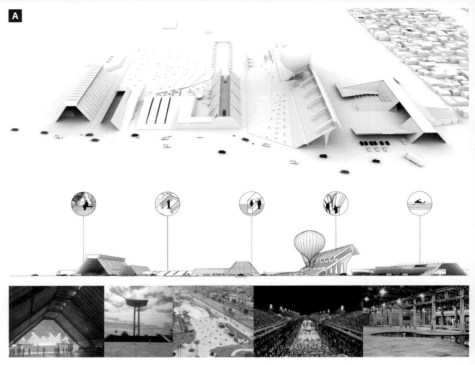

A

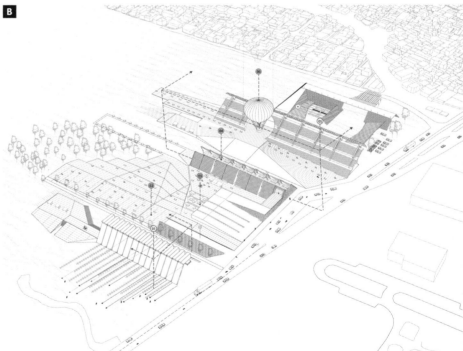

B

C

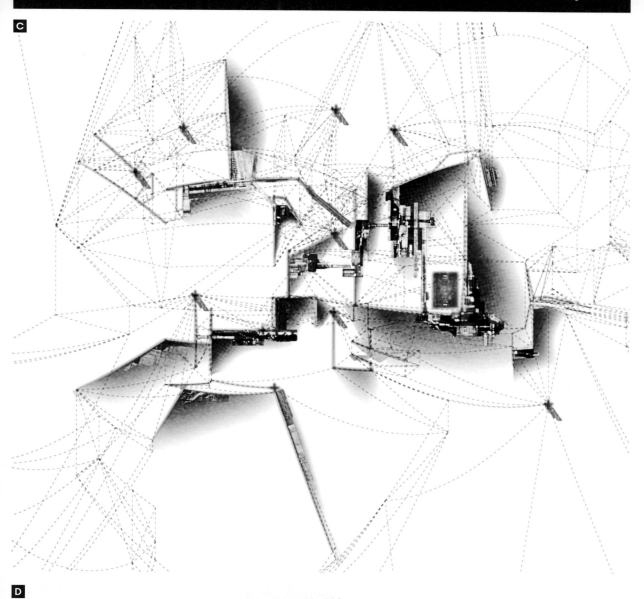

D

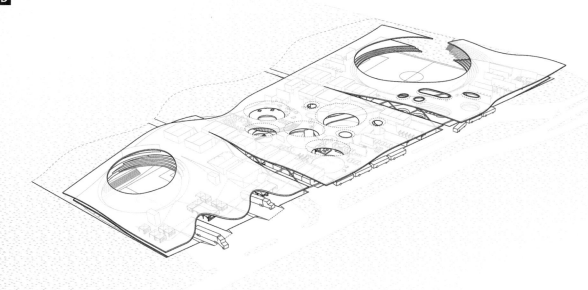

F

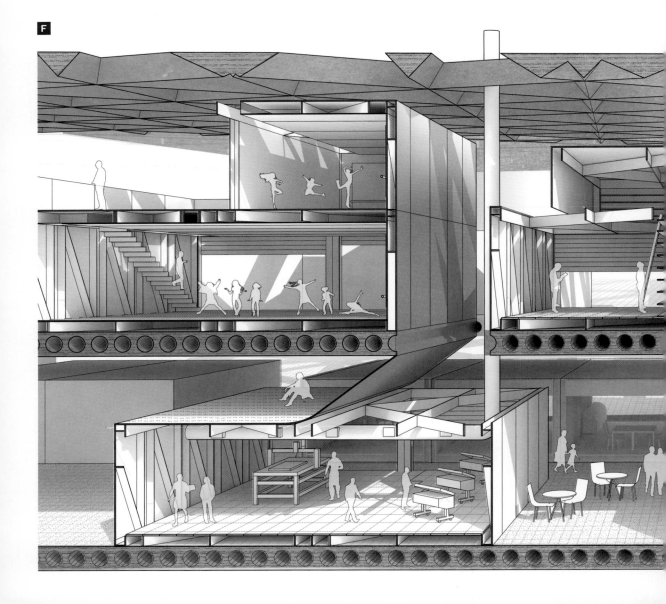

E

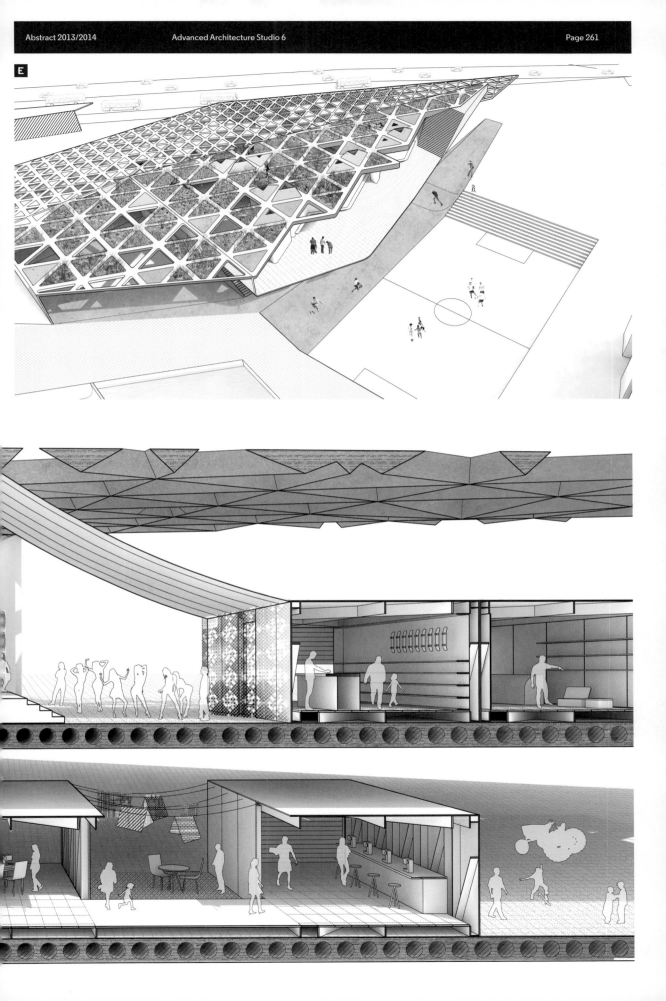

Jerusalem + the Occupation of Memory: Lifta

Advanced Architecture Studio 6
Spring 2014
Craig Konyk, critic, with
Nina V. Kolowratnik

Lifta is a small Palestinian village, divided by Western Jerusalem's Green Line, that was forcibly abandoned in the 1948-49 war, it has remained unoccupied for the last sixty-six years. Ironically, it is this unique condition of Lifta that has actually preserved it to this day. Jerusalem served as a laboratory for the investigation of the occupation of a memory landscape, and Lifta was our point of focus.

Today, many of Lifta's refugees are located in Ramallah, the West Bank, refugee camps and cities of neighboring Arab countries, as well as in East Jerusalem on former Lifta lands. For these refugees, Lifta remains a vivid memory landscape. Lifta represents the only Palestinian village in Israel where large parts of the built fabric remain intact and largely unoccupied until this day.

Ultimately, the results of the studio were responses to an understanding of what is the agency of an architect upon entering a situation as an outsider. The studio worked through the realities of the Israeli-Palestinian conflict developing architectural lenses through which to dissect spatial imperative beyond its present situation as simply a memory landscape.

Reece W. Tucker **A/B/C**
Geof Bell **D/E**

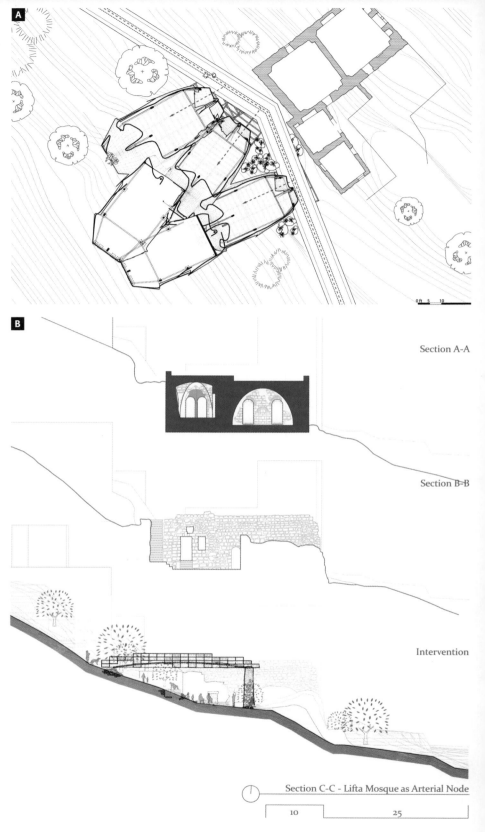

Section A-A

Section B-B

Intervention

Section C-C - Lifta Mosque as Arterial Node

10   25

Materialization of Information – Mumbai

Advanced Architecture Studio 6
Spring 2014
Frederic Levrat + Phillip Anzalone, critics, with Angie Jewon

How do we materialize information? What relation exists between the virtual, visual and physical environment? These questions are at the same time essential and not obvious. Can architecture play the role of an interface between the mind and the body, between the virtual and the physical? Clearly, the flow of information is constructed and organized, designed, just as our physical environment is. How should they relate? The studio was an extension of the Mindscape Lab and the Fabrication Lab, looking for possible expression of architecture from the influence of the information and visual world. What are the possibilities of architecture to address such conditions? The city and the architecture become a physical interface contextualizing virtual information into a physical space, negotiating between dimensions and, in return, producing information and knowledge. The process of the studio was collaborative and materialized. The studio designed and produced a full scale construction of a small information pavilion, built on the Mumbai promenade on Carter Road. The second part of the semester considered the main train station of downtown Mumbai, with the flow of almost three million passengers daily. This was a design-build studio that incorporated a built component in Mumbai in collaboration with Studio X Mumbai and Rajeev Thakker.

Bian Lin **A/B/C**
Katie Zaeh **D/E**

A

B

ROOF POSITION

By taking into the consideration of path for people to go through during the rush hour and normal hour, the roof edge is first defined by physical edge, then roof need to direct people to the sign, position also at the same time should take the columns positions and beams as support structure.

ROOF DETAIL

The roof structure rest go through the existing roof beams, by hanging down from the beams, multiple layers overlap together and all the other elements incorporate in a whole system, in the detail design, the frame hanging down from the beam.

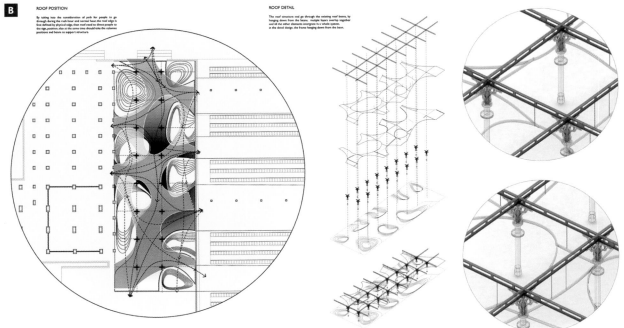

C

LONG SECTION STUDY

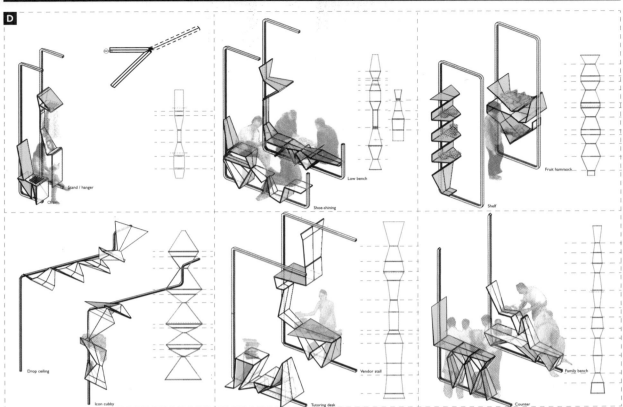

The Monograph Studio
Advanced Architecture Studio 6
Spring 2014
LOT-EK, Ada Tolla + Giuseppe
Lignano, critics, with
Thomas de Monchaux

The Monograph Studio invited students in their final semester to produce a pre-emptive documentation of all their future work: neither retroactive nor merely a manifesto. Students very rapidly generated, and documented to a standard book format, a very large volume of new work, and then collaboratively interrogated this same work. This process required both the reliance on, and defiance of, habituated behaviors. It staged a transformative experience in which the familiar traumas of the design process were accelerated and repeated, but then deeply reconsidered, to theoretically therapeutic effects. Five buildings were designed twice, requiring a commitment to decisiveness that revealed students to themselves.

The Monograph Studio was not a portfolio studio. A portfolio is comprehensive/a monograph is compromised; a portfolio is objective/a monograph is subjective; a portfolio is universal/a monograph is personal; a portfolio explains/a monograph mystifies; a portfolio hastens/a monograph hesitates; a portfolio is slick/a monograph is slippery; a portfolio is honest/a monograph is deceptive; a portfolio is defensive/a monograph is adaptive.

The Monograph Studio reminded us of the words of Samuel Becket, who in 1983 wrote: "All of old. Nothing else ever. Ever tried. Ever failed. No matter. Try again. Fail again. Fail better."

Jonathan Ivan Adamos Requillo A
Marissa Nava B
Bless Yee C

A

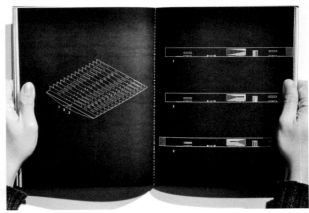

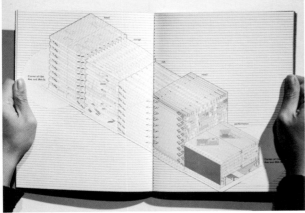

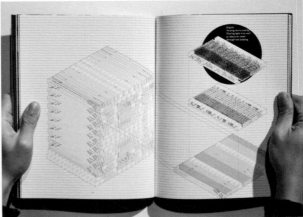

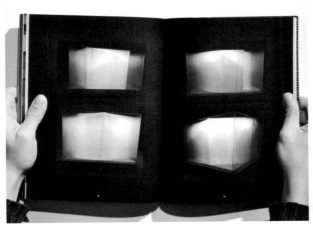

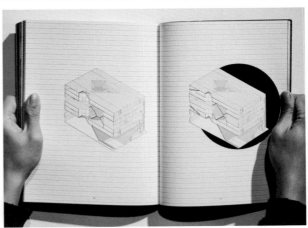

B

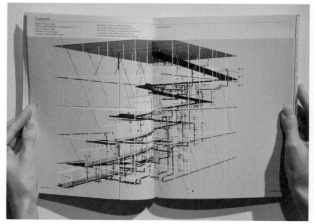

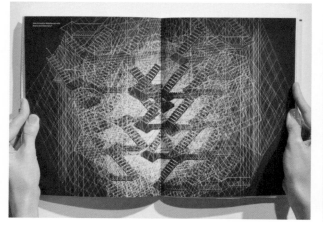

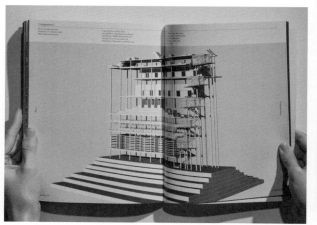

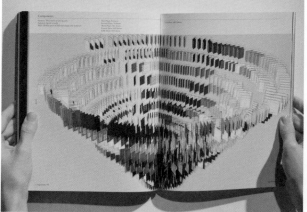

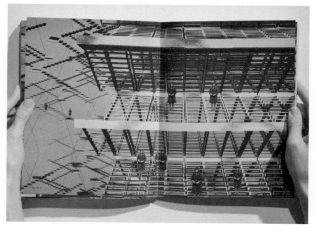

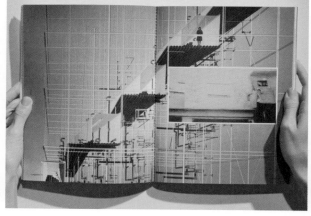

C

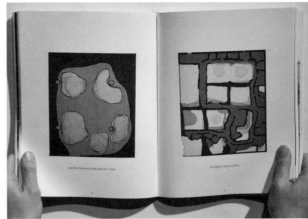

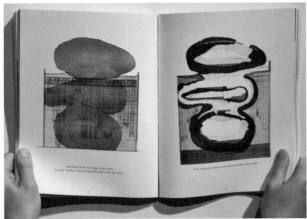

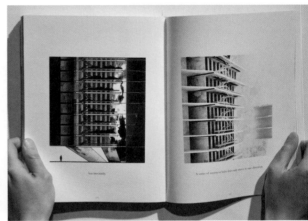

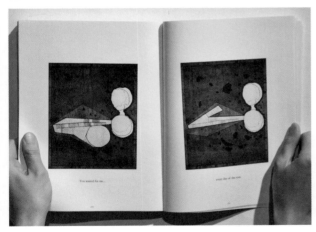

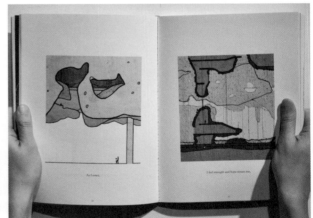

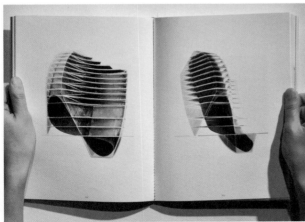

**Stress + Wellness: Design
Guidelines for Rio de Janeiro**
Advanced Architecture Studio 6
Spring 2014
*Hilary Sample + Vishaan
Chakrabarti, critics,
with Thomas Heltzel*

This semester students participated in an experimental research and design studio focused on the complex intersection between urban health, architecture, planning and development in the setting of Rio de Janeiro, Brazil. As one of the most modern cities in Brazil, it has experienced contemporary health crises that have sh aped its urban development and social and political landscape. As a studio, students researched typological and physiological forms within the stressed urban environment of Rio das Pedras. The studio prompted questions from how urban health has both historically and through the contemporary shaped this vibrant favela and the overall city of Rio to, similarly, how has the form of the city shaped the health and wellness of its population? This studio was as much a record of a search as it was a forum for creating design guidelines and proposals. The themes of stress represented the content of the studio and aimed to better understand situations of wellness in relation to design and development. The studio was structured through reading two scales; first students focused on Rio's urban context, infrastructures and building types and then studied the subject of design guidelines to focus on programmatic development in addition to environmental and material properties in designing a new health typology for the future, which included, but was not limited to, proposals for schools, housing, infrastructures, parks and opportunities for economic development particularly at the scale of microenterprises.

Vishaan Chakrabarti, Holliday Associate Professor with his seven Real Estate Development students participated in a weekly seminar. In addition, the joint symposium, Conversations about Public Health, Architecture and Cities

was held on April 22, 2014 at Studio X New York as a joint symposium between Columbia University's Mailman School of Public Health and GSAPP.

Dora Felekou +
Maria Lozano **A/B**
Georgios Kyriazis **C/D**
Talene Montgomery **E**

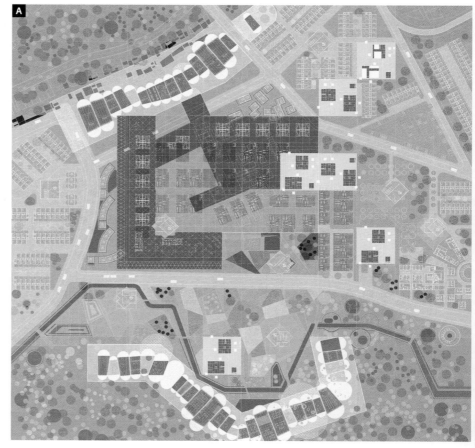

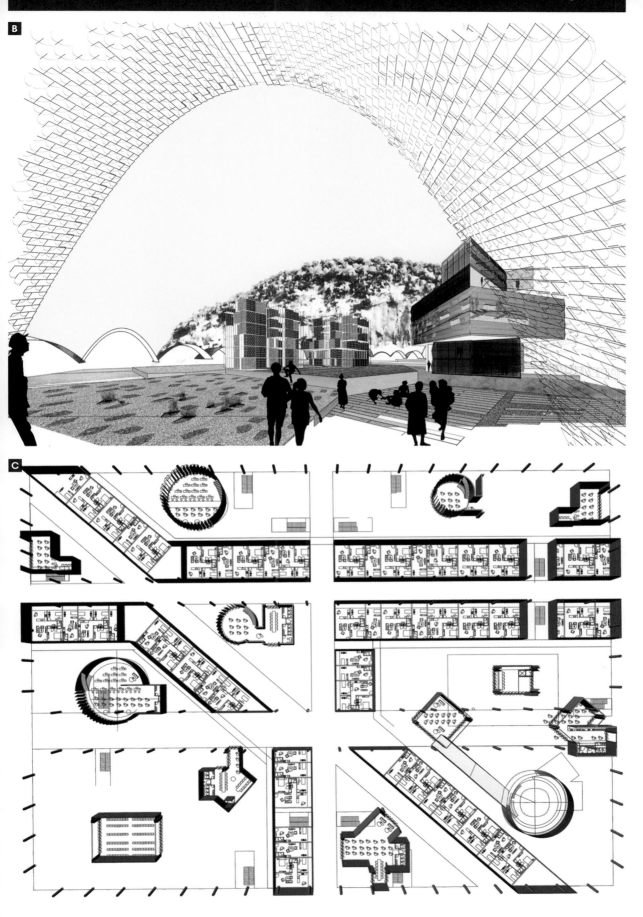

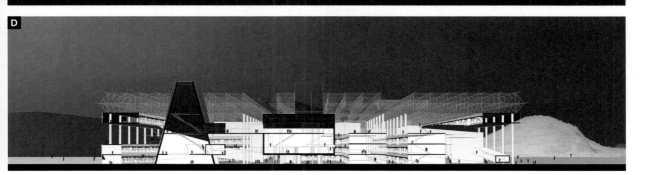

Studio X Istanbul
Advanced Architecture Studio 6
Spring 2014
*David Smiley, critic, with
Kyle Hovenkotter*

Design xChange proposed that the artisan and craft-based production work at the literal and metaphoric heart of Istanbul, rather than being squeezed out by global capital flow, could be expanded and architecturally transformed. Studio work focused on the invention of new recursive and blended formal-structural systems based on current production sites in the city – from the artisanal work places in the centuries old courtyard buildings, "hans," next to the Bazaar, to custom lighting buildings in older neighborhoods, to newer furniture showroom complexes and small-scale light industrial shops further out from the core. Secondly, the students catalyzed their work via new cultural programming – including neighborhood-focused arts, education, craft and recycling uses – to stake a claim in the changes and conflicts wrought by the city's new global positioning. More directly, the new projects connected to the Beyoglu neighborhood rose up from the coast and extended the public spaces central to remaking the "cultural valley" of the Golden Horn; the Design xChange site extended this cultural work along the coast in Karakoy and Galata – with spectacular views across the Bosphorus – and included the Istanbul Modern Museum, an exhibit center for the Mimar Fine Arts University, several massive, empty warehouses and Studio X. The Design xChange projects mixed globalizing social changes with local and regional capacities to create new opportunities for design, production and participation.

Nazli Ergani **A/B/C**
Natasha Amladi **D/E**
Sara Dionis Sevilla **F**
Seri Hieatt **G/H**

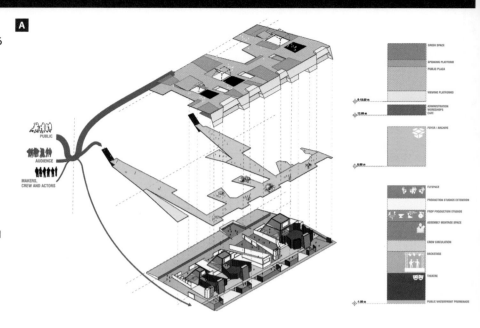

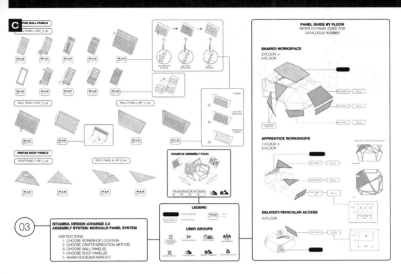

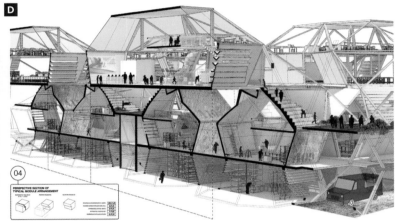

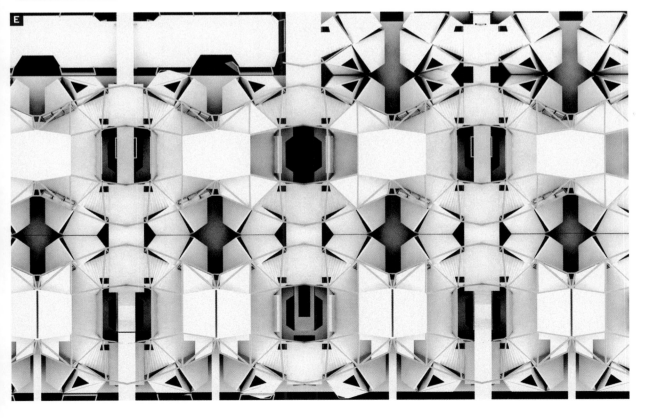

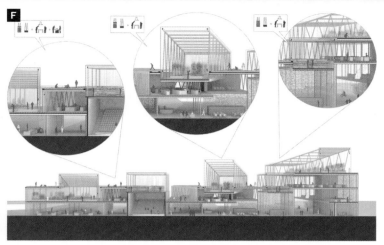

G

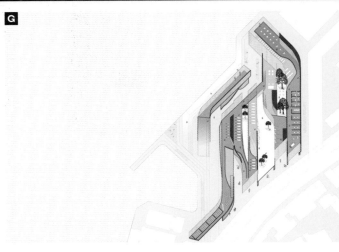

RIO, IDENTI-CITY: Producing Identity Driven Architecture

Advanced Architecture Studio 6
Spring 2014
*Galia Solomonoff, critic,
with Amy Maresko*

It is difficult to think about Rio without invoking images of Ipanema Beach, Burle Marx's sidewalks, colossal Christ or a crowded Carnival shimmering dance. Like a singular character, Rio as a city possesses all of the elements of an attractor, but also the thrilling potential of danger and engulfing quest.

Fareed Zakaria cautions us that our largest problems are a product not of our failure but of our success. In the world of capital, like in nature, what works spreads relentlessly. Architects, politicians, planners and developers attempt to reproduce the urban structures that worked in New York, Paris or Barcelona. Yet the formulas that have given us certain localized and time specific interventions are often elusive or insufficient, as every urban success has a particular layering of old and new, local and global that produced a certain ambiance and effect.

In Generic City (1993), Koolhaas describes a future city that is successfully dense yet indistinct. In this scenario, which Koolhaas positions as both an aspiration and a cautionary tale, people have blended beyond recognizable racial traces; cities have copied each other's salient traits; all territories, regardless of geographic or climatic challenges, have been conquered at a relentless pace, producing self-similar cities all over the globe. The Generic City, while thriving, could be confused with any other.

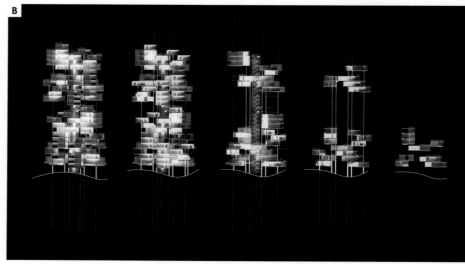

The Studio proposed to redesign the Moinho Fluminense site in Rio and positioned iconicity and identity as productive counterparts to density and capital expansion. Students questioned what of the existing should be kept, added to or discarded altogether, and whether key cities are able to provide a productive and stable identity and overtake nationalism or ethnic pride?

Chisom Ezekwo **A/B**
Eileen Chen +
Anastasia Tania **C/D**
Rong Zhao + Qiancheng Ma **E/F**

C

D

E

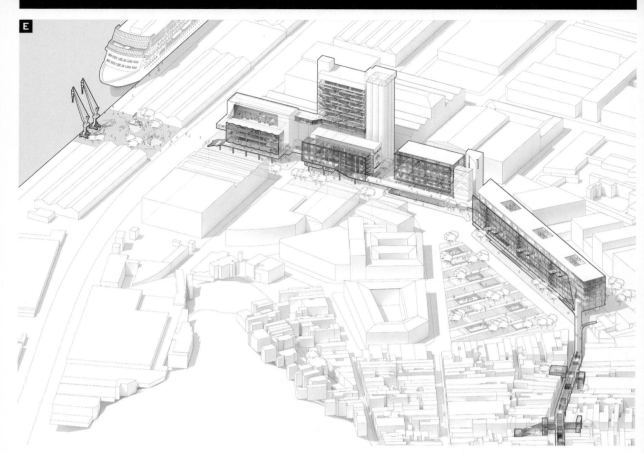

**The Dictionary of
Received Ideas**
Advanced Architecture Studio 6
Spring 2014
Enrique Walker, critic

This studio was the fourteenth installment in a decade-long project whose aim is to examine *received ideas*—that is, ideas which are uncritically accepted and repeated to the point of depleting their original intensity—in contemporary architecture culture. This ongoing series of design studios and theory seminars proposes to disclose, define and date—and in the long run archive—*received ideas* prevalent over the past decade, both in the professional and academic realms, in order to ultimately open up otherwise precluded possibilities for architectural design and architectural theory. To that end, it focuses on design operations and conceptual strategies—those which have outlived the problems they originally addressed—particularly in terms of the means of representation and the lexicon through which they are respectively articulated. This project took as precedent Gustave Flaubert's unfinished book, *Le dictionnaire des idées reçues.* Just as the latter, it set out to detect and collect received ideas and provide definitions—or a user's manual— to render them self-evident. Yet as opposed to the latter, arguably an inventory of potential exclusions, this project also sought to use—or to misuse—that collection of received ideas towards the formulation of other design operations and other conceptual strategies.

Laura Buck, Sean Myung Shin Kim, Alejandro Stein + Ray Wang **A/B/C/D**

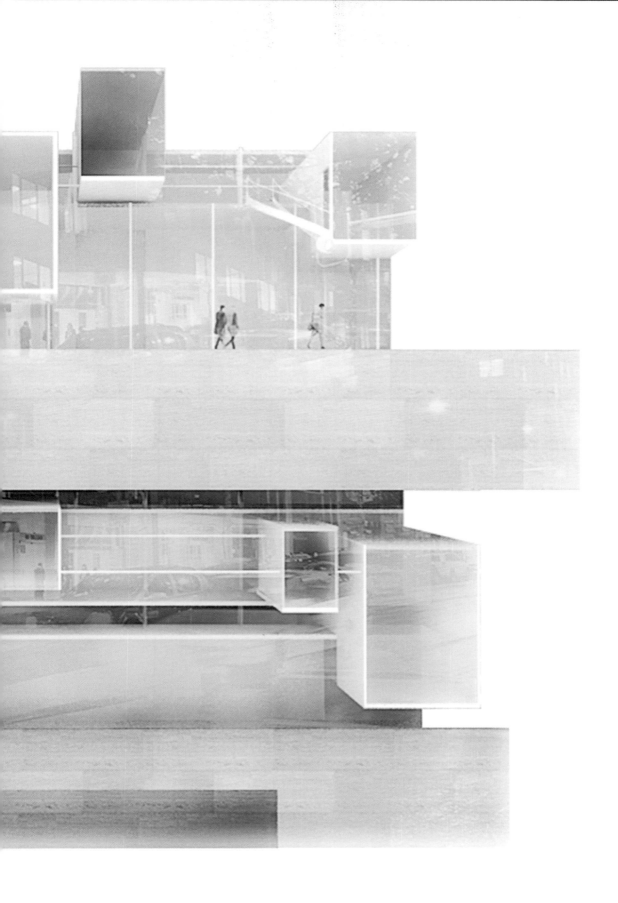

B

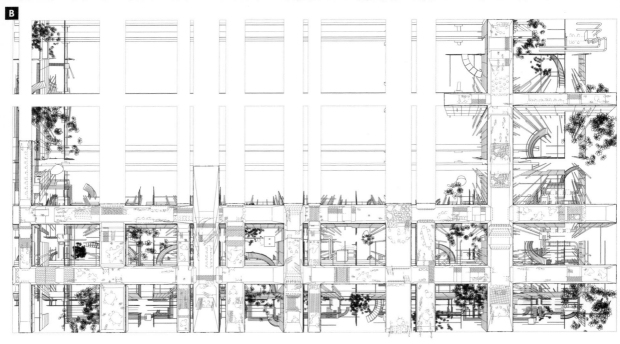

C

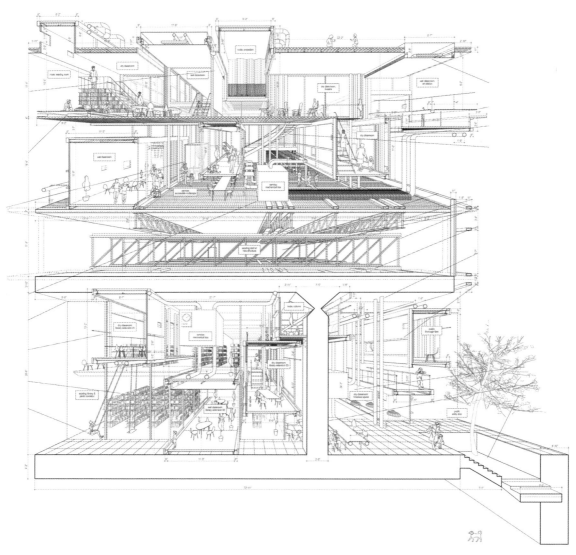

D Intersection
NODES   8 Types

N1 - READING NOOK

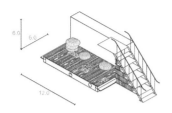

N2 - INDOOR GARDEN

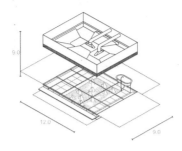

N3 - BOOKCASE CATWALK

N4 - CLASSROOM STORAGE

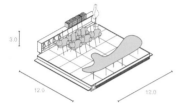

N5 - SUPPLIES STORAGE

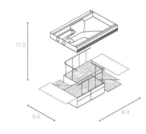

N6 - SINK TABLE

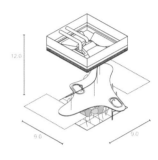

N7 - PROJECTION-BRIDGE

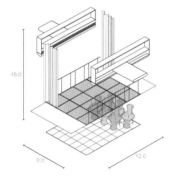

N8 - SLIDING STAIR

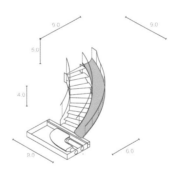

Collecting Architecture Territories: Beirut
Advanced Architecture Studio 6
Spring 2014
Mark Wasiuta, critic,
with Adam Bandler

This studio was the third iteration of the ongoing research project, Collecting Architecture Territories. The project tuned into one of the most significant developments reshaping the intersection of art and architectural practice over the last three decades: the veritable explosion of institutions and foundations that have emerged out of private art collections. The project proposed that the historical institution of the museum is undergoing a transformation that requires new forms of spatial, territorial and cultural analysis.

The studio traveled to Doha, Beirut and Amman, sites that sharply inflect notions of collection and that belong to distinct strata of access, mobility and circulation. Where private global art collections seem to share a frictionless economy in which objects, curators and collectors migrate more or less effortlessly, in the Middle East this mobility is often interrupted by precarious politics and territorial controls. If the global shuttling of Jeff Koons' balloon dogs describes a contemporary incarnation of the museum without walls, the Middle East institutions that operate through the management of extreme risk, and through the burden of extra techniques of containment, represent pockets of political, institutional difference. This is a not territory of museums without walls but a territory of museums both curtailed and defended by extra, supplemental walls, boundaries, check points and controls.

Andres Macera **A**
Margaux Young **B/C**
Wen Zhu **D/E**

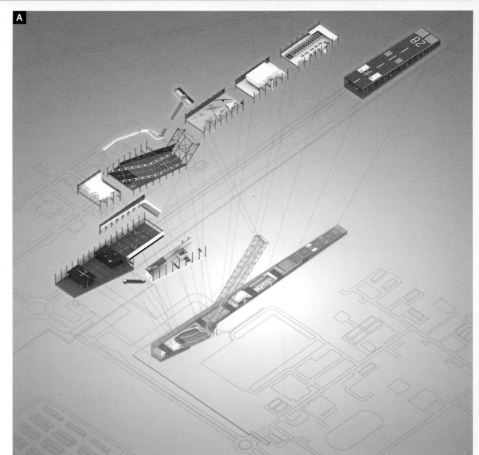

B

C

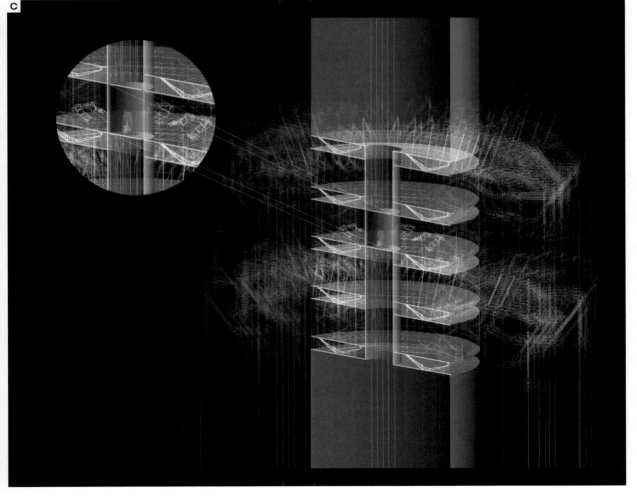

D

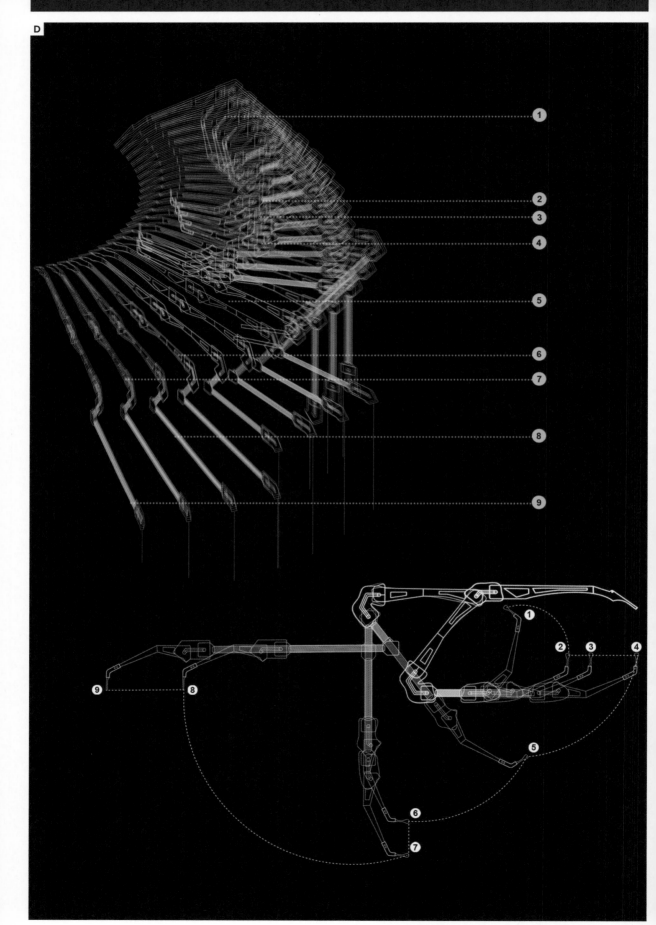

E

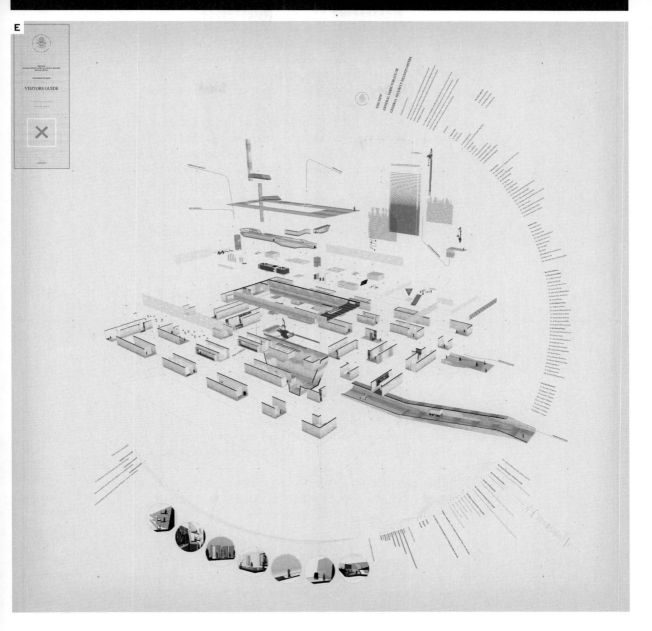

Master of Science in Advanced Architectural Design
Enrique Walker, director

The Master of Science degree in Advanced Architectural Design is a three-term program consisting of summer, fall and spring terms. The objective of the program is to provide outstanding young professionals who hold a Bachelor of Architecture or Master of Architecture degree the opportunity to enter into an intensive, postgraduate study that encourages critical thought in the context of design speculation. The program is viewed as a framework in which both academic and professional concerns are explored. Overall, the program emphasizes an experimental approach to research and architectural design rigorously grounded in multiple, complex realities. Specifically, the program seeks to:

1. Address the challenges and possibilities of global urbanization by exploring the city — and its architecture — in all its forms.

2. Engage in a complex definition of architecture, from the questioning of the program to the formulation of design strategies.

3. Produce architectural objects—both digital and physical — which reflect an open, critical engagement both with new and existing technologies.

4. Articulate architecture as a cultural practice that combines critical thought, design experimentation and ethical responsibilities in an interdisciplinary milieu.

5. Activate a wide debate on the contemporary conditions that critically affect the course of the discipline and the profession.

The program brings together a set of required studios with elective courses that are shared with other programs in the School and that promote intellectual cross-fertilization among disciplines. A required lecture course on the twentieth-century city and on contemporary architectural theory, exclusive to the program, provides grounding for disciplinary exploration in the studio. The advanced studios frequently utilize New York as a design laboratory—a global city that presents both unique challenges and unique opportunities. The program has long been a site for architects from around the globe to test concepts and confront changes that affect architecture and cities worldwide.

Replica Studio
AAD Studio
Summer 2013
*Cristina Goberna +
Urtzi Grau, critics*

This studio explored the potential of replicas, or Agonistic Copies, to open unexpected paths for the identification, confrontation and dissemination of current polemics in the field.

Architecture is subjected to a regime of originality, yet operations, having in common the recourse of already produced forms such as re-appropriation, détournement, objet-trouvé, mash-up, parafiction, remain unabsorbed and even taboo. While imitation and reproduction are the obvious roots of the last twenty or even six hundred years' excess of architectural shapes, the field has resisted to openly embrace copies and has thereby hindered its potential. To intentionally copy entails a radical reformulation of architectural imagination: it allows for a radical renunciation to form-making–since form is defined a priory–to focus on architectural knowledge yet to be discovered.

The current high-speed consumption of architectural imaginary entails the naturalization of issues that could otherwise be publicly contested. This domestication of architectural polemics, a general disinterest in discussion, and the automatic consensus it entails hinder the debates that generate advancement in the field. This studio proposed dissensus and friction as constructive tools of operation and design, explored through the investigation of three inter-related chapters: a study of copy methods, an exploration of agonism in architecture and the subsequent correction of an existing architectural work proved currently relevant for the field.

Che-Wei Yeh +
Nikolaos Vlavianos **A/B**
Li-Lin Lin + Chi Feng Wu **C**
Patrick Craine + Sheila
Aguilu **D/E/F**

A

B

C

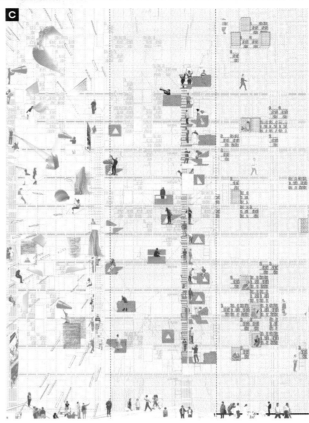

D

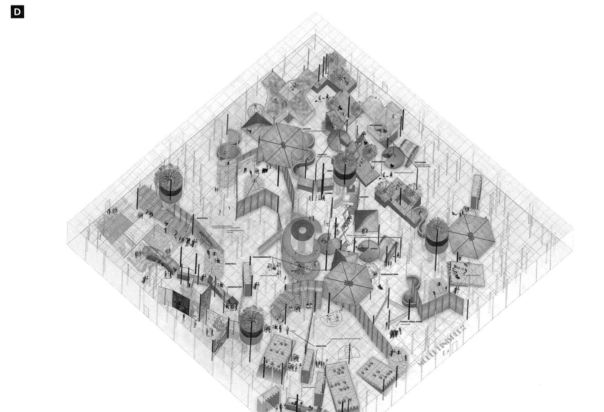

E

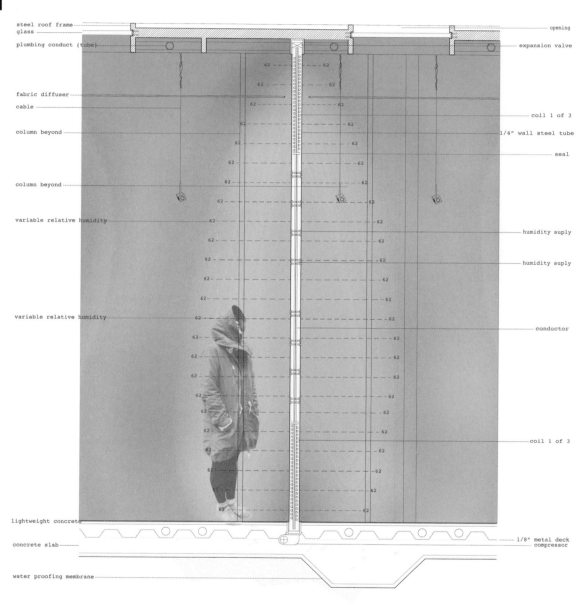

steel roof frame
glass
plumbing conduct (tube)

fabric diffuser
cable

column beyond

column beyond

variable relative humidity

variable relative humidity

lightweight concrete

concrete slab

water proofing membrane

opening

expansion valve

coil 1 of 3

1/4" wall steel tube

seal

humidity suply

humidity suply

conductor

coil 1 of 3

1/8" metal deck
compressor

F

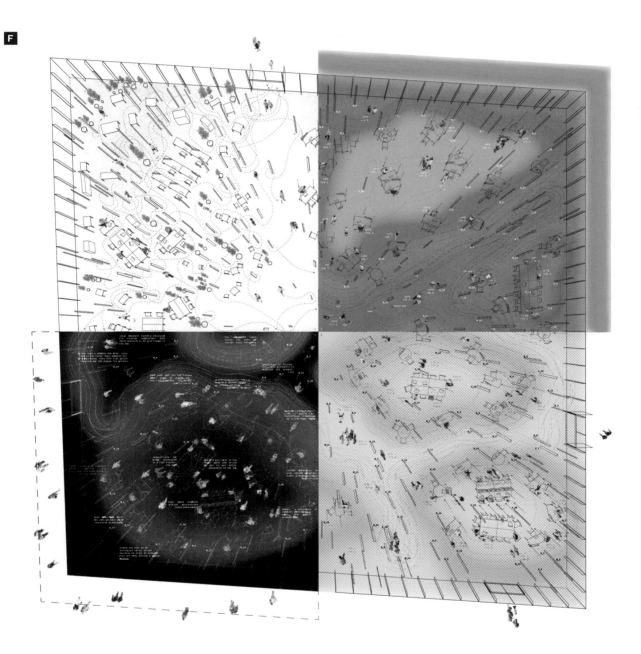

**Conditioned Urbanism:
Air Design for an
Urban Fitness Club**
AAD Studio
Summer 2013
*Phu Hoang, critic, with
Emanuel Admassu*

The studio researched and
investigated the role that "air
design" has in forming our
cities. "Air design" is the conditioning, or modification, of air
engineered to fill the volumes
within a building. From the
early technologies invented to
modify temperature and humidity, building systems are now
capable of modifying the air of
pollution, mold, odors, noise,
static electricity and even electromagnetic radiation levels.
The studio argued that the requirements of "air design" are
now too extensive to consider
it in service to the architectural
program. This conditioning
of air has led to a parallel
and invisible architectural
program with extensive impact
on the built environment.
   The "air design" of a
New York urban fitness club
addressed the process of
commodifying indoor air for
the commercial purposes of
health, shopping, dining and
recreation. This commodified
air conditioned the design of
a new type of urban fitness
club. The studio produced a
set of proposals that radically
reconsidered the program of
an urban fitness club through
design of the interior—as well
as exterior—airs. Students designed the spaces in between
architecture before designing the architecture itself.

Chisom Ezekwo +
Sara Dionis Sevilla **A/B/C**
Evan Collins + Kamilla
Csegzi **D/E/F**

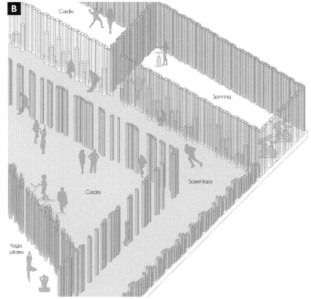

D

E

F

Learning from Food
AAD Studio
Summer 2013
Joaquim Moreno, critic

Food was the research engine of this studio; its lofty plan was to reinvent the domestic kitchen. It was a space to learn from the architecture of food and invent a new architecture for its locus solus, its singular place: the kitchen.

This research engine offered many different avenues from which to learn. From a Political perspective, it ranged from illegal farming to underground supper clubs. From a Logistics perspective, Siegfried Giedion's chapters on the mechanization of the organic and that of death are convincing about the intricacies between technological organization and food.

Food was also useful to decipher memory—personal and collective. Food happens; it does not exist in permanence. It is precious but impermanent, and its comforting memories are revived in the cycling repetitions of seasons, places and celebrations.

From a perspective of process, food is about fluidity–about changing and overlapping sets of processes that survive in recipes, loosely defined sequences of preparations and not fixed formulas.

The studio proposed a laboratory for taste, for its construction and production: a re-invented domestic kitchen. It was an opportunity to investigate the social and technical space of the kitchen from the point of view of food.

Mintra Maneepairoj **A/B/C/D**

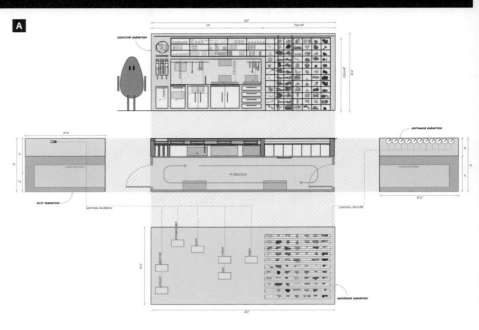

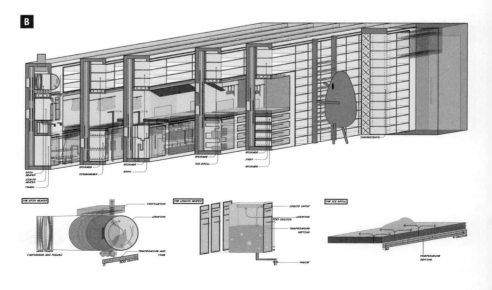

C

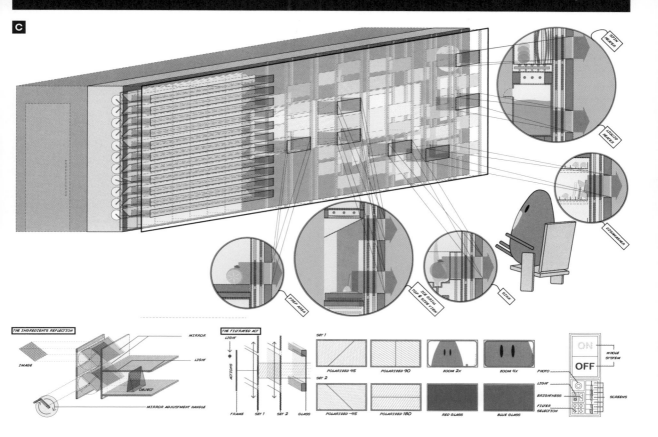

D

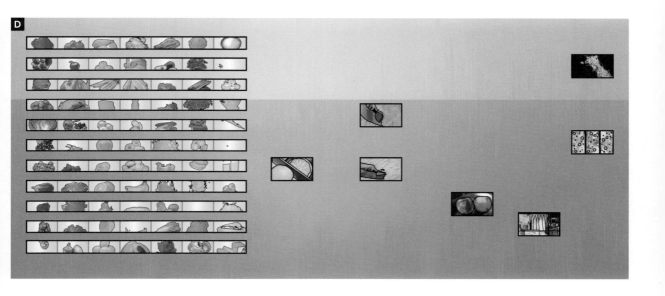

Epoch Value
AAD Studio
Summer 2013
Toshihiro Oki, critic,
with Carolina Ihle

Architecture that withstands the test of time by surviving the evolutions of society has a sense of value imbued in its core. Humans keep things of value and discard the others. People are highly creative beings with the ability to find new potential values, even as situations change. Buildings live or die under these conditions. This studio explored the notion of epochal value and how it could be part of an architectural vocabulary that was relevant to our ever-changing society and humanity. This architectural relevance was a search for the defining characters that we humans need for our 'spaces'–digging deep into the veiled realm of our intuition. It went beyond an architecture of current trends, fashions or authorship and reached for a broader understanding of our epochal time period. The search for epochal value was the search to understand the core meaning of our time.

Dina Mahmoud **A**
Ignacio Urquiza **B/C/D/E**
Marco Salazar **F/G**

D

E

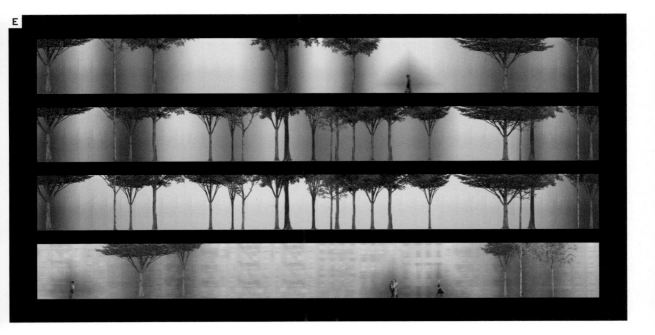

F

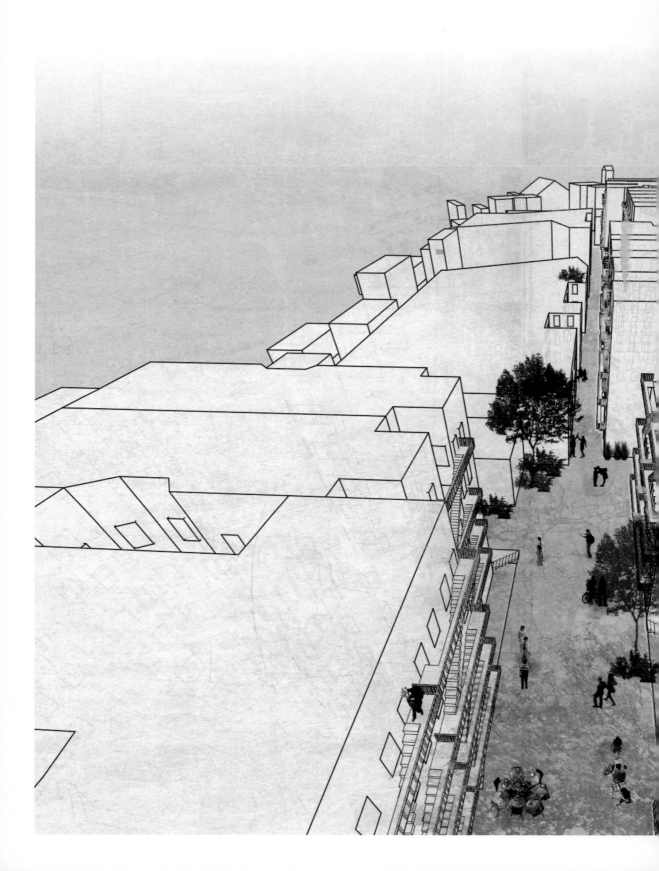

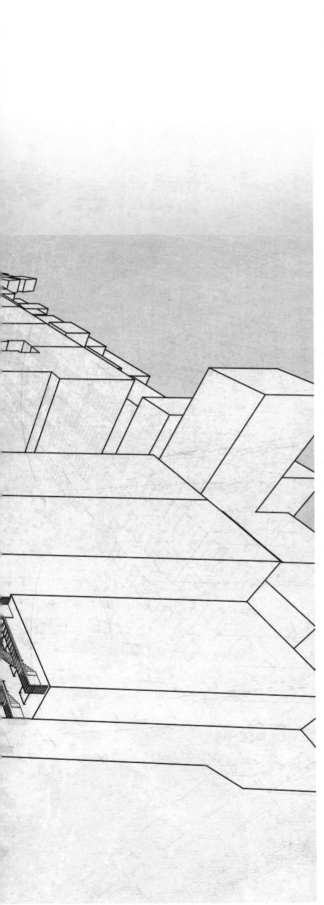

Metamorphic
AAD Studio
Summer 2013
Mark Rakatansky, critic

Morphe: form
Morphology: the study
of form and structure
Metamorphosis: the transmu-
tation of form and structure
This studio explored the experimental possibilities of metamorphosis – the transformative
invention of spatial form as
it is manifest in and through
social and cultural formations.

   We utilized one of the
world's most legendary collections of cultural form and
transformation, the Metropolitan Museum of Art, as a
site to explore new forms of
curatorial and informational
space-making. With the recent
development of many of New
York's primary cultural institutions, such as Renzo Piano's
Morgan Library/Museum and
Diller Scofidio + Renfro's Lin-
coln Center, the Met was prime
for a contemporary evolution.

   During the first part of the
semester, we experimented
with ways digital visualization in
museum settings might provide
groundbreaking opportunities
to expand the application and
accessibility of new informational systems. At the scale
of display architecture, the
museum environment was particularly geared to evolve ways
that these technologies could
provide interpretative information and multi-media visualization as the viewer looks through
fixed and mobile screens at
artifacts, models, paintings,
or period rooms. Student
projects focused on one of the
Museum's diverse collections.
Already imminent in each artifact in all these collections were
deep cultural and informational
networks that your architecture
drew forth with new spatial
and temporal relations.

Seri Hieatt **A/B**
Wei Ruoyu **C/D/E**

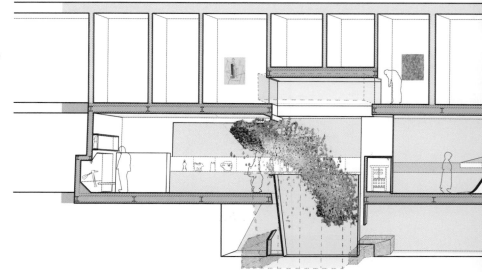

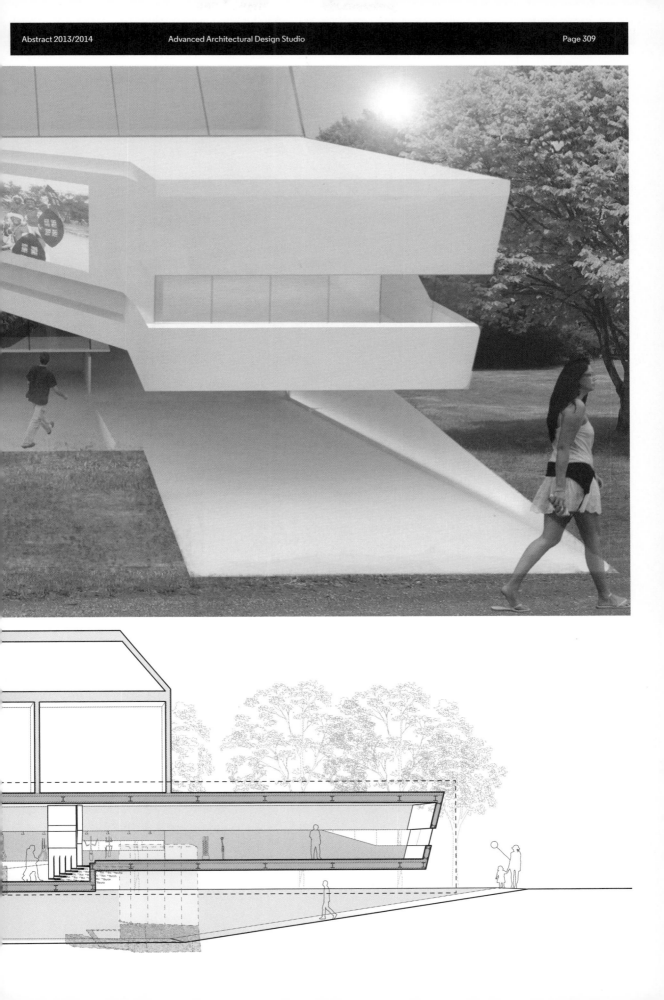

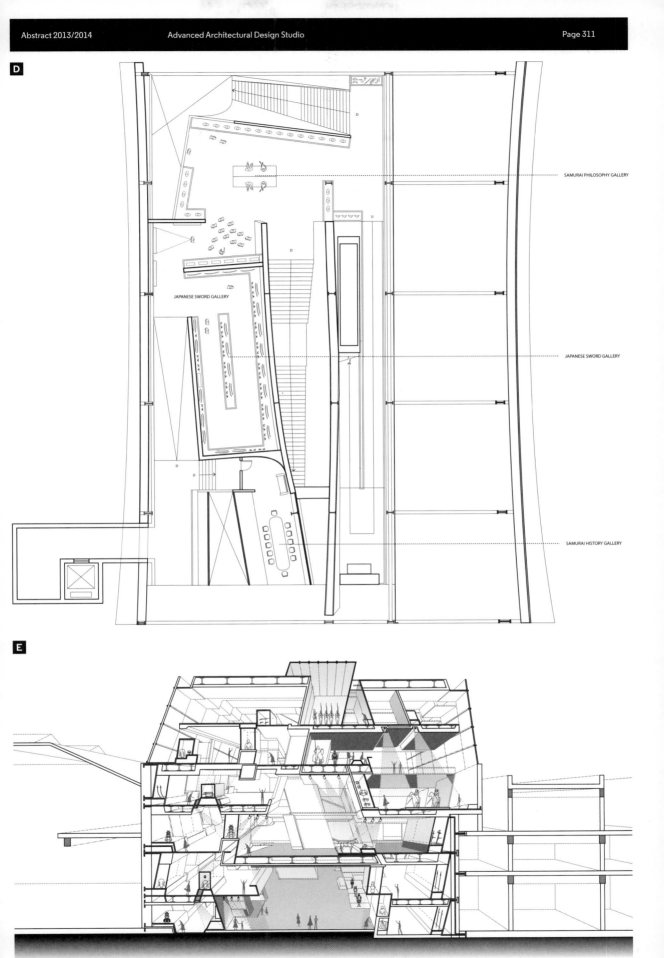

SAMURAI PHILOSOPHY GALLERY

JAPANESE SWORD GALLERY

JAPANESE SWORD GALLERY

SAMURAI HISTORY GALLERY

Public?
AAD Studio
Summer 2013
Jing Liu, critic

A question ever more frequently asked, but never more challenging and divisive is how can architecture make "public space"? However, probably precisely because of that, "public space" is called for in design briefs for almost all projects where tax or philanthropic money is being spent. It would be overly cynical to discount these questions as merely disingenuous chatter. But if one considers it a valid yearning for a common purpose, a coherent belief and attempts to answer to it, one should really start with the fundamental question: "what is public now?" Only once we have surveyed the extent of this question, we can follow with asking "what is public space?"

In the name of democracy, public calls for transparency, for immediate access to the objective "truth", which is proven to be nonexistent in any empirical form. "Public" ceases to have a singular image, so how can "public space" be organized? In this studio, students intuitively assembled into three groups. The first imagined this space as an assembly of various concrete topics and things of specificity, where people congregated, and discussion was encouraged – the passive one. The second imagined it as a puzzle of highly defined pieces, in which each piece was given its own freedom and internal structure; together, they formed a juxtaposed and jarring collage–the agonistic one. The third imagined the space to have multiple projective narratives, each coherent to its own logic and each open-ended. This space functioned as an island, separated from the here and now, where all were welcomed–the opportunistic one.

Begoña De Abajo,
Carlos Garcia, Yubo Liang +
Jiazhen Guo **A/B/C/D**

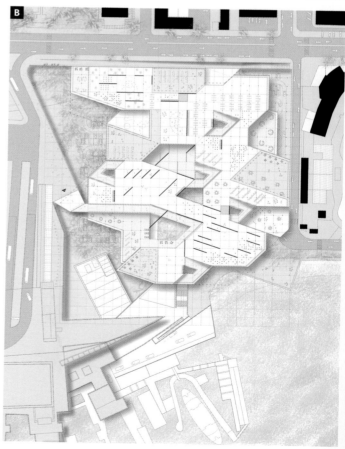

C

D

Fossil-Fuel-Free
AAD Studio
Summer 2013
Dan Wood + Chip Lord,
critics, with Sam Dufaux

The first part of the studio explored public space and infrastructure in New York City through the medium of video. Using minimal equipment–cell phones and iMovie software–we created an experimental video documenting one of New York City's great public spaces and dealing with themes of the future, optimism, climate change, public space and infrastructure.

Simultaneously, we carried out a group planning exercise for Governor's Island, which included identifying expected sea level change, modifying sea walls and imagining common spaces as an entirely new type of public space. This "crossed" with new sustainable infrastructure and technology to create a new kind of Piazza San Marco, in which water would come in rather than be kept out. Since the island was capable of receiving refugees from a Sandy type storm surge, these public spaces needed the potential to convert into a kind of pop-up city to house and serve displaced residents. No cares were allowed on the island; some alternative systems to move goods were designed or acquired.

The second part was an in-depth design of the research institute. This building took cues from the current crop of low-or zero-energy buildings, though with a more radical, forward-thinking and avant garde agenda, and served as a "vision" of how future buildings might look and perform.

Claudio Palavecino **A/B**
Jieun Lim **C/D/E**

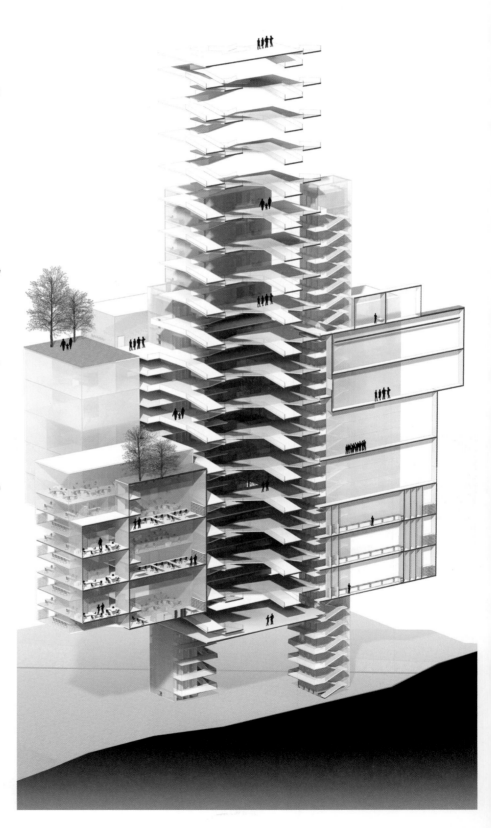

A

B

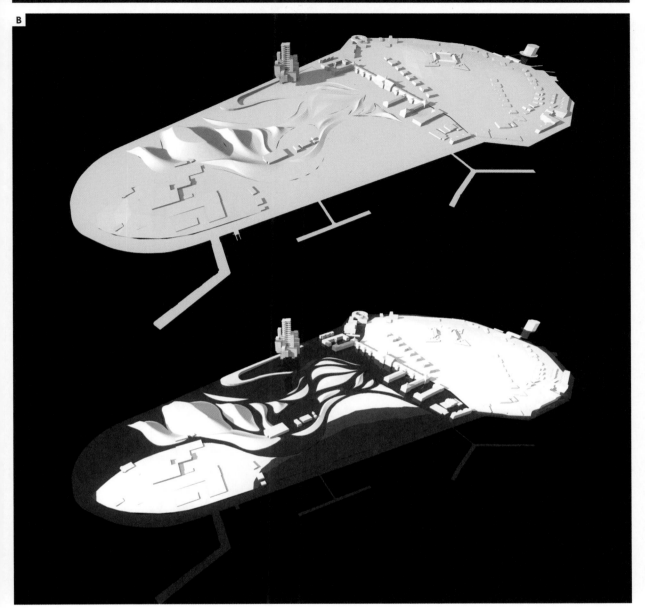

C

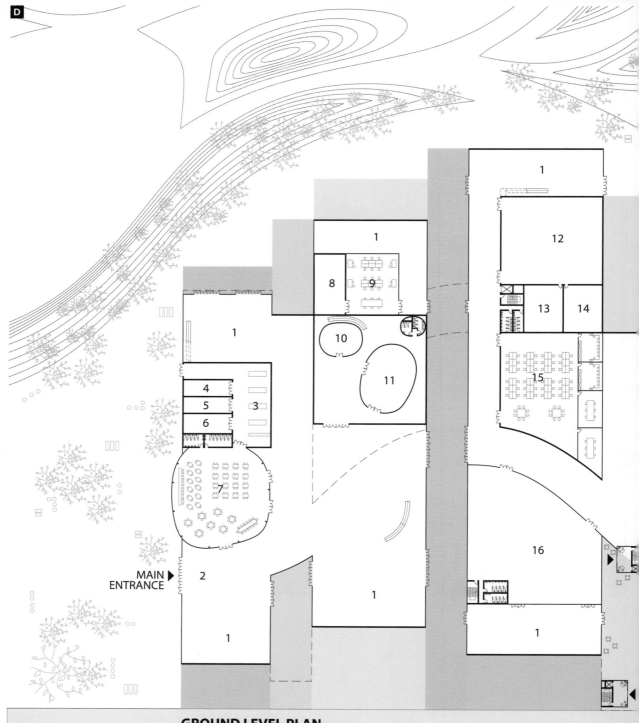

GROUND LEVEL PLAN

1. PUBLIC SPACE
2. LOBBY
3. KITCHEN
4. STORAGY
5. PANTRY
6. REFRIGERATOR
7. DINING
8. STORAGY
9. OFFICE
10. GALLERY ROOM1
11. GALLERY ROOM2
12. PROTOTYPE BUILDING SHOP
13. STORAGY
14. EQUIPMENT
15. ELECTRONIC DATA LAB
16. OPEN OFFICE
17. PRESENTATION ROOM1
18. PRESENTATION ROOM2
19. PRESENTATION ROOM3
20. INFORMAL MEETING SPACE

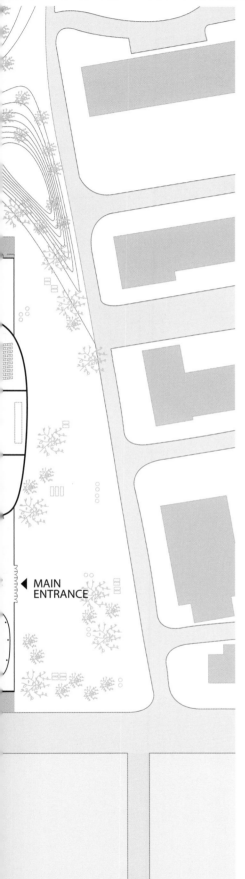

◀ MAIN
ENTRANCE

**Superpowering
Urban Enactments**
AAD Studio
Summer 2013
*Andrés Jaque, critic,
with Ernesto Silva*

The studio explored the
urban network's extension of a
number of open-to-the-public
devices as the site for architectural transformations. Places as
seemingly varied as nail salons,
funeral homes and public
baths, which tend to be disre-
garded or considered of less
significant urban value, gain
importance when studied as
part of networks of heterogeneous co-inhabitances. Through
detective fieldwork and group
discussion, students chose one
of these types of places to pursue further in their design project. The projects developed in
the studio focused on exploring
their hidden potentials in
the context of the greater
associated urban network.

Andrés Macera **A/B/C**
Emily Koustae **D/E**

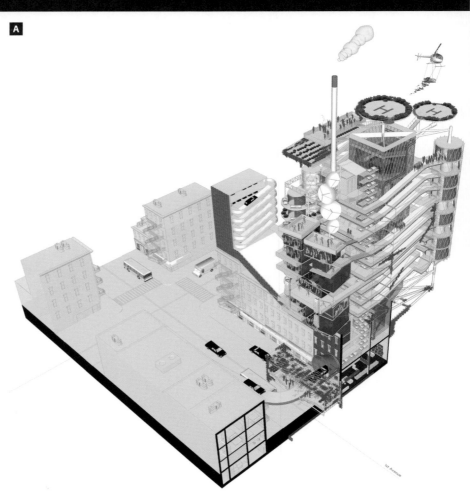

A

B

C

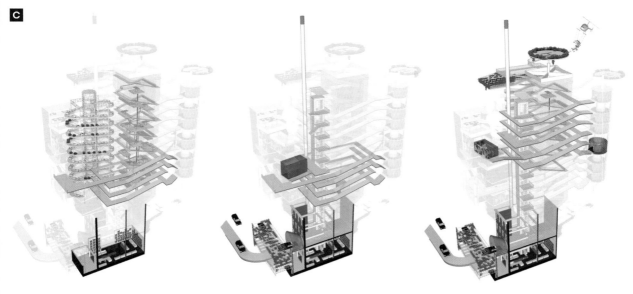

+ FUNERAL DIRECTORS CIRCUIT   + HINDU PROCESSION   + CATHOLIC PROCESSION

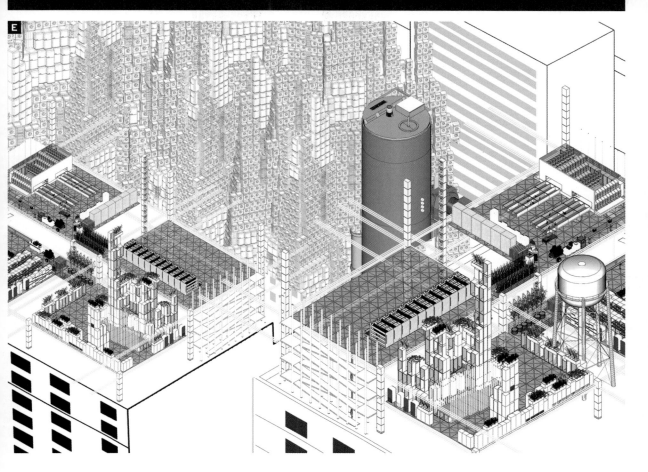

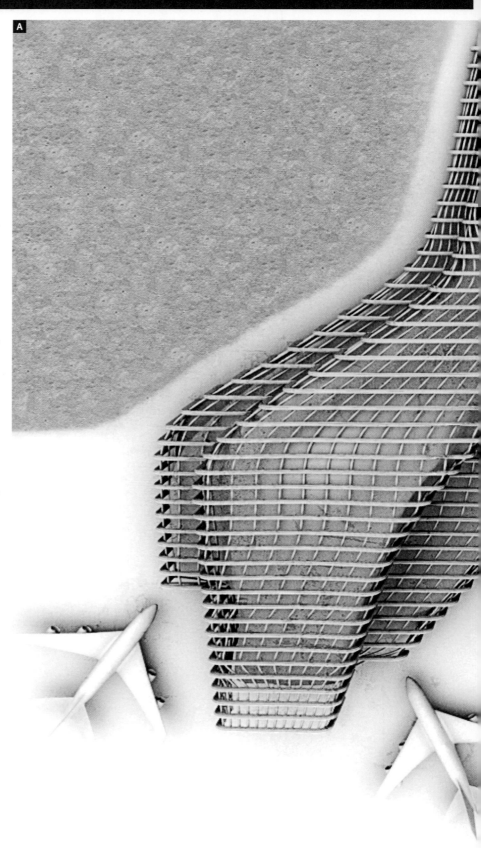

Very Fast Airports
AAD Studio
Summer 2013
Nanako Umemoto, critic,
with Hilary Simon

In the world of the terminal, the relentless and systematic exploitation of "free" or layover time between arrivals and departures gave rise to the advent of city-like agglomerations of uses for the in-transit population. In competition with the more common Central Hub model for such agglomerations, an alternate organizational model for the airport terminal has arisen in the last thirty years: a network of smaller secondary airports and metropolitan multi-airport systems rather than singular point destinations. This studio created architecture for these terminals. The students explored a replacement for Ibaraki International Airport, which stands as a link in a chain of airports spread throughout Asia in Japan, China, and Taiwan. The flattening or placelessness of airport space–the interchangeability of its stores, hotels and waiting rooms worldwide–is simply ahead of the same ineluctable processes everywhere else. Wagering that new publics might coalesce around new sensibilities and given the multiple impending crises on Japan's horizon, the studio suggested, in the most hopeful manner, a new cosmopolitan paradigm–in other words–new ways of life that cross regional and international boundaries, yet create their own sense of the artificial local through material effects.

Filippos Filippidis **A**
Junhee Cho **B/C**
Minjin Kim **D/E**

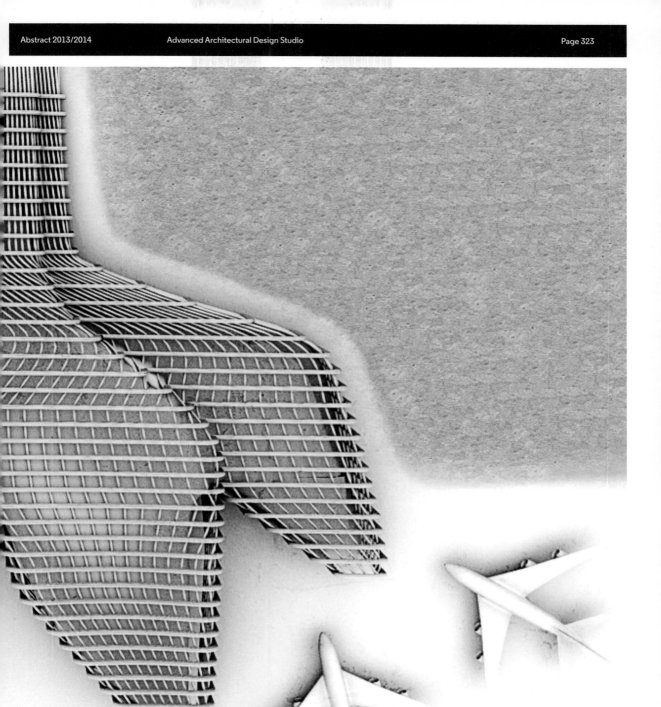

B   ■ structure forming method

■ structure transformation

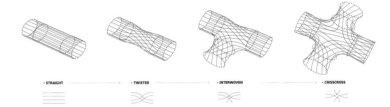

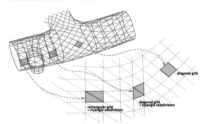

- STRAIGHT   - TWISTED   - INTERWOVEN   - CRISSCROSS

diagonal grid

rectangular grid
+ triangle subdivision

diagonal grid
+ triangle subdivision

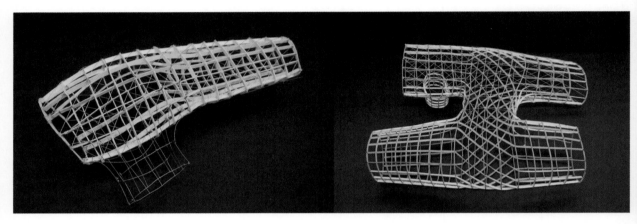

C   ■ double layer structure

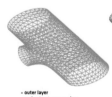

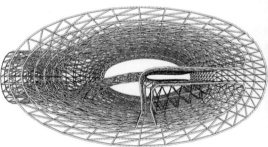

- outer layer
main structur + envelop

- inner layer
sub structure + interior space

- double layer structure

D

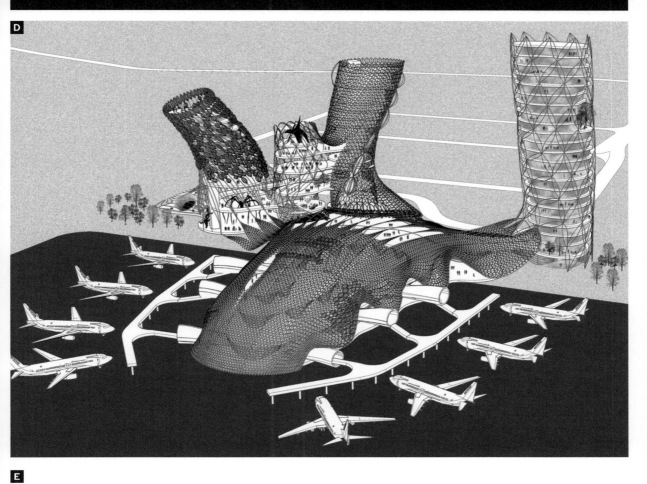

E

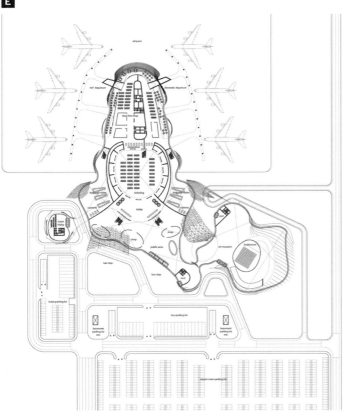

LEVEL +2.00M FLOOR PLAN   LEVEL +8.00M FLOOR PLAN

Necessary Architecture:
A Difficult Whole
AAD Studio
Summer 2013
*Kersten Geers + David
Van Severen, critics*

The Data Center is the most definitive, yet invisible, typology of our contemporary world. It is the densest spot in our digital universe, a physically invisible space virtually visited by many. As the collective spirit of the net becomes more and more in peril, these privately owned devices represent the pinnacle of our shared infrastructure; therefore, Data Centers are intrinsically collective infrastructures.

Unfortunately, the buildings themselves remain largely invisible. Subject to technical and environmental requirements, they tend to hide in the fringes of our world–fringes that are increasingly scarce. The Cloud, inhabitant of the data center, struggles with its own invisibility as the place where our valuable content is stored. Though both problematic, these dynamics offer an opportunity. As in our cities, what was formerly considered collective is increasingly privatized—one thinks of schools and communal offices. One might argue that Data Centers are amongst the few leftover opportunities that, because of their intrinsic content, have the potential to acquire collective meaning.

In this studio, Architecture without Content 4, we returned to the center of the city and investigated the potential of these enormous buildings if they were to be located on Roosevelt Island–formerly the outskirts of Manhattan, today the very center of New York.

Fernando Cena **A**
Rodrigo Valenzuela Jerez **B**
Sean Myung Shin Kim **C/D/E**
Esteban de Backer **F/G/H**

A

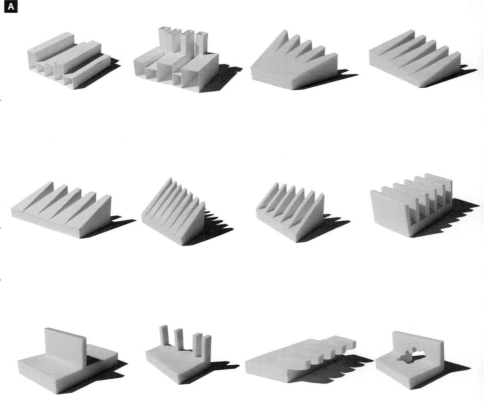

B

C

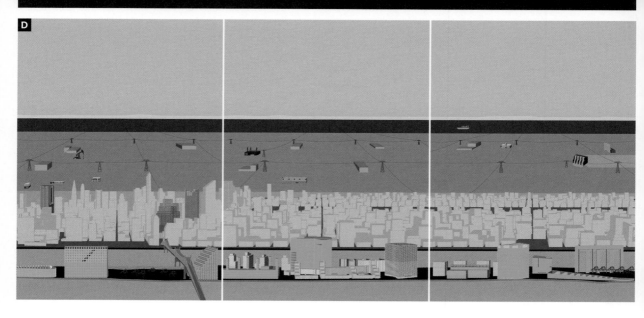

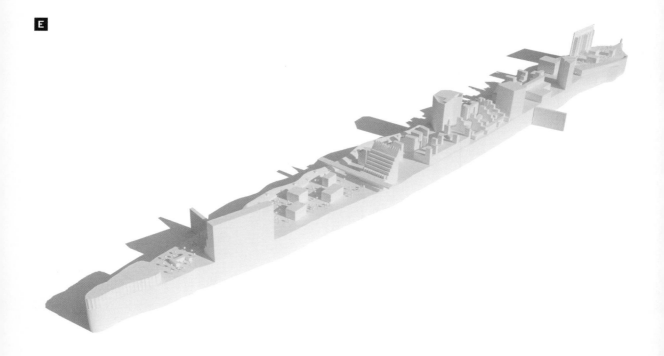

F

G

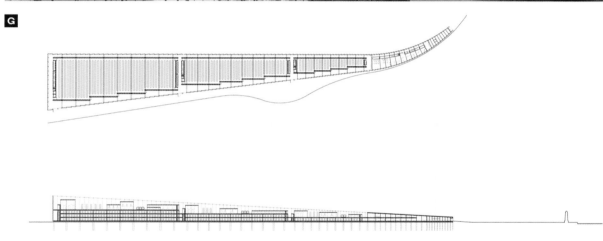

H

PHILLY REMIX
AAD Studio
Summer 2013
Keith Kaseman, critic,
with Diana Cristobal

PHILLY REMIX was an operational regimen geared as a spatial think-tank—an opportunity to critically imagine urban potentials in relation to architectural triggers, and especially vice-versa, through a mode of practice that utilized design motivation and spatial exploration at every step as the prime motive. Physical spatial constructs served as the core medium through which each desk-crit, group discussion, pin-up and review was fueled during the first half of the semester, allowing for the development of preemptive spatial interests to be wholeheartedly pursued prior to our first visit to Philadelphia. As such, this studio did not pursue "conceptual models" insofar as this term invokes the analogical representation of an idea or system. Rather, all models were to be considered spatial constructs to the extent that space is the idea. Studio participants collectively navigated a vast cloud of questions and ideas, which culminated in a diverse array of individually refined and physically communicated spatial projects. Ultimately, the fundamental mission of the Philly Remix was to exploit Philadelphia as a potential synthesizer for new spatial typologies and potential urban occupations that were yet to be imagined or pursued.

Georgios Kyriazis **A/B/C**
Theodora Felekou **D/E/F**

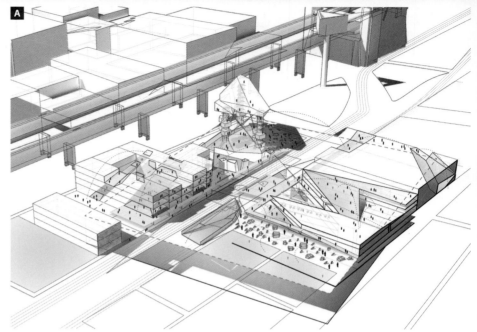
A

B

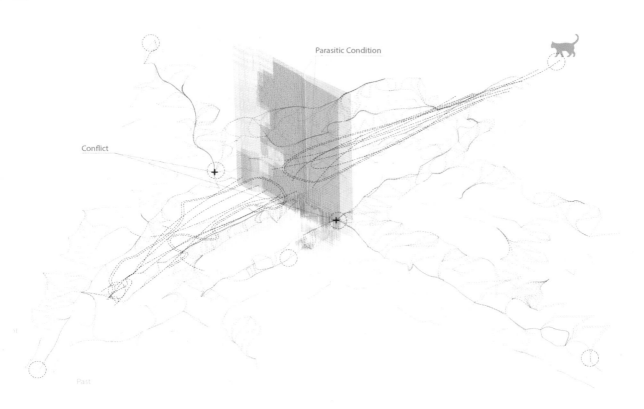

Green Line _ Nicosia _Densifying Edjes = Permeable Conflict

C

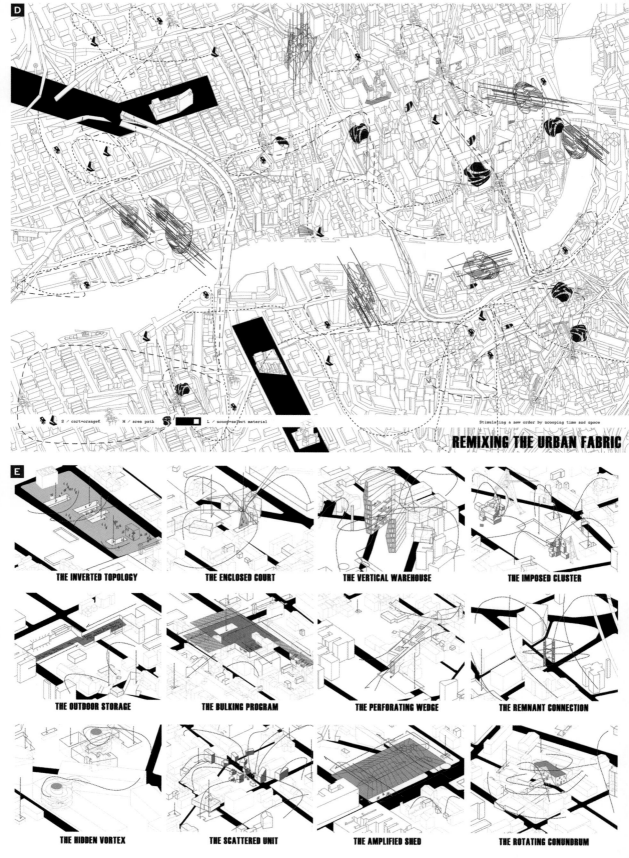

D

S / cart+orangeK   M / area path   L / scoop+select material

Stimulating a new order by scooping time and space

REMIXING THE URBAN FABRIC

E

THE INVERTED TOPOLOGY   THE ENCLOSED COURT   THE VERTICAL WAREHOUSE   THE IMPOSED CLUSTER

THE OUTDOOR STORAGE   THE BULKING PROGRAM   THE PERFORATING WEDGE   THE REMNANT CONNECTION

THE HIDDEN VORTEX   THE SCATTERED UNIT   THE AMPLIFIED SHED   THE ROTATING CONUNDRUM

REMIXING TYPOLOGIES

F

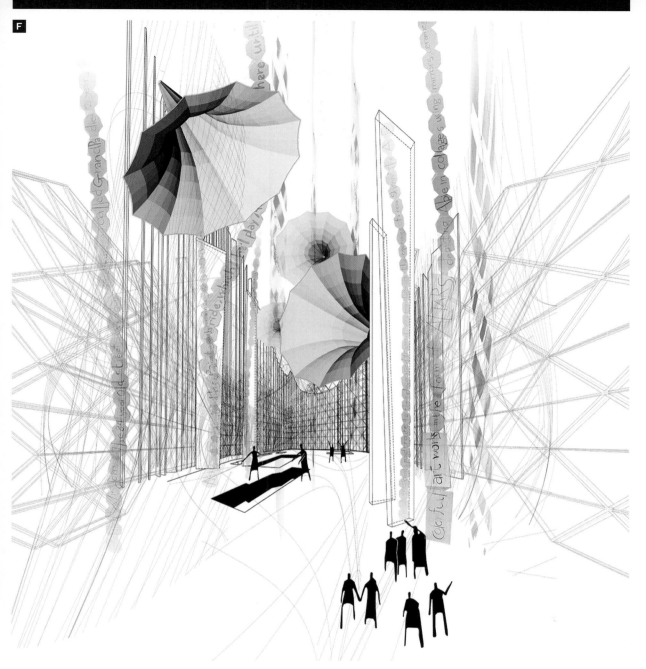

Present Futures: Micro-Social Networks + Macro-Urbanism in Istanbul + Moscow
AAD Studio
Fall 2013
Phu Hoang, critic, with Emanuel Admassu

The studio explored the relationship between the global metropolis and its embedded networks. The design research focused on the opposing scales of "micro" and "macro" networks and their roles in shaping the future of global cities. Citizen-based micro-social networks and governmental macro-urbanism are at odds over the future of the global metropolis. Today, the micro-networks of Facebook, Twitter and Instagram have become instrumental in the exponential growth of public demonstrations. The essential question the studio posed was: How can architects adopt the strategies of virtual social networks to affect change in the physical and material realm of the global metropolis?

In Istanbul, the recent widespread protests highlighted the importance of both physical public space and virtual public discourse. The demonstrations in Istanbul's Taksim Square were remarkable because they began from citizen dissent over the rights of access to their city. The studio took a critical look at an "urban renewal" development announced since the Taksim Square demonstrations. Galataport is an industrial waterfront area in Beyoglu, Istanbul slated to be razed for development into tourist, shopping and cultural programs. The studio proposed future visions for the site that created alternate futures to the current "tabula rasa" development.

Chih-I Lai + Tianhui Shen **A/B**
Heeyun Kim +
Jiazhen Guo **C/D/E**

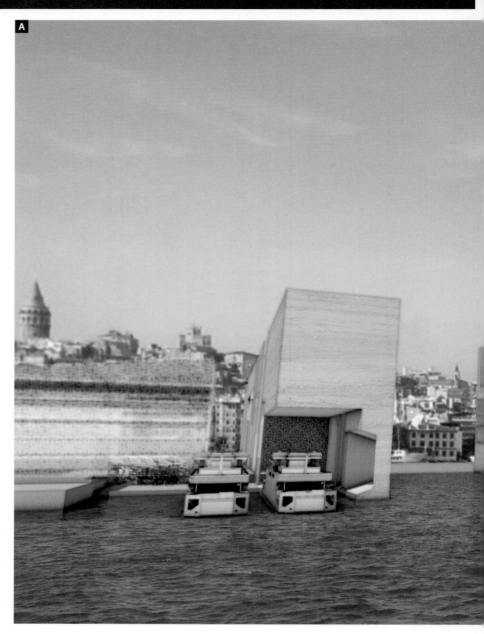

C

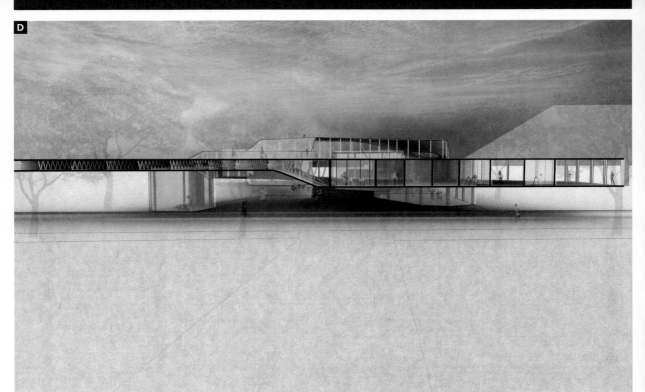

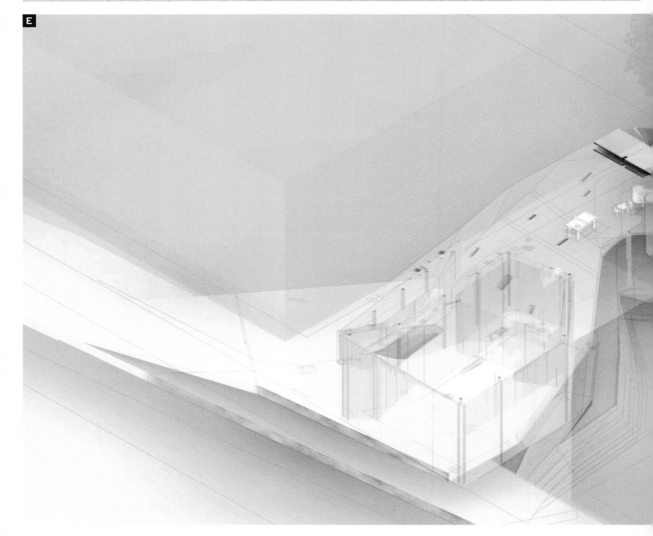

Global Cities: Thesis
Advanced Studio
AAD Studio
Spring 2014
Markus Dochantschi,
critic, with Carolina Ihle

Global Cities Thesis Studio was a platform to critically analyze the future of the twenty-first century city. This studio challenged students to envision solutions to both domestic and global issues that affect major international cities. Solutions were developed based on a comprehensive understanding of the mechanics and structure of a city and were strengthened through continuous communication with the Studio-X Global Network.

Concluding the one year thesis seminar, topics were independently selected by the students and were cultivated into urban strategies. These strategies aimed to address the issues affiliated with the exponential growth of a city. The expected surge in urban populations will transform today's modern cities through infrastructure, policy, culture, technology and globalization.

The only constraint given in the Global Cities Thesis Studio was to apply the proposed strategy to Rio de Janeiro, as a laboratory ground. Following the selection of the student's site and program, architectural projects were then developed at an urban scale. These same projects served as replicable models that could be deployed in other cities, testing the flexibility and durability of the concept.

Chih-I Lai **A**
Fengnuan Song **B**
Masha Drozdov **C**
Shin Hea **D**
Jiazhen Guo **E**

E

City-Bridge: Reconnecting the Urban
AAD Global Cities Thesis
Spring 2014
Chih-I Lai
Markus Dochantschi, advisor

This thesis aims to reconnect the urban infrastructure to adapt to the needs of the growing city. Rio de Janeiro is a global city: it is facing serious challenges such as growing population, increased demands for services, strained energy, water, sanitation and transportation infrastructure, growing slum areas, threats from climate change and limited resources. Rio's unique urban landscape is a mix of natural topography and informal settlements.

In the project, I proposed to construct a new type of infrastructure, which is the acupuncture in the neighborhood, will impact the environment and integrate with the existing fabric, intending to provide the disconnected hillside neighborhoods with much needed self-sufficiency. The proposed urban bridges attempt to reconnect the urban fabric while functioning independently from the rest of the city. They function as transportation, energy, waste collection, water supply, sewage treatment and recycling, and also allow for water-related public spaces. Unlike the urban centralized wastewater treatment plants, the new proposed system decentralizes the public space and treats grey water in an ecological way. The bridge system is accompanied by the conduits, which are adaptive to the growing city improving sanitation and creating more public space.

Live Happy Live Safe: When Urban Development Meets Natural Disaster
AAD Global Cities Thesis
Spring 2014
Fengnuan Song
Markus Dochantschi, advisor

Within the last decade, the number of natural disaster occurrences steadily rose. As a result, high levels of property damage and victim displacement were reported, especially in developed countries. This can be attributed to urbanization, which has a direct effect on population density and the increase of urban development. Rio de Janeiro is among those metropolises that suffer from such natural disasters. The geographical characteristics that make Rio such a beautiful city are inversely the direct causes of the disasters the city experiences; the mountains create mudslides, and the ocean and waterways attribute to flooding.

On the selected site, a golf course creates a division between low and high income citizens. However, this same golf course provides employment and healthcare opportunities for low-income individuals. Ultimately, a social and economic exchange is being implemented by this amenity.

Therefore, utilizing the remote areas of Rio's mountain range could help lessen the severity of damages caused by natural disasters. By decreasing the density of Rio's metropolis, we can easily isolate damaged areas without affecting the rest of the city, and so increase the population of the city without redefining the topographic characteristics of the city.

Generic Airport City
AAD Global Cities Thesis
Spring 2014
Jiazhen Guo
Markus Dochantschi, advisor

Like many other global metropolises, Rio de Janeiro suffers from aerial vehicle traffic efficiency. The Miami parking garage, Disney Parks and Heathrow International Airport are all examples of locations that follow high efficiency schedules. Unfortunately, as a result of society's rapid industrialization, accumulation of fortune and intelligence, the metropolis is no longer efficient. Issues that attribute to this problem are the lengthy commute times of travelers and the inability to fully utilize all aspects of an airport on a daily basis. When focusing on Rio, the airport of Santos Dumont is particularly hard to access because of traffic congestion during the day. At night, this area becomes a ghost town, with regards to staffing.

This thesis proposed a new mega structure system called "Airport City", which contains program that pertains to the individual's daily life along with a high efficiency runway. The design achieves urban efficiency through circulation planning; it takes only thirty minutes to either land or depart. The traditional linear plan for airport was changed to a vertical arrangement, reducing walking distances effectively. Thus, to some degree, the organizational tactics of this proposal could be applied to the city to increase general efficiency.

Immigrowth Rio de Janeiro: Cultural Integration through Architecture
AAD Global Cities Thesis
Spring 2014
Masha Drozdov
Markus Dochantschi, advisor

Today, immigrowth is present in any city in the world. It varies based on cultural segregation and is most prominent in a mixed community where different socioeconomic groups co-exist. Cities are most desirable places because of their density and variety of opportunities. The undesirable cities are the ones with segregated communities and missing or poor infrastructure.

In the case of Rio de Janeiro, the "successful" urban strategy for immigrowth refers to the upward and outward growth of favelas. They are viewed as a disturbance to the city as they consist of unsafe, unstable structures that in some cases have no utilities. Simultaneously, they are essential to the function and economic growth of the city.

I proposed a formal architectural typology that follows the strategy of the original settlements, learning from the shantytowns, but avoiding the downfalls. The master plan would provide the necessary infrastructure with access to easy maintenance, public spaces as well as new integrated housing for any of the new or existing Rio residents. The new infill is a critique of the modern romantic view of the favelas, taking into account future tourists who will want to see how the other half lives.

Tapestry of Events: Enhancing Peripheral Identities

AAD Global Cities Thesis
Spring 2014
Shin Hea
Markus Dochantschi, advisor

A metropolis consists of urban clusters that are juxtaposed and overlaid onto a city. Because urban clusters consist of intangible events as well as formal structures, a metropolitan identity is related to clusters and their events. To preserve identities, a new urban cluster with organized events can be proposed, and reconstructing and preserving one's social memories can be materialized in this cluster.

As this project is an architectural strategy for urban identities, the site was selected according to social values. Compared to a developed area with a standardized and unified identity, a peripheral boundary of a metropolis has infinite possibilities that could reveal true identities through autonomous vernacular events.

The architectural methodology began with an insertion of volumetric open spaces. Urban voids in the project designate categorized events and contain program according to scale and furniture. By planning voids on existing topography with circulation, current identities are materialized and enhanced. Furthermore, mixing and intertwining spatial structures can orchestrate a new type of identity and its preservation orchestrated within existing urban texture. This methodology is not only for a specific site, but also for general places in Rio de Janeiro to enhance its metropolitan identities.

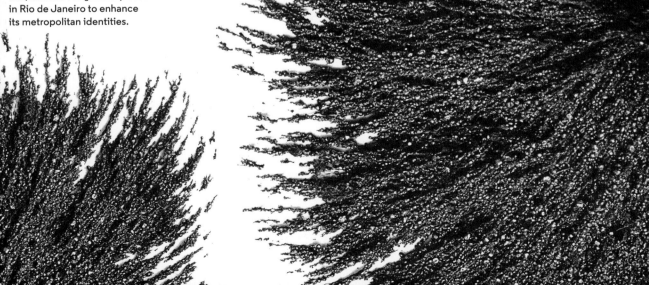

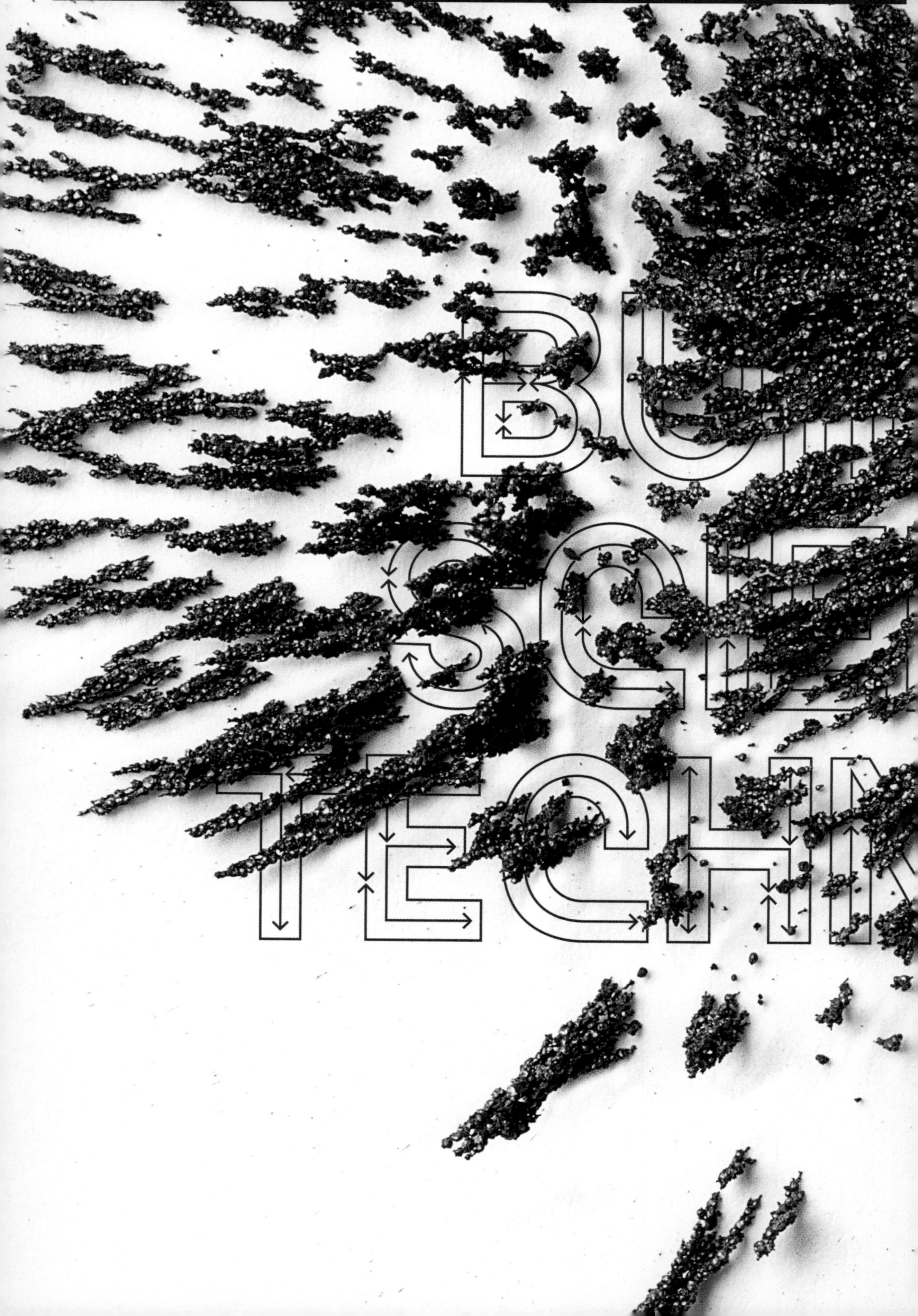

Building Science + Technology Sequence
Craig Schwitter, director

The Building Science and Technologies (BST) curriculum is based on the belief that architects benefit from having a knowledge of building physics and technical systems, not only as utilitarian ends in themselves, but also as a means to help develop a building's spaces, forms and expression. Building science and technology in the GSAPP teaching has been enhanced by a number of initiatives that introduce greater integration with the studio and history/theory classes. Teams of engineers are brought into Core Studios to offer feedback on student projects through the Roving Engineer program. The engagement with technology has become one of the central strengths of the studio program and a major source of inspiration to the wider initiatives at the school. All aspects of construction and building technology have become vital to both the school's core curriculum and its research culture.

The six-course BST required sequence begins with three core courses (Architectural Technology 1,2 and 3) that outline the structural, environmental and material conditions to which habitable spaces respond, describing physical determinants of technical building systems. Next, individual building systems—including structure, building enclosure, environmental conditioning and information management—are explored in depth. For each system studied, various design strategies, materials, fabrication techniques and didactic built works are explored. Field trips, laboratory demonstrations and short design problems are used to augment in-class study. As both a qualitative and a basic quantitative understanding of elementary systems are mastered, the curriculum shifts its focus onto increasingly complex systems serving entire buildings. The sequence's next two courses (Architectural Technology 4 and 5) help students develop an understanding of how technical-utilitarian systems are resolved, how they are integrated with other systems and how they inform a building's spaces and formal expression—first through in-depth case studies of an entire building and then by the preliminary design of a industrial-loft block. In both courses, students work in teams with structural, mechanical and building-envelope experts. The sequence's final course (Architectural Technology 6) is composed of an elective chosen by the student from a selection of classes taught by world-renowned experts in their field where students research a specific topic in-depth. The goals of the electives are threefold: to explore the potential of technological systems to impact design; to understand historical relationships among technology, philosophy, politics and architecture; and to take advantage of New York's professional practitioners working with state of the art technology. The diversity of views regarding architectural science and technology represented by the school's design and technology faculty is reflected in the elective offerings. Throughout the Building Science and Technologies sequences, students are encouraged to apply their growing knowledge to design problems posed in studio.

Architectural Technology 1
Building Science + Technology
Fall 2013
Craig Schwitter, instructor, with
Andrew Maier, Monica Blain,
Rebecca Riss + Scott Overall

Where does technology emerge in architecture? Is it through scientific formulae, through digital simulation or through experimentation in making? Does technology influence architecture, or has architecture always driven the necessary leaps in technology? To make architecture is to invent the future. In this course, we explored the fundamentals of building technology and what it meant to create bold, expressive and efficient built form and to gain the confidence to build these creations.

Architectural Technology I served as an introduction for the understanding of materials, construction techniques, structural and environmental systems in architecture, which are further explored through the Architectural Technology curriculum.

The fundamentals of building technology were explored through the historical progress in making in architecture, broadly split into the industrial, modern and digital eras. Materials and material applications were explored relative to each era and introduced through historical and transformative leaders in the development of technology. Student groups studied a specific technology leader, associated material and built examples through a semester long case study, including research presentations and physical models.

Technology + making derives from the individual, not merely the science. These critical connections and breakthroughs in invention were explored, and basic principles of building technology science were uncovered.

Aleeya Khan, Alexander Darsinos + Lauren Miyata **A**
Amanda Ortland, Jennifer Zeckendorf + SohEun Han **B**
Jason Danforth, Laura Dean, Riley MacPhee + Peter Mielnicki **C**
Mel Loyola Agosto, Woochan Jung, Makenzie Leukart + Tyler Henderson **D/E**
Mira De Avila-Shin, Emily Oppenheim, Sonya Ursell + Vincent Yan **F**
Yuchen Guo, Yu Wu + Boyuan Jiang **G**
Jesse Catalano, Manuel Cordero, Max Miller + Harrison Nesbitt **H**

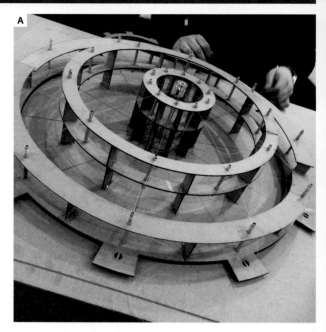

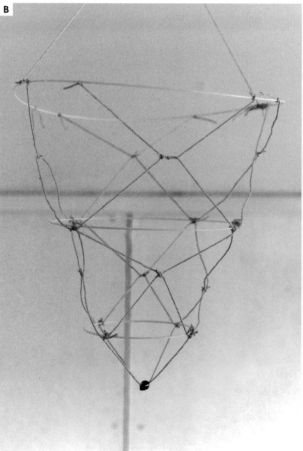

C

F

D

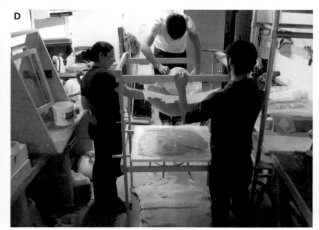

G

E

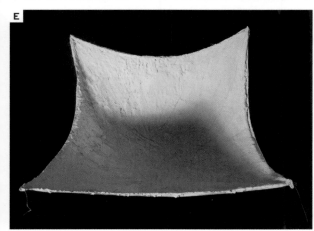

H

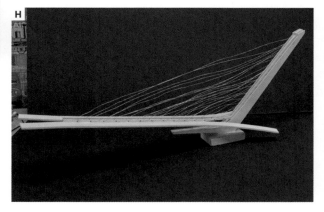

**Architectural Technology 2
Environmental Systems/MEP**
Building Science + Technology
Spring 2014
*Nico Kienzl, instructor, with
Scott Overall + Rebecca Riss*

This course addressed the
fundamentals and applica-
tion of environmental control
systems in buildings. Heating,
cooling, ventilation, lighting
and acoustics were discussed
based on the physical laws
that govern the exchange of
energy between building and
environment as well as how
they relate to human comfort.
Electrical, plumbing, fire
protection and circulation
were introduced in this context
as required systems to make
buildings fit for occupation.

Class time was divided into
lectures, hands on introduc-
tions of software tools and
quantitative methods, guest
lectures, as well as student
presentations of the assignments. Assignments combined
software and hand calcula-
tions in the application of
the principles introduced in
the lectures. Some assignments crossed over to the
design studio, and students
were encouraged to apply
lessons learned in this class
to their studio explorations.

Architectural Technology 3
Building Science + Technology
Fall 2013
*Will Laufs, instructor,
with Reece Tucker*

In Architectural Technology
3, students studied various
structural systems and how they
can be applied to support their
architectural designs. By visualizing the force-flow through
building volumes, students
developed opportunities to
use new materials and software
as an available part of their
technology toolbox in design.

Students established suitable
structural systems for various
architectural building types
and artistic visions based on
fundamental principles and
contemporary case study examples that go beyond well-known
standard systems and allow
room for plurality. Expression
and placement of structure was
understood not as a distant necessity during construction and
building approval process, but
as a rich opportunity to develop
integrated design solutions,
in which structural members
underline the overall expression of architectural context.

Paul Michael Graves,
Jonathan Yang, Mengxing
Wang + Dan Luo **A**
Jeffrey Montes, Laura Marie
Peterson + Damaskene
Danae Vokolos **B**
Lisa West, Athina
Zafeiropoulou,Walter Cain +
Daniel Watson De Roux **C/D**

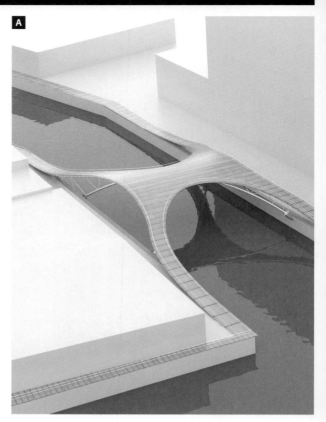

A

B

C

D

Architectural Technology 4
Building Science + Technology
Fall 2013
*David Wallance +
Jay Hibbs, instructors*

The semester was devoted to analyzing a prominent post World War II building. Using the building's construction drawings as the primary source of information, the investigation focused on the interrelationship between the structural, mechanical and enclosure systems, construction methods and materials and the architectural form. The examination of the building systems emphasized the way in which each system informs and impacts the others, as well as their ultimate effect on the creation of the architecture.

An objective of this part of the course was to understand the architect's attitude regarding building systems and how the architectural idea – intention – of the specific building was realized, reflected and amplified by the choice, manipulation, interaction and execution of the building systems.

Ekkaphon Puekpaiboon, John Kim, Xinyu Li + Bless Yee **A**
Ernest Pang, Janice Leong, Ho-gyum Kim + Meredith Wing **B**
Myung Jae Lee, Yongwon Kwon, Seuk Kim + Timime Tsang **C**
Xiaoxi Chen, Kyong Kim, Laura Peterson + Ivy Hume **D**
Megan Murdock, Sucheta Nadig, Ricardo Leon + Michelle Tse **E**

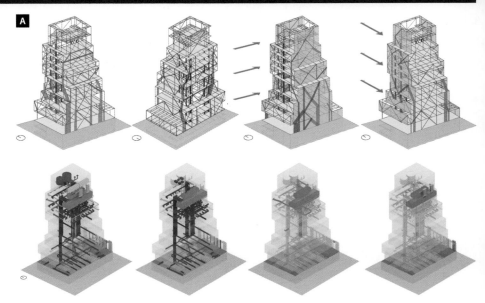

New Museum of Contemporary Art, SANAA

B

TYPICAL FACADE DETAIL IN LOWER LEVEL

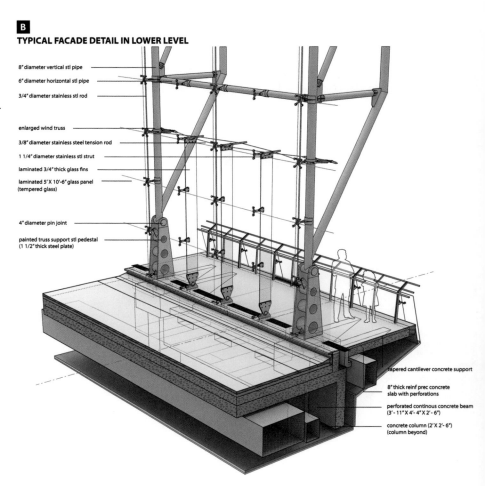

8" diameter vertical stl pipe
6" diameter horizontal stl pipe
3/4" diameter stainless stl rod

enlarged wind truss
3/8" diameter stainless steel tension rod
1 1/4" diameter stainless stl strut
laminated 3/4" thick glass fins
laminated 5' X 10'-6" glass panel (tempered glass)

4" diameter pin joint

painted truss support stl pedestal (1 1/2" thick steel plate)

tapered cantilever concrete support

8" thick reinf prec concrete slab with perforations

perforated continous concrete beam (3'- 11"X 4'- 4" X 2'- 6")

concrete column (2' X 2'- 6") (column beyond)

Inventors' Hall of Fame, Ennead Architects

C

MECHANICAL SYSTEM

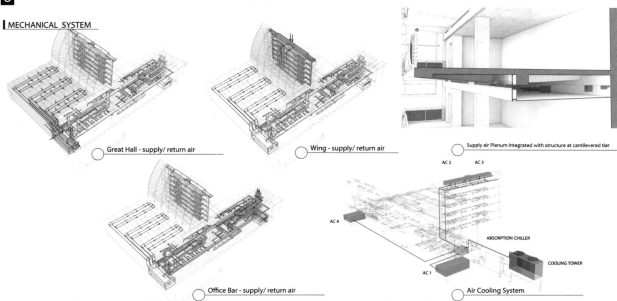

Great Hall - supply/ return air

Wing - supply/ return air

Supply air Plenum integrated with structure at cantilevered tier

Office Bar - supply/ return air

Air Cooling System

Rose Center for Earth and Space, Ennead Architects

D

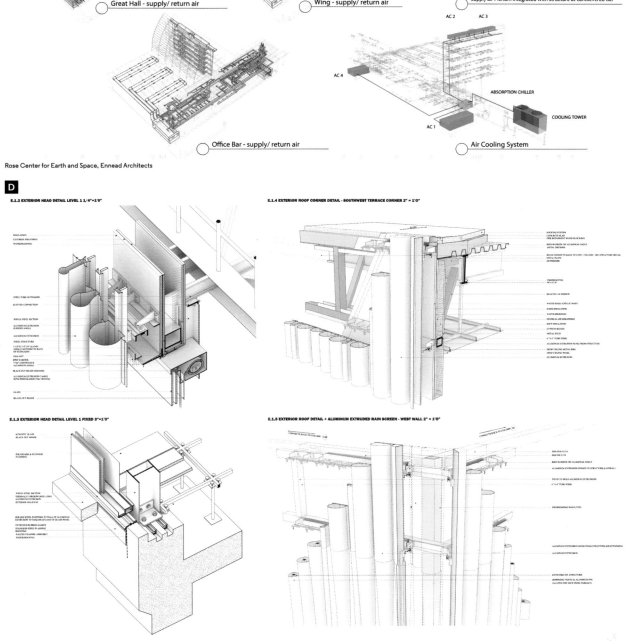

E.1.2 EXTERIOR HEAD DETAIL LEVEL 1 1/4"=1'0"

E.1.4 EXTERIOR ROOF CORNER DETAIL - SOUTHWEST TERRACE CORNER 2" = 1'0"

E.1.3 EXTERIOR HEAD DETAIL LEVEL 1 FIXED 3"=1'0"

E.1.5 EXTERIOR ROOF DETAIL + ALUMINUM EXTRUDED RAIN SCREEN - WEST WALL 2" = 1'0"

Wyly Theater, REX | OMA

E

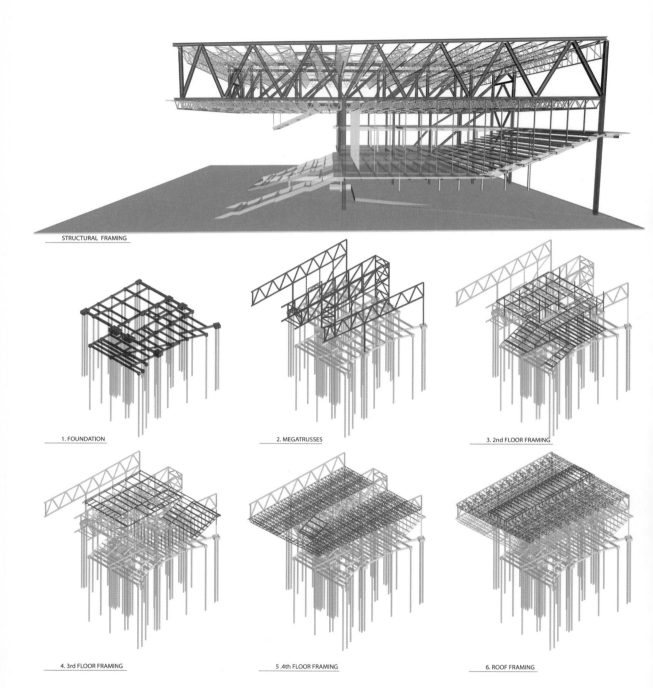

STRUCTURAL FRAMING

1. FOUNDATION

2. MEGATRUSSES

3. 2nd FLOOR FRAMING

4. 3rd FLOOR FRAMING

5 .4th FLOOR FRAMING

6. ROOF FRAMING

STICK SYSTEM

Institute for Contemporary Art, Diller Scofidio + Renfro

Architectural Technology 5
Building Science + Technology
Spring 2014
Jay Hibbs + David Wallance,
coordinators, Pat Hopple,
Anton Martinez, Elias Matar,
John Pachuta, Leo Argiris,
Seth Wolf, Kevin Lichten,
Scott Hughes, Sandra McKee,
Jason Stone, Robert Condon,
Russ Davies, David Dubrow,
Elias Dagher, Jeff Huang +
Fiona Cousins, instructors

Architectural Technology
5 was a technology class in
which a student's design skills
were an essential tool used to
synthesize the various technical
systems of a contemporary
building type into a coherent
expression of an architectural
intention. In order to focus attention on the problem of
expressing an architectural
intention through the choice
and development of building
technology, the course was
centered around a design
problem in which many of the
design issues students have
been preoccupied with in
studio work were eliminated.
The industrial loft building
program was selected with the
aim of limiting interior spatial
development to that which
one achieves by the articulation of the building envelope
and structural system and, to
a lesser (but still important)
extent, environmental systems.

Sareeta Dinesh Patel,
John Kim, Mondrian Hsieh +
Serdar Vardar **A**
Pachut Argiris, Sabrina Barker,
Chido Chuma, Rebecca Riss +
Lisa West **B**
Mimi Ho, Janice Leong,
Ernest Pang + Ekkaphon
Puekpaiboon **C**
Juan Pablo Azzares, Xiaoxi
Chen, Ivy Hume, Kyong
Kim + Carolina Ilano **D/E**

A

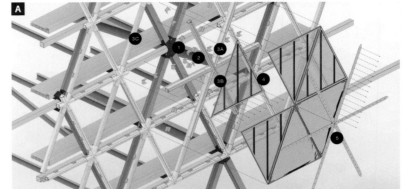

1   DIAGRID JOINT

2   C - CHANNEL
@ 4' - 8" O.C. TO
DIAGRID STRUCTURE

3A   CURTAINWALL
SUPPORT TUBE TO
C - CHANNEL

3B   CURTAINWALL
SUPPORT TUBE NODE

3C   CURTAINWALL
SUPPORT TUBE - SPAN
W/O C - CHANNEL

4   TRIANGULAR UNIT
W/ COVER MULLION
TO SUPPORT TUBE

5   DECORATIVE COVER
PLATE

B

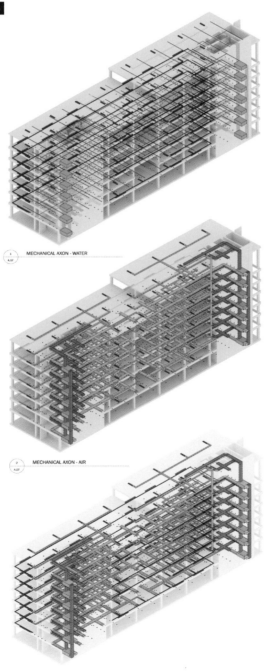

1   MECHANICAL AXON - WATER
A.07

2   MECHANICAL AXON - AIR
A.07

3   MECHANICAL AXON - ALL SYSTEMS
A.07

C

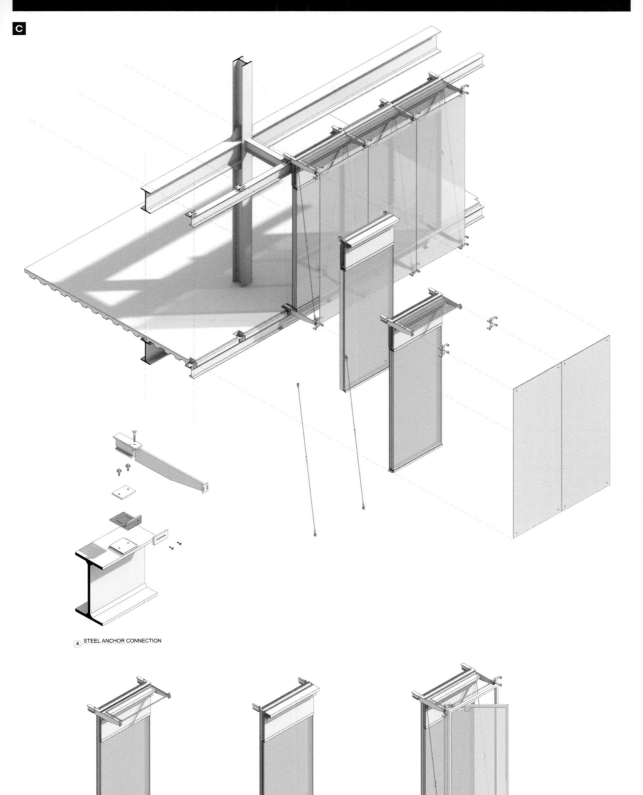

④ STEEL ANCHOR CONNECTION

① WINDOW WALL TYPE A

② WINDOW WALL TYPE B

③ OPERABLE WINDOW WALL TYPE C

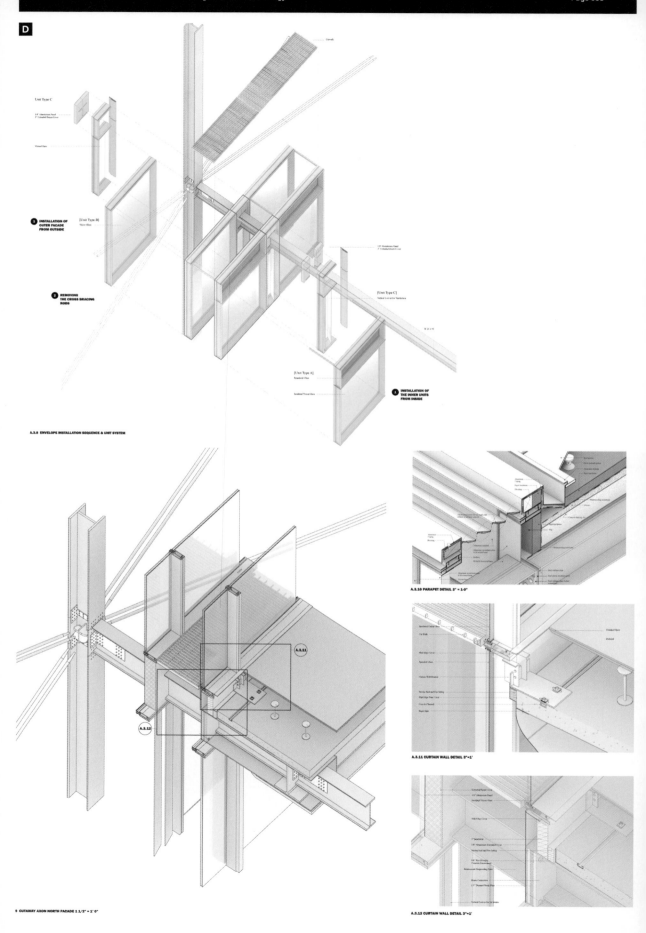

D

Unit Type C

Vision Glass

3 INSTALLATION OF OUTER FACADE FROM OUTSIDE

[Unit Type B]
Vision Glass

2 REMOVING THE CROSS BRACING RODS

[Unit Type C]
Vertical Louver for Ventilation

[Unit Type A]

1 INSTALLATION OF THE INNER UNITS FROM INSIDE

A.3.8 ENVELOPE INSTALLATION SEQUENCE & UNIT SYSTEM

A.3.11

A.3.12

9 CUTAWAY AXON NORTH FACADE 1 1/2" = 1' 0"

A.3.10 PARAPET DETAIL 3" = 1'-0"

A.3.11 CURTAIN WALL DETAIL 3"=1'

A.3.12 CURTAIN WALL DETAIL 3"=1'

E

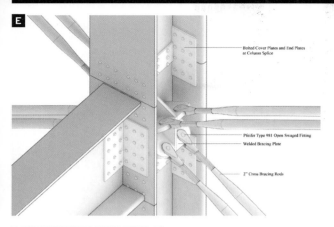

Bolted Cover Plates and End Plates
at Column Splice

Pfeifer Type 981 Open Swaged Fitting

Welded Bracing Plate

2" Cross Bracing Rods

S.2.1 STEEL CONNECTION 2ND AND 7TH FLOOR / SCALE 3" = 1-0"

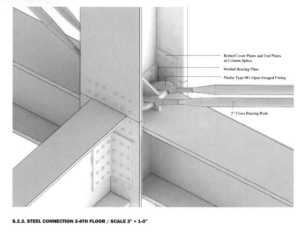

Bolted Cover Plates and End Plates
at Column Splice

Welded Bracing Plate

Pfeifer Type 981 Open Swaged Fitting

2" Cross Bracing Rods

S.2.2. STEEL CONNECTION 3-6TH FLOOR / SCALE 3" = 1-0"

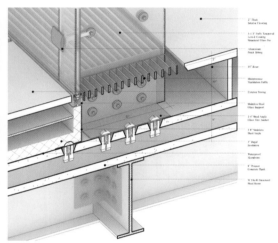

S.2.3 STRUCTURAL GLASS FINS ATTACHMENT / SCALE 3" = 1-0"

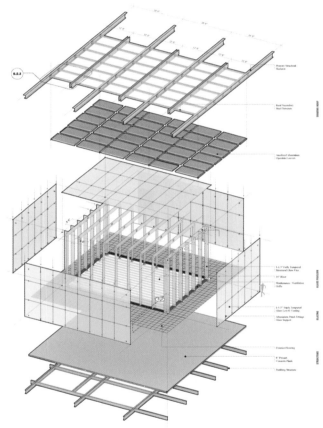

S.2.4 SHADING LOUVER SYSTEM / INSTALLATION SEQUENCE

S.2.5 GLASS PAVILION ASSEMBLY AXON

Optics of Architecture
Building Science + Technology
Spring 2014
*Phillip Anzalone, instructor,
with Arkadiusz Piegdon*

Optics can be used as a design tool to transform architectural spaces. While recent architectural theories and tools have focused on the quantitative aspect of space and design, the geometry and associated algorithms of formal aspects of space and matter, optics, in its relationship to architecture, operates on the qualitative aspect of our physical reality. By carefully exploring the potentials of science, technology, art and the culture of optics to alter our surroundings, designers can develop means to alter space. The optical relationship between light, material and space is a concept with a high degree of flexibility and fidelity, and, through empirical performance, operations can be a formidable architecture design element.

This course explored this relationship by staring at the foundations and first principles of optics, covering the electromagnetic spectrum, interaction with materials through transmission, reflections and absorption. From this foundation the lectures evolved to incorporate the applied aspect of optics such as perception, construction and other elements of the physical act of lighting. Finally, the practice of lighting in architecture was explored through the introduction of both simulation and analysis software, design methods for integrating light and design and control systems. Optics were thought of as a science, a technology and a philosophical and social concept.

Fast Pace // Slow Space
Building Science + Technology
Spring 2014
*Mark Bearak + Brigette Borders,
instructors*

Fast Pace // Slow Space used the concept of time to drive the design and fabrication of a meditative architectural folly. In today's cities people work not only at their place of business but also while mobile, utilizing the digital tools and infrastructure that allow us to stay constantly interconnected. While moving between fast-paced environments, people often have no chance to experience respite. This occurrence is even more amplified in Manhattan where space is premium, and the pace of life rarely slows down. This course tested high-speed construction against a space for meditation, relaxation and atmospheric therapy: a cohesive environment built upon the relationship between man and his built environment.

Parametric and computational software offer designers a high degree of specificity, which can be used to create complex forms, intricate details and material efficiency, yet high-level results become insignificant if construction methods are too complicated to be timely. Fast Pace/Slow Space focused on the marriage of complex form and logical assembly with detailing, hardware and construction methods informing design decisions from the onset. Student groups designed an installation or environment with slow pace sensibilities, while utilizing details that allow for high-speed assembly and disassembly.

Xiaoxi Chen, Benjamin Hochberg, Yasmina Khan, Isabelle Kirkham-Lewitt, Lucas Lind, Ji Nia, Sareeta Patel, Madhini Prathaban, James Stoddart + Athina Zafeiropoulou **A/B**
Margaux Young, Rashad Palmer, Dan Luo, Gemma Gene, Anna Vander Zwaag, Jenny Yuan Lin, Eileen Chen, Madeeha Merchant, Rebecca Riss + Gabriel Calarava **C/D**

C

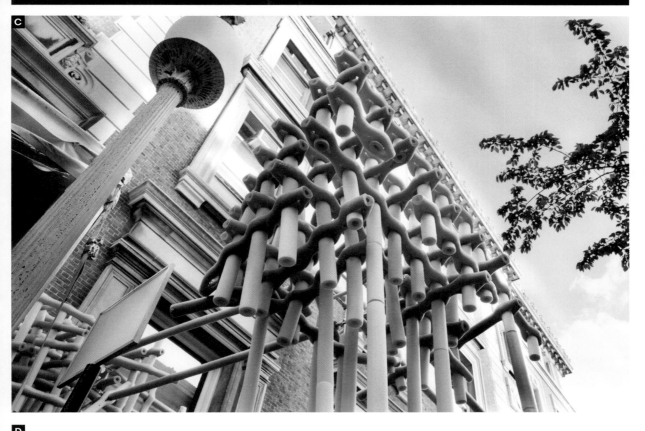

D

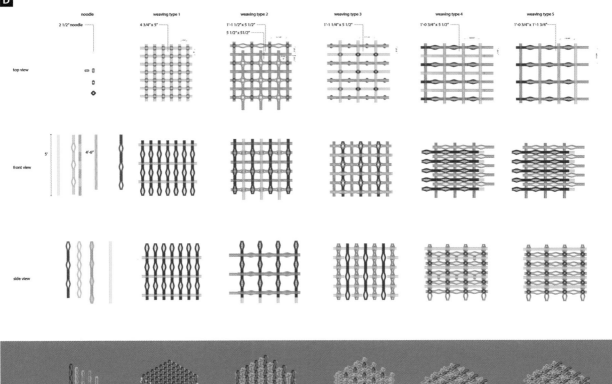

Digital Detailing:
Testing + Analysis
Building Science + Technology
Fall 2013
*Toru Hasegawa + Mark Collins,
instructors*

Innovation in design computation and fabrication has generated a new context within architects work. Digital modes of detailing, or specifying design intent, are increasingly scripted – generating millions of variations. In this torrent of new design information, search has become a necessary instrument in the designer's toolbox. For the next generation of structures, a critical understanding of concepts such as search, evolution and performance will be necessary to operate in this data deluge.

The goal of this building technologies seminar was to incubate a series of research proposals on the topic of performance-based design. We defined performance as optimally working within a defined context of measurement, including but not limited to structural performance, energy, lighting, acoustics and even aesthetics. The seminar explored several performance modeling platforms in a workshop environment. Supplementing this hands-on experience were lectures critically examining the potent roles that simulation can play in design projects and processes.

Andrew Nicolaides +
Ricardo Vega **A**
Albert Franco + Keonwoo Kim **B**

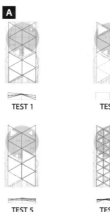
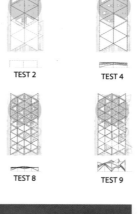

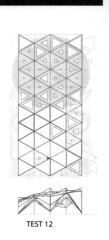

TEST 1   TEST 2   TEST 4   TEST 5

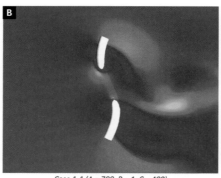
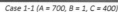

TEST 5   TEST 8   TEST 9   TEST 11   TEST 12

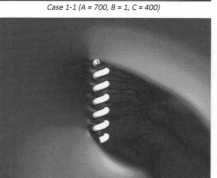

Case 1-1 (A = 700, B = 1, C = 400)

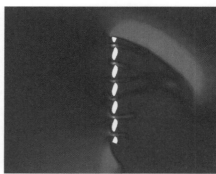

Case 2-1 (A = 100, B = 6, C = 400)

Case 1-2 (A = 700, B = 6, C = 400)

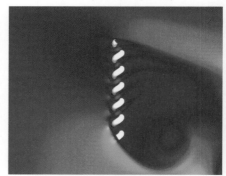

Case 2-2 (A = 500, B = 6, C = 400)

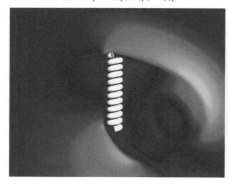
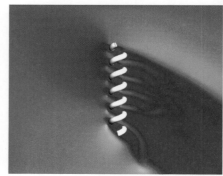

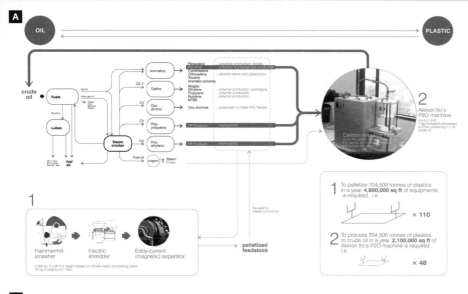

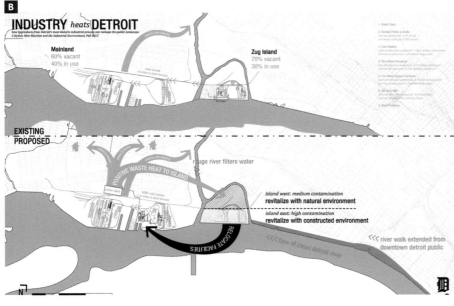

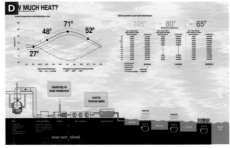

Man, Machine + the Industrial Landscape: Re-Imagining the Relationship between Industrial + Public Territories

Building Science + Technology
Fall 2013
Sean A. Gallagher, instructor, with John Barrett

Industrialized communities are prevalent in every corner of the world today; as a result, the global population is now more urban than rural. Over the next century, existing and developing metropolises will have to reconsider traditional relationships between industrial and public territories in order to accommodate and sustain an increased level of demand for space and services.

This course examined past and present strategies of meeting the growing industrial and infrastructural demands of our society. It identified areas in which industrial technologies and landscapes might be recalibrated to serve future infrastructural networks that establish new relationships between the public, local ecology and industry. The course framed an understanding of the means and methods of industrial activities ranging from mining to waste management with a focus on current and future techniques of material extraction, refinement and redistribution.

Students produced writings and drawings analyzing and re-imagining the current state and potential futures of industrial processes and sites. Students were encouraged to use their research assignment as a way of investigating interesting and unfamiliar industrial processes, but, more importantly, as a means to initiate a thesis for why and how architects can influence the necessary change in our urban environments.

Anastasia Tania **A/C**
Chelsea Hyduk **B/D**

Advanced Curtain Walls
Building Science + Technology
Spring 2014
Robert Heintges, instructor

This course offered an intense
exposure to the custom curtain
wall in a lecture/seminar and
technical studio format. The
intent of the course was to provide graduating students with
a comprehensive understanding of the technical concepts
and specific skills necessary to
undertake the actual practice of
designing, detailing, specifying
and administrating the custom
curtain wall. Although the
course emphasized current and
emerging technologies of the
curtain wall, discussion of specific technical issues and methodologies focused on those
aspects that directly inform
contemporary architectural
design. Case studies of contemporary examples were used
throughout to illustrate the
technical content of the course.

Juan Pablo Azares **A**
Reece W Tucker **B/C**
Tianhui Shen **D/E**

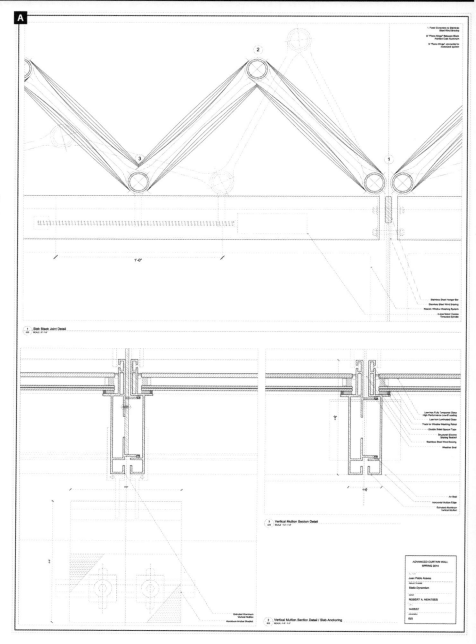

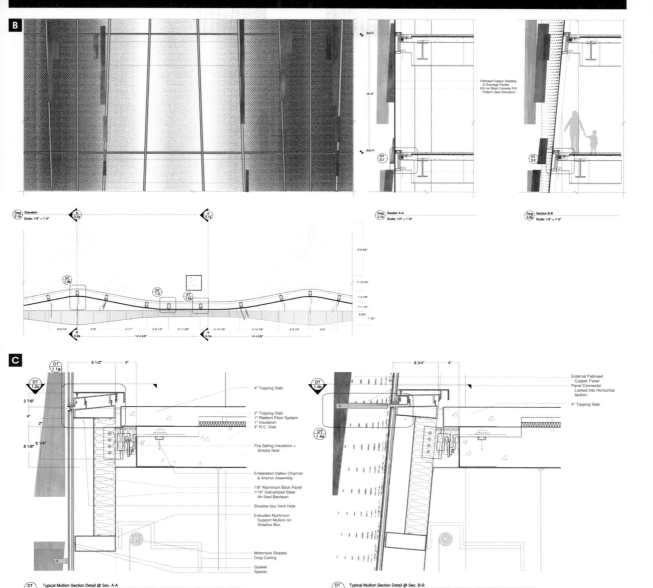

B

Patinaed Copper Shading & Drainage Panels IGU w/ Black Ceramic Frit Pattern (See Elevation)

Dwg 2.1b — Elevation — Scale: 1/2" = 1'-0"

Dwg 3.1b — Section A-A — Scale: 1/2" = 1'-0"

Dwg 3.2b — Section B-B — Scale: 1/2" = 1'-0"

C

4" Topping Slab

2" Topping Slab
1" Radiant Floor System
1" Insulation
8" R.C. Slab

Fire Safing Insulation + Smoke Seal

Embedded Halfen Channel & Anchor Assembly

1/8" Aluminum Back Panel
1/16" Galvanized Steel Air Seal Backpan

Shadow box Vent Hole

Extruded Aluminum Support Mullion for Shadow Box

Motorized Shades
Drop Ceiling

Gasket
Spacer

DT 3.1 — Typical Mullion Section Detail @ Sec. A-A — Scale: 3" = 1'-0"

External Patinaed Copper Panel Panel Connector Locked into Horizontal Mullion

4" Topping Slab

DT 3.2 — Typical Mullion Section Detail @ Sec. B-B — Scale: 3" = 1'-0"

D

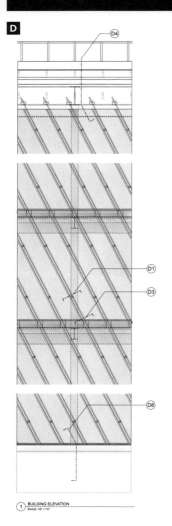

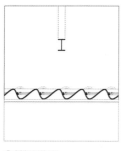

① BUILDING ELEVATION
SCALE: 1/2" = 1'0"

③ TYPICAL FLOOR PLAN
SCALE: 1/2" = 1'0"

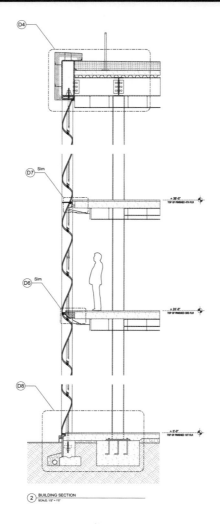

② BUILDING SECTION
SCALE: 1/3" = 1'0"

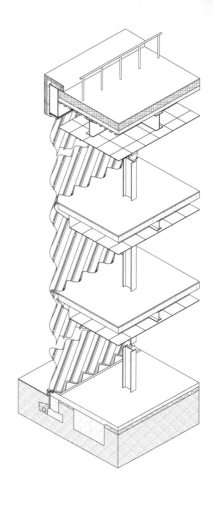

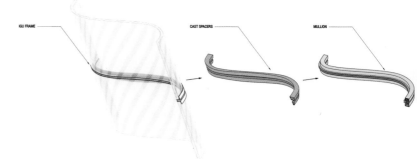

IGU FRAME   CAST SPACERS   MULLION

E

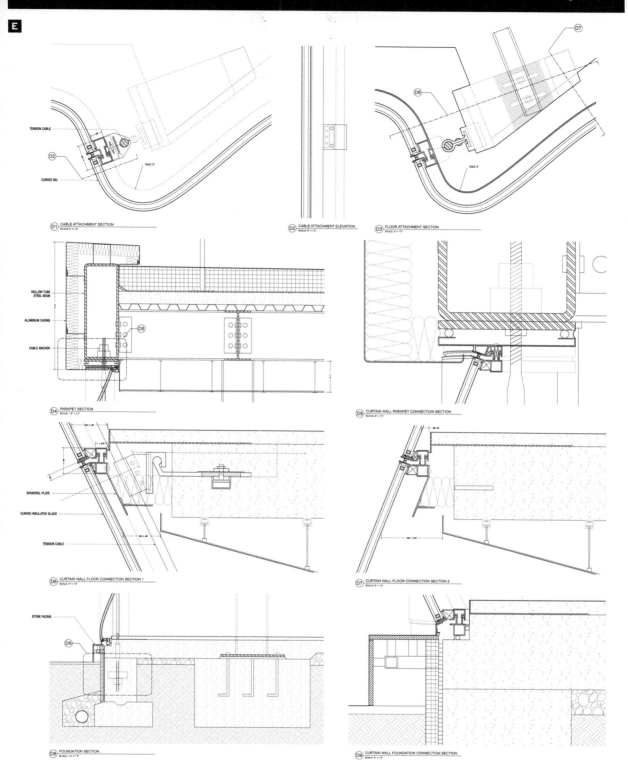

TENSION CABLE

D2

CURVED IGU

RAD 3"

D1 CABLE ATTACHMENT SECTION
SCALE 6" = 1'0"

D2 CABLE ATTACHMENT ELEVATION
SCALE 6" = 1'0"

D3 FLOOR ATTACHMENT SECTION
SCALE 6" = 1'0"

D6

D7

RAD 3"

HOLLOW TUBE STEEL BEAM

ALUMINUM CASING

CABLE ANCHOR

D5

D4 PARAPET SECTION
SCALE 1.5" = 1'0"

D5 CURTAIN WALL PARAPET CONNECTION SECTION
SCALE 6" = 1'0"

SPANDREL PLATE

CURVED INSULATED GLASS

TENSION CABLE

D6 CURTAIN WALL FLOOR CONNECTION SECTION 1
SCALE 6" = 1'0"

D7 CURTAIN WALL FLOOR CONNECTION SECTION 2
SCALE 6" = 1'0"

STONE FACING

D9

D8 FOUNDATION SECTION
SCALE 1.5" = 1'0"

D9 CURTAIN WALL FOUNDATION CONNECTION SECTION
SCALE 6" = 1'0"

Materials + Methods:
Concrete Procedures
Building Science + Technology
Spring 2014
Keith Kaseman, instructor

Concrete Procedures was
geared toward developing keen
levels of strategic sophistica-
tion in which one may both
comprehend and deploy
concrete in the world. Our fundamental goal was to cultivate
a diverse cloud of innovative
procedural demonstrations,
iterating through a working atmosphere biased towards agile
participation, experimental discovery, systematic refinement
and replicable specification.
With efforts within this course
including direct research, material experimentation, procedural trial and error, rigorous
refinement and comprehensive
documentation on-the-fly, the
most valued assets for participants to bring to this course
were curiosity and persistence.
Through this intensive hands-
on seminar, technical aptitude
with concrete rapidly accelerated over the course of the
semester, culminating in new
constructs that demonstrated
participants' customized
mastery of developed pro-
cedures. Dozens of concrete
samples developed throughout
the semester infected and
redirected team projects all the
way up to the final weeks, at
which time notions of potential
"success" or "failure" were still
unclear. Ultimately, a body of
unforeseen procedural work
with concrete was developed
and documented, all of which
was set to be compiled into
a larger open resource.

Dora Felekou + Pedro
Camara **A/B/C/D**
Robert Magdy Morgan +
Dina Mahmoud **E/F/G**

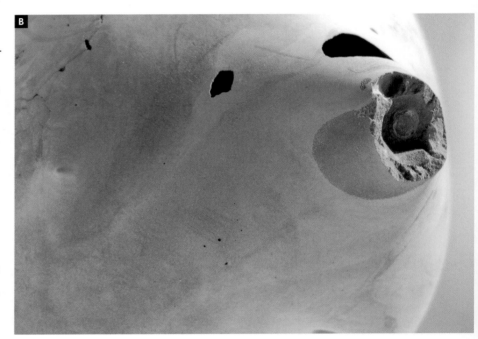

C

D

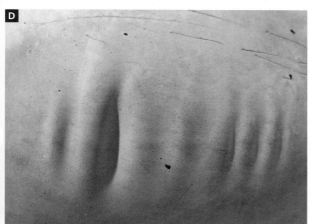

E

F

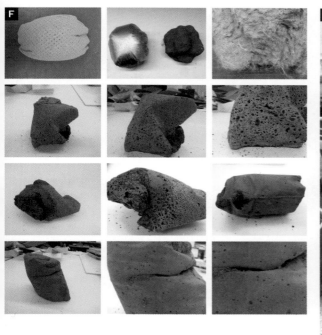

G

Exalted Structure
Building Science + Technology
Fall 2013
Zak Kostura, instructor

This class was not just about cathedrals, but, in cathedrals, we often find pure harmony between structure and aesthetic, where the structure itself is expressed in a way that adds spatial tension and heightens the experience of its occupants. We likewise see this in the thin concrete shells of Felix Candela, the cast iron bridges of Thomas Telford, the sweeping fabric roofs of Jörg Schlaich and the hyperboloid towers of Vladimir Shukhov.

The implementation of such structure requires intimate knowledge of the principles and precedents of the assembly, as well as the unique construction considerations and analytical techniques used to validate its performance. An analysis of these aspects confirms that these assemblies exist not only because of their compelling form, but also because of the ability of early designers to prove that these could be built using conventional construction techniques at reasonable cost and perform adequately throughout their useful lifetimes, despite their unique and unusual configurations.

Students gained a holistic understanding of these essential characteristics through group-based research and design projects. Groups selected an existing assembly, which they explored through four class modules: principles and precedents, analysis, construction and innovation. Each group prepared and delivered a presentation to the class at the end of each module.

Jordan Anderson, Whitney Boykin, Della Leapman + Lindsey Wikstrom **A/B**
Rand Abdul Jabbar, Natasha Amladi, Juan Pablo Azares + Alejandro Stein **C**

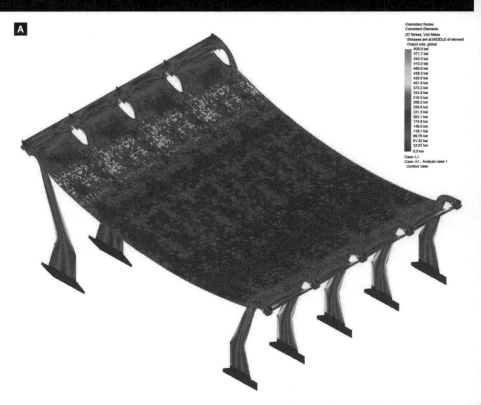

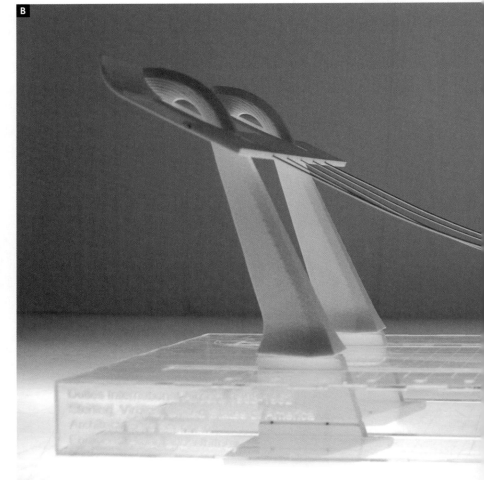

C

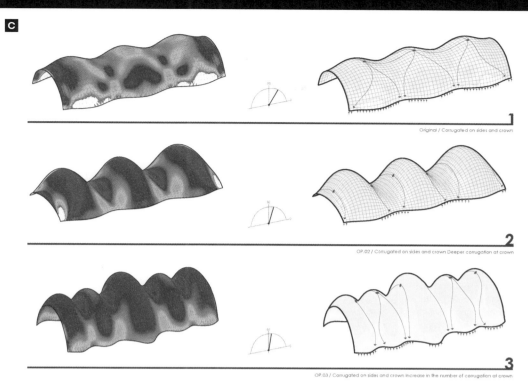

Original / Corrugated on sides and crown
1

OP.02 / Corrugated on sides and crown Deeper corrugation at crown
2

OP.03 / Corrugated on sides and crown Increase in the number of corrugation at crown
3

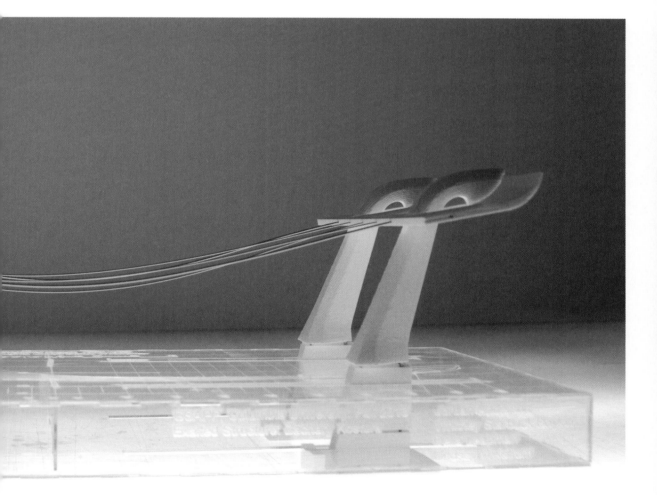

Workflow: Designing Industry
Building Science + Technology
Fall 2013
Scott Marble, instructor

This seminar was aimed at students interested in rethinking architectural practice. It was based on the premise that any significant change in the architectural, engineering and construction industry would come through a disruptive shift in the culture of the industry driven by the next generation of architects...the students. It was less about how practice and industry work now and more about how it could work in the future. Students were exposed to the most current thinking on the structure of industry with an emphasis on the role that digital communication tools are having in its reorganization. Students were encouraged to think creatively and critically about future options to architectural practice and its relationship to industry – in essence, how to design a practice.

Lingyuan Jiang **A**
Sunjana Thirumala Sridhar **B**

A

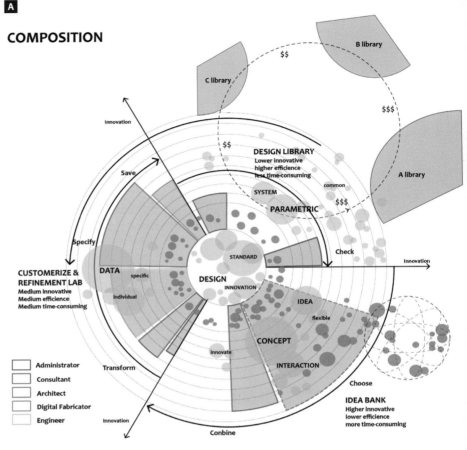

B

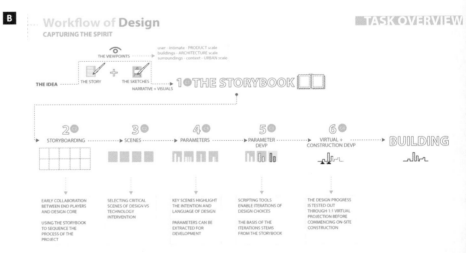

11

Architecture + The Sustainable
Building Science + Technology
Summer 2013
Davidson Norris, instructor

This course was offered to students interested in sustainable design who do not have architectural design backgrounds, skills or ambitions. The purpose of the course was to familiarize students with core architectural design strategies and mechanical/technical systems that can make buildings more resource efficient, all while creating an architectural environment that is, for its occupants, thermally comfortable, psychologically affective, sustainably instructive and architecturally poetic.

Each class explored the technical requirements, sustainable opportunities and design implications of a particular sustainable strategy, technique or technology. The idea was to incrementally familiarize students with the broad range of sustainable building design options but also to alert them to the critical need to evaluate, mix and trade off these technologies as the integrated sustainable building design developed.

Assignments required students to apply each week's design strategy and/or technology to a new High School of Sustainable Design. For the final project, students assumed the role of the school's Project Manager for the City of New York and developed a comprehensive brief to inform the school design team of the project's broad sustainable objectives as well their suggestions of appropriate design and technical solutions.

Acoustics
Building Science + Technology
Spring 2014
Raj Patel, instructor

The course began with an overview of the history of human interaction with sound in the built environment. Fundamentals of acoustics, sound, noise and vibration were explained over a series of three classes, using images, video, listening, sound creation, sound visualization and sound measurement. This was followed by an assignment entitled "Boom Box," for which students had one week to apply the teaching so far, to construct a lightweight sound isolating enclosure for a loudspeaker.

The next two classes focused on listening with a field trip to two significant sites in New York City where sound plays a pivotal role in the experience, followed by a visit to the Arup SoundLab to experience acoustic environments and how sound is used proactively in the design process.

Classes then investigated sound and space, thinking about how different types of buildings sound as well as understanding the impact that sound, noise and vibration have on design in the built environment. In the final assignment students brought all this knowledge together to deliver a project called "Sound Space" in which students delivered a project built around sound as the core driving concept.

Architectural Daylighting
Building Science + Technology
Spring 2014
Davidson Norris, instructor

This course focused on daylight as a prime generator and articulator of architectural space. Students began with the key relationship of light to the eye and its perception and then shifted to the primary relationship of the sun to the building over time. From there, students investigated the basic means by which daylight interacts with both the environment and the building. After that, the class focused on the architectural control of daylight – shading. Finally, the course examined various perimeter and core strategies that can provide daylight to the interior and drive it deeper and discussed various advanced daylighting systems and technologies.

Advanced Energy Performance
Building Science + Technology
Spring 2014
Craig Schwitter, instructor,
with Andrew Maier

Energy is increasingly a driving factor behind architectural design. Sustainable design today is giving way to resilient design buildings that not only use less energy, but also are more robust in the face of challenges from climate change. Our approach to reduction of carbon and driving efficiency in buildings will be critical over the next few decades as design and standards evolve to new regulation, social pressures and changing climate conditions. Design for energy efficiency must start to be integral to design processes, not simply an added element.

This course explored the integration of three primary aspects of built form: energy use, envelope design and lighting. The lecture topics covered advanced concepts of energy performance and their application in computational modeling supported by industry professionals. Case studies of contemporary approaches to resilient and effective design strategies were reviewed as a conceptual framework for the individual student design and analysis projects. The student projects analyzed the performance of an existing architectural project, and they proposed solutions and/or analysis based on climate zones, energy conservation measures and performance targets, while adhering to the architectural intent.

Christopher James Botham **A**
Geof Bell **B/C/D**
Zaw Lin Myat **E**

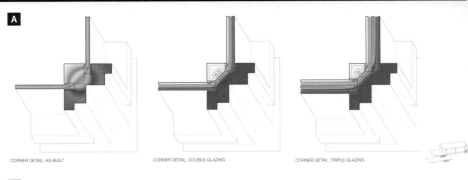

CORNER DETAIL: AS-BUILT   CORNER DETAIL: DOUBLE-GLAZING   CORNER DETAIL: TRIPLE-GLAZING

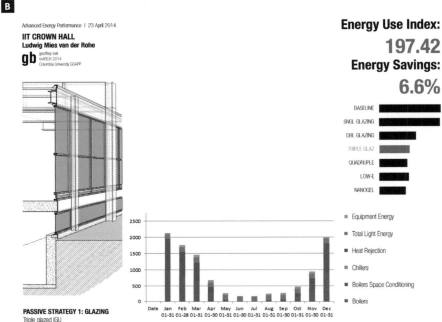

PASSIVE STRATEGY 1: GLAZING
Triple glazed IGU

Energy Use Index:
197.42
Energy Savings:
6.6%

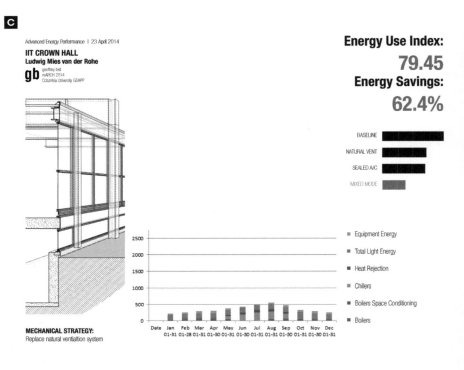

MECHANICAL STRATEGY:
Replace natural ventilation system

Energy Use Index:
79.45
Energy Savings:
62.4%

D

Advanced Energy Performance | 23 April 2014

IIT CROWN HALL
Ludwig Mies van der Rohe

gb geoffrey bell
mARCH 2014
Columbia University GSAPP

Energy Use Index:
197.42
Energy Savings:
6.6%

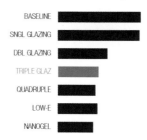

BASELINE
SNGL GLAZING
DBL GLAZING
TRIPLE GLAZ
QUADRUPLE
LOW-E
NANOGEL

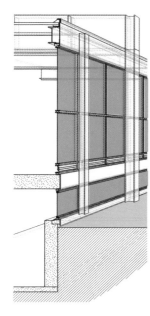

PASSIVE STRATEGY 1: GLAZING
Triple glazed IGU

- Equipment Energy
- Total Light Energy
- Heat Rejection
- Chillers
- Boilers Space Conditioning
- Boilers

| Date | Jan 01-31 | Feb 01-28 | Mar 01-31 | Apr 01-30 | May 01-31 | Jun 01-30 | Jul 01-31 | Aug 01-31 | Sep 01-30 | Oct 01-31 | Nov 01-30 | Dec 01-31 |

E

COMPARISON
BASELINE

TOTAL INTERVENTIONS

Exterior Skin
Triple-Paned Panels

3ft Base added
Concrete with 8"
Insulation

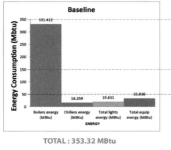

Baseline

Energy Consumption (MBtu)

Boilers energy (MBtu) 331.412 | Chillers energy (MBtu) 16.359 | Total lights energy (MBtu) 19.831 | Total equip energy (MBtu) 33.838

ENERGY

TOTAL : 353.32 MBtu

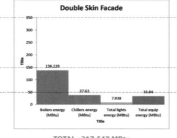

Double Skin Facade

Boilers energy (MBtu) 138.139 | Chillers energy (MBtu) 37.63 | Total lights energy (MBtu) 7.938 | Total equip energy (MBtu) 33.84

Title

TOTAL : 217.547 MBtu

REDUCED
Boilers Energy by 58.32%
Total Lights by 59.97%

INCREASED
Chillers Energy by 56.52%

TOTAL : -38%

3ft Concrete Base Addtion

Energy Consumption (MBtu)

Boilers energy (MBtu) 128.125 | Chillers energy (MBtu) 35.451 | Total lights energy (MBtu) 7.712 | Total equip energy (MBtu) 33.838

ENERGY

TOTAL : 205.126 MBtu

REDUCED
Boilers Energy by 64.34%
Total Lights by 61.11%

INCREASED
Chillers Energy by 53.85%

TOTAL : -42%

Surface, Screen + Structure
Building Science + Technology
Fall 2013
*Joseph Vidich + Reto Hug,
instructors, with Heidi Werner*

This course focused on the design and digital fabrication of stainless steel panelized sun screening systems. The course used the Adidas Sport Performance Store at 610 Broadway as a case study building. The screens were designed to perform as functional shading systems as well as ornamental expression, engaging with the city while branding the Adidas store. Students were challenged to design thoughtful solutions that graphically, spatially and functionally resolved their concepts within a given set of intrinsic and extrinsic constraints. These included but were not limited to light transmittance, thermal expansion, CNC machine limitations, assembly logistics, structural loading and cost analysis. All design work was reviewed with a structural engineer in order to analyze the forces that acted globally on the cladding system as well as locally at each connection detail. The full-scale prototypes were designed and built using Solidworks, a parametric sheet metal modeling software. Every project was optimized and fabricated through at Maloya Laser with the use of their 4,000-watt laser cutter. In addition, details and secondary structures were fabricated at the GSAPP Digital Fabrication Lab.

Jose Cruz, Young Jun, Heeyun Kim, Albert Franco, Pari Agarwal + Keonwoo Kim **A/B**
Katie Zaeh, Tiffany Rattray + Madeeha Merchant **C**
Louis Jin, Hogyum Kim, Brittany Roy + Rashad Palmer **D**

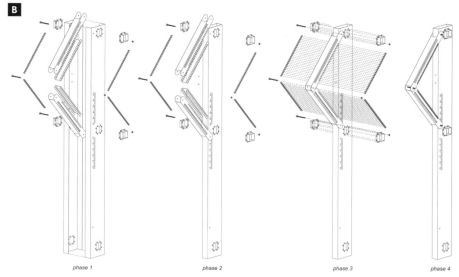

phase 1   *phase 2*   *phase 3*   *phase 4*

Modular Architecture: Strategy/Technology/Design
Building Science + Technology
Fall 2013
David Wallance, instructor

We are about to experience an unprecedented and transformative change in the way we design and build our cities. Over the last decade, interest in modular architecture has surged, and architects are increasingly called upon to design multi-story urban buildings using modular techniques. To design in a modular language requires both a fundamental shift in thinking at the conceptual level as well as a working knowledge of modular technology. The main focus of this course was a design problem in which the students developed a modular solution to a pod hotel with ground floor mixed use on a site located along the Gowanus Canal in Brooklyn. In order to gain familiarity with concepts of modular architecture, the first three classes consisted of lectures and a tour through a local modular manufacturing plant.

Students worked on the design problem in teams of four. After the introductory lectures and factory tour, there were weekly meetings to review progress. The weekly critiques emphasized conceptual clarity and technical rigor. The final presentation was a fully developed design, including details and three-dimensional analytical drawings.

Paul Payet-Godel,
Marc Mascarello,
Mark Pothier +
Hanxiao Yang **A/B/C**

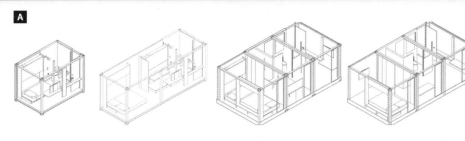

A

Basic Unit   Premium Unit   Extended Stay Unit   Accessible Unit

B

DIAGRAMS

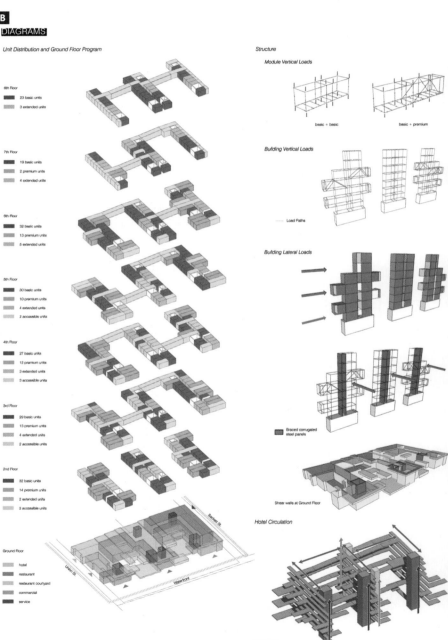

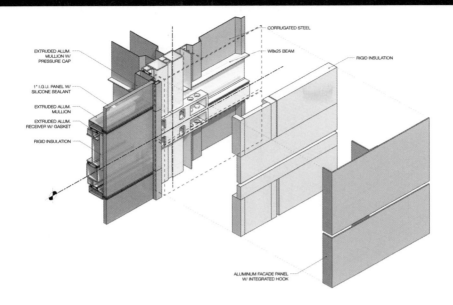

CORRUGATED STEEL

W8x25 BEAM

RIGID INSULATION

EXTRUDED ALUM.
MULLION W/
PRESSURE CAP

1" I.G.U. PANEL W/
SILICONE SEALANT

EXTRUDED ALUM.
MULLION

EXTRUDED ALUM.
RECEIVER W/ GASKET

RIGID INSULATION

ALUMINUM FACADE PANEL
W/ INTEGRATED HOOK

EXPLODED AXONOMETRIC DETAIL AT MODULE CORNER CONNECTIONS
3" = 1'-0"

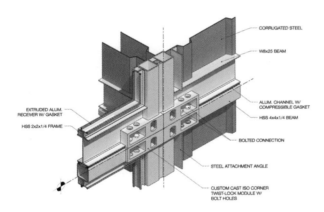

CORRUGATED STEEL

W8x25 BEAM

ALUM. CHANNEL W/
COMPRESSIBLE GASKET

HSS 4x4x1/4 BEAM

BOLTED CONNECTION

STEEL ATTACHMENT ANGLE

CUSTOM CAST ISO CORNER
TWIST-LOCK MODULE W/
BOLT HOLES

EXTRUDED ALUM.
RECEIVER W/ GASKET

HSS 2x2x1/4 FRAME

STRUCTURAL AXONOMETRIC DETAIL AT MODULE CORNER
3" = 1'-0"

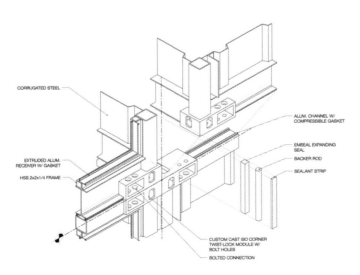

CORRUGATED STEEL

ALUM. CHANNEL W/
COMPRESSIBLE GASKET

EMSEAL EXPANDING
SEAL

BACKER ROD

SEALANT STRIP

EXTRUDED ALUM.
RECEIVER W/ GASKET

HSS 2x2x1/4 FRAME

CUSTOM CAST ISO CORNER
TWIST-LOCK MODULE W/
BOLT HOLES

BOLTED CONNECTION

STRUCTURAL AXONOMETRIC DETAIL AT MODULE CORNER
3" = 1'-0"

History / Theory
Kenneth Frampton, director

The History/Theory curriculum of the GSAPP stresses a broad social and cultural approach to architectural discourse. Architectural history is not seen primarily as stylistic evolution, but rather as the consequence of a complex interaction between artistic, socio-economic, technological and ideological vectors. Most instructors of architecture history at GSAPP have both professional and academic degrees. The overall intent is to place the relationship between theory and practice in a broad historical perspective.

The course offerings are structured to provide students with an opportunity to acquire a general overview of contemporary architectural history and, at the same time, a degree of specialized knowledge in areas of their own choosing. Where the former is dealt with through a required lecture sequence, the latter is met through specialized seminars. The architecture history classes within the GSAPP are supplemented by classes in the Department of Art History and Archaeology. In this regard, students are especially encouraged to take art history courses examining pre-1750 and non-Western topics. Students may also take courses in other departments of the University, such as history and philosophy, providing they meet basic distribution requirements of the GSAPP program.

Architecture History 1: 1660-1860
History/Theory
Fall 2013
Mary McLeod, instructor

The objective of the two se-mester sequence Architecture History 1 and 2 was to provide students with a basic critical understanding of major de-velopments in European (and to a lesser extent, American) architectural history during what is sometimes considered the modern period, from the late seventeenth-century to the post-World War II era. The course emphasized moments of significant change in architec-ture, whether they be theoreti-cal, economic, technological or institutional in nature. Each lecture usually focused on a theme, such as positive versus arbitrary beauty, enlightenment urban planning, historicism, structural rationalism, social utopianism and so on.

History of Architecture 2: Twentieth Century Architecture, 1895-1965
History/Theory
Spring 2014
Kenneth Frampton, instructor, with Justine Shapiro-Kline

The course traced the history of modern architecture and its transformation under the influ-ence of two major forces: the process of modernization and the development of ideology. The first of these derives from the material changes brought about by technology and industrialization; the second stems from the received idea of progress and from the utopian legacy of the Enlight-enment. The period covered runs from the high point of the Art Nouveau to the death of Le Corbusier. The European Avant-Garde is given a par-ticular emphasis. Rather than being a continuous chrono-logical account, the course was structured around a series of thematic episodes, which correspond to chapters from Modern Architecture: A Critical History, the comprehensive text covering the period.

Arab Cities in Evolution
History/Theory
Fall 2013
Amale Andraos, instructor

While the Middle East and the Arab World in general, have for too long occupied the world's center stage for its endless conflicts, this past decade has simultaneously shed light on it as another kind of 'hot spot'—one that has fostered radical experimentation in architecture and urbanism. From leading the wave of 'instant urbanism' to building the first zero carbon city, the MENA region has also witnessed a resurgence of new social housing and institutional buildings, led major recon-struction and preservation efforts as well as re–affirmed for the world the importance of public space through its recent democratic revolutions.

While much of the contem-porary urban and architectural production in the Arab World continues to be wildly broad-cast, too little is presented as a context through which to read this ebullient production, con-trasting the region's emerging and struggling cities while situ-ating the work within a long his-tory of complex exchanges re-gionally as well as between East and West. Working through specific discursive lenses—fo-cusing in particular on issues of representation, post World War II developmental strategies, Pan Arabism and environmen-tal orientalism—the seminar built a repertoire of references through which to apprehend the present transformations.

New Spaces of Housing
History/Theory
Spring 2014
Michael Bell + Brian Loughlin, instructors

Section 42 of the United States Internal Revenue Service's tax code was designed in 1986 to be a source of innovation: an in-centive and an entrepreneurial aspect for affordable housing development. Low-Income Housing Tax Credits (LIHTC) quickly became the main source of capital for afford-able housing. Federal plans for affordability were constituted by deferred rather than direct revenue; the policies were intended to both spur housing creation and abet innovation. Yet, since their inception afford-able housing has assumed a more traditional appearance. Housing questions and in particular low income or Public Housing issues have been cast into hardened political posi-tions since the inception of the public housing in the 1930's. But today whether the one makes an argument from the left or the right, housing and the actual development means are largely adjudicated via market factors; it is architectur-ally built in the same manner as market rate housing. The social aspects of policy--as economics--are metered by a financial practice of real estate and are effectively narrowed. This seminar explored the implications of this scenario and more so its implications if any for architecture.

Japanese Urbanism
History/Theory
Spring 2014
Lynne Breslin, instructor

The class was conducted as a laboratory. Tokyo was studied and situated in the seeming contradiction of universalizing technologies and romantically preserved particularities. We began with Edo and demon-strated its basis and diversion from other Japanese cities in the early seventeenth century. The course focused on the modern city and concentrated on the tension of western influ-ence and modernism, the twin spears and legacy of Meiji Japan. The ideas, forms and formulations studied directed in class presentations and research. Visual analysis of artifacts, such as maps, adver-tisements, photographs and art were also used. Students were responsible for two small as-signments and one major class presentation. For the second half of the course, students were asked to locate a map of a Japanese city from any period and read the map for the class. The goal was to help students read a different culture, through its most complex form—a city.

Latin American Architecture: 1929-2012
History/Theory
Spring 2014
Carlos Brillembourg, instructor

Beginning in 1492, America was a source of exchange between European sources as interpreted by Priest-Architects and Amerindian cultures. During the sixteenth century printed books were used by the priest/architects as sources of architecture for the churches they were building for the King of Spain or Portugal. Edicts given by the King established codes for urbanism and individual buildings were drawn and rendered for approval in Seville or Lisbon. "The Laws of the Indies" established a common language in all the Spanish/Portuguese Colonies from California to Patagonia.

The modern movement in the Americas is both a natural continuity of this process and a fundamental rupture of this tradition. Architecture built using Amerindian or mestizo labor with or without the Islamic building traditions original to Southern Spain, influenced the iconography of the modern movement in Brazil, Venezuela, Cuba and Mexico. Using contemporary mapping strategies, we created a cultural map of import/exports and influence/counterinfluence between the cities North/South and East/West. The different patterns of these cultural exchanges were analyzed and their stories were gathered.

Agency, Ideology + Critical Practice
History/Theory
Spring 2014
Jordan Carver, instructor

The goal of this seminar was to develop critical frameworks for understanding architectural production and for each student to claim a position within the broad field of "spatial practice." In order to do this, the class focused first on readings concerning the role of authorship, ideology and criticism. We then turned our attention to some of the more recent arguments within the architectural discourse concerning criticism and the use of theory. Finally, we investigated how the concerns of the class are being raised—or not—and how new techniques of practice are being developed and deployed by several contemporary architectural thinkers often associated with "alternative" or "critical practice"—terms that are, of course, up for dispute.

Traditional Chinese Architecture
History/Theory
Spring 2014
Chang Liu, instructor

Instead of an introduction from macro- to micro order, this course dissected the highest achievement in traditional Chinese architecture, timber structure, by starting from the carpenter's "playgame," the wood puzzles, and interpreted original designs concerning planning, gardening and proportioning.

The course covered four major components of the Dougong bracket–constructed virtually at present and suggested to be made of wood in the lab when conditions permit–making individual timber structures, in the formation of building complexes steered by ritual and mysticism and interpreting interior design, residential complex design and garden design.

The course integrated lectures on the topics of Dougong, timber structure and layout of complex gardens with seminars to allow students to saturate better into this cultural context. Materials on which the discussions were based included firsthand data and media ranging from architectural presentations and representations of the eighteenth to nineteenth centuries to measurements of historic buildings including 3D scan data, from historical pictures by gentry scholars and craftsman to related historical literature.

Forming Alliances + Dismantling Oppositions
History/Theory
Spring 2014
Alberto Foyo, instructor

The course focused on re-visiting and re-formulating primordial architectural concepts. Using a comparative approach we explored primordial binary relations that affect our critical stand in the field of architecture. Genetic-cultural, natural-manmade, archaic-sophisticated, rural-urban, tradition-modernity, technique-technology, are but a few symbiotic dichotomies that in our epoch have all too often become antagonistic concepts played against each other in pathological opposition. A concerted effort was placed on understanding these dichotomies as complementary and not as oppositional as a way to increase the 'critical density' of our design processes. Conversely the course aimed at finding antidotes to arbitrary design decision making. The pedagogical intent was to foster the critical use of language as a generative tool that can inspire more holistic and meaningful design decision-making and consequently stimulate students' freethinking; that is to let go of the use of language as a codified sound bite; a sound bite that increasingly fosters stereo typified thinking.

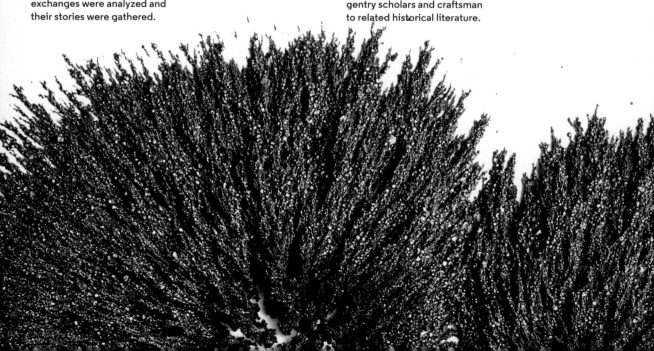

Germanic Culture + the Predicament of Modernity: Politics, Philosophy + Architecture, 1848-1988
History/Theory
Fall 2013
Kenneth Frampton, instructor

This course was based on a sequence of technological, ideological, cultural and political transformations that took place under the sign of modernity and modernization between 1848 and 1988. The first of these otherwise arbitrary dates is predicated on the so-called liberal revolution that took place in Frankfurt and in other continental European city-states in 1848. The year 1988 marks the publication of Gianni Vattimo's provocative philosophical text, The End of Modernity.

Each participating student was responsible for making a presentation and leading that week's discussion in collaboration with the instructor. Thereafter students were expected to write the presentation up in the form of an essay for submission at the conclusion of the semester.

Studies in Tectonic Culture
History/Theory
Spring 2014
Kenneth Frampton, instructor, with Justine Shapiro-Kline

The tectonic proffers itself today as a critical strategy largely because of the current tendency to reduce architectural form to a spectacular image. This emphasis on structure and construction may be seen as a response to the postmodern preoccupation with the scenographic.

This lecture course traced the emergence of the tectonic theory and practice in the evolution of nineteenth and twentieth-century architecture. In so doing, it examined the role played by structure and construction in the development of modern form. It addressed the so-called autonomy of architecture not only in terms of space and form, but also from the standpoint of the poetics of construction, as this has made itself manifest over the past 150 years.

Global Metropolis
History/Theory
Spring 2014
Douglas Gauthier, instructor

Our world is a global metropolis, much like a bazaar or a Luna Park, in which equal activity occurs between the market stalls, the rides as well as the games as within them. But what are the global, urban, regional boundaries of a global metropolis and how are they measured? What are the prostheses that allow for an understanding of the space of the global metropolis? What are the representational machineries, or conventions, to provide access and measure the space of the global metropolis? Using fragments of vital metropolises turned megalopolises in today's global network—New York, Moscow, Beijing, Rio, Johannesburg and Mumbai—this course re-defined and re-imagined a future global metropolis. This course was comprised of four basic components: class discussions, Studio-X talks, team presentations and architecture firm visits to New York practices involved in projects in China, South America, Africa and/or Russia. Global Metropolis was defined by the developed matrix of six cities, six topics, five studio-X's, six office visits, fifteen discussion topic readings, twenty-plus background readings and four group presentations.

Art Power + Space in the Middle East
History/Theory
Spring 2014
Mario Gooden, instructor

The Arab world with its socio-political tensions and contradictions, and rising conservatism coupled with a chronic political turmoil provides a rich laboratory for such artists. Yet, young Arab artists are looking for answers to the ever more complex trajectories of postmodernity than one might find at these auction houses.

The 'art boom' started backwards in the Arab world. The art market flourished in the oil-rich Gulf states– where only a fraction of the Arab population resides–before the art support systems set in. The 'boom' euphoria spread before school curricula, museums, art critics or even art scholars began to grapple with the relevant questions.

For example, contrary to the common belief, what is new in Arab contemporary art is not just the mediums being employed but rather it is the image in all its forms that Arab artists have subverted while creating spaces for interpretation and engagement with the art.

The seminar examined the production, consumption and dissemination of Middle Eastern art and the subversive strategies of artists to engage in new spaces for social and political critique. The seminar uncovered pedagogies and methodologies for artistic practices to locate new sites of meaning in contested territories and among contradictory landscapes.

Exotic Moderns: City, Space + 'Other' Modernities
History/Theory
Spring 2014
Jyoti Hosagrahar, instructor

This seminar explored the fragmented, complex and paradoxical urbanism of contemporary cities in Asia, Africa and Latin America, in the context of globalization and colonialism. What does modernity mean in cities outside the conventional West? In an interconnected world of global flows, how do we understand and engage with questions of difference? We examined what happens when global modernity engages with particular places, localities and traditions. We began with the premise that modernity, claimed and defined by the West, was fundamentally global and that colonialism and modernity are connected. From these perspectives we explored the cultural and symbolic dimensions of spatial transformation. The seminar focused on the ways in which globality and locality reconcile when local settlement practices and spatial cultures encounter universal ones. While recognizing our subjective position within the Western academe, we critically examined dualities such as 'traditional' and 'modern,' 'West' and 'non-West,' 'Orient' and 'Occident,' as culturally constructed categories that frame professional understandings and interventions in architecture and urbanism. The course integrated a historical and cultural understanding of the architecture and urbanism of specific places with theoretical considerations of postcolonialism.

Imperatives of Urbanism
History/Theory
Spring 2014
Jeffrey Inaba, instructor

The urban design proposals done during the early part of an architect's career are informative of the architects' intellectual stakes in architecture as a whole. They reveal their priorities as designers and thinkers and, to that extent, are of relevance to architecture debates today. The arguments they make for the project's realization shed light onto what they believe to be disciplinary issues that need to be urgently addressed. To that extent, the imperatives they describe for urbanism bring to light what they believe to be imperative for architecture itself.

Contemporary Chinese City
History/Theory
Spring 2014
Jeffrey Johnson, instructor, with Min Chen

During the past two decades, China's economic growth has fueled an unprecedented urban expansion. Never before at this scale and sustained pace has the world experienced such a project. This growth is projected to continue at an accelerated pace as more and more rural Chinese migrate to the urban areas. By 2030, China's urban population could balloon to almost 1 billion people, nearly double what exists today. This seminar explored how the mechanisms of this rapid urbanization have created new urban models, and how the resultant forms and patterns might influence cities of the future as the world becomes ever more urbanized. The seminar was organized by topic, with each session dedicated to a specific subject or phenomenon. The course utilized multiple source disciplines to discuss each topic, including film, architecture, urban planning, landscape, politics, film, etc.

Researching Research
History/Theory
Spring 2014
Janette Kim, instructor

This seminar examined the history and theory of applied research practice in recent architecture and urbanism and, in turn, experimented with the production of novel techniques of inquiry.

Research is everywhere. Architects make materials, incite public action, archive urban life and invent design protocols. They sidestep traditional models of practice, at times, to launch unsolicited provocations into the world and, at others, to join forces with foundations and government think tanks. The dominance of research practice today can be attributed in part to the rise of computing technologies—consider data mining, the search engine and rapid prototyping. Architects today also seek new tools to grasp the volatility of markets and climates and to fathom neoliberal governance and mobile populations. Still, many research methods are not new, and extend to a history of invention and spirit of curiosity in the field.

This course was structured around a series of topics, each focused on a technique or protocol of applied research. For each topic, we examined texts and projects to evaluate their implications for contemporary practice. Topics such as 'Test Subjects,' 'Conflict of Interest,' and 'Degrees of Certainty,' for example, examined the ethical implications of real-time testing, the influence of research funding sources and degrees of fidelity in quantitative analysis.

Post-War Japanese Architecture
History/Theory
Fall 2013
Kunio Kudo, instructor

'The country is destroyed; yet mountains and rivers remain same. Spring comes to the city; with full grass and trees again.' Toho

The United States' loss of the Pacific War was unprecedented, but the Japanese one was far beyond it both in built infrastructure and human casualties. Devastation was limited not only to Hiroshima and Nagasaki, but also to Tokyo, Osaka, Yokohama and Kobe. Smaller local cities flared up with napalms from B29 carpet-bombing night after night. Tokyo's causalities were said to be between 150,000 to 200,000 on the night of March 10, 1945 alone, but those numbers continue to be disputed as too conservative. Cities and infrastructures were completely flattened, and children walked the streets barefoot. The homes that survived were clouded with shared families.

This seminar examined the postwar Japanese Ash to Diamond saga in architecture and urbanism. A country, once devastated by war, stood up to rebuild its land, cities, people and new architecture. The current events of Japan were also covered, following the horrific aftermath of the Tohoku Great Earthquake on March 11, 2011.

Traditional Japanese Architecture: Re-Defining the Form of Tradition
History/Theory
Spring 2014
Kunio Kudo, instructor, with Whitney Starbuck Boykin

As a society, Japan dramatically changed and dynamically evolved between 311 and 2011. It is no longer a country of stainless purity of self discipline, as described by Ruth Benedict in her legend "The Chrysanthemum and The Sword." No excuse was previously allowed for any failure, but now all are excused with self-justification and aggressive self-assertion. Is this apparent change a paradigm shift or yet another disguising layer to respond to new global reality? However, in craftsmanship including building-industry, the tradition is not only being sustained but also further implosively deepened and developed in meticulous nano-order and practical precision to adapt to the customer's widening individualized demands and computer applications. It is a divine zone where human, machine and computer form a Trinity. It is a tenaciously sustainable living and growing tradition, where matter becomes spirit. This semester, we focused on re-examining in detail zen-tinted aesthetic associated with the tea ritual and tectonic in built form and building process.

World Architecture Project: Representing the Chinese Built Environment in Context + Print
History/Theory
Fall 2013
Amy Lelyveld, instructor

The seminar examined the shape and habits of English language in-print coverage of the Chinese built environment over the last 100 years—a period matching China's post-imperial history. This investigation ran in tandem with the second project of the course, the very real opportunity of designing a shift in the character of this discussion going forward.

The Chinese journal World Architecture has been in print for just over 30 years—a span of time coincident with China's journey from the first post-Mao rural economic reforms to the country of today where more than half of its population is for the first time urban. The journal was the first to introduce Chinese architects to international content. WA's appointment of an English language editor was a purposeful mirroring of their original "opening up to the world" view that creates the opportunity for a curated and demanding representation of its built environment and, as deliberately, offers a basis for wider professional exchange.

The journal's 50,000 strong circulation and respected position is a tremendous platform. How should it be seized? This seminar explored the factors relevant to the potential of this opportunity, including: Content: the issues covered and the stories to be told; Precedent: the ways these stories have been covered, by whom and to what effect; Theory: the structure of the in-print discourse here and there; Promotion: what will be advertised and to what end; Audience: how to engage professionals, academics, historians and theorists both "here" and "there"; and the Lacunae: what has yet to be discussed or thought. The seminar will be instrumental in shaping the journal's editorial strategy. Its findings will be published in the magazine as the opening foray of what must be a much richer conversation.

Building China Modern / 1919-1958: Experiments for a New Paradigm
History/Theory
Spring 2014
Amy Lelyveld, instructor

The search for an architecture that is both Chinese and modern has been under way for more than a hundred years. At the beginning of the last century, many countries were looking for just such a new language of building—one that could be both culturally specific and international. But China started this grappling early that it continues to this day. This architectural quest has run parallel to changing ideas of what China represents, both as a place and a nation.

The seminar examined experiments in Chinese building during three important periods: around the May 4th movement of 1919, in Nationalist China from 1927 through 1948 and during the inaugural years of the People's Republic. Each period had its own distinct mindset, but, in all of them, the reimagining of Chinese architecture was considered of paramount importance.

The class introduced the language of traditional Chinese architecture in conversation with caches of related primary source material from the deep resources of Columbia's research collections. It used such primary resources and assigned readings to explore case study "experiments" in modern Chinese building—buildings which broke with certain aspects of tradition while safeguarding others—in terms of "new," "modern," "Chinese," "character," "type" and other discourses.

Architectural Visualization 1900-2000
History/Theory
Spring 2014
Reinhold Martin, instructor

This lecture course considered the history and theory of architectural visualization throughout the twentieth century across a variety of cultural contexts. The approach was thematically chronological. Key episodes in the development of international modernism and its aftermath were presented and analyzed with respect to the construction of architectural knowledge, interactions between drawing and building, the circulation of ideas and imagery and globalization. The course bridged between the history and theory of modern architecture, the history of technology and theories and practices of visualization. Though formally a history and theory lecture, the course therefore brought together concerns shared among different aspects of the GSAPP architecture curriculum, including visual studies, the technology sequence and the design studios. A further goal of the course was to introduce students to the material infrastructures and interfaces through which architectural discourse and techniques move across a variety of national, cultural, and geographic boundaries, both historically and in the present. The history of architectural visualization in the twentieth century is also a history of globalization. Problems and effects of visual translation, standardization, reproduction, transformation, site and circulation were therefore emphasized.

Politics of Space: Cities, Institutions, Events
History/Theory
Spring 2014
Mary McLeod, instructor

This seminar explored the relation between space, power, and politics in the urban environment from the Enlightenment period to the present. In contrast to some Marxist approaches that see architecture primarily as an ideological reflection of dominant economic forces, this seminar investigated how power is actually produced and embodied in the physical environment. In other words, space and architecture are seen as active participants in the structuring of our daily lives and relations, not merely as passive reflections of political and economic institutions. Two theorists were critical to this exploration: the philosopher and sociologist Henri Lefebvre and the philosopher/historian Michel Foucault. Lefebvre's work, which draws heavily on both Marxism and existentialism, introduced the notion of daily life as a critical political construct. Lefebvre saw the city and architecture as integrally contributing to power relations and viewed the urban festival as an important strategy in overcoming the monotony of what he called "the bureaucratic society of controlled consumption." Foucault, on the other hand, rejects Lefebvre's humanism and emphasis on subjectivity in his analysis of the relation between space, power and social institutions. Both theorists, however, share a skepticism towards Enlightenment rationality, and both attempt to counter the traditional Marxist/Hegelian emphasis on historical time by placing a new importance on space. The writings of more recent theorists were also examined with regard to issues concerning the politics of space.

Contemporary Theory + Criticism of Architecture, 1960-Present
History/Theory
Spring 2014
Mary McLeod, instructor

This seminar examined some of the theoretical and critical approaches current in architecture debate from 1960 to the present. The course focused in particular on the question of meaning in architecture, beginning with approaches influenced by semiology and structuralism to establish an architecture of greater signification, and concluding with recent trends influenced by poststructuralist theories that challenge the possibility of architecture meaning. The last class addressed the current reaction against theory, and the emergence of anti-theoretical "theories"–technological determinism, Neo-Pragmatism, etc. Certain classes considered general theoretical approaches, usually originating in philosophy or literary criticism; others examined specific currents in architecture in relation to these theoretical approaches. Seminars were structured primarily around the assigned readings.

Sustainable Futures
History/Theory
Fall 2013
Kate Orff, instructor

World-changing. That is what we all want to be doing and that is why we study sustainability, architecture, urban design, management and policy. Inaction. We tend towards it, bogged down by contrasting perceptions, overwhelmed by biased opinions and made apathetic by the scope of the challenge at the heart of imagining post-oil futures and scenarios. Curiosity. What is the role of design thinking? Design. We are all designers. Our forum brought together the realms of science, policy and design to address complex questions of environment and development with fresh thinking and a creative approach grounded in research, experimentation and pilot projects. Built environment. We discussed the concept of sustainability on global, regional and local scales, focusing on the role of cities and on targeted ideas that work, imagining scenarios of a post-petrochemical era future.

This seminar intended to marshal sophisticated thinking in design and policy towards developing a toolkit of strategies and scenarios for change. Through a focus on both speculative projects and tried case studies, the seminar highlighted the reciprocity between thinking and making, researching and doing, desk work and fieldwork - the idea and the thing.

Twelve Dialogical + Poetic Strategies for the Millennium
History/Theory
Fall 2013 + Spring 2014
Yehuda Safran, instructor

Inspired by the insight that simply thinking of a certain musical phrase effects one's body no less than if one actually hears it, this seminar set out to introduce the possibility of an Archimedean point that allows each individual to extricate his/herself from any set of conventions, preconceived ideas or paradigms. Each week we introduced a pair of dialectically connected concepts. We practiced a conceptual analysis—something in the spirit of Paul Feyerabend's "anything goes" on one hand, and the systematic meditations of Husserl's Phenomenological Reduction on the other hand. Indeed, sometimes we found in more recent writers—Paul de Man and Derrida—several critical discourses and poetics derived epistemologically from Husserl's insight, not unlike an earlier generation of Russian Formalism. Above all, with the introduction of several poets and writers together with architects and painters grasped more clearly the possibility of learning a measure of Socratic irony in order to create other poetic strategies.

Vauban's Military Urbanism
History/Theory
Fall 2013
Victoria Sanger, instructor

Sébastien Le Prestre de Vauban (1633-1707), military engineer to France's King Louis XIV, continues to be a central figure in urban history. He built an exceptionally large and unified corpus of fortified cities: nine new towns and one hundred sixty cities in total. Because the cities had a military function and were located on the borders of France, historians have mistakenly seen them as marginal derivatives of Paris and Versailles. This course showed the importance of seeing French town planning from the vantage point of the frontier. The sheer quantity of Vauban's output catalyzed trends in all European cities developing since the mid-fifteenth century. The needs to administer the military and civilian population of these towns profoundly affected urban politics and planning in the interior as well as at the borders. The course began with the origins of the bastion and its effect on town planning in the Renaissance period. It concluded with a study of the impact of this approach to cities in the eighteenth and nineteenth centuries in France and America. Thereby raising the question of the degree to which the Baroque city had military underpinnings, based on considerations of national defense, power relations and a culture of surveillance.

European Urbanism + Cartography from the Sixteenth to the Eighteenth Centuries
History/Theory
Spring 2014
Victoria Sanger, instructor

This course took cartography as a point of departure for understanding the major changes in European cities in the Early Modern Period. It examined how maps document their built environment and function as carriers of deeper scientific, political and rhetorical meanings. We studied a very exciting period of urban, political, and scientific expansion; one that in many ways set the stage for mapping and planning in the twenty-first century.

The first half of the course involved readings, discussions and lectures about the different techniques of cartography and the major urban trends of the period. Students then choose from a list of significant maps of major European cities in Avery Library and other New York collections. The second half of the course consisted of group presentations of case study cities and their most famous maps—Paris, London, Amsterdam, Rome and Besançon.

Health + Cities: Health Acts, Types + Forms in Architecture + the City
History/Theory
Spring 2014
Hilary Sample, instructor

This seminar focused on the complex intersection between design and health by examining particular modern and contemporary architectural typologies and their urban contexts and infrastructures. Cities formed through the programmatic development of their public spaces often as a direct result of public health and the intertwining of urbanism and architecture. This seminar approached the history of design, architecture and technology through a close reading of select models of architecture, propositions for cities, urban infrastructures, manifestos and policies associated with general health and wellness. It aimed to encourage students to reflect upon innovative building types and unusual urban projects. At the heart of the seminar was the core understanding of modern and contemporary architects and the architecture and urbanisms they have produced with respect to health and environment. Students were exposed to such building types and the political, social and cultural manifestations that prompted their development, including a reading of their urban contexts from Post World War II to the present. The development of an architectural health type was explored through specific building types including but not limited to hospitals, sanatoriums, rehabilitation centers, clinics, senior housing, daycares, health headquarters, pharmaceutical companies and playgrounds. This seminar took up historical, socio-political and cultural aspects of architecture's progressive relationship to disease and health, trauma, wellness and globalization. Students were asked to consider the twofold aspects of urban health: that of a city being in a state of sickness or health, and what physical effects are produced within the city. What forms of architecture play out in relation to health?

Professional Practice
History/Theory
Fall 2013
Paul Segal, instructor

The purpose of this course was to give students an understanding of the framework and processes by which designs become buildings. Topics included the relationship between Owners and Architects and Owners and Contractors, covering the duties, obligations, rights and remedies of each. Additionally, the course covered the public constraints or the public/private relationships by which individuals (owners and architects) have their rights limited for the sake of the public good. Through these topics students learned how to protect their designs from concept to realization, as well as some of the ethical and moral issues of practicing architecture. Active student participation and debate was required.

New York Global
History/Theory
Summer 2013
David Grahame Shane, instructor

The course objective was to see contemporary New York through a global lens that included the history of global urbanization in the last sixty years. Four main points were emphasized in this macro history of globalization linked to the micro history of New York: 1) New York was initially in a rivalry with Moscow to be the model for a contemporary, post-colonial metropolis in the competition between the two Cold War, nuclear, super powers; 2) New York rapidly distinguished itself from its rival transforming from a metropolis into megalopolis, a suburban network city of thirty-two million stretching from Boston to Washington, recognized by Jean Gottmann in 1961; 3) This transformation impacted the inner city, in abandoned areas like the South Bronx, but also spurred urban innovations from Jane Jacobs in favor of dense urban neighborhoods; 4) The shrinkage of New York in this period also lead to the involvement of artists in the city, the Green Thumb movement and a growing ecological awareness.

Italian Renaissance Architecture 1400-1600: Regola + Invenzione
History/Theory
Fall 2013
Daniel Sherer, instructor

The course provided a historical overview of the major figures of Italian Renaissance architecture from 1400 to 1600—Brunelleschi, Alberti, Leonardo, Bramante, Raphael, Antonio da Sangallo the Younger, Michelangelo, Peruzzi, Giulio Romano, Sanmicheli, Sansovino, Palladio and Serlio. Stressing the dialectic of rule and license implicit in the revival of the classical code, we studied the diverse cultural and artistic factors that entered into the project of forging a new language based on antiquity. Topics covered included: the social and cultural implications of the link between architecture and humanism; the role of architecture in elaborating new urban strategies, chiefly in Florence; the search for a new type of canon that simultaneously presupposed and challenged the authority of Vitruvius and the study of ancient buildings; the emergence of new conventions of graphic representation based on orthographic and perspective projection; the transformation of architecture by print culture, whose mechanical reproduction of image and text revolutionized the dissemination of theory; the division of architects into three major categories, derived from their training as masons, painters or sculptors; the assertion of an unprecedented cultural status for the architect constituted by novel concepts of authorship; the relation of architecture to new uses of visual representation that helped inaugurate the modern era.

Urban History 1: Configurations of the City from Antiquity to the Industrial Revolution
History/Theory
Spring 2014
Daniel Sherer, instructor, with Sucheta Nadig

The course traced the development of the European city from classical antiquity to the Industrial Revolution, ending with the formal repercussions of ideal schemes and the effects of capitalism on urbanization in the New World. Focusing on the configuration of architecture in urban space, it followed the evolution of the city through a complex series of exchanges between typological, morphological and topographical factors. The first part of the course addressed the typological transformation of the agora and acropolis and the parallel articulation of paradigmatic urban forms from fifth-century Athens to the rise of the Roman republic. We then studied the formal and functional dimensions of domestic, civil and sacred architecture in the Roman Empire from Augustus to Constantine. Turning to the medieval period, we examined continuities and discontinuities between classical and Christian conceptions of the forma urbis, concentrating on practices of typological functionalization and the ideological use of spolia in Split, Constantinople and Venice. This was followed by a discussion of new urban strategies and architectural languages associated with utopian schemes, aristocratic and communal use of public space and the rise of new towns in the Italian Renaissance. The second part of the course charted the emergence of new urban models and related architectural interventions from the inception of the Baroque era to the end of the ancien régime. Focusing initially on the interplay of street axes and monumental nuclei in the Rome of Sixtus V, we traced their transformation in the Enlightenment schemes of London, Paris, Philadelphia and Lisbon, in light of eighteenth and nineteenth-century theoretical debates on the relationship among nature, reason and the city. The course ended with a contrast of monumental and capitalist urban development exemplified by Washington D.C. and New York City.

Architecture as Concept
(from 1968 to the Present)
History/Theory
Spring 2014
Bernard Tschumi, instructor

The "Architecture as Concept" seminar took as its starting hypothesis the idea that there is no architecture without a concept and that concepts are what differentiate architecture from mere building. The seminar attempted to demonstrate that the most important works of architecture in any given period are the ones with the strongest concept or idea, rather than simply those with the most striking form.

The seminar discussed projects or buildings from 1968 to the present in terms of their ability to mark the history of ideas and concepts in architecture. It also discussed differences between concepts, "partis", diagrams and compositions, as well as between concepts, precepts and affects. For the architecture of the past forty years, the course identified several major concepts and asked students to form a position in relation to them, "for" or "against." Through this method, students questioned the moral, ideological, economic or formal standards of the architectural discipline today.

Facing Energy
History/Theory
Spring 2014
Troy Therrien, instructor

Most culpable in this crime of identity theft is architecture. Modernization has tuned architecture into an efficient machine for consuming energy under the radar of human sensibility, or more precisely, the most efficient, as architecture accounts for more than half of global energy consumption. It is thus the greatest lever through which to affect energy, yet this possibility is surrendered so long as it remains a black box.

Responding to this hypothesis, we approached energy through the object and concept of the interface. Funded by the GSAPP Future of Energy initiative, students worked in small groups to define, design, develop, deploy and test an architectural energy interface with a budget to manage and dispense. Each group developed a position on the topic of energy and a strategy that led to a corresponding interpretation of the interface. Whether a poster, book, installation, app, appliance, campaign, service, blog or symposium, the objective was to define, measure and create impact. That is, to actually enter the live debate, assemble an audience – whether a limited group of "influencers", the media or a massive global community – and produce measureable effects.

To support this ambition, the pedagogy was accordingly dual: part history/theory seminar to identify and develop a position on the landscape of the contemporary energy discourse and situate it in a historical context, and part product design workshop. We paired traditional discursive methods with contemporary approaches culled from practices of entrepreneurship, technology, design, communication and creative and innovation consulting, including brainstorms and workshops led by guests from companies such as Google, IDEO, Nike and Kickstarter. We began by collectively building a common inventory of tools for each team to subsequently leverage as the focus shifts to producing the interface.

Network Culture
History/Theory
Fall 2013 + Spring 2014
Kazys Varnelis, instructor

Network City explored how urban areas developed as ecosystems of competing networks since the late nineteenth century. Networks of capital, transportation infrastructures and telecommunications systems centralize cities while dispersing them into megalopolises, e.g. larger post-urban fields such as the megalopolis of the Northeastern seaboard, the Great Lakes region or Southern California. Such territories are key players in the geography of flows that structure economies and societies today.

Cities can be thought of as communications systems or networks, but these are products of historical development. To this end, the first half of the course surveyed the development of urbanization since the emergence of the modern network city in the late nineteenth century while the second half focused on conditions in contemporary urbanism. Throughout, we used New York as a key test case. Like cities, buildings also function as networks. In this sense, the city is not just as a network but rather an internet (originally "internetwork") of buildings. We considered the demands of cities and economies together with technological and social networks on architectural program, envelope and plan. Throughout the course, we explored the growth of both city and suburb not as separate and opposed but rather as a whole.

Metropolis
History/Theory
Summer 2013
Enrique Walker, instructor

The modern metropolis—caul-dron of social transformation, technological innovation and aesthetic experimenta-tion—is inseparable from the equally modern notion of an international avant-garde. However, in the course of their myriad encounters through the twentieth century, both categories—the metropolis and the avant-garde—have become virtually unrecog-nizable. In their place have emerged new configurations, new challenges, and new pos-sibilities. This course examined the arguments architecture has formulated for—and through—the city after metropolis. This is the global city, the financial capital of advanced capital-ism. But it is also the city after the city—the result of massive urbanizations stemming from regional and global migrations, as well as massive dispersals that trace back to the decades immediately following the Second World War. The course scrutinized in detail architec-tural objects and the debates surrounding them, positioning these objects within the cities they imagine. In each case, we traced multiple, genealogi-cal affiliations—the alliances forged, the subjects conjured, the pasts constructed, the futures projected, the others excluded—and find a decisive realignment of the ways in which architecture and urban-ism operate, as well as multiple opportunities to re-imagine the city—architecture's recurring dream—yet again today.

Arguments
History/Theory
Summer 2013
Pep Avilés, Chris Cowell, Ignacio González Galán, Diana Martinez, Joaquim Moreno, Alexandra Quantrill, Daniel Talesnik + Norihiko Tsuneishi, instructors

This course examined the production of architectural knowledge through the lens of current intellectual projects in the field. Organized around a series of case studies, and focusing particularly on spaces outside the realm of building—from exhibitions to installations, from journals to books, from re-search projects to educational projects—the main goal of this course was to interrogate ongo-ing projects for these spaces, and in turn to examine different positions within the discipline. In brief, the course scrutinized the formulation of agendas and projects—that is, arguments—and the way in which they take part in the advancement of architecture. This course took on four spaces of architectural production—books, collec-tive exhibitions, individual exhibitions and journals—and devoted two sessions to each. Each session was divided into two parts. The first, conducted as a seminar, and supported by selected readings—with the course instructors operating individually—examined a specific space of architectural production. The second, con-ducted as a guest lecture, and followed by an open debate—with the course instructors operating as a team—interro-gated a project for that space. The ultimate aim was to engage current debates within the field.

Guest lectures by:
Kersten Geers, Andrés Jaque, Pedro Gadanho, Greg Lynn, Craig Buckley, Pier Vittorio Aureli, Ana Miljački and Alfredo Brillembourg.

The Dictionary of Received Ideas
History/Theory
Spring 2014
Enrique Walker, instructor

This seminar was the fifteenth installment in a decade-long project (2006—) whose aim was to examine received ideas—in other words, ideas that have been depleted of their original intensity due to re-current use—in contemporary architecture culture. Based on Gustave Flaubert's unfinished project, Le dictionnaire des idées reçues, this ongoing series of theory seminars and design studios proposes to disclose, define and date—and in the long run archive—re-ceived ideas prevalent over the past decade, both in the professional and academic realms, in order to ultimately open up otherwise precluded possibilities for architectural design and architectural theory.

Program
History/Theory
Spring 2014
Enrique Walker, instructor

This seminar examined the trajectory of the notion of *pro-gram*. Specifically, it focused on the various terms coined in the field of architecture since the fifties to describe—in fact, to reduce—actions in space: from *function* to *behavior*, from situation to event, from use to *organization*. The seminar was structured upon twenty exemplary projects regarding questions of program. Each session interrogated two of these projects and scrutinized the concepts they articulated, the objectives they pursued, the critiques they entailed and the practices they implied. Ultimately, the seminar at-tempted to trace a genealogy of design strategies formulated to *program* architecture.

Collecting Architecture Territories
History/Theory
Spring 2014
Mark Wasiuta, instructor, with Marina Otero + Elis Mendoza

Collecting Architecture Ter-ritories examined one of the most significant developments reshaping the intersection of art and architectural practice over the last three decades: the veritable explosion of in-stitutions and foundations that have emerged out of private art collections. The project proposed that the historical institution of the museum is undergoing a transformation that requires new forms of spatial, territorial and cul-tural analysis. Starting with this transformation it asked what new conditions of collection and organization beyond its walls the mutation of museum signals. The project considered architecture both as an agent that organizes, supports and informs a range of contempo-rary collecting practices, but also increasingly as an object of collection in its own right.

The seminar asked students to develop descriptive strate-gies for elucidating the spatial-ity and territoriality of new regimes of collection. Students considered diverse factors such as new art-architectural prac-tices, the globalization of the art market, initiatives for urban development, practices of pres-ervation, cultural policies, finan-cial investments and tax laws. In each case, the task was to identify the forces that appear most relevant to architecture presently, but also to reflect on what role architecture is play-ing within these new territories and regimes of collection.

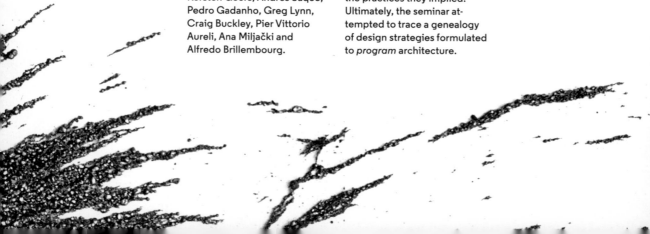

Indigenous Eco-Technology + Bio-Cultural Conservation
History/Theory
Spring 2014
Julia Watson, instructor

In the past, the vernacular of traditional peoples has inspired innovation in the field of architecture, however the equivalent for landscape remains unexplored. While ecological principles mainstream design discourse and terms like resilience supersede sustainability, our understanding of the consequences of these theories and the practices they inspire, remains unknown. For designers, terms such as diversity, reciprocity, feedback and resilience have ambiguous spatial and ecological consequences. However, they can be informed by the breadth and depth of knowledge observed in the societies of our ecological dwellers as resilience is innate in the indigenous understanding of the environment.

This seminar explored the global shadow conservation network composed of indigenous landscapes and their living systems, in search of ecological innovation and vernacular models of preservation. Through subtle ecosystem modification and ecological mimicry, indigenous and traditional peoples have become the critical inhabitants of ecosystems that conservationists are so anxious to protect. A synthesis of recent evolutions in the fields of ecology, environmental systems, biodiversity conservation and sustainability were accompanied by explorations of both classified contemporary material technologies and unclassified indigenous living systems. In this broader context, we conducted investigations into new materialities and preservation models, through a global exploration of existing indigenous innovations.

The History of Architectural Theory
History/Theory
Fall 2013
Mark Wigley, instructor

Architecture emerges out of passionate and unending debate. Every design involves theory. Indeed, architects talk as much as they draw. This class explored the way that theory is produced and deployed at every level of architectural discourse from formal written arguments to the seemingly casual discussions in the design studio. A series of case studies, from Vitruvius to Cyber-Chat, from ancient treatises on parchment to flickering web pages, were used to show how the debate continues to adapt itself to new conditions while preserving some relentless obsessions. Architectural discourse is understood as a wide array of interlocking institutions, each of which has its own multiple histories and unique effects. Students in this course explored "how" and "why" these various institutions were put into place, tracing their historical transformations up until the present to see which claims about architecture have been preserved and which have changed.

Thinking Race, Reading Architecture
History/Theory
Fall 2013
Mabel O. Wilson, instructor

Thinking Race, Reading Architecture examined the nascent topic of the racial in architecture. Students in the course closely read primary treatises and manifestos, scholarly essays and books, along with drawings, models, buildings and urban plans to trace a genealogy of how the racial shaped modern architectural discourse and practices. Students examined how and why the racial evolves in western philosophy, as found in the writings Kant, Hegel and others, from which architectural theory and history derives its frameworks. The course charted a history of the racial to comprehend its presence in the writings and projects of various architects, theorists, and historians including Thomas Jefferson, Viollet-le-duc, Gottfried Semper, Adolf Loos, Le Corbusier and others. One objective of the seminar was to understand why the discipline and profession of architecture have been resistant to recognize how the racial has been part of its discursive genealogy. The study of gender and sexuality in architecture served as a model for how to interpret the category of the racial in these theories and projects. Over the course of the semester, Professors Charles Davis of UNC Chapel Hill, Irene Cheng of CCA and Adrienne Brown of University of Chicago shared their research with the seminar.

Modern Housing
History/Theory
Fall 2013
Gwendolyn Wright, instructor

Housing has been a prime site for experiments throughout the history of modern architecture. Today's modernists recognize that innovation does not preclude comfort, delight and familiarity. Nor is there a single standard: housing or dwelling is at once a universal human need and a diverse panoply of forms and social conditions.

This seminar explored key themes and examples of 20th- and 21st-century modern housing. We focused on fundamental questions about continuities and innovations. How have architects addressed cultural norms about "home" and "housing" over time? We ranged across multiple scales from the individual body, the room and the wall to larger composites of housing complexes, production systems, social services, environmental factors and economic challenges.

The first half of the class surveyed and compared a broad range of examples from iconic social-democratic housing estates of Europe in the 1920s and progressive American enclaves of that era, to more recent prefab prototypes in Sweden, informal barrios in Caracas, the mix of market-rate and social housing in Amsterdam and affordable housing in the United States. Students in the Housing Studio worked with students from other programs and other departments across the university.

Students presented research projects during the last third of the class. They also commented on one another's presentations with great insight, which quickly lifted the level and self-awareness of everyone's work. Topics included UN-Habitat proposals for the Middle East, John F.C. Turner's work in Latin America, contemporary projects in Sao Paulo's favelas, UDC projects in Brooklyn, Joseph Eichler's suburbs in northern California, Chinese gated communities, post-WWII and more recent housing projects in Mexico City, barracks for illegal immigrants and the use of recycled materials in recent housing.

History of the American City
History/Theory
Fall 2013
Gwendolyn Wright, instructor

This course explored the volatile, seemingly chaotic yet cohesive forms of American cities, which have long been the quintessence of the modern metropolis: a synthesis of raw unregulated development, precise professional master plans, broad-based cultural and transnational exchanges, and unexpected local anomalies. Lectures began with colonial-era origin myths, then 19th-century developments and focus on the 20th-century metropolis. Each class took up a specific historical epoch and formal typology (housing, commerce, finance, industry, etc.), juxtaposing general trends across the country with a focus on one particular city. We covered both unique creations and generic spatial forms, problems and creative inventions.

While the last lecture concentrated on contemporary cities, every class examined repercussions of earlier decisions on the present day. Who decides where 'downtown' is located? How have Americans envisioned homes – and housing? What are Americans' attitudes about the natural environment, especially in cities? How does infrastructure affect the efficiency and equity of a city? We emphasized a fundamental aspect of historical inquiry: the past affects what is possible in the present and what people can imagine about the future.

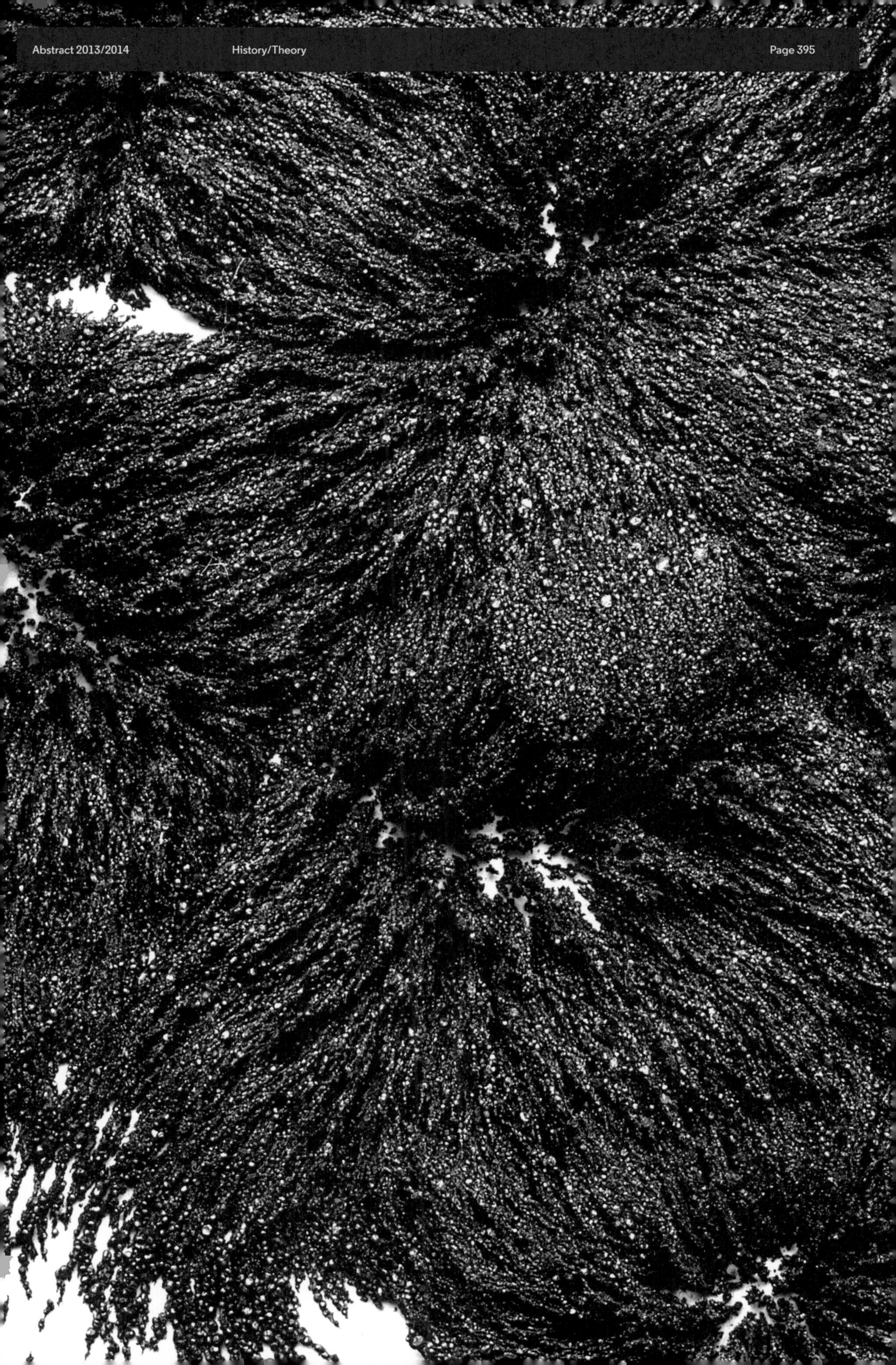

Visual Studies
Laura Kurgan, director,
Joshua Uhl, coordinator

In the last fifteen years, architecture has been exposed to a radical set of changes in its visual toolkits and its technological environments. New hardware and software, often imported from other fields and emerging at a dizzying pace, have digitized and automated techniques of architectural drawing, modeling and production; multiplied networks of communication into diverse infrastructures and media; increased the accuracy of analytic imaging; and expanded databases and methods of data collection. Architecture, because its core techniques are not simply its own, cannot wall itself off from the many other disciplines and practices—ecology, the military, science, geography, popular culture—with which it shares, and from which it often borrows, its tools.

Today, what can be defined as visual in design has multiplied exponentially and forced us to rethink all of our projects and practices. Visual studies now spans all the disciplines of the GSAPP, such that a wide range of tools and techniques are available in an expanded matrix of courses. The core of the curriculum emphasizes collaboration among disciplines, studios and seminars.

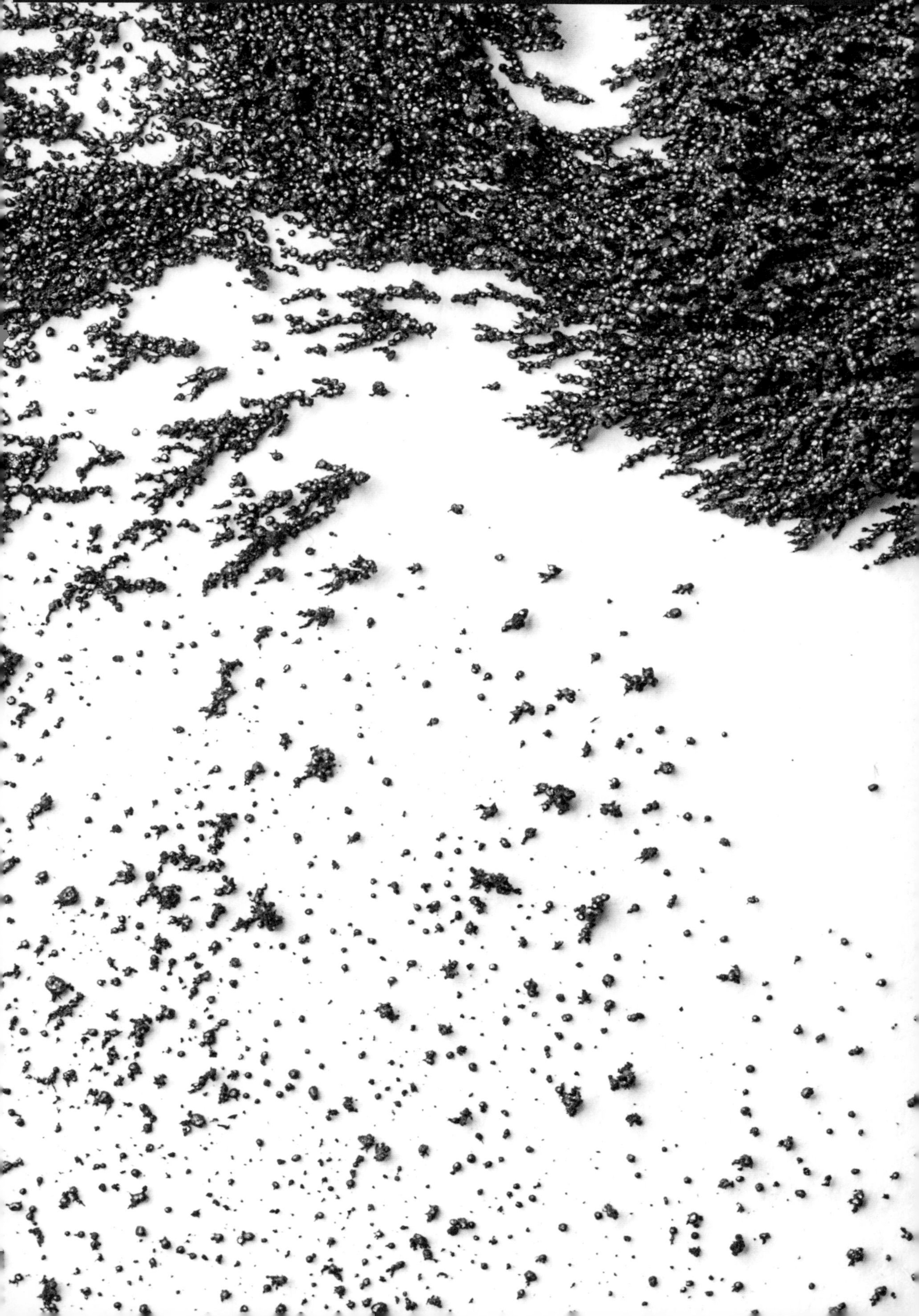

Architectural Drawing + Representation 1
Visual Studies
Fall 2013
Joshua Uhl, Cristina Goberna + Danil Nagy, instructors, with Ray Wang, Lorenzo Villagi, Bika Rebek, Abe Bendheim, Mondi Hsieh, Susan Bopp, Skylar Bisom-Rapp + Jordan Meerdink

Architects do not make buildings; we make drawings. Our drawings can be descriptive when they are generated to convey a particular set of formal conditions, and they can be prescriptive when they act as tools used to interrogate adjacencies and spatial relationships. In either case, a well-crafted drawing becomes a feedback loop for the architect, allowing one to interrogate their design, respond to the drawing and further their proposal.

Architecture's history of projection-based representation developed a certain level of stasis in its evolution over the last half a century. However, recent shifts to a 'paperless' architecture continue to have a profound impact on the field of architecture and its modes of representation and analysis. Beyond severing the longstanding relationship of the line to paper, the extraction of the vector to a virtual realm is accompanied by a simultaneous influx of data.

In this course, we engaged drawing's new temporal nature and tried to harness its potential. What does it mean to make a drawing in the 'Post-Projection' era? What is lost when an understanding of the constructed nature of a drawing is gone, and the tools of projection are relegated to a secondary role? What can be gained through understanding these tools more completely and then re-appropriating them in contemporary investigations?

Alexander Darsinos **A**
Jason Danforth **B**
Joann Feng **C**
Maxwell Miller **D**
Yuhong Du **E**
Yue Zhong **F**

A
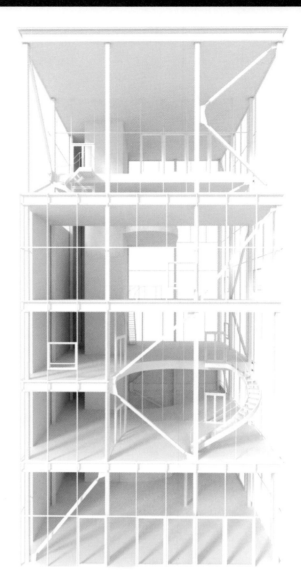

B
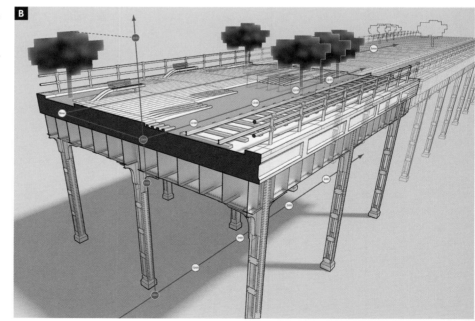

C

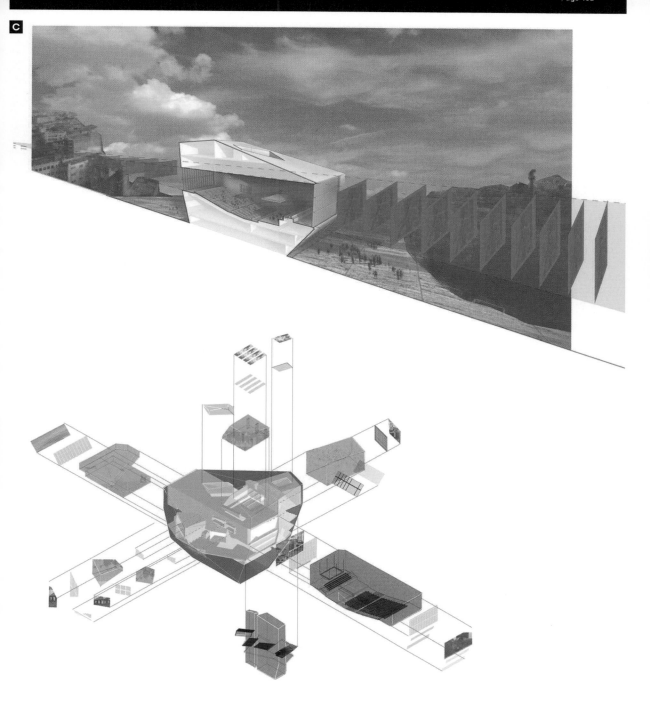

D

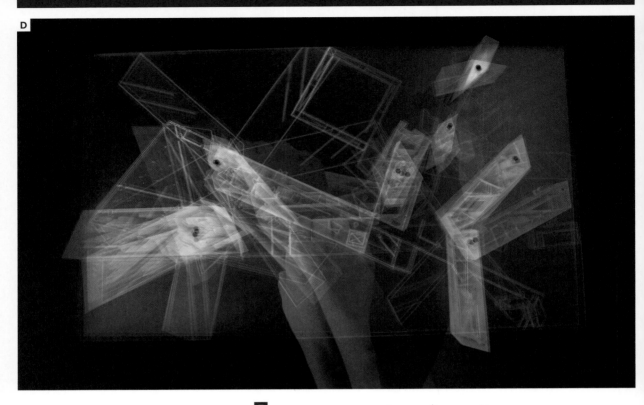

E

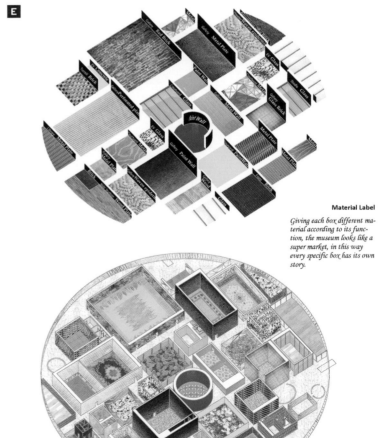

Material Label

Giving each box different material according to its function, the museum looks like a super market, in this way every specific box has its own story.

Museum? Supermarket?

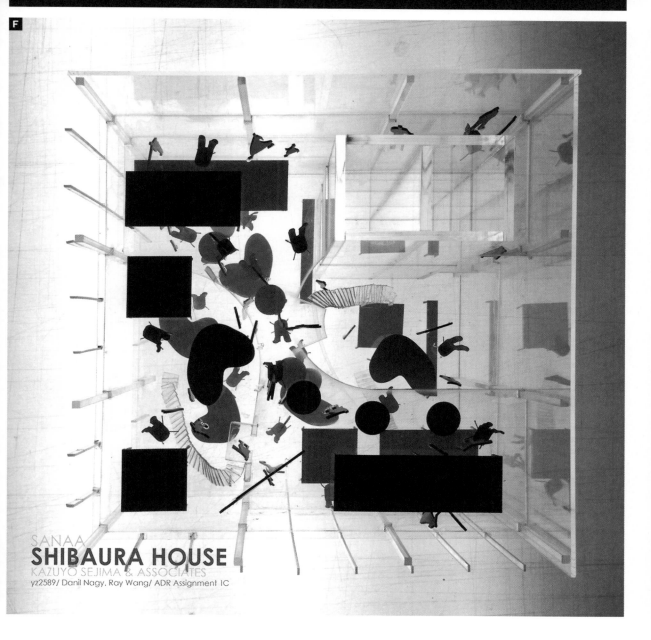

SANAA
SHIBAURA HOUSE
KAZUYO SEJIMA & ASSOCIATES
yz2589/ Danil Nagy, Ray Wang/ ADR Assignment 1C

**Architectural Drawing +
Representation 2**
Visual Studies
Spring 2014
*Laura Kurgan, director,
Danil Nagy, Katie Shima +
Jason Vigneri-Beane, instruc-
tors, with Skylar Bisom-Rapp,
Susan Bopp, Mondrian Hsieh,
Chelsea Hyduk, Jordan
Merdink, Bika Rebek,
Lorenzo Villagi + Ray Wang*

Visualization tools and drawing
have changed radically over the
last century, in both the practice and pedagogy of architecture. The course charted these
shifts, beginning with the pre-
sumption that there are strong
links between old and new
media, analogue and digital
methods, drawing with pencils
and drawing with software.

   Given the indispensible role
of visualization in facilitating
and communicating design
ideas, this course introduced
students to and addressed a
range of questions about multiple techniques of architectural
visualization. This semester,
we asked what the larger
implications of visualization are
for architecture, for contemporary visual culture and for
the move from modernity to
postmodernity and beyond?

   While the focus of the course
was on the production, tools
and techniques of drawing,
the intent of the course was
to foster active engagement
between the history and theory
of visualization, the practice of
drawing and the design studio.
The connections, although not
always direct, were intended
to allow first year students to
think about how visual tools
have an impact on their design
methods, which is to say, that
the utilization of techniques
and tools are not neutral
choices in the practices of
drawing, design or pedagogy.

   The course also addressed
how the audiences for viewing
and methods for distributing
visualization have changed, not
only through the network, but
also politically and aesthetically. The sharing of the work produced by students via blog and
cloud media, as well as through

the traditional reviews of work
in situ, was critical to creating our own audience for the
work produced in this course.

Caitlin Magill **A**
Boyuan Jiang **B/C/D/E**
Xiaoyu Wang **F/G/H/I**
Justin Lui **J**
Chang Qi **K/L**
Yuchen Guo **M**
Zaw Lin Myat **N**

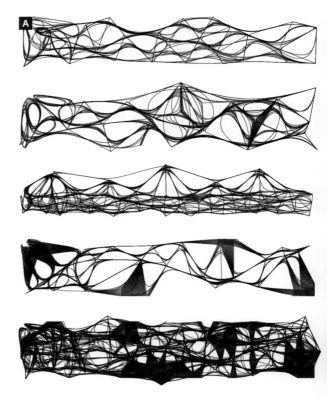

B

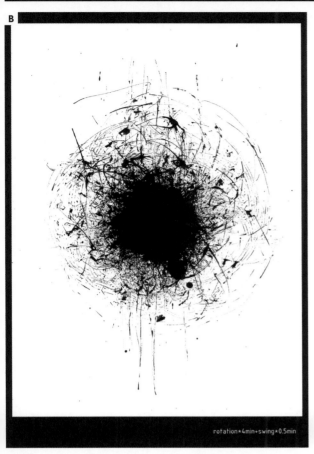

rotation*4min+swing*0.5min

C

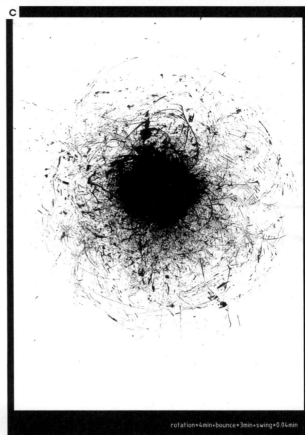

rotation*4min+bounce*3min+swing*0.04min

D

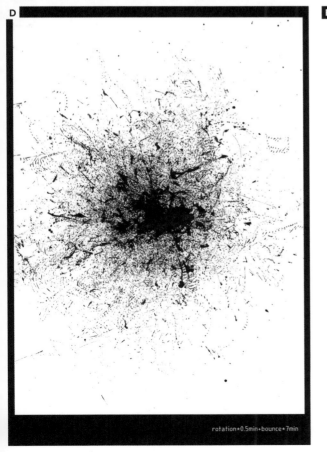

rotation*0.5min+bounce*7min

E

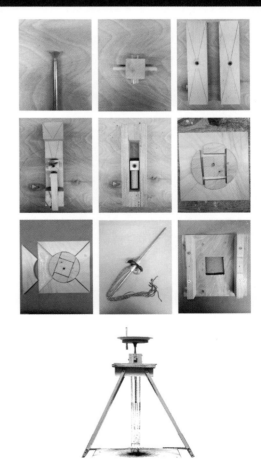

F

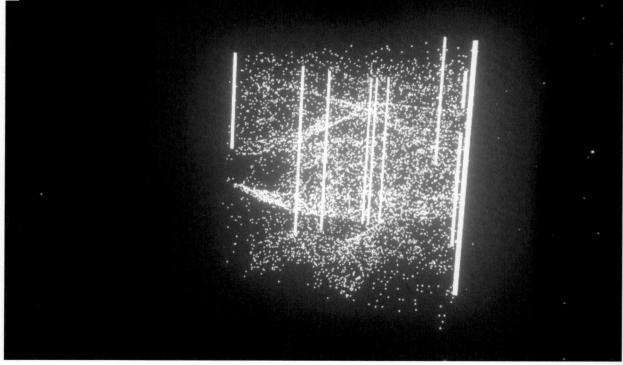

G

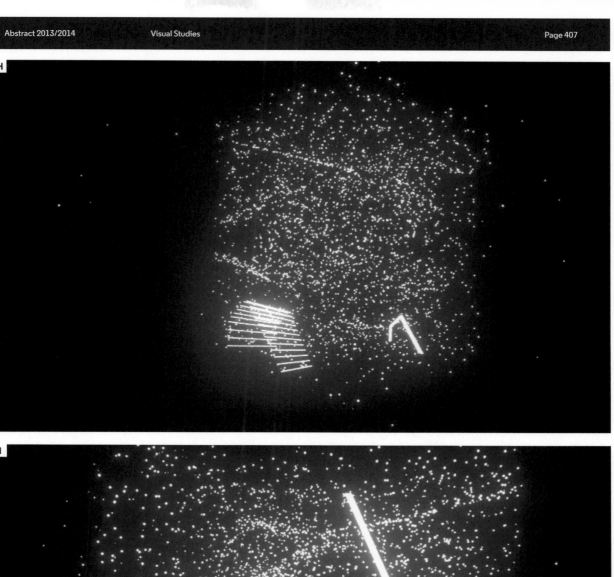

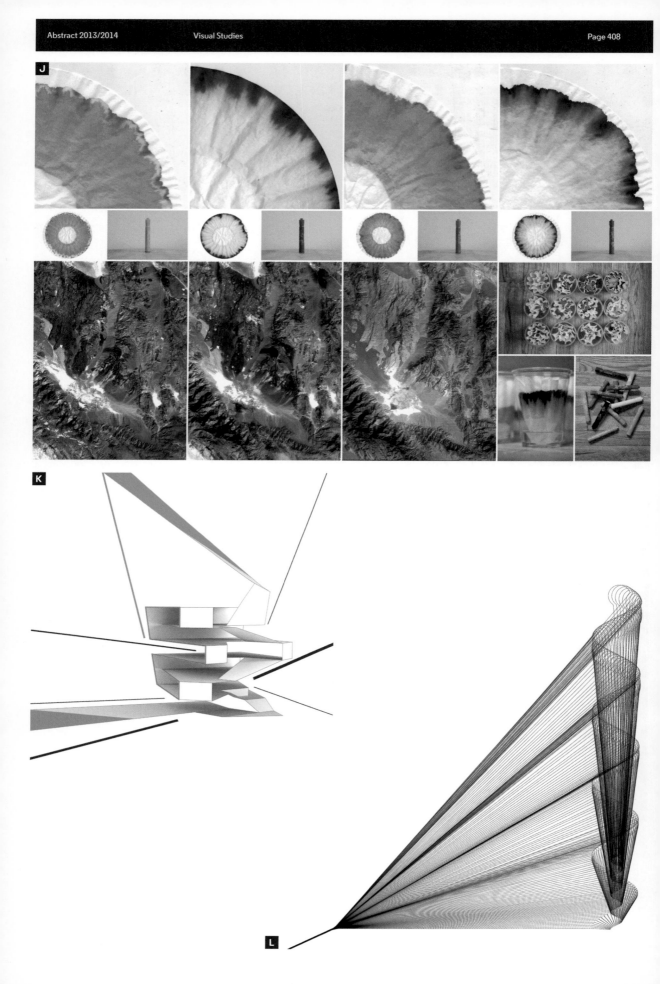

M

N

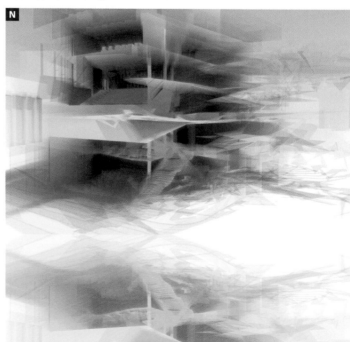

Architectural Photography 1 + 2
Visual Studies
Fall 2013
Erieta Attali, instructor, with Michael Bosbous

The scope of this course focused on using the medium of architectural photography as a critical tool for analyzing and representing buildings. By contextualizing and framing the relationship between an architect and his or her work, it becomes easier to understand the intent behind the design process. Architectural photography helps us to understand the creator's ideas and intentions and can provide us with insights into a building's meaning. It not only provides us with documentary evidence but also serves as a stimulant for the critical mind. On a practical level, the class taught soon-to-be architects what to expect and what to desire from documentation of buildings they might design in the future.

Professor Attali led each class as an open critique tailored to individual strengths and interests. Students were expected to produce work for every class for review so that, by the end of the semester, each student would ideally build up a portfolio of work centered around an individualized project. The class also incorporated the work of past and contemporary landscape and architectural photographers, drawing from their example and talent for inspiration. Photo I was largely an introductory course, while Architectural Photography 2 delved more thoroughly into the discipline.

Emily Koustae **A**
Cheng Zhou **B**
Mintra Maneepairoj **C**
Nazli Ergani **D**
Yue Zhao **E**

B

C

D

E

Architectural Photography: Night
Visual Studies
Spring 2014
Erieta Attali, instructor, with Michael Bosbous

Since the Renaissance, artificial illumination has been used to alter our perception of the built environment. During the twentieth century, it became an inextricable part of the design process. Architecture of the night has even contributed toward the fulfillment of the modernist dream for an architecture of intangible forms. Now, the once cold and sturdiness of a structure's materials can be transformed into a floating apparition by the building's light, shadow and color that can only exist after dark.

From its infancy, photography has proven to be an important means of documentation and aesthetic appeal. Urban photography pioneers such as Alfred Steiglitz and his peers were key in the development of a technical and aesthetic photographic language that influenced their followers, the design community and the general public. By ignoring mere topographical representation, these photographers embraced the technical imperfections of this medium–darkness and artificial light–and produced images of striking aesthetic and cultural impact. These pioneers used designed building lighting and ambient city lighting to change our perception of modern urban cityscape.

This course gave students the opportunity to engage in a similar quest, asking them to approach photography as a medium to interpret aesthetic intent and express subjective understanding of building or urban space after dark. In doing so, they produced a series of night images that covered a range of architectural themes: cityscape, urban landscape, residential, commercial and public spaces.

Parametric Realizations
Visual Studies
Fall 2013 + Spring 2014
Mark Bearak + Brigette Borders, instructors

Parametric Realizations outlined the process of generating a parametric model or algorithm using Rhino.script and Grasshopper and turning that model into a physical reality. Material exploration and prototyping formed a critical component of testing the design, and material failures were both challenged and embraced. The projects integrated components of the digital fabrication into their protocol, in order to test the limits of both tools. The course focused on the scale of a product, and students designed and manufactured a physical object, as well as created a branding strategy.

Tanya Lucia Griffiths, Albert Hsu, Andres Macera + Minglu Zheng **A/B/C**

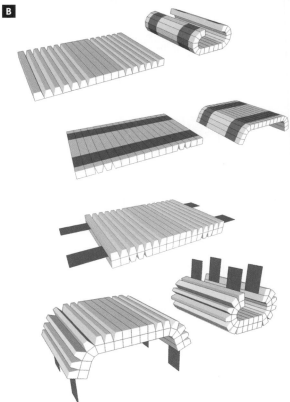

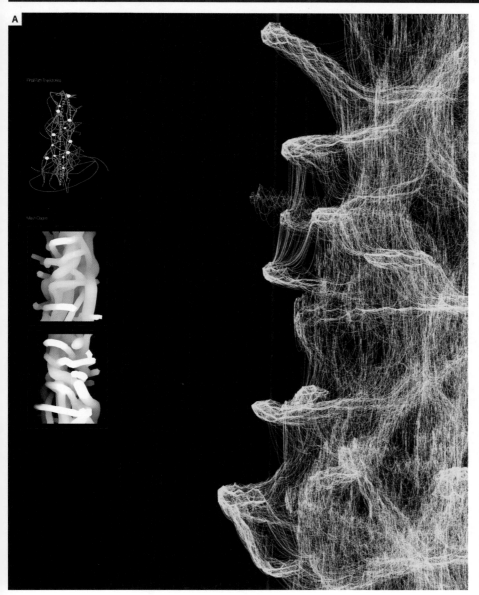

Encoded Matter: Workshop in Computational Craft
Visual Studies
Fall 2013 + Spring 2014
Ezio Blasetti, instructor

This workshop investigated non-linear systems and self-organization in the design and prototyping of architectural immersive environments via computational generative methods. At present, computational techniques are predominantly employed in the optimization, rationalization or surface decoration of more traditionally created forms and spaces. This research instead focused on the inherent potential of computation to generate space and of algorithmic procedures to engage self-organization in the design process. Encoded matter operated as an open source design laboratory, investigating these areas at the scale of a temporary spatial construct: a pavilion. Participants engaged closely with computational processes in order to develop an aesthetic and intuition of complexity that resides in a balance between design intent and emergent character.

Encoded matter proposed a parallel study between material behavior and computational systems. The participants were encouraged to conduct and document a series of material 'experiments' in dialogue with their computational research. A critical parameter in this workshop was to develop the potential beyond finite forms of explicit and parametric modeling towards more non-linear algorithmic processes. The goal was the development of an exquisite and novel architectural language that is inextricably tied to the process of its own production.

Allen Ghaida + Carlos Garcia Fernandez A
Bian Lin, Zhen Dong + Haocheng Yu B
Nicolaos Vlavianos + Hamid Reza Malhooz C

B

C

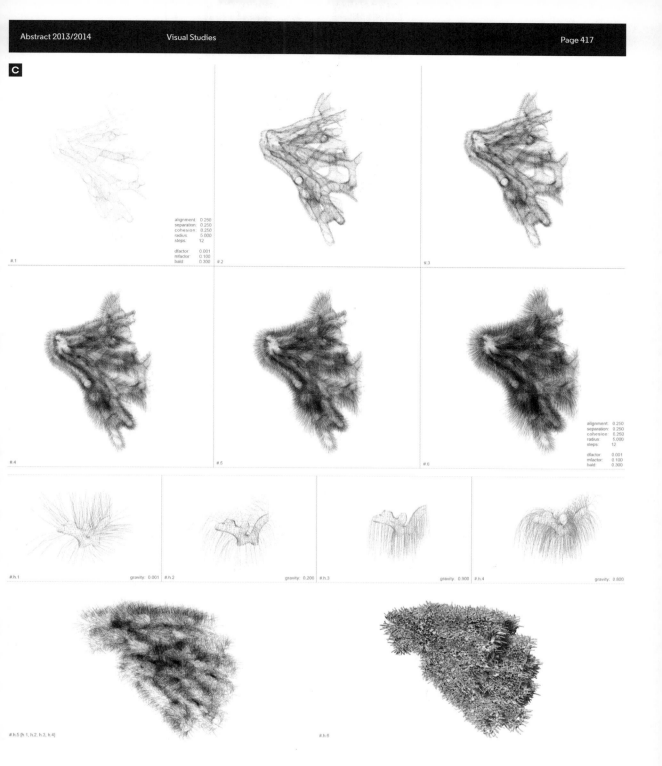

alignment: 0.250
separation: 0.250
cohesion: 0.250
radius: 5.000
steps: 12

dfactor: 0.001
mfactor: 0.100
bald: 0.300

#.1   #.2   #.3

alignment: 0.250
separation: 0.250
cohesion: 0.250
radius: 5.000
steps: 12

dfactor: 0.001
mfactor: 0.100
bald: 0.300

#.4   #.5   #.6

#.h.1   gravity: 0.001   #.h.2   gravity: 0.200   #.h.3   gravity: 0.900   #.h.4   gravity: 0.600

#.h.5 [h.1, h.2, h.3, h.4]   #.h.6

Approaching Convergence
Visual Studies
Spring 2014
Biayna Bogosian +
Maider Llaguno, instructors

Through the development of information technologies our relationship with objects and the built environment has become intrinsic, defining a material semiotic that allows the world to become a live information platform. The rise of digital methods in architectural design, real-time environmental sensing, physical computing and simulation platforms for environmental analysis has produced a renewed interest in the relationship between architecture, social dynamics and natural phenomena. This suggests the integration of environmental aspects into the design process not through the reproduction of pre-existing typologies, but through the development of site-specific environmental prototypes.

This course focused on the integration of environmental data – anthropogenic data and climatic data – in the convergence of varied and disparate computational platforms into design workflows. Maneuvering explorations through, between and within multiple applications, the students launched into agenda-driven opportunities for advanced and fluid inter-operations, outputting geometric systems from the environmental big data. In this advocated methodology, where the distance between generation and evaluation substantively compresses, the students navigated across multiple digital platforms with an amplified ability to both explore options across an expanding design-space and achieve depth and speed of analysis.

Allen Ghaida **A/B**
Gao Zhao, Xu Yao, Li-Ling
Lin + Tietong Lu **C/D**

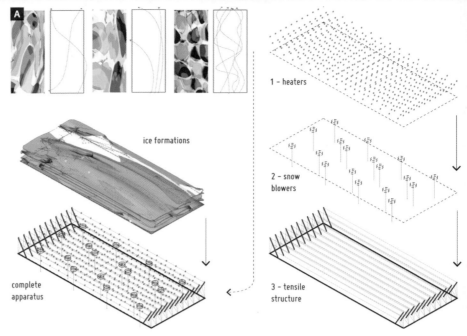

A

1 – heaters

ice formations

2 – snow blowers

complete apparatus

3 – tensile structure

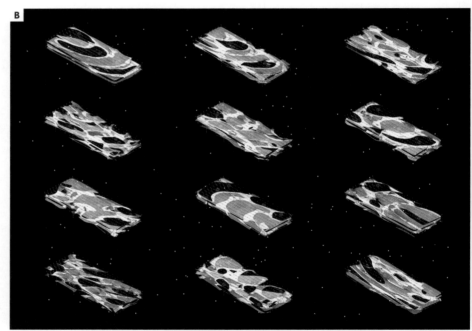

B

C

D

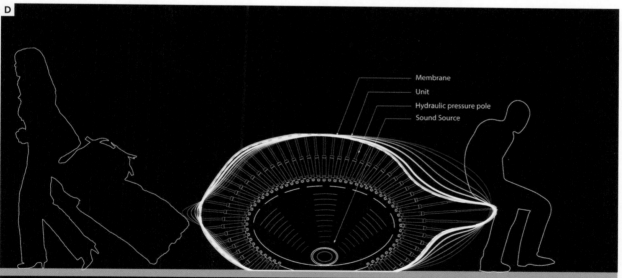

Membrane
Unit
Hydraulic pressure pole
Sound Source

6:00 AM

8:00 AM

10:00 AM

12:00 PM

2:00 PM

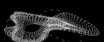

4:00 PM

6:00 PM

8:00 PM

10:00 PM

12:00 AM

Techniques of the Ultrareal + Imagining the Unreal
Visual Studies
Fall 2013 + Spring 2014
Joseph Brennan + Phillip Crupi, instructors, with Geof Bell

The current abundance and use of 3D modeling software has caused techniques of perspective to be an afterthought. Rendering is most often used to produce images for final presentations. In the Techniques of the Ultrareal and Imagining the Ultrareal, the students were encouraged to use rendering not only as a method for presentation, but also as a method to be implemented early and often within their design process. Students learned not only the skills to create photorealistic images but also workflow and file management techniques. This class looked for inspiration from renderings, as well as all types of media, including photography, art and cinematography.

Bryan Kim, Cheolho Kim + Kangsan Danny Kim **A**
Donyanaz Nazem **B**
Sabrina Barker **C**
Lindsey Wikstrom **D**
Serena Li **E**

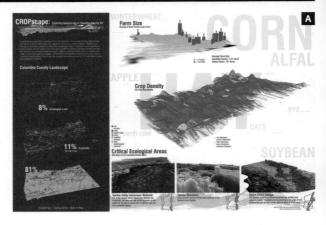

Field of Play: Agency in Mapping Site
Visual Studies
Fall 2013
Brian Brush, instructor

This class investigated techniques in GIS for visualizing spatial data as instrumental geometry for design within the conceptual framework of "territory."

Territory, in the historic sense, suggests the establishment, management, and documentation of political or administrative geographies – the quintessential representation of which has been, and continues to be, the map. In the context of contemporary architectural design, however, territory suggests a constructed condition that articulates the reciprocal spatial relationships between politics, environment, landscape, information and architecture that define a site.

Geographic Information Systems – GIS – is the primary digital platform for documenting these relationships through spatial mapping. Furthermore, GIS can be used as a powerful tool for design by creating instrumental geometry embedded with socio–geographic meaning that can qualify conditions of territory beyond what mapping alone can afford. The products of GIS can be descriptive and analytical representations of a site that simultaneously perform as generative manifolds for the creation of architecture indelibly connected to place.

This class used GIS as the primary computational platform for collecting, creating, interpreting and representing 2D and 3D geographic data in service of articulating spatial territories of a site for design. The class was an exploration of successive territorial–topological dialectics including but not limited to: polygon area-assemblages, volumetric–vertical compositions, point–density mapping, raster surface–topography, vector surface contouring and point/line–network tracings.

Field of Play 1 + 2
Visual Studies
Spring 2014
Brian Brush, instructor

Architecture is a discipline of cultural and artistic production characterized by the negotiation of imagined possibilities with significant real constraints. One such constraint, the constraint of site, tasks the designer to distill, through various interrelated processes of observation, abstraction, representation and materialization, an infinite realm of possibilities into what can be achieved at a particular place and time. Site is not limited to the conventional notion of a demarcated plot of land on which to build a building. Site is also the social, cultural, political, economic, environmental, historic and technological contexts within which a project is situated. Moreover, site is not limited to a single location but is extensive, incorporating and indexing distant related locations as prototypical instantiations of a larger territorial condition. Architects qualify these conditions of site through the collection, creation and interpretation of spatial data. The manifestation of this data in physical form is an essential part of architectural design. This course investigated techniques for visualizing geographic and spatial data as instrumental geometry for design. The objects of investigation were spatial mappings translated and transformed for fabrication of a full-scale, site-specific architectural intervention. As a manifestation of contextual data flows, the intervention tested architecture's ability to communicate information critically and thoughtfully in the public domain.

Crystal Yuehin Ng **A**
Sukwon Lee **B**
Yue Zhao **C**

B

INVINCIBLE BANK VERSUS VULNERABLE BANK

FIELD OF PLAY / FALL 2013 / SUKWON LEE

The most crucial factor of a bank is the security of users' money. Although the digitalized banking system has deducted a crime of the bank robbery, it is still remaining as an attractive wallet for criminals. In our investigation, we are going to find physical factors which determine and effect on the level of security for the bank. These factors mainly focus on the physical environment including trees and heights of buildings surrounded. Height factors and trees may cast a shadow and play a pivotal role in blocking the visibility from pedestrians and guards. In this investigation, we narrowed down the scope of the site into a certain district of Broadway in order to set relatively the same condition.

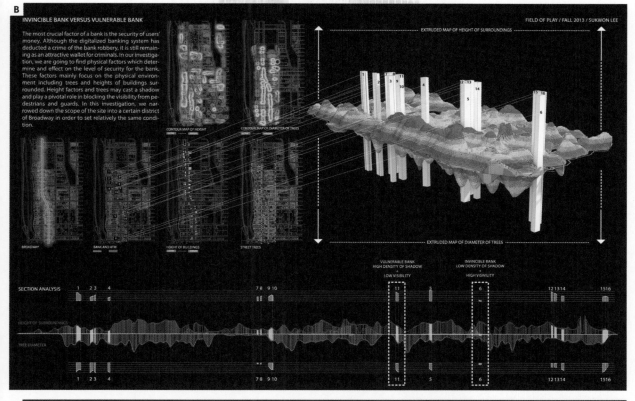

EXTRUDED MAP OF HEIGHT OF SURROUNDINGS

CONTOUR MAP OF HEIGHT   CONTOUR MAP OF DIAMETER OF TREES

BROADWAY   BANK AND ATM   HEIGHT OF BUILDINGS   STREET TREES

EXTRUDED MAP OF DIAMETER OF TREES

VULNERABLE BANK   INVINCIBLE BANK
HIGH DENSITY OF SHADOW   LOW DENSITY OF SHADOW
LOW VISIBILITY   HIGH VISIBILITY

SECTION ANALYSIS

HEIGHT OF SURROUNDINGS

TREE DIAMETER

C

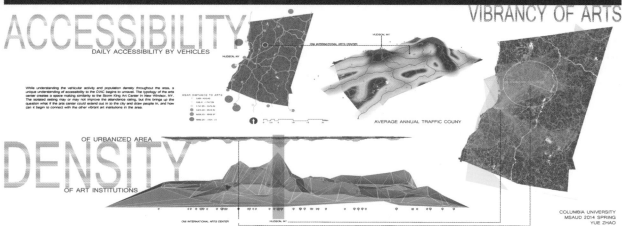

ARTS SPOTTING

UNDERSTANDING THE ARTS
IN COLUMBIA COUNTY, NY

The purpose of this project is to assess Omi International Arts Center as a model of public gathering spot in Columbia County, NY, which helps promote social interaction and a sense of fine art community. I identify the geographic and social characteristics of the Omi International Arts Center through functionality, correlation with other county art institutions, connectivity and density, visualizing the data. I frame the methodology of defining a good public space, and to better understand the potential in terms of future development and expansion.

Taking the Omi International Arts Center as study model, the success of an arts center depends on the vibrancy and diversity of its own services and activities. The arts atmosphere created with other nearby art centers, art schools museums and studios within approachable distance, reflects the possibility of potential collaborations and active learning.

12 ARTS CENTERS   5 ART SCHOOLS   13 MUSEUMS   37 STUDIOS

ACCESSIBILITY

DAILY ACCESSIBILITY BY VEHICLES

VIBRANCY OF ARTS

While understanding the vehicular activity and population density throughout the area, a unique understanding of accessibility to the OIAC begins to unravel. The typology of the arts center creates a space making similarity to the Storm King Art Center in New Windsor, NY. The isolated setting may or may not improve the attendance rating, but this brings up the question what if the arts center could extend out in to the city and draw people in, and how can it begin to connect with the other vibrant art institutions in the area.

NEAR DISTANCE TO ARTS

HUDSON, NY   ONE INTERNATIONAL ARTS CENTER

AVERAGE ANNUAL TRAFFIC COUNT

OF URBANIZED AREA

DENSITY

OF ART INSTITUTIONS

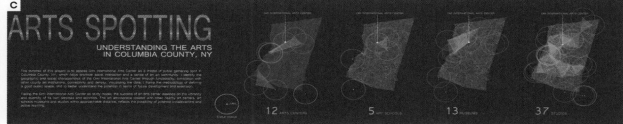

ONE INTERNATIONAL ARTS CENTER   HUDSON, NY

COLUMBIA UNIVERSITY
MSAUD 2014 SPRING
YUE ZHAO

Craft in the Digital Age
Visual Studies
Fall 2013 + Spring 2014
Nathan Carter, instructor

What is the role of craft in architecture? The skills of the architect are now dedicated to the digital. The making and testing of a project can take place entirely in the computer, but without an intimate understanding of materials and techniques of making, the architect's digital work has limited efficacy. Making and testing belongs within the larger feedback loop of design.

The aim of the class is twofold: to explore craft, developing a personal understanding of materials, tools and techniques to directly inform the design process and to frame this exploration in a larger context of analog and digital design and fabrication, highlighting efficiencies and limitations and rethinking the orchestration of the two by the designer.

The class was structured around weekly, hands–on exercises in the Fabrication Shop. Students became proficient with a number of tools and tested construction and joinery techniques. We discussed tolerances, material properties and constraints and work–flow/logic.

The final project was to design and fabricate a multi–person Seating Unit that demonstrated an understanding of materiality, tools and techniques developed from our exploration of craft. This could be one piece at a larger scale to accommodate multiple people, or it could be a development on the aggregation of multiple single person Seating Units.

Andrew Maier **A**
Bryan Kim + Sabrina Wirth **B**
Dichen Ding **c**
Ebberly Strathairn **D**
Makenzie Leukart **E**
Vahe Markosian **F/G**
Zachary Maurer **H**

A

B

C

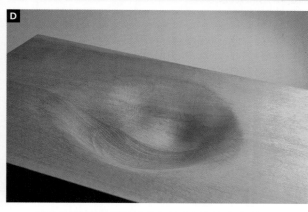

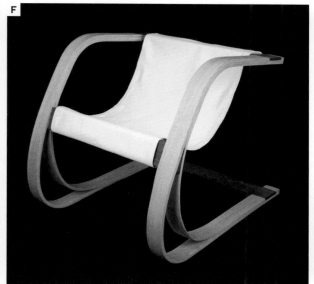

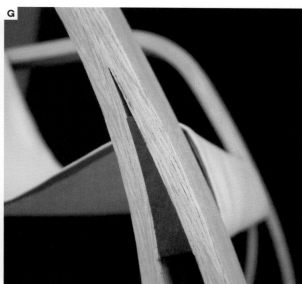

Graphic Presentation 1
Visual Studies
Fall 2013 + Spring 2014
Ken Meier + Yoonjai
Choi, instructors

Architecture starts and ends as graphic design.

The Graphic Architecture Project is a way of thinking about the intersection of the flat and the deep. Over the past few years we have been looking at how design concepts like branding, display and advertising affect the practice of architecture.

This semester we want to examine, in rather minute detail, aspects of presentation: that is the visual rhetoric employed to convey design concepts. We are especially interested in how diverse forms of representation—plan, section, elevation, perspective, diagram, rendering—combine with typographic language in complex graphic and discursive narratives.

We investigated these conceptual issues through extremely practical assignments. In so doing, this class introduced basic 2D design as a component of complex message making. In the first half of the semester, we focused on 2D composition and typography. We examined the details of letterforms and investigated type design and typesetting from a historical and visual perspective. We also considered typographic hierarchy and systems and looked at the composition of graphic space using both typography and images.

In the second part of the semester, we began with a lesson in simple but refined typesetting, followed by assignments that dealt with layered content, working with more sophisticated design systems. We continued to explore the use of grids for managing complex information and for the graphic articulation of two-dimensional space. Using the visual and conceptual tools developed in the first section, we combined graphic devices with narrative content.

Hajeong Lim **A**
James Stoddart **B**
Laura Buck **C**
Alissa Anderson **D**
Jessie Baxa **E**
Sara Dionis Sevilla **F**

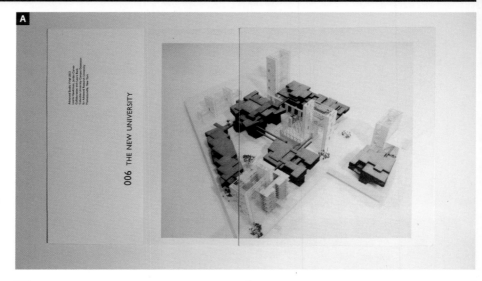

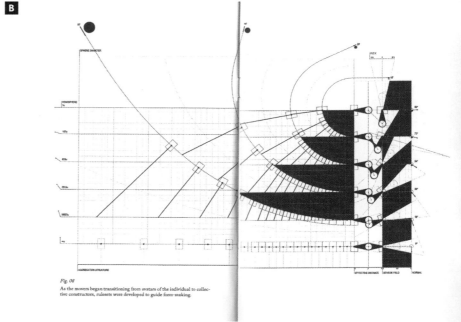

Fig. 08
As the movers began transitioning from avatars of the individual to collective constructors, rulesets were developed to guide form-making.

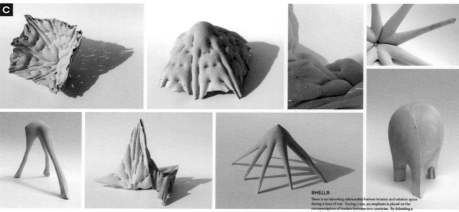

SHELLS
There is an interesting relationship between interior and exterior space during a time of war. During a war, an emphasis is placed on the circumscription of borders between two countries. By delimiting a boundary, a country is specifying its interior. In that same motion, however its interior becomes vulnerable. The interior space of one country becomes a target for another country. Space, at that time, is both interior and exterior. It is turned inside out, or hugging itself. The above casts explore the idea of coupled volumes. Spaces formed by each others curvature.

D

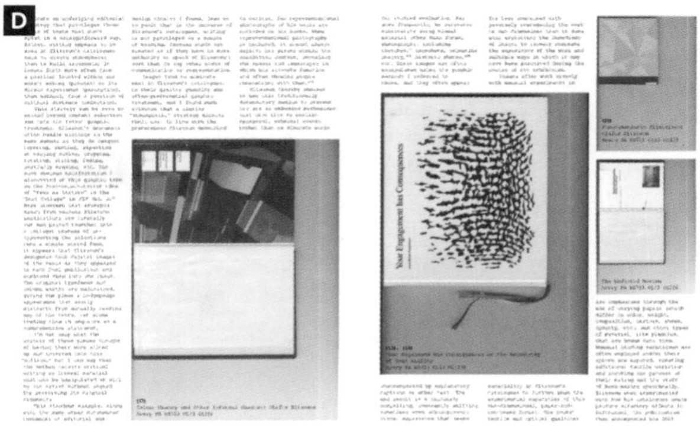

E

36

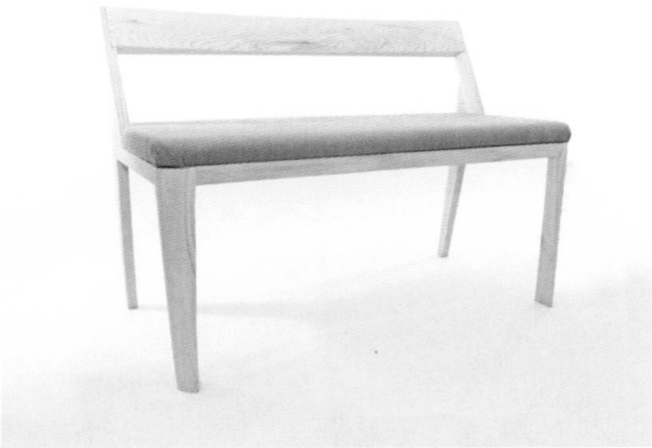

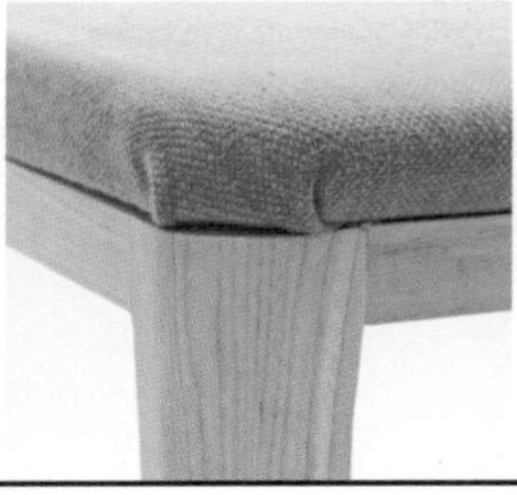

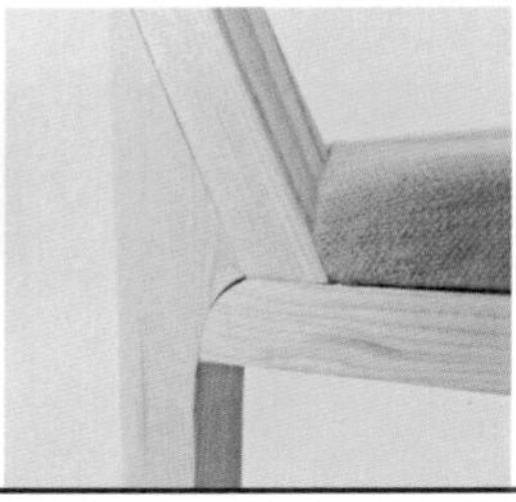

37

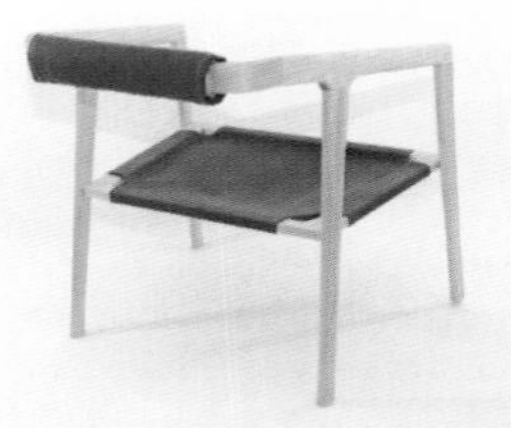

Bent wood lounge chair

Craft in the Digital Age

GSAPP Spring 2013, Professor: Nathan Carter

Final seating unit for two

2 unique joint conditions

The design and fabrication of furniture allows me to investigate the subtlety of connections and form at the user scale. Traditional craftsmanship informs how I approach digital fabrication, construction, and detailing: find a balance between functionality and refined form without feeling limited by the tool.

My work has been focused on investigating the strength and subtleties within each material I use. While my ultimate concern is the product, the insights gained about how to harness the full potential of my tools has pushed my understanding of construction and developed an innovative approach to achieving the end result.

F

SCENT THERAPY

URBAN FITNESS CENTER IN DUMBO, NEW YORK CITY

Combining thorough research as well as design, this studio integrates "air design" into architectural practice. The conditioning of air has led to a parallel and invisible architectural program that focuses on the in-between spaces of buildings (both exterior and interior) and has an extensive impact on the built environment. The studio's goal was to address the changes that architecture will inevitably experience if we actively design the conditioning of air. Since air design is a key aspect of an urban fitness center, this program is chosen as the starting point for all the proposals.

Relative humidity acts as a filter, modifying the perceived scent intensity of the city. Understanding scent therapy's capability to alter people's mood and cognitive function, scent was instrumentalized to design a new fitness experience focused on the well-being of both body and mind. The boundaries between inside and outside and different programs dematerialize to generate various conditioning perimeters that regulate scent and humidity exchange. The scent track—an inside-out program—negotiates between these different perimeters and serves as the major structural spine of the building. The walls of the Scent Therapy Center act as filters negating or augmenting scents generated inside and outside the building.

The fitness center program is organized in three categories: acceleration, suspension and mixture. It is arranged horizontally by contradicting the site border scents, and vertically according to the ideal relative humidity. The acceleration program, comprises activities in which scent intensity is higher than relative humidity intensity. The suspension program, comprises activities in which relative humidity is higher than scent intensity. And finally, the mixture program comprises activities in which there is an equal relationship between relative humidity and scent intensity.

Columbia GSAPP . Critic: Phu Hoang. Summer 2013 . Published.

(Left) Exploded axonometric. Conditioning perimeters description
(Top Right) Underground plaza view
(Middle Right) Aerial view Scent Center
(Bottom Right) Structure diagram

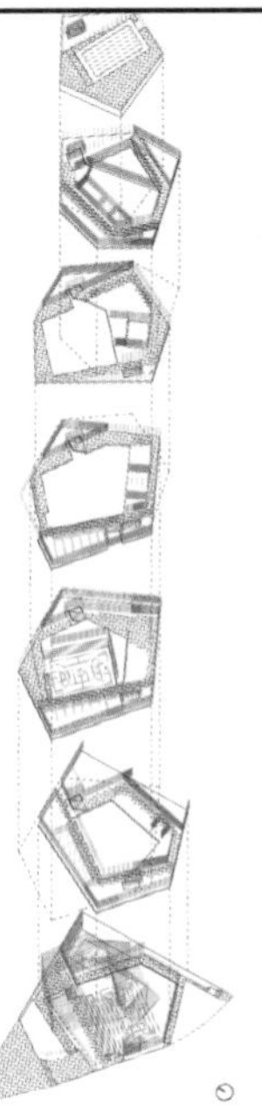

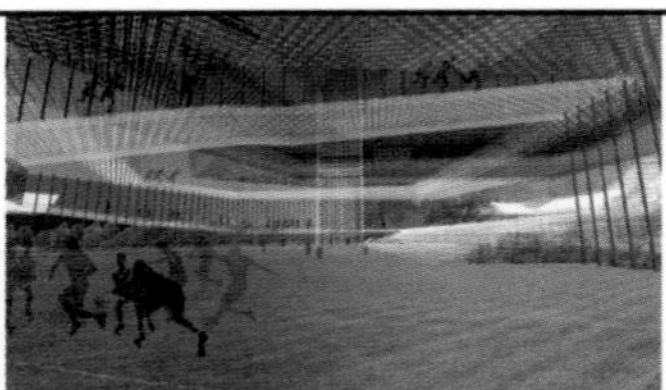

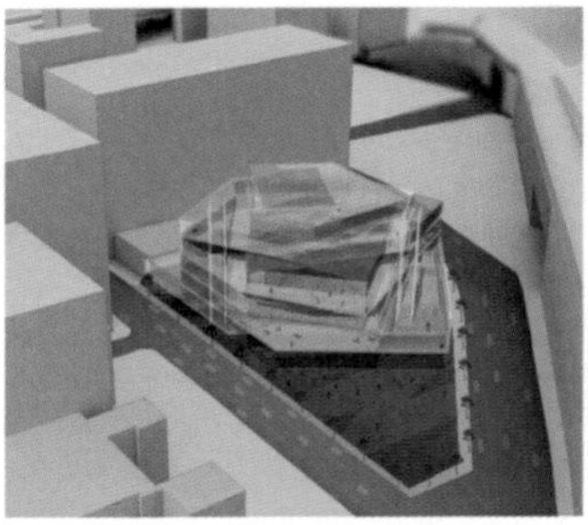

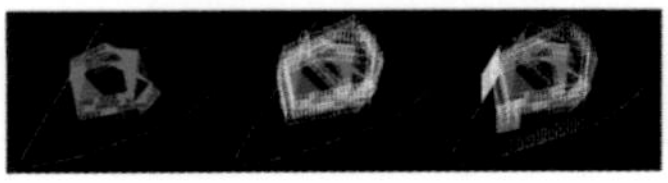

14 THE ARCHITECTURE OF THE (IN)VISIBLE

SCENT THERAPY 15

Graphic Presentation 2
Visual Studies
Fall 2013
*Terri Chiao + David
Yun, instructors*

*[S]ince nothing can enter
architecture without having
been first converted into
graphic form, the actual
mechanism of graphic
conversion is fundamental.*
Stan Allen, *Diagrams Matter*

The Graphic Architecture
Project is a critical investigation
into the intersection of architectural design and graphic
form. All ideas are communicated through mediated representations — whether in the form
of speech, text, image, form
or action. In architecture and
urban design, the graphic presentation of complex ideas is
essential in shaping how information is produced, received
and, ultimately, experienced.

As complex forms of draw-
ing, both the map and the
diagram have an important
function in the process of
designing. Because they are
reductions, both forms may
reveal an essential truth not
visible in the realm of the real.
The diagram is the reduction
of an idea to its most brutal
contradictions: it depicts
relationships, and the map
reveals adjacencies. But
beyond their declarative and
clarifying functions, maps and
diagrams are visual objects in
their own right and, therefore,
worthy of a closer look.

This class looked specifically
at diagramming and graphic
communication through
the lens of the architectural
process. The course focused
on key touch points in the
process from pre-design to
post-occupancy that helps to
frame visual representation
throughout the design process.

Chisom Ezekwo **A**
Jonathan Ivan
Adamos Requillo **B**
Marissa Naval **C**
Yu Hsuan Lin **D**

For instance, the
intersection
between Front
and Main streets
and analyzed
how scents
related to each
other and to
humidity.

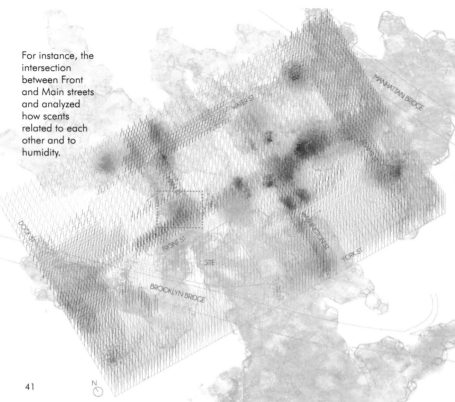

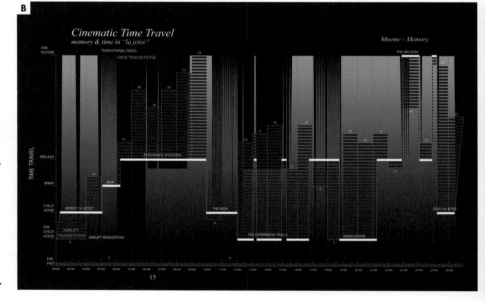

C

NETWORK OF INTERACTIONS

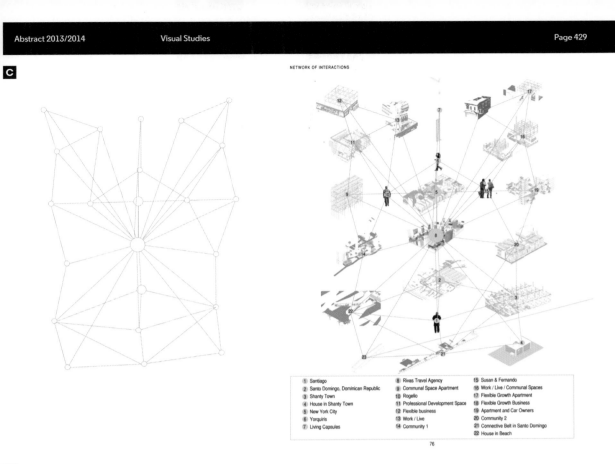

1 Santiago	8 Rivas Travel Agency	15 Susan & Fernando
2 Santo Domingo, Dominican Republic	9 Communal Space Apartment	16 Work / Live / Communal Spaces
3 Shanty Town	10 Rogelio	17 Flexible Growth Apartment
4 House in Shanty Town	11 Professional Development Space	18 Flexible Growth Business
5 New York City	12 Flexible business	19 Apartment and Car Owners
6 Yorquiris	13 Work / Live	20 Community 2
7 Living Capsules	14 Community 1	21 Connective Belt in Santo Domingo
		22 House in Beach

76

D Regional Route

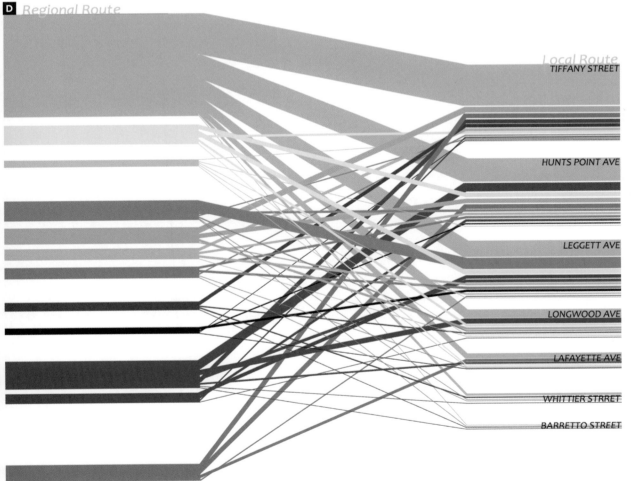

Local Route
TIFFANY STREET

HUNTS POINT AVE

LEGGETT AVE

LONGWOOD AVE

LAFAYETTE AVE

WHITTIER STRRET

BARRETTO STREET

Search: Advanced Algorithmic Design
Visual Studies
Fall 2013 + Spring 2014
Mark Collins + Toru Hasegawa, instructors

Architects work with computers every day but rarely achieve a true synthesis of machine automation and human design thinking. This workshop promoted simple, visual programming as a vehicle for designers to take their ideas to the next level. We achieved this by collaborating with the computer at its most potent level: code.

Design computation encompasses a broad range of approaches and techniques. Using object oriented programming and Processing – an open source programming environment – as a starting point, the seminar explored the practice and promise of these new means of design conception through a process of experiment, play and re–wiring. The results of the class were visualizations that revealed hidden algorithmic logic at work inside each code. Object-oriented programming was a crucial part of the seminar's approach to algorithms by providing a rich, flexible language to model complex systems and visualize their outcomes.

The seminar promoted the notion that design through computation is necessarily a search process. Generative computing brings with it entirely new ways of solving problems, new modes of expression and new challenges in managing the torrent of design information that one can generate. The seminar introduced key terms and concepts that addressed issues, such as design solution space, emergence and artificial life, to critically assess our role as both actors and objects in this new reality.

Arkadiusz Piegdon **A**
Filippos Filippidis +
Hamid Reza Malhooz **B**
Shalini Amin **C**
Zhen Dong + Bian Lin **D**

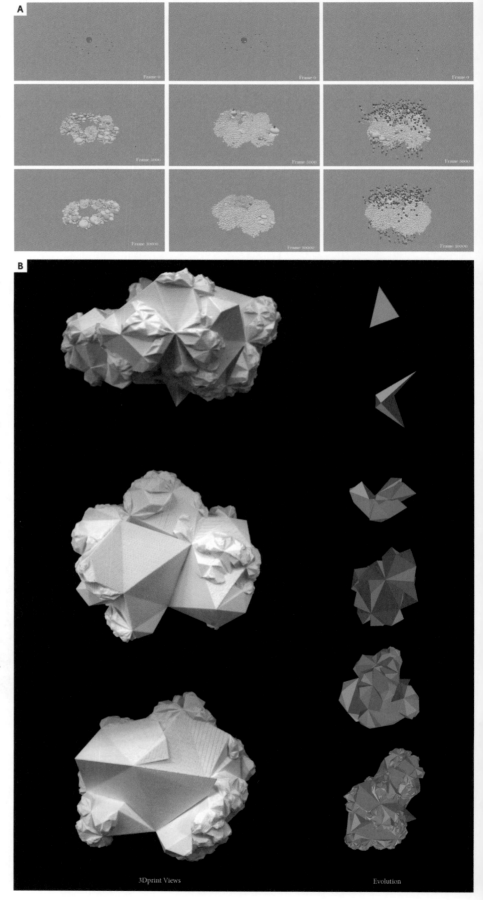

3Dprint Views   Evolution

C

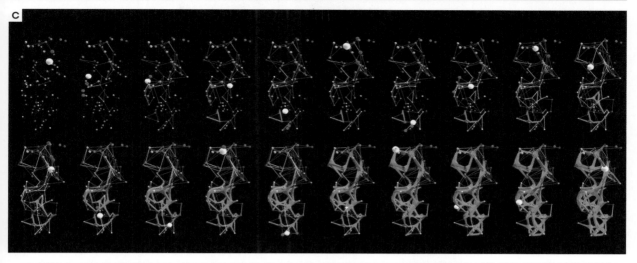

D

Appitecture
Visual Studies
Spring 2014
*Toru Hasegawa +
Mark Collins, instructors*

Mobile phones, in particular the current generation of smart phones, are an expansive platform for spatial computation. Taking on the role of software developer, the architect is well poised to deliver compelling experiences that build strong connections between information and space. Space can be mapped, tagged, generated, shared and experienced through the device's considerable sensing and processing capabilities. The platform enables us to design experiences that are simultaneously embedded in real and virtual worlds. The goal of this seminar was for each student to develop a "spatial app" – a loose description to incubate architectural thinking across mobile devices.

Melodie Yashar A
William Bodell +
Filippos Filippidis B
Yi Wu C

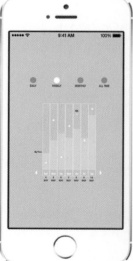

Beyond Prototype
Visual Studies
Spring 2014
Jason Ivaliotis, instructor

The relationship between the components of structure and the components of enclosure is conventionally considered to be mutually exclusive. However, in an environment where material efficiency and speed of fabrication is becoming increasingly important, there exists an opportunity for the architect to intervene within the fabrication process to assimilate both structure and envelope into one hybridized system that abolishes exclusivity and attains a higher level of efficiency. This course encouraged and enabled students to use digital software as a generative tool and the laser cutter, CNC Mill, plastic bender and welder as a means to bring virtual systems into the physical realm. Emphasis was placed on using the digital fabrication machines to extract forms from conventional, flat sheet stock that was transformed using cutting, bending and folded manipulation in order to create a topological network of elements: a homogenous, self supporting mesh. Students operated across multiple platforms to devise a completely automated design and fabrication process. The research objectives of this course encouraged students to devise functional design applications, establish contextual relevance for their component systems and propose realistic fabrication scenarios based on quantifiable material and mechanical constraints. Components were extracted from the digital realm, built at full scale, tested and reevaluated, effectively taking us beyond prototype.

Lines Not Splines: Drawing is Invention
Visual Studies
Fall 2013 + Spring 2014
Christoph A. Kumpusch, instructor

Drawing is not the form; it is the way of seeing the form. Degas

To draw does not simply mean to reproduce contours; the drawing does not simply consist in the idea: the drawing is even the expression, the interior form, the plan, the model. Look what remains after that! Ingres

This intensive workshop–formatted course was rooted in three propositions: that drawing is as much a way of seeing as it is a means of representation, that drawing is not bound to digital versus analog categorizations and that drawing remains the primary vehicle to record, communicate and create architecture.

We reviewed the "Top Twenty Great Architectural Drawings," as a series of case studies linked to a film project on the drawing process. We attempted drawings of one line and drawings of 1,000 lines in the same spans of time. We drew what we see, what we cannot see, what we want and what we wish we could achieve. The word "rendering" had no place in this seminar.

Students surrendered their typical drawing habits in favor of a rigorous drawing routine, which challenged notions of style, assumptions about "start" and "finish" and ideas about surface, shadow and scale. Diverse media were deployed; subjects included studio work, urban fragments, body parts and inward visions. Students left the course with sore hands, bright minds and a thick portfolio of new work.

Metatool
Visual Studies
Spring 2014
Dan Taeyoung, instructor

Metatool was a course about creating experimental design tools by utilizing Grasshopper as a software environment and meta-tool: a tool that enables the creation of other tools.

The course was grounded in a solid technical understanding of Grasshopper and hovered around a set of critical history and theory texts as well as group discussions. Each new experimental tool resulted from an examination of an existing design tool and was oriented towards the creation of a new design process within Grasshopper.

The custom created Grasshopper component Hairworm was used in conjunction with Github, a cloud-based platform for sharing code. The course was the starting seed for the Grasshopper Exchange, a new online-based tool arsenal. Over the duration of the course, students collectively amassed this shared database or 'arsenal' of new Grasshopper-based tools into a suite of experimental design processes that could enable and augment new, experimental design possibilities.

Integrated Parametric Delivery
Visual Studies
Fall 2013 + Spring 2014
John Lee, Brian Lee + Mark Green, instructors, with Tian Hui

Emerging technologies in architectural design find their own time and place to be implemented. Too often the tool controls the design. When utilized effectively, advanced parametric design methodologies will facilitate numerous iterations, enabling a more resolved final product in a time-restricted setting. Designers often favor one tool over another, mainly out of familiarity. This workshop insisted on interoperability between various platforms, magnifying the strengths of each tool. We investigated the process of integrating multiple parametric tools simultaneously into a single architectural project.

Myung Jae Lee + Sukwon Lee **A**
Pei Chia Hsu, Tanya Lucia Griffiths + Pari Agarwal **B**
Yao Xu, Ruoyu Wei + Wen Wu **C**
Young Won Chi, So Yae Beak + Ji Eun Lim **D**

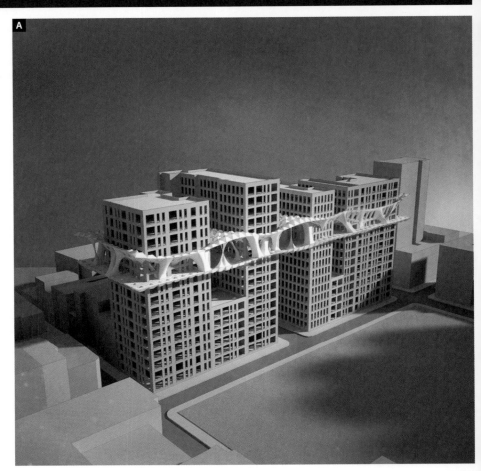

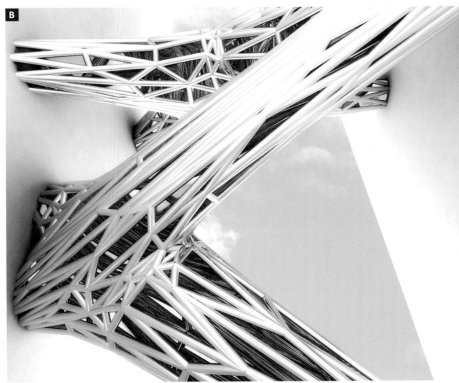

C

PANEL 748
Rotation Angle = 24
Diagonal = 7.07'

PANEL 792
Rotation Angle = 60
Diagonal = 8.49'

PANEL 831
Rotation Angle = 60
Diagonal = 8.49'

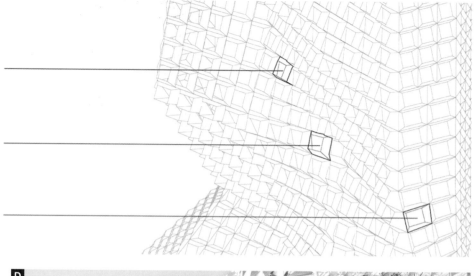

D

View from main street

Re–Thinking BIM
Visual Studies
Fall 2013 + Spring 2014
John Lee, Brian Lee +
Mark Green, instructors

What is the place of BIM in architecture? Is it only meant for production, or can architectural design benefit from the real time feedback of Building Information Models? BIM can, and will, change the profession; this generation is responsible for how that will happen. Without the constraint of professional demands, students in this course were able to explore BIM strategies, which in the workplace would not be possible. These virtual buildings require that architects be extensively aware of all aspects of design. The intention of this workshop was to develop a thorough understanding of BIM, most importantly how we could intervene in the BIM process not to let it be strictly about efficiency, but instead utilize its capabilities as opportunities for design. How is the time, gained from these tools, re-appropriated? How can the concepts of parametric modeling infiltrate, magnify and redefine the design process? Using software that forces rigor, can we learn from it and re-apply their logic to other aspects of what we do?

Often out of familiarity, architects favor one design medium over another. This workshop insisted on interoperability between various platforms, magnifying the strengths of each tool. We investigated the process of integrating multiple parametric platforms simultaneously into a single architectural project. Students used Autodesk Revit, Autodesk Vasari, 3DS Max, Rhinoceros and associated plugins to create a parametric architectural system with embedded variability. A direct relationship with Autodesk was established, which allowed for an exchange with the software developer.

Bryan Kim, Cheolho Kim + Jaeyoung Park **A**
Chih-I Lai, Kuan-Yi Ho + Zhengda Hou **B**
Minjin Kim, Junhee Cho + Monica Rhee **C**
Seri Hieatt, David Hui + Elizabeth Labra **D**

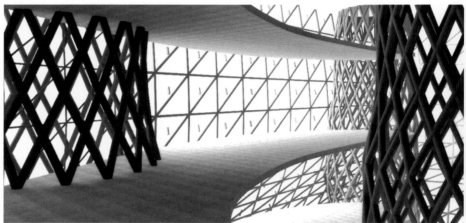

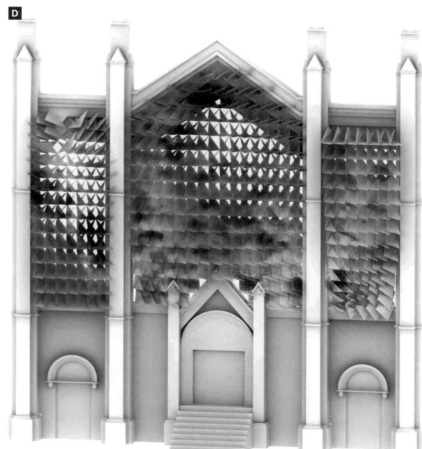

Hacking the Urban Experience
Visual Studies
Fall 2013 + Spring 2014
John H. Locke, instructor

This course sought to assert the relevance of the fabrication skills at our disposal as potentialities for social and environmental relevance. Through the re-appropriation and re-imagining of existing urban conditions, the students designed and fabricated a working prototype that embraced the messy reality of our city and promoted community involvement. The students pushed the notion that learning occurs through making, doing and interactivity, while giving primary focus to the designing of experiences in lieu of objects. At the conclusion of the course the students produced a full-scale urban intervention and observed and documented their relevant successes or failures.

Material workshops were held to encourage students to explore constructions from inflatables to parametric agglomerations using quotidian materials. Ultimately, the student came out of the course with a healthy respect for two core concepts: firstly, an increased skill in the use and applicability of the building skills we developed for solving design issues using unorthodox materials in unconventional settings; and secondly, that there is an opportunity for architects to regain lost relevance by inserting themselves through unsolicited proposals into the public consciousness as stewards of urban well being.

John Lee, Jack Tao +
Sonia Turk **A**
Kelly Neill, Claire Bian, Jesse McCormick, Richard South +
Stephan Van Eeden **B**
Michael Schissel, Kelly Neill + Jack Tao **C**
Yong He, Yu-Hsuan Lin, Taylor Miller + Jack Schonewolf **D**

Drawing after the Computer
Visual Studies
Spring 2014
Babak Bryan, instructor

Starting with a virtual model, this half-course explored the act of drawing as more than an act of extraction/reduction/excision. Embedded within the desires of the act of drawing is an attitude towards exploration/explanation/valuation. Specifically, through a series of explorations, the students interrogated the artifact of the virtual model in drawn form to question and explore the value of a trace. A record of progress/iteration/evolution of design principles was documented and codified. In the end, an assessment of the value of this production was made and the ultimate necessity for this form of representation was fundamentally critiqued, or at least a speculation towards it was framed.

In the six-week course, students were asked to prepare at least four iterations of an existing design. Weekly meetings included a brief presentation of a particular aspect of drawing followed by an open discussion of sharing the iterative progress of the work. The attitude within the course was that of a laboratory, in which experimentation and new thinking were encouraged. In the end a final presentation was made speculating on the benefits of their findings.

Modeling after the Computer
Visual Studies
Spring 2014
Babak Bryan, instructor

Though the distinction between a model and a drawing has never been more blurred, the primary purpose for creating each mostly remains distinct. Models are seen as physical representations of a final construction and drawings as the coding that enable these constructs to be made. This section attempted to further exploit the contemporary blur between these forms of representation while still valuing the coding and evaluating benefits found primarily in drawings. Specifically, this course explored a hybrid form of physical drawing, through which physical principles were explored and tested.

Through a series of weekly explorations, the students produced a model/drawing that either examined underlying principles of construction, or better represented the complete spatial qualities of how a space is used/occupied/experienced that could not readily be made in a 2D medium. While digital fabrication techniques such as CNC-fabrication, thermojet printing or laser cutting were permitted, manual methods of construction were equally valid. In either case the goal was to explore the process of making the physical rather than just simply exporting final forms.

The students prepared at least three iterations of an existing design. Weekly meetings began with a brief presentation of a particular aspect of modeling followed by an open discussion sharing the iterative progress of the work. The attitude within the course was that of a laboratory where experimentation and new thinking were encouraged.

Adaptive Formulations 1
Visual Studies
Fall 2013 + Spring 2014
Adam Modesitt, instructor

Computer aided design has enabled designers to easily generate and visualize complex shapes and systems. Double curved surfaces (eg. blobs) and other complex geometries have been associated with computer-aided architectural design since its inception two decades ago. However, while such forms are now common in architectural practice, there is still a disconnect between the ease of generating computer-assisted 3D models and the complexity of construction. Computer generated-geometry still generally consists of idealized mathematical surfaces that have no relation to the process of building fabrication.

In the past decade, and increasingly over the past several years, computer software and hardware has begun to enable architects to model some of the complexity inherent in the fabrication of irregular architectural forms. Computers have not yet radically changed the process of construction, but rather they enable architects and engineers to intelligently manage the complexities and limitations of architectural fabrication.

This course explored the use of CATIA and parametric modeling as an architectural design tool. We examined what it means for architectural design to manage and control large data sets, complex geometries and systems. We explored questions about the limits of computer modeling in scale, material and resolution.

Adaptive Formulations 2
Visual Studies
Fall 2013 + Spring 2014
Adam Modesitt, instructor

Researchers in fields like Biomimetics and Systems Engineering discovered relationships embedded within complex systems of seemingly unrelated components or, in the case of natural systems, plant and animal life. These relationships can be shown to enhance the whole, perhaps improving the resiliency of the system to changing conditions or reducing waste of limited resources. Another common theme in complex systems, particularly natural systems, is adaptive growth. Research aimed at modeling natural systems resurged in the 1980's with 'genetic algorithm' optimization techniques showing promise.

How do we build a system to adapt? What does it adapt to? This workshop investigated the formulation of an adaptive system based on optimization methodologies. The notion of optimality–generally understood to be a singular, mathematical minimum–was reconsidered as a catalyst for design. A rigorous definition of optimization was applied, translating a 'generalized design model' into a 'performance design model.' Students used parametric formulations to develop relationships and dependencies between design elements in a 3D modeling environment.

The workshop covered fundamental principles of structural design, parametric formulation and optimization theory. Students used finite element analysis (FEA) software for structural analysis and testing, Microsoft Excel and optimization software to conduct optimization studies.

Datamining the City 1 + 2
Visual Studies
Fall 2013
Danil Nagy, instructor

This seminar focused on developing strategies for data mining large datasets from the web and processing them spatially to derive new knowledge about the city. Lectures provided students with a theoretical and historical basis for this kind of research, as well as training in the specific tools that were used. Techniques explored in the class included coding of custom web-scraping applications for gathering data from the web, GIS-based tools for spatial analysis and online interactive mapping and visualization. The primary tools for the class were Python and QGIS, but several other free and open source tools were also presented.

To fulfill the requirements of the class, students worked in groups to produce original research projects exploring a chosen urban issue. After selecting an issue, each group identified an online data source they wished to use, created custom scripts to collect, organize and analyze this data, spatially analyzed the data within a GIS and used their data and analysis to create provocative visualizations that made some conclusion about their chosen issue. The projects of the Fall 2013 semester focused mainly on the Pearl River Delta and culminated in an exhibition at the Shenzhen/Hong Kong Bi-city Biennale that opened in December 2013.

Daniela Jacome,
Alexander Ehlers Rosenthal +
Yimeng Sun **A**
Meagan Aaron, Chieh Chih
Chiang + Zhengda Hou **B/C**
Xin Fu, Jean Qin Gu +
Fan Guo **D**

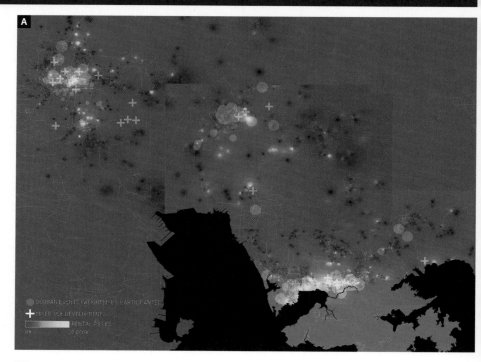

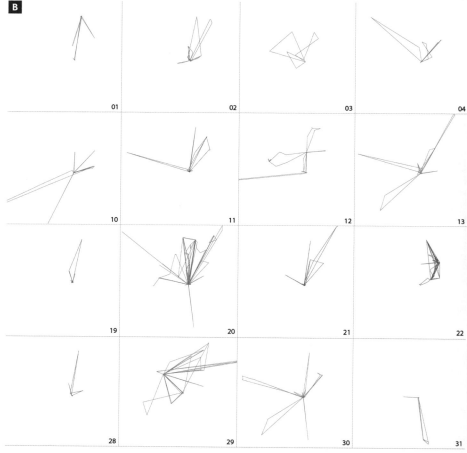

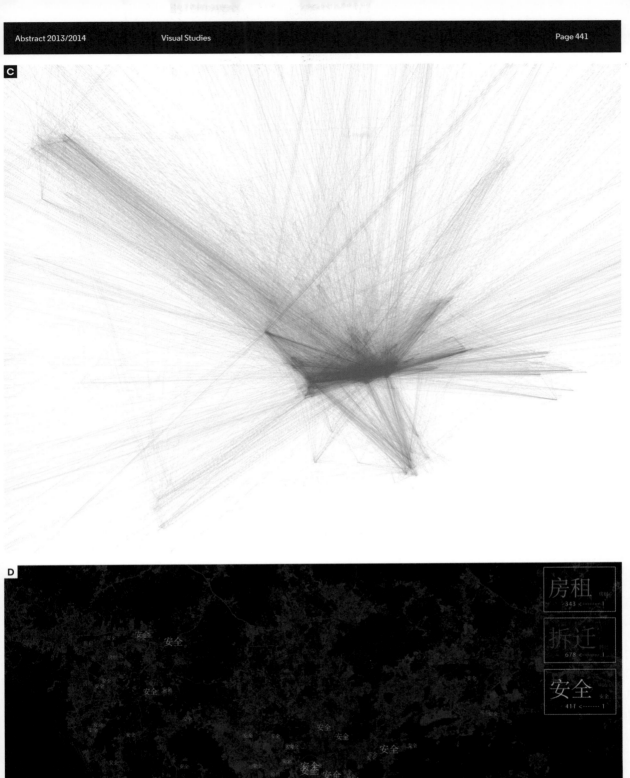

Intelligent Systems /
Interactive Architecture
Visual Studies
Fall 2013
Andrew O. Payne, instructor

This class focused on hardware and software prototyping techniques; primarily focusing on a wide range of sensing and actuation modalities in order to build novel, interactive, architectural prototypes. Through a series of fast-paced lectures and technical workshops, students were exposed to topics relevant to this domain including: microcontrollers and programming, sensor technologies for interactive environments, mechanism design, robotics and motor control, fabrication methodologies, parametric design, computer vision and signal analysis and interactive prototyping techniques. Using remote sensors, microcontrollers and actuators, students were asked to build virtual and physical prototypes that were able to intelligently respond to one or more dynamic pressures found within Avery Hall. The teams were asked to focus on the concept of prototyping– both digitally and physically–as a means to explore intelligent control strategies, material affects and the parameters that effect dynamic systems.

Minjin Kim, Junhee Cho,
Filippos Filippidis +
Hamid Reza Malhooz A
Mondrian Hsieh +
Bika Rebek B/C
Sareeta Patel + Kelly Neill D

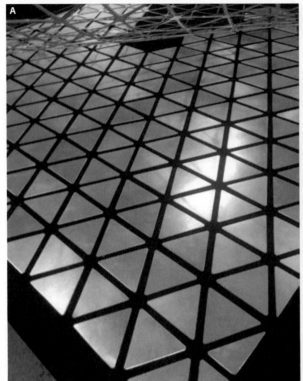

C

D

Site to Site – Site to Web + Web to Site
Visual Studies
Fall 2013
Troy Conrad Therrien +
Chris Barley, instructors

Architecture is online. Recent achievements in ubiquitous computing, machine intelligence, deep learning, ambient locative media, mobile and embedded devices, machine to machine systems and other forms of the "Internet of Things", coupled with the proliferation of cheap networked sensors and actuators has brought us to a moment in which architects no longer have the comfort of speaking of connected environments in the future tense. The technologies for connecting and orchestrating physical spaces digitally are not simply accessible, they are pedestrian, yet have not fully penetrated either the architectural imaginary or the space of architecture production. This course aimed to do both simultaneously.

In Session A, students designd and built the furniture, climate control, lighting and display systems, surfaces and other objects to address one or more segments of the above programmatic spectrum of OfficeUS. Powered by a $35 Raspberry Pi mini–computer running Node.js on the Linux operating system, these objects produced and consumed digital information, collecting information about and producing effects in their environment. Students also designed the technical protocols and representation systems for tapping into these inputs and outputs.

In Session B, students focused on developing applications on top of the platform, parts of which were distributed to locations around the Studio–X global network. Students studied these physical spaces and designed a strategy for the deployment and installation of the objects of the platform. That is, students redesigned these spaces using our platform. They had access to the entire network of distributed objects to design and implement applications that affect the way in which these spaces

are used and, consequently, the forms of architecture production these spaces support.

The course was highly collaborative, as the following students all worked collectively on the projects throughout the semester: Christina Badal, Maria Drozdov, Kirk Finkel, Allen Ghaida, Yong He, Wei Huang, Dina Mahmoud, James Quick, Katherine Samuels, Leo Shaw, James Stoddart, Ebberly Strathairn, Yifeng Wu + You Zhou.

Site to Site **A/B/C/D/E**

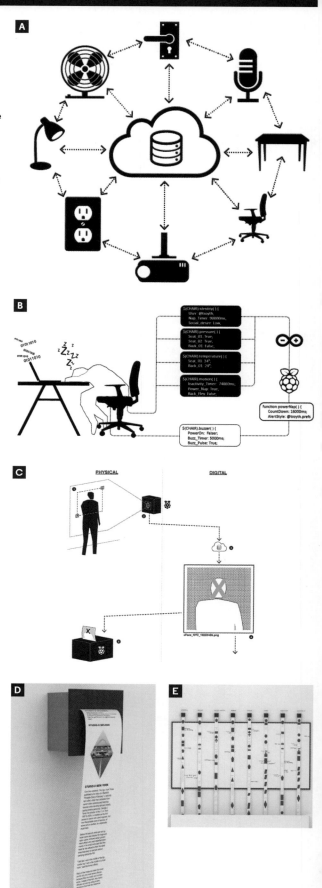

Other Design Seminar
Visual Studies
Fall 2013 + Spring 2014
Michael Rock + Oana Stanescu, instructors

In this seminar we considered the challenges of multiple screen experiences focusing specifically on the design and narrative possibilities of a mobile theater designed for moving image and sound. We researched the history of the multi–screen theater and the artistic, financial, technical and design constraints that might shape possible outcomes. The class consisted of readings, class discussion, research presentations and a concept design presentation. We also worked directly with artists, producers and promoters to better understand the programmatic needs.

The Topological Study of Form
Visual Studies
Fall 2013 + Spring 2014
José Sánchez, instructor

Architectural form has traditionally been implemented neglecting the mathematical underlay of post-Euclidean geometry. With the advent of advanced time-based computer modeling techniques, architects are able to embed quantifiable data into the architectural design process. Using the inherent dynamics of the architectural program, we can generate traditional diagrams. Since these diagrams carry the ever-changing programmatic behavior of a building, generative geometry derived from programmatic connections allow designers to create unique geometrical formations. Based on this approach to design, this course studied morphology using the time-based mathematical models inherent in modern software-based digital tools.

Simulation as the Origin of Tangible Form
Visual Studies
Fall 2013 + Spring 2014
José Sánchez, instructor

This workshop focused on generating visual constructs dealing with the notion of simulation and representation. We undertook simulation as the origin of a reality, not as a representation of a formal construct, which can deal with the generation of behavioral models and abstract events without a tactile origin, hence avoiding representing an environment or event. The simulation spawned sequential representation of unknown events that progressively yielded the generation of a tangible fabric.

Cinematic Communication
Visual Studies
Fall 2013 + Spring 2014
John Szot, instructor

This workshop focused on digital video as a tool for dissecting and reinventing the physical environment. It was designed to introduce students to the architectural potential within the advanced features of Adobe Premiere and basic functions of Adobe After Effects. Presentations and discussions throughout the workshop were organized around two brief assignments that covered advanced pre–production techniques, advanced motion graphics and basic compositing techniques.

Students prepared short films to fulfill assignment requirements after receiving technical and theoretical instruction on various aspects of video production. Sessions alternated between the presentation of technical material in the form of workshops and screenings of student work side–by–side with class discussion of concepts related to the class topic.

The semester was divided evenly between two assignments. Daily sessions included technical presentations on the basic functions of each software package as applicable to the current assignment and group discussion in which completed assignments were critically analyzed and evaluated.

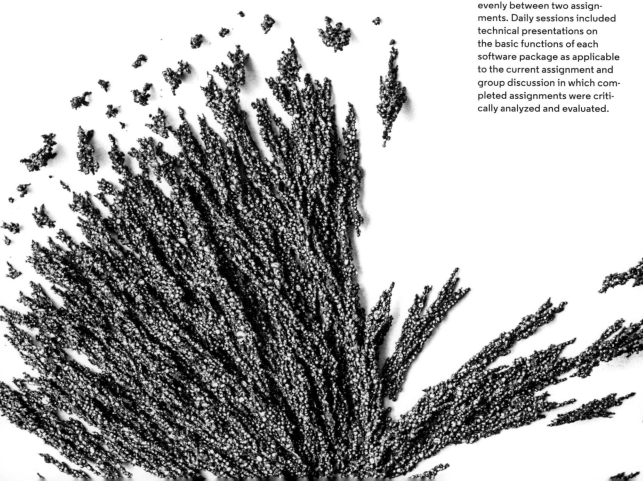

Drawing with Data
Visual Studies
Summer 2013
Joshua Uhl, instructor

Computing in architecture has changed methods of representation, retooled construction techniques and made communication of complex information instantaneous. In this state of ubiquitous computing, the architect is asked to not only grasp these new technologies but to shape them into the built environment. As the edge between the virtual and real become increasingly thin, the architect must not only be proficient in this interactivity, but also tool it toward new ideas and potentials that are rife within this expanding territory.

Drawing With Data investigated the concepts, techniques and working methods of computer aided 'drawing' in architecture. Students studied the operative relationship between 2D and 3D data, exploring the reaches of their analytic and representational potential. While the class was a foundational course in architectural computing, it built on the student's advanced ability to question, shape and interrogate space and time.

The full-semester course focused on a project that was generated primarily with the use of Rhinoceros and 3dsMax. After the initial development of a virtual model, we investigated tools to further the analytic and representational capacity of the data within the model. Studies took place in the form of drawings, physical models, images and animations. There was one assignment with 4 milestones. As a companion to the course lectures, the class held weekly Tutorial Sessions.

Mintra Maneepairoj **A/B**
Theodora Felekou **C/D**

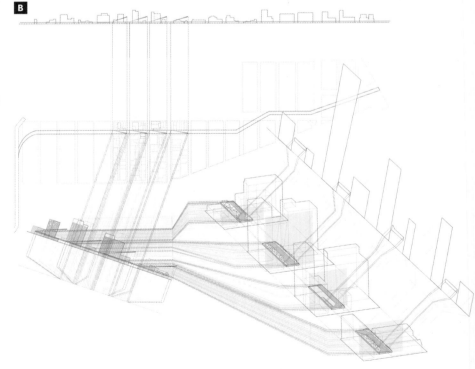

C

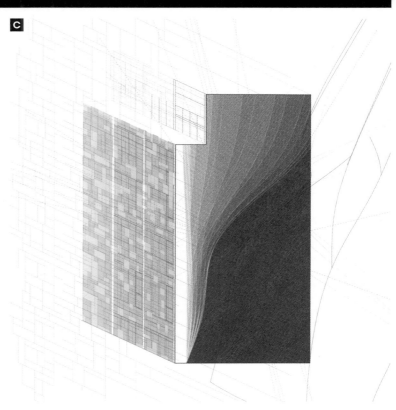

D

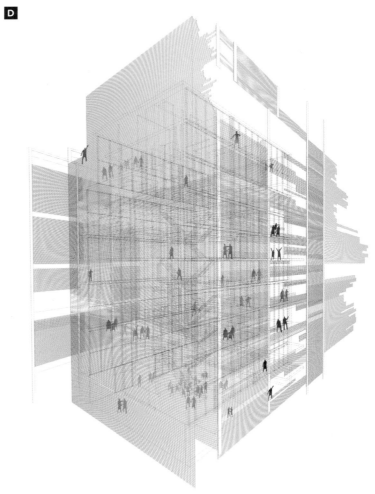

X-Information Modeling
Visual Studies
Fall 2013
Luc Wilson, instructor

This course examined the maturity of the twenty-first century metropolis by moving past conventional benchmarks and preconceptions of growth to develop flexible design systems. These systems are founded on a holistic approach to economic, environmental and social problems that allowed for speculation on possible futures for the city. Using this methodology termed X-Information Modeling or XIM, students leveraged parametric design tools to create systems that strategically integrated diverse objectives and, through Grasshopper for Rhino, visualized potential scenarios for a more informed decision making process.

Students created custom evaluation tools using Grasshopper for Rhino to investigate one of two questions in the context of Midtown Manhattan: is it possible to measure the experience of public space, and is there a sustainable density? Session A was research oriented with students looking at zoning, real estate value and the environment to understand the competing objects of the design and development process. Through this process students were asked to create new drawing types that effectively communicated the intent of their parametric design systems for evaluation and critique.

Session B was design oriented with students focused on creating unique parametric massings to continue investigations of Session A. Galapagos, a single objective optimizer in Grasshopper, was used to test thousands of parametric massing iterations, with students evaluating the results using the custom evaluation tool from Session A.

Christopher James Botham + Sangyoon Kim **A**
Diego Rodriguez + Vahe Markosian **B**
Juan Pablo Azares, Eileen Chen, Jim Stoddart + Ray Wang **c**

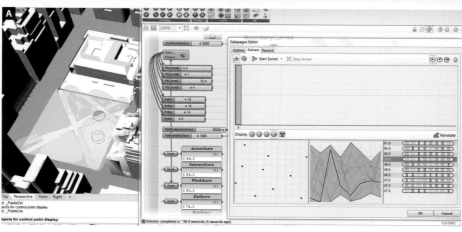

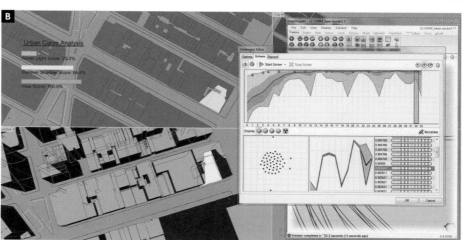

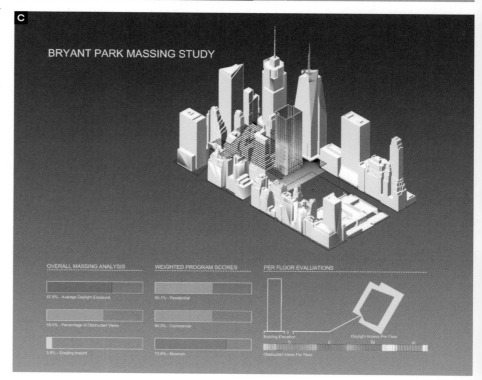

A
MILETUS

CHICAGO / BARCELONA

MANHATTAN

SALT LAKE CITY / PUDONG

BEIJING

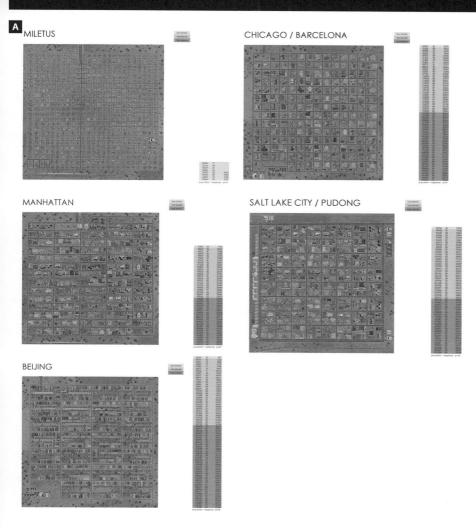

**Algorithms + Urbanisms:
SimCity**
Visual Studies
Spring 2014
Luc Wilson, instructor

This course investigated the range of algorithms, metrics and benchmarks increasingly used today for tracking the performance of cities using SimCity as the framework for experimentation. Students used the metrics available in SimCity to evaluate historic, ideal and contemporary cities and then developed additional evaluation criteria--both quantitative and qualitative--lacking in SimCity but critical for understanding the performance of cities. Through this process, we discussed the underlying assumptions and algorithms of SimCity and the influence on general understanding of the design of cities. This course pushed students to understand, hybridize and eventually develop their own urban design theories and evaluation tools through imaginative elaborations on the game SimCity. To start each student was assigned a historic or ideal city--such as 1850's Paris or Broadacre City--and a contemporary city--Hong Kong or Laguna West, California--to analyze and evaluate using SimCity. Next, students identified elements from the historic, ideal and contemporary cities and hybridized them in SimCity based on the collected. Finally, based on the hybridization, students developed their own urban design proposals using SimCity to iterate, test and experiment.

Qiancheng Ma **A**
He Sang **B**

B

Designing Interactive Narrative through Data Visualization
Visual Studies
Spring 2014
Annelie Berner, instructor

Our world is brimming with data and always has been. Now, more than ever, we have the ability to record and access massive amounts of information and free tools to work with those records. In this course, we delved into why a set of data requires depiction, researched how to uncover the story within a data set and strived to integrate our visualization with its narrative. We explored both the simplest method to represent a set of data, as well as how to draw out and represent the specific character of that dataset. We discussed various methods of representing data and learned to design interactive data visualization on the web. We worked with data using the d3/javascript framework and understood its integration with HTML and CSS. Students were also introduced to physical and audial data representation and encouraged to pursue final projects in these areas of output as well as web-based output.

The course had two main goals: to provide grounding in the design of elegant and meaningful data visualizations and to provide a technical introduction to implementing data visualizations using D3 and web technologies.

Future Craft: Radical Sustainability in Product + Ventures
Visual Studies
Spring 2014
Amanda Parkes + Leonardo Bonanni, instructors

From sweatshop fires to superstorms, society is coming to terms with the reality that business-as-usual is unsustainable–socially, economically and environmentally. A new generation of goods and services is emerging to address humanity's needs as they continue to grow. Future Craft looked at new ways of making things, from the way materials are sourced and manufactured to the way customers are considered. We were interested in re-configuring industry, its systems and services. This class looked at ways to reshape business, technology and design to create new, radically sustainable products and companies.

In the first half of the semester, students learned the latest methodologies for evaluating environmental, social and financial impact. The second half of the semester was a proposal and prototyping session, during which students prepared fleshed out proposals for production or companies.

Special Topics in Fabrication: Design Machine + Field Fabrications
Visual Studies
Fall 2013 + Spring 2014
Josh Draper + Eric Hagan, instructors

Digital Fabrication has revitalized the idea of the Architect as Maker. While new software and workflows have made digital fabrication accessible, its potential to intervene in practice is only fully realized at the level of the CNC machine. What might become possible if Architects designed and built their own machines? Agendas involving material, performance and computation could be embedded instead of inherited. New architectures could become possible if control extends to this foundational level.

Formworks combined casting with computational techniques through the production of a Design Machine – an original and specific CNC machine. Using the Firefly plug–in for Grasshopper, the Arduino microcontroller and servo devices such as stepper motors and linear actuators, students made their own CNC machine from the ground up to produce a system of non–repetitive castings.

Formworks was staged in two sessions over the semester. The first session, Design Machine, introduced students to mechatronics techniques using Firefly, Arduino and two basic servo devices – stepper motors and linear actuators. Students made a prototype servo device, which formed the basis of a larger system, to mechanically and computationally demonstrate a system of non–repetitive but parametrically related castings. In parallel, students were introduced to various casting techniques. The second session, Field Fabrications, iterated the prototypes, producing a larger array of robust servo devices. Full castings were made using the system. The course focused on pre–cast curtain walls to maximize the graphic qualities of the process.

Biomaterials: Sustainable Fabrication + Living Forms
Visual Studies
Fall 2013
Amanda Parkes, instructor

Current fabrication methods for the development of materials are energy intensive in production and unsustainable in nature, often utilizing non–renewable fossil fuel resources for production and transportation necessities. New methods in growth and aggregation, which use living organisms in the production of materials, present possibilities for materials that can be immediately intertwined with natural cycles of waste and renewal.

This course investigated new materials and new creation processes for biomaterials, which present an alternate future for building that taps into the natural processes of living things for growth and fabrication. A biomaterial can be defined as a substance that has been engineered to take a form, alone or as part of a complex system, through control of interactions with components of living systems, encompassing elements of biology, chemistry, materials science and tissue engineering. We investigated concepts including mycelium bricking systems, 3D fabrication using live silk worms, solar 3D printing from sand and textiles grown from bacterial cellulose.

The course format was research focused with weekly hands on lab demonstrations and experiments. Students read and interpreted high level scientific papers, but from a designer's perspective. The course featured an all day field trip to Evocative, a manufacturer of mycelium bricking for architectural systems.

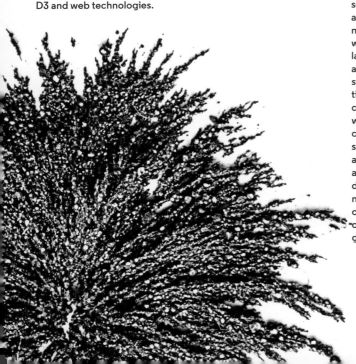

**Body Craft: Form,
Function + New Material**
Visual Studies
Fall 2013
Amanda Parkes, instructor

Human–centered design has
emerged as one of the tenets of
contemporary culture. Studies
in ergonomics have taught
designers to revere the form
and abilities of the body as the
standard for analysis in interaction. Yet, our notion of the body
is changing. New technologies
allow our bodies to become
enhanced, augmented,
expanded in functionality and
altered in form. Ubiquitous
and embedded technologies
allow the devices we carry
and the garments we wear to
converge into a 'secondary
skin' which functions as an
extension of ourselves creating our own mobile personal
environment. In addition to
this convergence, new tools for
creation are allowing designers to explore biomimickry in
their design process in more
transformative and temporal
ways. Blurring the line between
wearables and structures, this
course explored evolving issues
in 'universal design' and how
our changing concept of the
body alters how and what we
strive to design for ourselves.

The course mixed studio
design work with lectures,
readings, discussion and
critique. Through a combination of producing objects and
engaging in critical reflection,
students were encouraged
to develop a design practice,
which innovated technically
in process and materials.

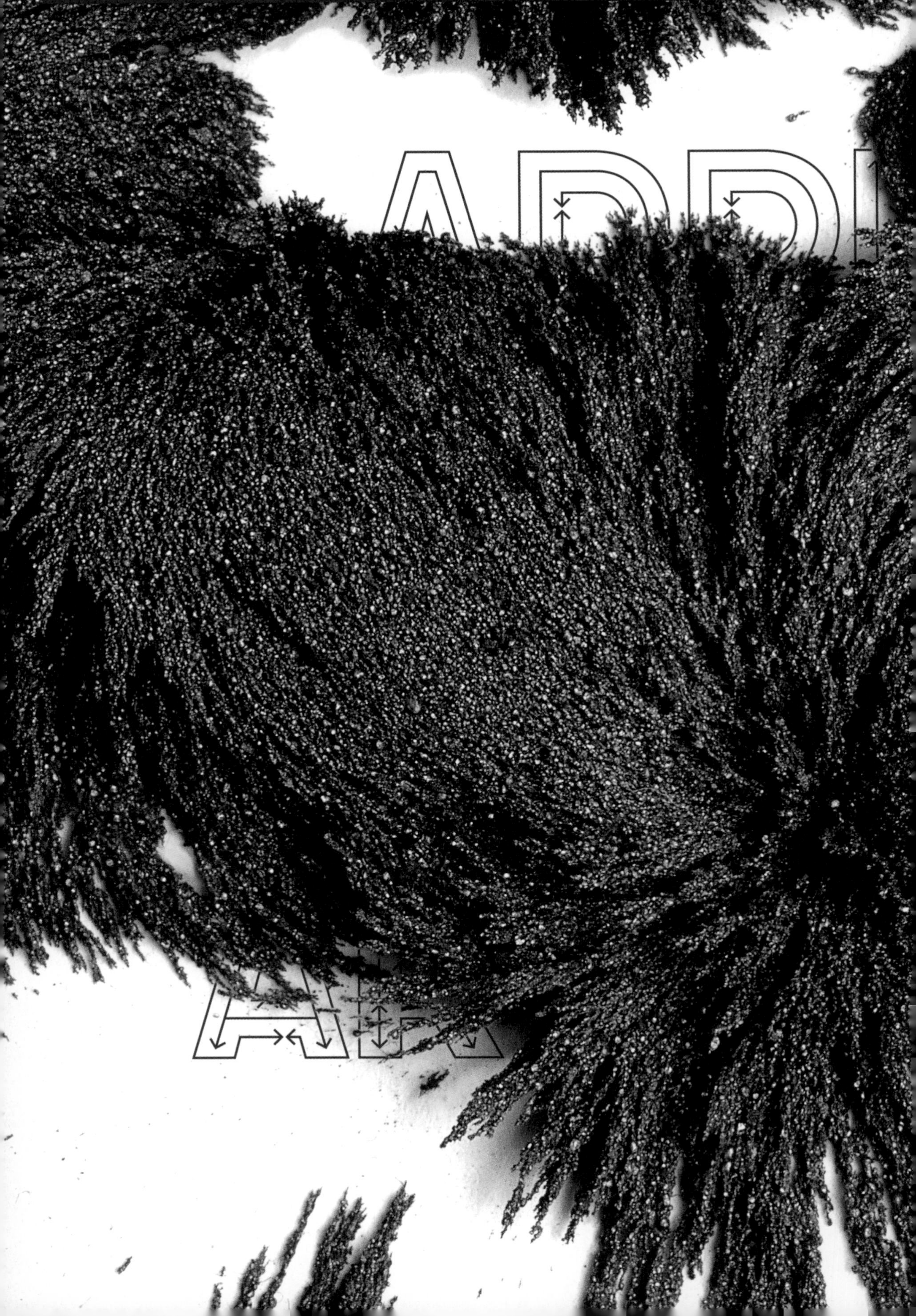

Applied Research Practices in Architecture
Janette Kim, *director*

To engage emerging global societies, climate change and increasingly complex notions of the public sphere, new graduates in architecture must be prepared to navigate a multi-disciplinary profession. Architects not only design, but also must develop new forms of expertise.

Applied architectural research produces rigorous and speculative interpretations of issues facing the built environment. Researchers expand upon techniques of the discipline and critically adopt methods from other disciplines. As an applied practice, research promises to engage contemporary actors, sites and techniques, combining experimentation with inquiry into researchers' ethical responsibility.

Applied Research Practices in Architecture, ARPA, supports students in the development of independent, applied research projects. The initiative, started in 2007 as Advanced Architectural Research, enables students to establish core ideas central to their future, independent practice. ARPA is dedicated to the idea that architectural practice can be driven not only by commissioned projects, but also through the initiation of original inquiry.

Translations from Drawing to Drawing

Diana Cristóbal +
Maria Esnaola
Janette Kim, advisor

Architects spend most of their time making representations of buildings, rather than constructing buildings themselves. Hence, we were interested in drawings as pedagogical instruments that are able to transmit – AND even modify – the argument and the physical reality of an object. This research did not aim to invent new methods of representation, but to re-understand the graphic imaginarium that architects have used up to today for the generation of concepts in the design process.

[1] We believe that representation in architecture is not neutral. The use of each method of representation implies a specific understanding of an object and, it could be argued, even an ideological stand. Therefore, we claim that we need to be in control of representation for the transmission and evolution of ideas. There is no consciousness in the way we represent today, and the proliferation of the hyperrealistic rendering is the clearest symptom of that. Representation is in crisis today.

[2] The way we represent has changed with the rise of the digital world. Today, the process of the digital image has become a complex process involving different agents and software. The drawing is constructed as a series of layers that are superimposed to an initial model built in a three-dimensional logic. As a result of this superimposition of information, the original object ends up disappearing. The layers erase the architecture behind.

Representation in architecture is a way of reformulating ideas. Through a drawing exercise this research aimed to explore the relationship between new architecture ideas and identifiable ways of drawing. To this end an as found object – a pre-existing architecture – was redrawn in order to discover what ideas each representation technique enhances. Each method induced the transformation of the object that is being represented in a particular manner.

Diana Cristobal + Maria Esnaoa A/B/C/D/E

C

D

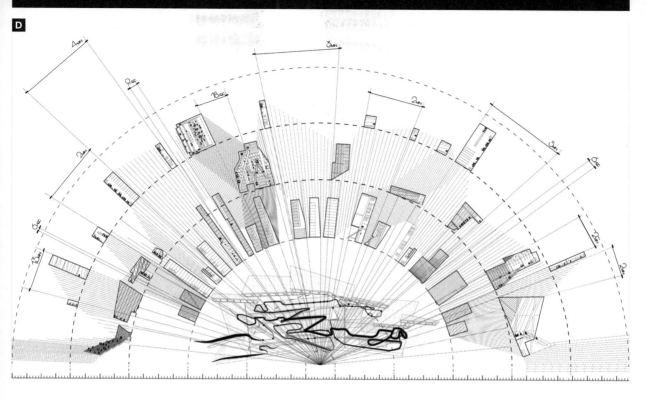

E

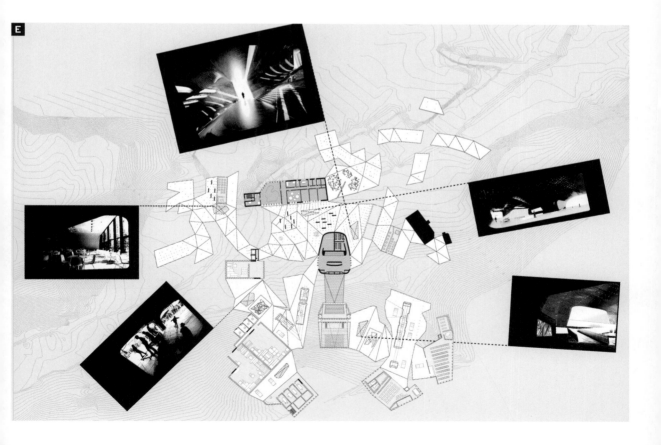

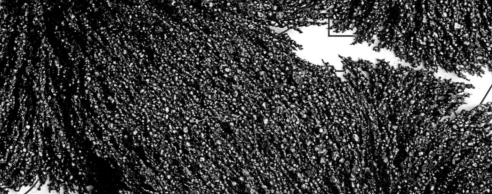
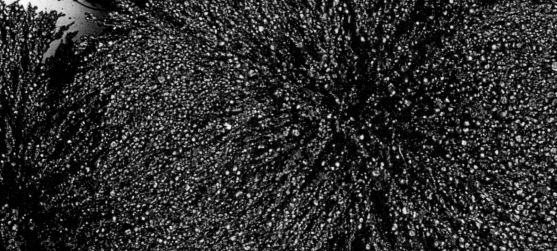

Architecture Ph.D. Program
Reinhold Martin, director

The Ph.D. program in architecture is oriented toward the training of scholars in the field of architectural history and theory. Its structure reflects a dual understanding of the scholar's role in the academy: as a teacher and as a researcher making an original contribution to the field, with an emphasis on expanding and reinterpreting disciplinary knowledge in a broad intellectual arena. Course requirements give entering students a solid foundation in historical knowledge and theoretical discourse, with sufficient flexibility to allow the initiation and pursuit of individual research agendas. The program's focus is on the history and theory of modern and contemporary architecture and urbanism in an international and cross-cultural context, from the mid-eighteenth century to the present. Within this, a wide range of research is supported through the expertise of the faculty and through strong relationships with other departments throughout the University and beyond.

Ph.D. Committee:
Barry Bergdoll
Vittoria Di Palma
Kenneth Frampton
Mary McLeod
Jorge Otero-Pailos
Felicity Scott
Mark Wigley
Mabel O. Wilson
Gwendolyn Wright

Architecture, Technocracy, Silence: Building Discourse in Franquista, Spain
Architecture Ph.D.
Program Thesis
Fall 2013 + Spring 2014
María González Pendas, candidate

This dissertation examines the emergence of a distinct form of architectural culture in Spain during the Franquista regime (1939-1975) and draws connections between the modernization of architecture and the ideological and institutional evolution of the dictatorship. Throughout its thirty six year span, the fascist Sate led by Francisco Franco transitioned from a military autarky to a technocratic state of sorts, all the while retaining the ultraconservative, Catholic and authoritarian values that were essential to its inception. Opus Dei cadres who came to control the governing and cultural apparatus of the regime led this particular process of reactionary modernization. This dissertation reveals ways in which buildings, architects and ideas about the built environment participated of this shifting scenario, arguing that the intersection of aesthetics and politics assumed the paradoxical discursive form of silence. If architects undermined the symbolic aspirations of their designs by means of abstraction and the formal and technical tropes proper to modernism, there was also a foreclosure of critical discourse and an emphasis on building as disciplinary domain. Through a series of analysis of buildings that remain silenced in the history of architecture—or emptied out of their ideological significance and that include the Tarragona Government Building and the National Pavilion for Expo'58—I make them speak of the politics of Franquismo, of the architecture culture they encompassed and of the ways in which silence was instrumental to both.

Modernity's Body, 1850-1930: The Architecture of Norm + Type in East Central Europe + German Africa
Architecture Ph.D.
Program Thesis
Fall 2013 + Spring 2014
Hollyamber Kennedy, candidate

At the 1930 World Energy Conference in Berlin, the architect Herman Sörgel unveiled his technological vision for Atlantropa—a new Mitteleuropa, a 'postnational' state represented by an infrastructural map that linked the 'arid' lands of Africa and the Middle East to the industrial centers of Central Europe. Under the banner of an 'efficient' hydroelectric colonialism, an expanded Germany would absorb the 'surplus populations' and raw materials of the African continent and the Middle East. For Sörgel, it was a matter of risk management: threatened by American capital to the west, and "the Yellow Menace" to the east, Atlantropa would draw its power along an extended north south span that stretched "from pole to pole," dissolving the Westphalian border system in a flood of synthetic light. It would be, Sörgel argued, a modern electrical deluge: "Instead of dividing walls: binding power lines! Only a common interlinking with a high-voltage network achieves a European Union." Drawing on the work of Phillip Sarasin and Roberto Esposito, I argue that Sörgel's map conceptualized the immunitary principle at the core of sovereign power—the problem of the conservatio vitae first expressed in Hobbesian legal theory—as an infrastructural practice. As such, Sörgel's presciently postcolonial 'world building' exercise stands as a key example of 'border discourse' central to the development of architectural modernism in Central and East Central Europe.

Exporting Zionism: Architectural Modernism in Israeli-African Technical Cooperation, 1958-1973
Architecture Ph.D.
Program Thesis
Fall 2013 + Spring 2014
Ayala Levin, candidate

This dissertation explores Israeli architectural and construction aid in the first decades of sub-Saharan African states independence. In the Cold War competition over development, Israel distinguished its aid by alleging a postcolonial status, similar geography and a shared history of racial oppression to alleviate fears of neocolonial infiltration. I critically examine how Israel presented itself as a model for rapid development more applicable to African states than the West, and how the architects involved negotiated their professional practice in relation to the Israeli Foreign Ministry agendas, the African commissioners' expectations and the international disciplinary discourse on modern architecture. While architectural modernism was promoted in the West as the International Style, Israeli architects translated it to the African context by imbuing it with nation-building qualities such as national cohesion, labor mobilization, skill acquisition and population dispersal. Based on their labor-Zionism settler-colonial experience, as well as criticisms of the mass construction undertaken in Israel in its first decade, the architects diverged from authoritarian "high modernism" to accommodate the needs of weak governments.

This research is supported by the International Dissertation Research Fellowship of the Social Science Research Council, and the Institute for Religion, Culture and Public Life at Columbia University.

Feminism in American Architecture, 1968-2000
Architecture Ph.D.
Program Thesis
Fall 2013 + Spring 2014
Andrea J. Merrett, candidate

My project – an examination of the impact of feminism on American architecture from the late 1960s through the 1990s – explored the ferment that shook architecture during these pivotal decades. Second-wave feminism emerged out of the turmoil of the late 1950s and early 1960s and was well established as a movement by the time women in architecture began organizing associations and conferences in the early 1970s. From early concerns about improving their numbers and status in the profession, feminist architects and architecture scholars expanded the knowledge of women's involvement in the built environment and challenged the boundaries of the discipline. The 1990s saw a proliferation of scholarship and academic conferences, which, reflecting a broader shift towards theory in architecture and feminism, took up gender and discourse analysis. Through careful archival work, supported by extensive interviews, I sought to uncover the history of the feminist movement in architecture and assess its present-day legacies.

**Savage Mind to Savage
Machine: Techniques +
Disciplines of Creativity,
1880-1985**
Architecture Ph.D.
Program Thesis
Fall 2013 + Spring 2014
Ginger Nolan, candidate

This project reexamined histories of modernist design by proposing to view them through a
theory of "semiotic apartheids,"
traces of which can first be de-
tected in early strains of European liberal political philosophy
and epistemology, eventu-
ally manifesting themselves
through the putative binary of
conscious versus unconscious
processes of production. In the
twentieth century, the categories of conscious and unconscious thought became pivotal
to formulating new semiotic
and aesthetic technologies,
such that a peculiar association
between technics and "savage
thought" came to underlie new
methods of artistic production
in Western Europe and the United States. This thesis argues
that class inequalities under
capitalism have been linked
to the ongoing formulation
of these two distinct—albeit
tacit—constructs of epistemic
subjectivity: one whose creative intellectual processes are
believed to constitute personal
property, and one whose creative intellectual processes—because these are deemed rote or
unconscious—are not regarded
as the property of those who
wield them. This is despite
the fact that the unconscious
psyche or, the "Savage Mind,"
was, at the same time, repeat-
edly invoked by modernist
designers in their efforts
to formulate creative technologies that tended towards
digital modes of production.

Architecture + Urban Design Program
Richard Plunz, director

Columbia's Architecture and Urban Design program exploits the pedagogical potential of the design studio as a form of design-based inquiry. To explore how the city is thought, projects are seen as critical instruments to focus on topics in contemporary urban design practice. All three studios emphasize a multi-scalar approach to the urban site –local, neighborhood, metropolitan, regional and global – and approach Urban Design as an inter-disciplinary practice that engages with and negotiates between different actors in the urban dynamic.

In general the curriculum is focused on the futures of cities that have come of age in the modern industrial era and now face the transition to new forms and meanings, in dialogue with new cities in development. Particular emphasis is placed on questions of urban infrastructure and urban ecology. A dialogue is woven between New York City and other world capitals with analogous contemporary conditions, moving between recent theoretical debate on future urbanism and applied projects that directly engage the realities of transformation of the post-industrial city. In this way, the program attempts to engage both the daily reality of our urban condition and the theoretical abstraction of current academic debate. Within this position, Urban Design is pursued as a critical re-assessment of conventional approaches relative to questions of site and program, infrastructure and form-mass, as they have come to be defined by Urban Design practice during this past century. The Urban Design curriculum is unique as a coherent pedagogic position on the role of architecture in the formation of a discourse on urbanism at this moment of post-industrial development and, indeed, of post-urban sensibility relative to the traditional Euro-American settlement norms.

By proposing an expanded architecturally-based teaching model for urban design, the program advocates working from the "ground up," rather than adopting "a top down" master-planning approach. It takes advantage of architecture's traditional concerns for site specificity, spatial experience, construction logics, economics of organization, morphology and physical form, while also engaging forms of knowledge associated with disciplines such as urban planning, urban ecology and landscape design. In this sense, the program is considered experimental, exploratory and unorthodox in comparison to the established canons of the traditional architectural design studio.

The sequencing of the studios is intended to build the linguistic substructure that is essential to urban design thought and practice. The use of language evolves from how representation of the urban site determines the quality of site knowledge – representation – to more specifically how discourse on the city determines interpretations of its past and projections of its futures – discourse – to the invention of the strategic languages of public engagement involving operational mechanisms for urban transformation at both the formal and programmatic levels – public synthesis. This sequence asserts that the grounding conditions of an urban design project – site and program – are complex mechanisms that must be actively and critically constructed rather than simply accepted as "givens" beyond a designer's control. While each Urban Design studio presents students with differing urban conditions and programming opportunities, all three semesters together reinforce the program's commitment to help individual designers to develop rigorous Urban Design tools and methods, to acquire a working language to communicate Urban Design ideas and to enhance the critical skills needed to test and refine urban design strategies.

**Urban Design Studio 1:
Transformative Urban Systems**
Architecture + Urban Design
Summer 2013
*Kaja Kühl, coordinator,
Earl Jackson, Tricia Martin,
Walter Meyer, Michael
Piper + Emily Weidenhof,
critics, with Kevin Lê*

The first urban design studio introduced students to an urban design process, where site and program were not a given, but were treated as principal variables of urban design thinking. Working in multiple scales as well as multiple time frames was an integral part of this investigation to design an intervention that followed a critical hypothesis for the future of the City.

The five boroughs of New York City are used as a laboratory for experimenting with this process that re-thinks, re-shapes and re-generates the city in the twenty-first century. Public space and public infrastructure were central concerns of this urban design studio. In the summer of 2013, the studio explored the role of the urban designer to envision resilient and resistant infrastructure that allow New Yorkers to face the challenges of future hazards without sacrificing the quality of life in the city. Following the destruction of Super-Storm Sandy, students developed proposals for five neighborhoods in New York City that were vulnerable to future flooding and sea-level rise: Hunts Point in the Bronx, Red Hook in Brooklyn, the Rockaways in Queens, Lower Manhattan and the East Shore of Staten Island.

Priscilla Coli, Adi Efraim,
Taehyung Park + Wen Wu **A**
Crystal Yuehin Ng, Daniela
Jacome, Emmanual Lopez +
Yu-Hsuan Lin **B/C**
Faisal Almogren, Ximing Chen,
Yili Gao + Sangyoon Kim **D**
Jing Peng, Nasim Amini,
Tyler Cukar + Zuhal Kuzu **E**
Juan Guzman Palacios,
Wu Yi + Shirley Dolezal **F/G**
Lu Feng, Abhimanyu Prakash,
Jimena Romero + Yi Tang **H/I**
Xin Fu, Jihan Lew, Tiantina
Ren + Duyoung Yoon **J**
Yue Zhao, Cheng Zhou,
Shixiu Wang + Nico Rios **K**

A **ROOF PLAN**   **PLAN GROUND FLOOR**

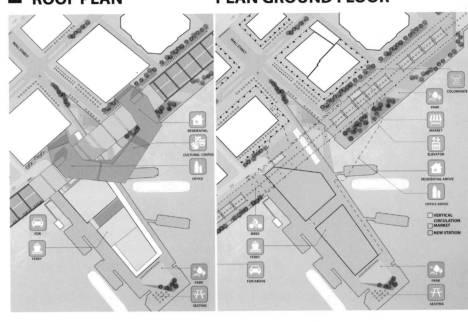

B

HIGH PERFORMANCE EDGE

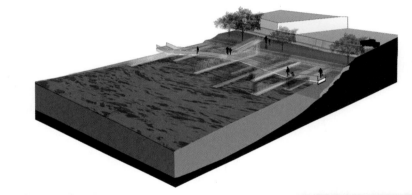

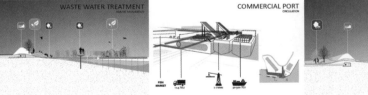

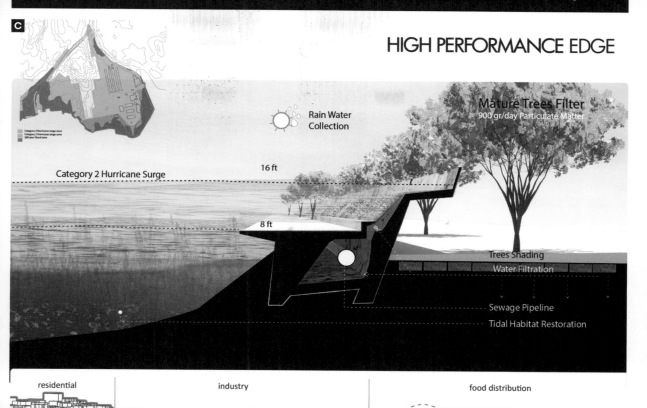

HIGH PERFORMANCE EDGE

Rain Water
Collection

Mature Trees Filter
900 gr/day Particulate Matter

Category 2 Hurricane Surge   16 ft

8 ft

Trees Shading

Water Filtration

Sewage Pipeline

Tidal Habitat Restoration

residential   industry   food distribution

Category 3 Hurricane surge zone

Category 2 Hurricane surge zone

100 year flood zone

E

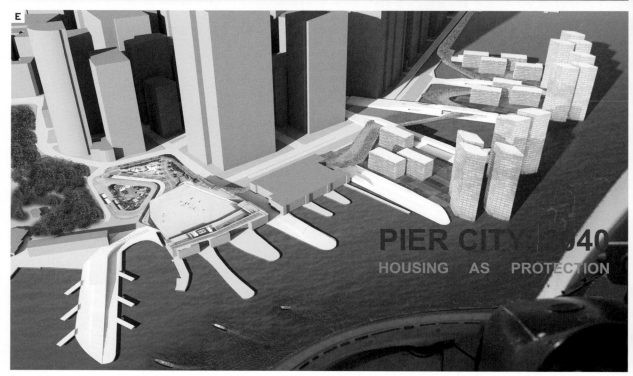

PIER CITY 2040
HOUSING   AS   PROTECTION

F

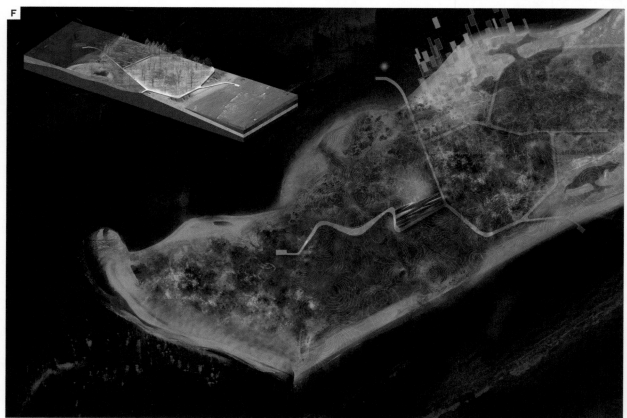

G

H

I

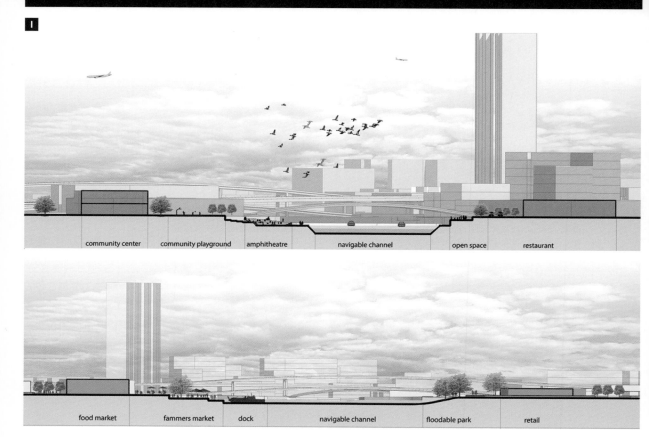

community center   community playground   amphitheatre   navigable channel   open space   restaurant

food market   fammers market   dock   navigable channel   floodable park   retail

J

TYPOLOGY

RESIDENTIAL   BUNGALOW   COMMERCIAL

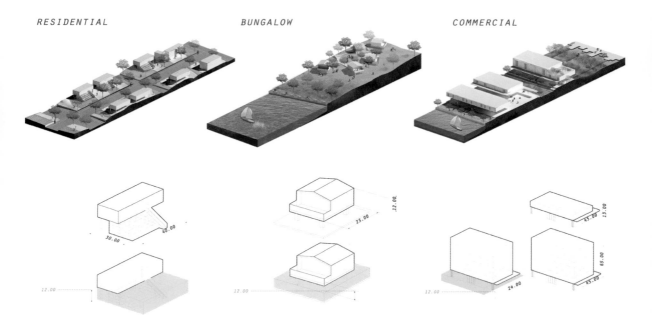

URBAN/LIFE/SUPPORT

Architecture + Urban Design
Fall 2013
*Skye Duncan + Justin G. Moore,
coordinators, Lee Altman,
Danielle Choi, Alison Duncan,
Dongsei Kim, Christopher
Kroner + Sandro Marpillero,
core faculty, Nadereh Nouhi
(Economic Development) +
Guilherme Lassance
(GSAPP Visiting Scholar),
embedded critics*

The Fall Urban Design Studio explored American Cities and their regions, accepting the premise that the practice of Urban Design is fundamentally interdisciplinary and collaborative. It is the result of a kinetic relationship between physical design, environmental considerations, public policy, culture and economy, which operate at scales that often exceed the limits of a specific site, city or region. The studio collectively examined the influence exerted by these various factors and the immense impact they have in contributing to the conditions of urban environment, including its public and private spaces, its programs and the perceived quality-of-life for its communities. Examining the relationship between health and the built environment, the students were charged to creatively explore, interpret, expand and challenge the definition of 'health' in how it relates to cities and to their 'competitive advantages.'

Following an analysis of national cities, the 'Urban/Life/Support' studio embarked on a semester to collectively explore the available 'resources and exchanges' within, around and between two primary urban sites: New Rochelle in Westchester County and East Harlem in New York City. By considering key actors and their specific interests, students engaged in the social, political, environmental, economic and physical forces acting upon the sites, identifying opportunities for design interventions, treatments and prevention strategies to ensure a dynamic and healthy future for the region.

City of New Rochelle, Department of Development Research Fellows: Ankita Chachra, Ryan Jacobson + Kristina Ricco

Jing Deng, Wagdy Moussa, Wen Wu, Priscila Coli + Shirley Dolezal **A**
Zahraa Alwash, Ximing Chen, Hanisha Dandamudi, Yili Gao + Daniela Jacome **B**
Maria Belen Ayarra, Faisal Abdulaziz Almogren, Ji han Lew, Xin Fu + Yue Zhao **C**
Abhijeet Shrivastava, Hugh Shixiu Wang, James Zhou, Sangyoon Kim + Yi Tang **D**

A

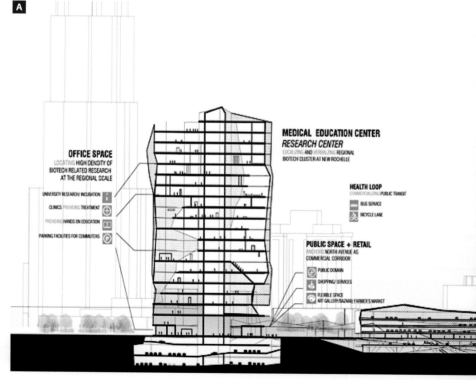

OFFICE SPACE
LOCATING HIGH DENSITY OF
BIOTECH RELATED RESEARCH
AT THE REGIONAL SCALE

UNIVERSITY RESEARCH INCUBATION
CLINICS PROVIDING TREATMENT
PROVIDING HANDS ON EDUCATION
PARKING FACILITIES FOR COMMUTERS

MEDICAL EDUCATION CENTER
RESEARCH CENTER
LOCALIZING AND VERBALIZING REGIONAL
BIOTECH CLUSTER AT NEW ROCHELLE

HEALTH LOOP
CONNECTING PUBLIC TRANSIT
BUS SERVICE
BICYCLE LANE

PUBLIC SPACE + RETAIL
ANCHORS NORTH AVENUE AS
COMMERCIAL CORRIDOR
PUBLIC DOMAIN
SHOPPING SERVICES
FLEXIBLE SPACE
ART GALLERY/BAZAAR/FARMER'S MARKET

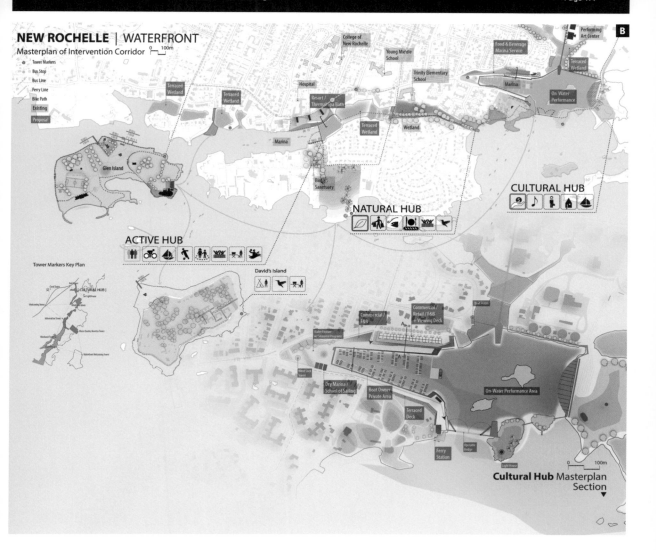

NEW ROCHELLE | WATERFRONT
Masterplan of Intervention Corridor

0 ___ 100m

- Tower Markers
- Bus Stop
- Bus Line
- Ferry Line
- Bike Path
- Existing
- Proposal

Tower Markers Key Plan

ACTIVE HUB

NATURAL HUB

CULTURAL HUB

David's Island

Glen Island

Bird Sanctuary

College of New Rochelle

Young Middle School

Trinity Elementary School

Hospital

Resort / Thermal Spa Bath

Terraced Wetland

Wetland

Food & Beverage Marina Service

Performing Art Center

Terraced Wetland

Marina

On Water Performance

Marina

Commercial / F&B

Commercial / Retail / F&B + Viewing Deck

Water Feature w/ Seasonal Programs

Wind Sock Tower

Dry Marina / School of Sailing

Boat Owner Private Area

Terraced Deck

On-Water Performance Area

Operable Bridge

Ferry Station

Light House

Cultural Hub Masterplan Section
▼

0 ___ 100m

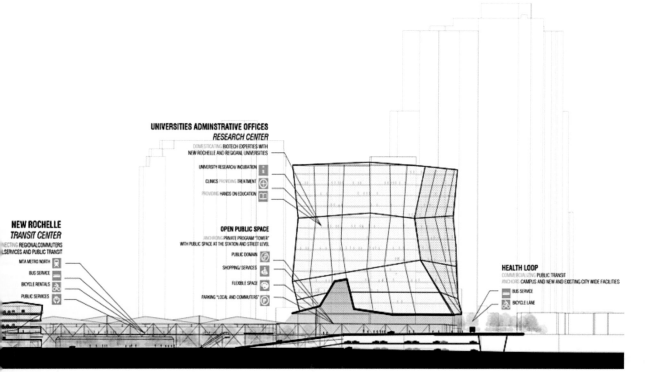

UNIVERSITIES ADMINSTRATIVE OFFICES
RESEARCH CENTER
DOMESTICATING BIOTECH EXPERTIES WITH NEW ROCHELLE AND REGIONAL UNIVERSITIES

UNIVERSITY RESEARCH INCUBATION

CLINICS PROVIDING TREATMENT

PROVIDING HANDS ON EDUCATION

NEW ROCHELLE
TRANSIT CENTER
CONNECTING REGIONAL COMMUTERS RAIL SERVICES AND PUBLIC TRANSIT

MTA METRO NORTH

BUS SERVICE

BICYCLE RENTALS

PUBLIC SERVICES

OPEN PUBLIC SPACE
ANCHORING PRIVATE PROGRAM "TOWER" WITH PUBLIC SPACE AT THE STATION AND STREET LEVEL

PUBLIC DOMAIN

SHOPPING/ SERVICES

FLEXIBLE SPACE

PARKING "LOCAL AND COMMUTERS"

HEALTH LOOP
COMMERCIAL IZING PUBLIC TRANSIT ANCHORS CAMPUS AND NEW AND EXISTING CITY WIDE FACILITIES

BUS SERVICE

BICYCLE LANE

C

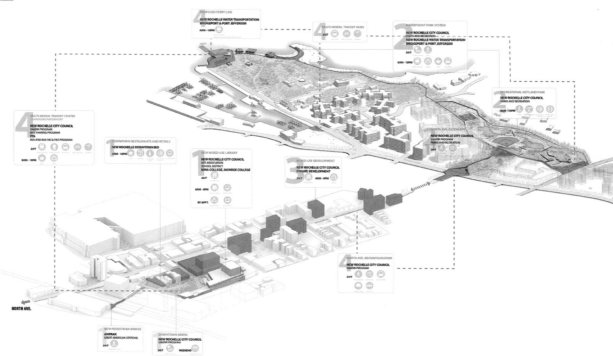

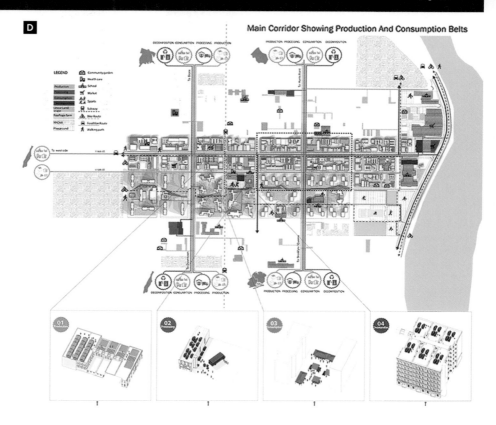

Main Corridor Showing Production And Consumption Belts

Three Densification Modes: Delhi, Kisumu + Medellin

Architecture + Urban Design
Spring 2014

Richard Plunz, coordinator, Victor Body-Lawson, Viren Brahmbhatt, Juan Esteban Correa Elejalde, Michael Conard, Petra Kempf, Geeta Mehta + Kate Orff, critics

The subject of this Studio was a comparative urban dialogue between New Delhi, Kisumu and Medellín. Like dynamic cities everywhere, they share concerns about the form of their continuing expansion and the consequent mandate for compact growth. This particular dialogue is of interest given the diversity of character and context of each, within the broad context of development in the "Global South." The New Delhi mandate involved densification of the Lutyens Plan for the original colonial city, long considered an international landmark in early twentieth century urban design. In question was the evolution of this culturally significant and highly formalized hallmark: from its ceremonial significance as new Capitol of India to expanded meaning as center of a new commercial metropolis. The Kisumu mandate also entailed urban densification, but with sharply contrasting origins and formal characteristics evolving out of the commercial functionalism of an early twentieth century port city. In question was the upgrading of areas along a rapidly growing growth corridor, within municipal resource constraints. The Medellin mandate entailed densification of the "informal sector" periphery, within the context of a city recently transformed by new political will and substantial investment. In question was the next phase of development for a city that has become an international "textbook" case in terms of innovative urban design initiatives and projects. For each of the three cities, detailed study sites were carefully chosen as particular "fragments" that served as windows through which to view the larger question of their respective development modes and to comparatively explore "saturation" levels of density within the respective urban contexts.

Site 1: Kisumu, Kenya

Kisumu dates from the early twentieth century as a British colonial era enterprise. In 1901 a major port facility was constructed at this location as the terminus of the Uganda Railway facilitating commerce via Lake Victoria. Within Kenya's rapidly urbanizing context, Kisumu arrived at a current population of over 500,000, making it the third largest city in Kenya. In 1963, when Kenya achieved independence from Britain, only eight percent of the population was urban; now it is over thirty five percent and is projected to be fifty percent by 2050. Culturally it lies within the international territory of the Luo peoples within the Lake Victoria basin. Today it enjoys a strategic position as a business center for East Africa and as an agricultural center surrounded by fertile lands that produce abundant sugar and rice. The port makes Kisumu a gateway from Kenya into the Great Lakes Region, connecting to Uganda, Tanzania, Burundi, Rwanda and the Democratic Republic of Congo. A new rail connection under construction connecting Kisumu with Nairobi, Mombasa and Malaba will considerably enhance commerce. Agriculture in the region remains vital, with numerous new initiatives including fish farming and coffee production. Kenya's recently adopted new constitution, devolution of power to the counties and its growing and robust economy made this a dynamic time for urban design initiatives in Kisumu.

Site 2: Delhi, India

Delhi, India's "National Capitol Region" has grown to over 22 million, making it one of the largest urban conurbations in the world. Urbanized in various fragments over the last two millennia, New Delhi is one of the eleven districts of Delhi and has remained relatively immune to developmental pressure until the present because of its enormous cultural and political significance as the Capitol complex for India. It dates from the famous plan designed by the British architects, Sir Edwin Lutyens and Sir Herbert Baker (1911-1931). This entirely new urban complex was to house all of the government functions that were moved from Calcutta and remains today as a highly formalized expression of the British colonial planning conventions at the height of empire. With a population of 250,000, New Delhi remains a municipal entity within the much larger Capitol Region. Given the hyper-development context of Delhi, there is growing pressure for redevelopment of New Delhi and for study of the potentials for densification within the Lutyens plan. Proposed changes to the Lutyens plan are controversial, such that to date no such comprehensive urban design study has been completed.

Site 3: Medellín, Colombia

With a population of 2.4 million and an urban agglomeration of more than 3.5 million, Medellín is the second largest city in Colombia and among the most important in Latin America. It was founded as a Spanish colonial outpost in 1616. In 1826, toward the end of the Spanish colonial period, it was designated as the capitol of a large region comprising parts of present-day Colombia, Venezuela, Ecuador and Panama. The nature of its strategic location relates to natural resource extraction, initially gold and with the commercialization of a high quality coffee production. From the early twentieth century until the 1970's, it was the most important industrial region of the country. Changes in the global economy, including cheaper labor elsewhere, plunged the city into a crisis with a proliferation of drug trafficking and its related violence that made it one of the most dangerous places on earth. The renewal of the city in recent years as a global player in spite of the geographical restrictions, gives evidence of its well-known culture of innovation and entrepreneurship. These characteristics are precisely what brought the society together to change the environment that violence had imposed on the city during the 1980's and '90's – an effort that involved civil society, industry, culture and the public sector. The situation was reversed in a return to a very innovative city. Broad issues were addressed including social inequality and lack of inclusion for economic opportunity. This reversal makes Medellin a valuable case-study for cities everywhere and, as such, in 2013 it was awarded in 2013 City of the Year award by the Wall Street Journal and Citi Global Competition, as the most innovative city of the world precisely for its efforts to repay a social debt by providing the best quality urbanism, architecture, civic amenities and infrastructure for the poorest population. In 2014 it hosted the World Urban Forum where social equity was a principal topic.

Delhi, Cultural Waterscape: Silvia Vercher, Maria Belen Ayarra, Zahraa Mahmood + Marco Alejandro Sosa **A** Delhi, Soft City: Jimena Romero, Jimena Gonzolez-Sicilia + Feyza Koksal **B** Medellin, Leveraging Infrastructure: Ye Zhang, Candy Ye Tang, Abhijeet Shrivastava + Hugh Shixlu **C** Medellin, Placemaking for Innovation: Ninoshka Rachel Henriques, Daniela Andrea Jacome, Abhimanyu Prakash + Joel Nicolas Rios **D**

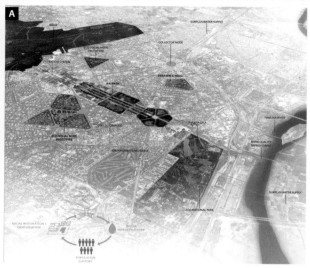

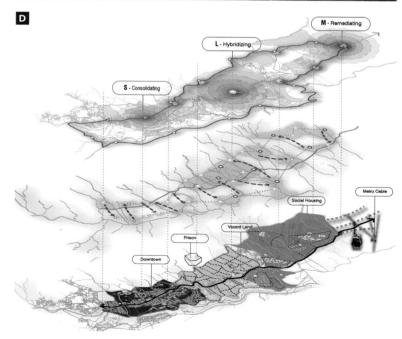

**Infrastructure, Resilience +
Public Space**
Architecture + Urban Design
Fall 2013
*Morana M. Stipisic +
S. Bry Sarté, instructors*

Why focus on cities? And why at this moment in time? What is changing at the intersection of infrastructure and public space? What are the opportunities to redefine and improve urban livability informed by integrated infrastructure? How can our evolving cities better work with energy, water and ecological systems and what are the metrics to track their success? How can we lower carbon levels while stimulating densification? How can cities utilize eco-efficiency? Why is the traditional sector-specific planning process not suitable for twenty first century urban development?

These and similar questions were analyzed within this seminar. We looked into the complexity and intertwined nature of infrastructural systems, political structures and public space, as well as elaborated on their causal relationship. Urban resilience was also a recurring theme.

This seminar was intended to strengthen participants' ability to simultaneously view the 'big picture' while finding appropriate contributions at the 'fine grain.' Exploration of urban design approaches, methods and tools were structured to deepen participants' understanding of the interconnected workings of resilient urban systems. The aim of the seminar was to enable participants to gain critical skills for designing and proposing healthy urban transformation at this critical moment in time.

Juliana Azem Ribeiro de Almeida, Juan Guzman, Grace Pelletier + Katherine Samuels **A**
Fan Guo, Lu Feng, Kenneth Mata + Hugh Shixiu Wang **B**
Yuehin Ng, Wen Wu, Du Young Yoon + Yu Zhang **C/D**

A **WETSCAPE DISTRICT**
a more resilient and sustainable neighborhood

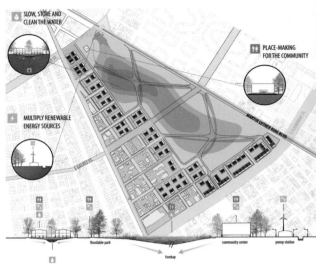

SLOW, STORE AND CLEAN THE WATER

PLACE-MAKING FOR THE COMMUNITY

MULTIPLY RENEWABLE ENERGY SOURCES

CREATING A NETWORK OF WETLANDS

ACTIVATING PUBLIC SPACE

BRIDGING THE COMMUNITY

B

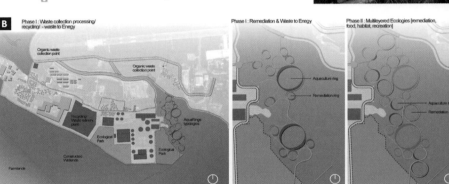

Phase I : Waste collection processing/ recycling/ - waste to Enegy

Phase I : Remediation & Waste to Enegy

Phase II : Multileyered Ecologies [remediation, food, habitat, recreation]

Phase I : Waste collection processing/ recycling/ - waste to Enegy   Informal settlements decentralized system

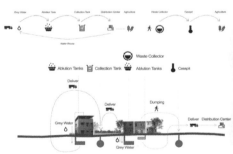

Waste Collector

Ablution Tanks   Collection Tank   Ablution Tanks   Cesspit

Waste = food = energy - loop system

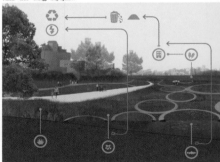

C

San Francisco Eco District
NEIGHBORHOOD: CONNECTION IMPROVEMENT

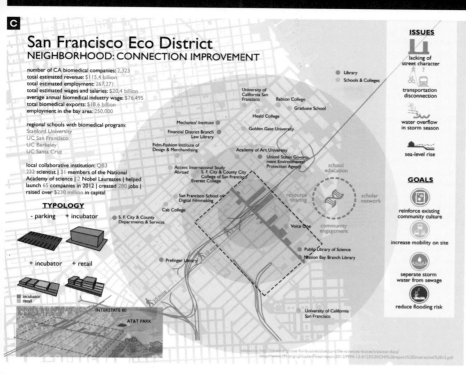

number of CA biomedical companies: 2,323
total estimated revenue: $115.4 billion
total estimated employment: 267,271
total estimated wages and salaries: $20.4 billion
average annual biomedical industry wage: $76,495
total biomedical exports: $18.6 billion
employment in the bay area: 250,000

regional schools with biomedical program:
Stanford University
UC San Francisco
UC Berkeley
UC Santa Cruz

local collaborative institution: QB3
232 scientist | 31 members of the National
Academy of science | 2 Nobel Laureates | helped
launch 65 companies in 2012 | created 280 jobs |
raised over $230 million in capital

TYPOLOGY
- parking   + incubator

+ incubator   + retail

incubator
retail

ISSUES

lacking of
street character

transportation
disconnection

water overflow
in storm season

sea-level rise

GOALS

reinforce existing
community culture

increase mobility on site

seperate storm
water from sewage

reduce flooding risk

D

San Francisco Eco District
BLOCK: SYSTEM INTEGRATION

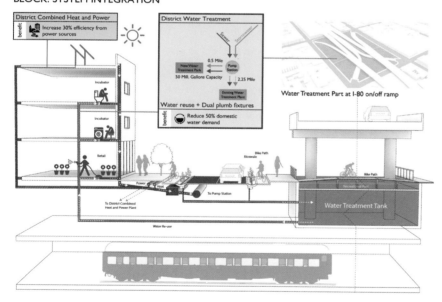

Water Treatment Part at I-80 on/off ramp

Reading New York Urbanism
Architecture + Urban Design
Summer 2013
Michael Szivos, Liz Barry +
Phu Duong, instructors,
with Brandt Graves

This seminar focused on three
critical questions embedded
in the title: What is reading?
What is New York? What is
urbanism? The intention was
to develop an understand-
ing of New York by exploring
its urban patterns through a
cinematic lens. Students were
asked to capture and represent
their nuanced understanding
of New York City's urbanisms.
A cinematic approach framed
the course to look beyond
spatial or formal conditions:
to view the city as a network
of dynamic forces, pressures,
intensities and flows. Students
built the capacity to engage
audiences through short format
videos that employed narrative-
based film sequences and
motion graphics. ArcGIS Suite
instruction introduced in this
course provided students with
a foundation for interrogating
and extracting urban data. This
process involved identifying
a system's logic, its working
pieces, its changing uses and
the livelihood or conflict it
presented within the context
of the post-industrial city. This
seminar culminated in ninety
second videos composited with
Adobe AfterEffects to demonstrate the dynamic effects that
render physical, temporal and
experiential design dimensions.
   Final projects were completed in groups of two. As
the final projects were videos,
archive submissions were formatted as five scene filmstrips.

Urban Theory + Design in the Post-Industrial Age
Architecture + Urban Design
Summer 2013
Noah B. Chasin, instructor

Urban Design Seminar 1 was intended as an introduction to the theoretical, critical and formal vocabularies of postwar urbanism throughout Europe, the U.S. and beyond. The class was arranged thematically and, in a larger context, chronologically. The rise of a new urbanism as a result of rapidly proliferating technological and industrial advances was seen as the backdrop against which various urban design strategies were deployed. From suburban sprawl to the Team 10 critique of interwar functionalism, from megastructures to semiotic models, from New Urbanism to X-Urbanism, students measured the merits of various paradigms—and their critiques—against one another in an effort to understand the processes that provide the structures and infrastructures for built environments. Of particular concern was, on the one hand, the paradoxical nature of designing for an unknown future population, and, on the other, the role of self-organization as an increasing viable source for urban morphology.

Urban Preconfigurations: New York / Global
Architecture + Urban Design
Fall 2013
Michael Conard, instructor

The accelerated rate of unprecedented urban change fueled by the proliferation of information technologies and service industries challenges traditional and theoretical Urban Design paradigms, pedagogies and practices. Conventional practice and normative conceptions of fabric are challenged in the context of variant conditions such as sprawl, generic landscapes, informal settlements, preservation districts, marginalized centers, disused industrial zones and the environmental questions of climate change, obesity and peak oil. Metaphors for chaos, complexity, biourbanism, junk space, fluidity, transparency and dynamism have flourished. Yet the ability of these constructs to engage the drivers of urban form and urban policy change remain unclear and suspect. The seminar introduced students to the logic of Western market driven development; to the means and methods in which design in the contemporary city is conceived, created and regulated; and to historical and contemporary land-use controls.

Form + Fabric Negotiations
Architecture + Urban Design
Spring 2014
Skye Duncan, instructor

This seminar investigated the various tools, processes and systems of negotiation involved in the shaping of urban form and fabric. Participants learned about the numerous stakeholders involved in Urban Design projects and their complementary and sometimes competing interests. Using New York as the birth place, the seminar discussed the history and fundamentals of zoning – how, through land use and bulk regulations, zoning provides one of the key frameworks for shaping our built environment. The course explored how zoning influences Urban Design, how it can in turn be informed and shaped by design and how it can act as a tool to promote growth, to protect character or to revitalize neighborhoods. Participants investigated a variety of local and global policy mechanisms that relate to important urban themes, including waterfront access, fresh food access, public health, sustainability, affordable housing and public space quality. These themes explore how negotiation processes can leverage private investment for public benefit and how sometimes blunt tools of zoning can become more nuanced to take into account the specificity of place and local context or provide the platform to enhance opportunities for social and cultural enrichment. We explored methods of translating the often verbal-based policies into visually-based tools, how to supplement zoning with Urban Design guidelines. With the foundation knowledge of these various negotiating mechanisms, the course culminated in a critical analysis and a developed needs assessment that informed a proposal for a transformative and innovative zoning strategy for a given context.

Digital Modeling for Urban Design
Architecture + Urban Design
Summer 2013
Phu Duong + Christoper Kroner, instructors

This course served as an introduction to fundamental techniques for urban design representation. The primary objective was to provide an entry point into current software applications that enable contemporary urban design practices. Digital Modeling for Urban Design supports the content and theoretical material framed by the Reading New York Urbanism seminar. Students learned to visualize their ideas about various urban conditions through three dimensional digital modeling and animation completed in Maya. In order to work through three dimensional modeling skills students were asked to design public spaces for the city. Surface tectonics manifested the flows, forces and pressures found and analyzed in New York City. These models were envisioned as a collection of prototype paths, pavilions and gardens.

Advanced Digital Modeling for Urban Design (ADMUD)

Architecture + Urban Design
Fall 2013
Jose Isaias Sanchez + Robert Brackett II, instructors

This seminar extended the 3D modeling and animation curriculum for Urban Design at the GSAPP. It advanced the Maya skills taught in Digital Modeling for Urban Design during the first semester of the MSAUD program. Fundamental knowledge of Maya was a prerequisite to this course. Advanced DMUD explored time-based modeling and generative geometry technologies applicable to urban modeling, analysis and representation that prepared graduates with innovative ways to deploy data to inform the creative process relevant to contemporary design practices. The course focused on methodologies for exploring zoning and fabric related modeling.

Asian Urbanism + Public Space Now

Architecture + Urban Design
Spring 2014
Geeta Mehta, instructor

In this seminar urbanism in Asia was examined through the lens of public spaces and the public realm. While public space is important everywhere, it is more so in densely populated Asian cities and critical in low-income neighborhoods and informal settlements there. While the intensity and scale of urban growth in Asia is one of the most exciting developments in recent history, it is also resulting in erosion, privatization and loss of public spaces, as well as the consequences thereof.

Three cities that were the focus of the seminar - Tokyo, Shanghai and Mumbai - are among the largest in the world. The urban public realm in these cities is the most articulate expression of politics, power, money and class, which have defined these cities at specific moments in history. Asian cities like these are also the arenas where the Millennium Development Goals of poverty reduction and environmental sustainability will be either achieved or missed.

The course considered the issues and design of micro-level neighborhood public spaces as well as monumental and iconic public spaces within the broad context of Asian lifestyles and rising expectations, urban form, history, physical and socio-economic infrastructure, governance, environmental sustainability and social equity.

Fabrics + Typologies: NY/Global

Architecture + Urban Design
Fall 2013
Richard Plunz, instructor

This course explored the meaning of urban building typology and fabric in the evolution of cities worldwide. It questioned the canons of architectural and urban historiography that tend to overemphasize the isolated monument rather than fabric. Students scrutinized the evolutionary history of anonymous urban fabric, often created by the uncelebrated architect or builder, and which comprises the major building volume of this and all cities. The focus was on the culture of housing with the intent to grasp the political and tectonic devices that lead to specific fabrics in specific urban contexts. The city became a crucible to be understood both forwards and backwards in time, from extant present-day realities to underlying formational causes and vice versa. Beginning with New York City, this exercise in urban forensics was played back for other global cities. Seminar participants translated the technique and values learned from the New York case to case studies embedded in their own local knowledge, culminating in a final forum in which comparative projected architectural transformation of fabrics became the basis of critical discourse.

Public Space + Recombinant Urbanism

Architecture + Urban Design
Spring 2014
David Grahame Shane, instructor

This seminar examined how cities evolve and develop public space and density over time in cycles of expansion and decline. The emphasis was on the urban actors who generate these spaces. The first part of the course was based on a close reading of Recombinant Urbanism and an in-class discussion of related issues. Cities were seen as complex systems involving multiple actors, energy and information flows, resulting in diverse urban forms and systems of self-governance. The second part of the course concentrated on city models, Urban Design and public space case studies, tutorials and student presentations. Students were required to develop digital group presentations at the end of the semester, through modeling a city and selected public spaces that were assembled into a website based on the seminar research.

Critical, Curatorial + Conceptual Practices in Architecture Program
Felicity D. Scott + Mark Wasiuta, directors

The Masters of Science in Critical, Curatorial and Conceptual Practices in Architecture offers advanced training in the fields of architectural criticism, publishing, curating, exhibiting, writing and research through a two-year, full-time course of intensive academic study and independent research. The program recognizes that architectural production is multi-faceted and diverse and that careers in architecture often extend beyond traditional modes of professional practice and academic scholarship, while at the same time reflecting and building upon them.

The CCCP program is structured to reflect this heterogeneity and the multiple sites and formats of exchange through which the field of architecture operates while at the same time sponsoring the ongoing critical development and interaction of such a matrix of practices and institutions. The program's emphasis is thus on forging new critical, theoretical and historical tools, and producing new and rigorous concepts and strategies for researching, presenting, displaying and disseminating modern and contemporary architecture and closely related fields. The program is aimed primarily, but not exclusively, at those with a background in architecture who wish to advance and expand their critical and research skills in order to pursue professional and leadership careers as architectural critics, theorists, journalists, historians, editors, publishers, curators, gallerists, institute staff and directors, teachers and research-based practitioners. Applicants might be seeking further academic training or specialization after a professional degree or years of teaching, or even at mid-career. They might also have worked in a related field and be seeking an academic forum to develop additional specializations in architecture. The program also provides the highest level of preparatory training for application to Ph.D. programs in architectural history and theory.

In addition to their coursework and workshop-based presentations by visiting curators, critics, exhibition designers and directors of institutions, CCCP students undertook assistantships with the directors of exhibitions, print publications and public events at the GSAPP. They also initiated exhibitions and research projects both on campus and beyond.

CCCP Colloquium 1: Documents + Discourse

Critical, Curatorial + Conceptual Practices in Architecture
Fall 2013
Mark Wasiuta, instructor

The seminar interrogated the current status of theory, its recent history, its application, its utility, as well as the anxieties that it has often fostered within and outside architecture. It examined how, through new research and methodological approaches, the conceptual parameters of architectural history, theory, criticism and practice have been expanded and how canonical figures and their works have been recast in distinct terms. The seminar read a series of architectural and theoretical texts that offer important conceptual and intellectual tools for addressing architecture's relation to technology, media, ecology, sexuality, spatial politics and a range of other problems and directions. The ambition of the seminar was twofold, aiming both to expand our familiarity with contemporary debates and to provide a focused forum for ongoing discussion regarding the articulation of new sites and strategies for research, writing and practice.

This fall the seminar approached contemporary critical discourse through the filter of documents and documentation. In specific historical examples, and through a range of theoretical texts the status, definition, use and authority of documents for architecture, architectural history, architectural exhibitions and architecture's other media practices was examined and assessed. Through the question of the document the seminar surveyed a range of methodologies and approaches that have served to define, demarcate or redirect the stakes of the discipline over the last decades.

CCCP Colloquium 2

Critical, Curatorial + Conceptual Practices in Architecture
Spring 2014
Mark Wigley, instructor

Taught by the Dean of the school, this course emphasized forging new critical, theoretical and historical tools, and producing new and rigorous concepts and strategies for researching, presenting, displaying and disseminating modern and contemporary architecture and closely related fields.

CCCP Thesis

Critical, Curatorial + Conceptual Practices in Architecture
Fall 2013 + Spring 2014
Adam M. Bandler, coordinator

The second year of the CCCP program is dedicated primarily to the research and writing/production of a final thesis. This can take the form of: a written thesis on a historical or theoretical topic; a portfolio of critical writings; a print-based demonstration and visualization of rigorous, original research or; it can involve the conceptualization, design and a detailed prospectus and documentation for, or when feasible the production of, an exhibition, publication, institute, major event, web-based initiative, time-based project, etc. Each student conducts his/her research independently, under the supervision of a faculty advisor, as well as participating in mid-term and final reviews each semester with feedback offered by the CCCP Director, advisors and invited critics.

Sayyida Zaynab Cultural Park for Children: The Architecture of Abdelhalim I. Abdelhalim + the Making of the Egyptian Neoliberal State

Critical, Curatorial + Conceptual Practices in Architecture Thesis
Fall 2013 + Spring 2014
Ashraf Abdalla
Reinhold Martin, advisor

The Cultural Park for Children in Cairo, a project sponsored by the Egyptian Ministry of Culture and designed by Egyptian architect Abdelhalim I. Abdelhalim, won the Aga Khan Award for Architecture in 1992. Located in the historic district of Sayyida Zaynab, a "poor and underdeveloped" area in Cairo, the park was hailed by the jury as a "three-dimensional history lesson," and the architect was praised for his innovative approach to community development. Subsequently, the project became a showpiece for "modern Islamic" architecture and "community-based" design processes for many Egyptian and international architects and critics.

The history of the park, from its inception, has been written in the struggle between the local community and the state. Abdelhalim intended for the cultural park to be a catalyst for urban transformation and social change within the "underdeveloped" and "alienated" surrounding community. Against forces of exclusion by the authoritarian and bureaucratic state, seen as an accomplice to western modernization and global forces, Abdelhalim aimed to include and empower the local community by connecting them to their "Islamic" past, built environment and park. By evoking "Islamic" imageries from the surrounding historical sources and activating local participation through community rituals and festivals, the architecture of the park produced forms, which stood for distinct cultural identity, and visual patterns, which guided the organization of the park. The ensuing failure of the project's intentions has been attributed to the power of the centralized state at preventing the community from engaging with the cultural park, both in its production and appropriation.

Testing Territory: A History of Spatial Strategies Along the Rio Grande
Critical, Curatorial + Conceptual Practices in Architecture Thesis
Fall 2013 + Spring 2014
Caitlin Blanchfield
Reinhold Martin, advisor

Architecture can cast predictable characters. Territory can be a familiar stage. Narrative can fall into line. The border between the United States and Mexico is a space whose script is as entrenched as the walls that limn it, the tunnels that circumvent it and the codes that interdict or enable passage across it. So, what can a space that does not fit this bill tell us about the nature of borders and their relevance today? How does the making of a transbounded territory reinforce, circumvent and throw into relief politics of space and nation-state, ideologies of land management and the scales— from supranational to local—at which territory is produced? What spatial possibilities are opened up if we recast the protagonists and antagonists of conflict and contestation?

Transbounding territory and history, this thesis destabilized notions of borders, access and transnationality through a close-grained examination of three contiguous national parks: Big Bend National Park in Texas, Cañón Santa Elena in Chihuahua and Maderas del Carmen in Coahuila. By assembling a constellation of historical moments, archival documents and contemporary voices the thesis traced the emergence and implementation of a scientific method in the management land, from the nation-building projects of post-progressive pre-war years, to NAFTA-underwritten research ventures. Resource extraction, infrastructure development and population distribution on national and supranational levels were written into the landscape here, and always subject to the micro-movements of local communities—from coveys of yellow-billed cuckoos to trespass cattle, from fluoride miners to geology students.

Behind the Gates: New Forms of Private Enclavism in India
Critical, Curatorial + Conceptual Practices in Architecture Thesis
Fall 2013 + Spring 2014
Devina Kirloskar
Anupama Rao, advisor

"Paradise on earth", "Buy a flat-get a city free" and "Live a luxurious life" scream the billboards advertising for the townships and gated enclaves that proliferate along the highways across cities in India. They promise a new and improved lifestyle that is defined by luxury and convenience targeting specifically the new consumers of these spaces— the Indian Middle class. The paradox of the dense urbanity of the traditional Indian city against the backdrop of the utopian landscape of these private enclaves alludes to a change in the perceptions of this community and their aspirations.

The architecture, however, of these spaces is unique, and in many ways it connects to global trends of gated communities as well as India's own historical lineage of gated-ness and exclusion in cities. The peculiarities of these enclaves are revealed through the built architecture—the high rise vertical model, large suburban utopias, the gated-ness and its celebration, the enforcement of the gates, the urbanized landscapes, construction of nature, swimming pools, gyms and manicured lawns, organized labor, the relationship to the informal and the exceptions and inequalities in land laws and zoning regulations.

The ambition of the thesis was to put together a montage of realities and experiences in these urban spaces that are read in conjunction with the top down infrastructural policies to reveal a larger story of social exclusion and urban asymmetry. The focus was mainly on "Integrated Townships" in the periphery of Pune.

Codifying Violence: Sites of the Mexican War on Drugs
Critical, Curatorial + Conceptual Practices in Architecture Thesis
Fall 2013 + Spring 2014
Elis Mendoza
Reinhold Martin, advisor

In 2006, only eleven days after taking office, Mexican president Felipe Calderon announced the Operación Conjunta Michoacán, a strategy that would derive in the so-called "War on Drugs", transforming the cities and towns along the north of Mexico into perpetually contested places.

This work argued that the evident failure of the war on drugs provoked a change in strategy: from a battle against drug trafficking to a battle for the way this moment will be portrayed and understood in the future independent of its outcome. It is an ongoing war for territory, not just in its physical form but also in the media, the society, the academic world, the international community and the future. All the actors in this transformed war display actions that involve more pressing matters than just the commercialization or distribution of illegal drugs.

The territory, the images and the bodies are symbols that narrate a complex structure of violence. The "war against the Narco" has become the "war against violence," though it is not clear who is the perpetrator, who are the responsible parties and who are the victims. This thesis aimed to uncover and question the changes in the discourse and portrayal of this conflict.

Exceptional Territory: The Case of Diego Garcia
Critical, Curatorial + Conceptual Practices in Architecture Thesis
Fall 2013 + Spring 2014
Gregory Barton
Laura Kurgan, advisor

This thesis focused on territory as a conceptual construction and its relationship to the nation-state, particularly its structural role as an advantageous ensemble in theatres of war. Territory is something made both through acts of demarcation(/delineation) and designation(/declaration). That is to say, the myriad contours of territory not only are defined by geospatial limits and technological capabilities but also are a function of such linguistic variables as speech acts and legislative items. Through mapping and language, territory was investigated as multiscalar, relational and enabling; the extraordinary instance of Diego Garcia – a joint United States-United Kingdom island military installation in the Indian Ocean – provided a case study to explore and problematize the questions and possibilities of territorial capacity, integrity and sovereignty. Cartographic research navigated the geopolitical vectors and institutions that Diego Garcia inhabits and exploits in order to extrapolate more broadly the mechanics and instruments by which a state creates and utilizes territory as paranational operational space, often breaking or disregarding its own laws and international obligations in the process.

Remapping Istanbul Cosmopolitanism Now: Control, Agency + Identity in Transnational Global Transition

Critical, Curatorial + Conceptual Practices in Architecture Thesis
Fall 2013 + Spring 2014
Javairia Shahid
Kazys Varnelis, advisor

Shahid: Could you point out on this map where Taksim is?
Tafokoon: Right about here (pointing to a spot on the map)
Shahid: Oh, I missed it. Wait, it says something else, in Arabic. It does not say Taksim on the map.
Tafokoon: Yeah, it does not.
Shahid: Where is this map of Istanbul from?
Tafokoon: I found it in a book, a collection of maps of Istanbul at the University of Virginia.
Shahid: Do you know how old the map is?
Tafokoon: I do not remember exactly, but 1907 I think.
Shahid: That is decades before the Gezi uprising.
Tafokoon: Yes.

Every time we refer to the Occupy Gezi Movement in Istanbul, it seems some discursive precautions need to be taken because of the sensitivity of the topic. This project aimed to elucidate the side of the city produced through Occupy Gezi by positioning the politics of memory, history and urban imaginaries of Istanbul in its globalizing context and the global rise of the memorialization industry. Within this context, the project traced the conception of the 'other' neo-'Orientalist' framing of the subject and its 'representation' and presents a counter-method of history practices.

Remains of National Identities: Twin Houses by Javier Carvajal in Somosaguas, 1967

Critical, Curatorial + Conceptual Practices in Architecture Thesis
Fall 2013 + Spring 2014
Javier Anton
Kenneth Frampton, advisor

"Absorbing Modernity 1914-2014" is the theme that Rem Koolhaas proposed for the national pavilions that participated in the 2014 Venice biennale. This biennale advanced the provocation that under globalization national characteristics are being eroded in favor of the almost universal adoption of a single modern language in a single repertoire of typologies. Taking their own national perspective, each pavilion contributed to the creation of a global overview of architecture's evolution over the course of a century into a single, modern aesthetic, while uncovering unique national features and mentalities that continue to exist. In words of Rem Koolhaas:

In 1914, it made sense to talk about a "Chinese" architecture, a "Swiss" architecture, an "Indian" architecture… One hundred years later, under the influence of wars, diverse political regimes, different states of development, national and international architectural movements, individual talents, friendships, random personal trajectories, and technological developments, architectures that were once specific and local have become seemingly interchangeable and global. Has national identity been sacrificed to modernity?

This thesis dealt with the absorption of modernity in Spain. Contextualizing the historical, social, political and economical situation of the country, it made use of the film technique as a tool to display how that absorption has been blended with remains of national identities through a particular case study: the twin houses that Javier Carvajal built in Somosaguas in 1967. As Koolhaas recognized, the transition to what seems like a universal architectural language is a more complex process than we typically acknowledge, involving significant encounters between cultures, technical inventions and ways of remaining "national."

Virtual Spaces: A Digital Archive of Unbuilt Works

Critical, Curatorial + Conceptual Practices in Architecture Thesis
Fall 2013 + Spring 2014
Katia Davidson
Mark Wasiuta, advisor

Contemporary architectural projects are almost entirely conceived in the virtual realm of 3d modeling. Long the standard medium, it facilitates the implementation by offices of digital renderings — the animated variety of which allows for the building to be not only understood, but also experienced by an audience untrained in reading traditional architectural documentation. With current technologies, an entire environment can now be imagined, realized and recorded by virtual means with increasing ease and expertise. This, along with growing expectations by both clients and the public, has resulted in a rising amount of animated visualizations executed by both designers and developers throughout the building practice.

This thesis aimed to dissect both the strategy of documenting projects through digitally constructed narratives and the space of production surrounding it through an online, interactive platform. By establishing a lexicon of both visual and descriptive terms through an intimate examination of their construction, this thesis created an alternative index to both read and analyze this growing form of representation and its impact on the architectural practice. Through a rigorous exercise in cataloguing, the goal was to unveil the peculiarities and complexities behind this growing medium as well as chronicle the media in which it is both disseminated and preserved.

Capital Artifacts: Critical Structures of Auralization

Critical, Curatorial + Conceptual Practices in Architecture Thesis
Fall 2013 + Spring 2014
Maximilian Lauter
Mark Wasiuta, advisor

Auralization connotes the imagining of an aural event, distinct from sonification as a process of mapping datum to audible signifiers, or the modulation of sound on a multidimensional axis of compositional techniques for representation. As a set of practical and conceptual tools, these systems are built upon advancements in psychoacoustics and our sonic imaginary evolves with these applications. The integration of artistic processes in computer music and data visualization offer specific communicative capacities, and their intersection implicates new notions of transmission, translation and fidelity. Operating on the thresholds of perception and calculation, the efficacy of these strategies are tested within various spatial design practices, and are augmented by artistic practices contextualized within a discourse of 'glitch' aesthetic and methodology. Glitch refers to an unpredictable error, but it has become increasingly unclear if that error resides externally or occurs internally.

This project cultivated a critical language and taxonomy for expanding notions of auditory display to examine the productivity of these noise-based methodologies—glitch being the referent and object for the perception of difference. How are we to understand the cross-disciplinary influence of auralization on the social aspects of perceptual capital and cultural capital? What are the functional implications of an immersive aural architecture embedded and encoded within the institutionalized museum and the urban stage of the city? As both steganographic and unintended interferences are unavoidable characteristics of globalized information flow, cultural politics and spatial perception, the lossiness has become a source of production. Application of these notions to scientific and artistic practice is paramount if we are to decode the future city.

San Salvador, El Salvador: A Portrait of Spatial + Social Fragmentation

Critical, Curatorial + Conceptual Practices in Architecture Thesis
Fall 2013 + Spring 2014
Sabrina Wirth
Clara Irazábal, advisor

Like many Latin American cities, San Salvador, El Salvador is characterized by its fragmented urban planning and challenges with safety. The city is divided between public spaces only used by one social class, and enclosed private spaces occupied mainly by another. It has been 22 years since the signing of the Peace Accords in 1992, and the beginning of a second consecutive presidential term that represents the FMLN party, the rebel group with whom the government signed the treaty. How has the El Salvador's capital, San Salvador, changed since the end of the war? The structure of the city, or the lack thereof, represents a city full of insecurity and disorganization. Since cities are designed to reflect the way we live, how does the disorder of the city reflect the social conditions of its population, and how does it affect the way people view their city? This project aimed to present the spatial and social fragmentation of San Salvador through the narratives of its inhabitants in the form of a documentary. The main themes it focused on were: mobility/transportation, public space and communication. While this documentary presented one part of a complex issue of San Salvador, the goal was to stimulate a dialogue that could potentially lead to social action in the future.

The New Image of Human: Architecture as a Virtual + Psychological Habitat.

Critical, Curatorial + Conceptual Practices in Architecture Thesis
Fall 2013 + Spring 2014
Vahan Misakyan
Mark Wigley, advisor

This thesis used the notion of the human to explore and elucidate the underlying infrastructural condition of the presumably impending global state—surveillance and dataveillance—and observed this condition as a spatial context in which to understand the status of the human.

The thesis defined the accumulative ubiquity of surveilable mediums and their interconnected agglomeration, as the infrastructural condition of surveillance and dataveillance. It viewed this condition as a continuous context surrounding humans, which encloses and mediates all spatial relations between humans. Using concepts of medium, observation, interface, control and convergence, it elucidated upon synergic spaces fusing humans and the surveillance infrastructure, as well as the interdependent progression of humans and the infrastructural condition of surveillance and dataveillance. This reading externalized a hierarchical order of the created context in which the disposition, reconfiguration and segregation of humans takes place.

Taking it to the Street: The Art of Public Life

Critical, Curatorial + Conceptual Practices in Architecture Thesis
Fall 2013 + Spring 2014
Tanya Gershon
Mabel Wilson, advisor

I heard the rhythm. As I navigated through hundreds of people rushing between the trading stalls and the spazza shops on the narrow streets of Johannesburg's Central Business District (CBD) only one sound rose above the hum of the traffic and the street traders. "Ayah ayah." Three women dancing and singing at the busiest intersection on Bree Street. They seemed to stop people for a moment, captivating passerby's with their energy and spirit. I stood and watched the entire performance not able to move as their music filled the surrounding blocks and their song and dance had their own sense of power over the space that they occupied. These women were artists, seasoned performers, full of passion for their craft. As everyone dispersed, I asked a man what the foreign lyrics meant. He paused and replied, "they are singing about laundry detergent."

While millions of rand a year is channeled into capital art projects with the aim of transforming Johannesburg's highly contested inner-city, the artists and agencies falter in their objective by not weaving their projects into the existing communities and vibrant beat of street in the CBD. While large squares and parks remain vacant, the street maintains a vibrancy and energy that pulsates throughout the day reinforcing the sidewalks and street corners as the real public space in a city wrought with a tumultuous history of spatial politics. This thesis explored the following questions: How can we harness the talents of street performers to create community in areas that they already reside? How can we use their knowledge of the city to create more meaningful site-specific interventions rather than perpetuate fragmented "public" infrastructure?

Re-emerging Complexities: A Microhistory on Contemporary Social Lives of Young Chinese Artists Residing in New York City

Critical, Curatorial + Conceptual Practices in Architecture Thesis
Fall 2013 + Spring 2014
Sirui Zhang
Kazys Varnelis, advisor

Since the late twentieth century, a plenty of Chinese artists travelled abroad to study, debut and practice in Europe, North America and Japan. Rather than obtain a transcultural experience, or to exile from cultural revolutions, such relocations were mostly based on the aspiration to seek the contemporary, for the reason that contemporary art in China was regarded as undeveloped or rather unsynchronized with the western or the contemporary world.

The specific goal of traveling abroad defined the primary pattern of the artists' social lives. Many of them chose the metropolitans like Paris and New York City as their destination, where has the largest audiences and the updated theories. It was also random. The certain places of meeting, the barrier of language and the cultural identity limited the number of potential targets for the expansion of their social networks. It forced them to be acquainted with people from comparatively distant fields, which would not happen frequently in their homeland. Recently, such patterns have subtly changed through the tremendous economic growth and increasing interests in Chinese

art alongside today's complex social networks. More and more young Chinese artists are traveling abroad. Though the whole population of artists is still comparatively small, their social trajectories and intersections take place not only in the salons and galleries of twenty years ago, but also various places online. The carrier of the social networks overlap new mediums of contemporary art, architecture and other forms of visual arts, through a new way of general art production and the interdisciplinary communication.

To contour the social lives of overseas young Chinese artists, instead of depicting a overall image, I interviewed 3 to 5 Chinese contemporary artists residing in New York City at length, and conducted a microhistory based on the interviews and other relevant surveys. By doing so, this thesis discussed the characters of the artists' relocation, social networks and how these affected the form of art and the general art production in an interdisciplinary language.

Historic Preservation Program
Andrew Dolkart, director

The Historic Preservation program welcomed another class of high-caliber students this year, with several pursuing dual degrees in Urban Planning and Architecture. Historic Preservation held the James Marston Fitch Colloquium in November, a day-long colloquium that attempts to discover and define the leading edge of the discipline. The Historic Preservation Program hosted scholars from around the globe to discuss preservation practice in the contexts of engagement between East and West.

First year students worked on studio projects at Yorkville in the fall, using Woodlawn Cemetery as a laboratory. For Studio 2 in the spring, the students split into three different studio projects: analyzing revitalization potential for Roosevelt Island, strategizing adaptive reuse for the Red Hook Grain Elevator in Brooklyn and recommending landmark districts in Yorkville. Second year students kept busy with coursework and thesis writing. Emily Barr, Jee Eun Ahn, Max Yeston and Tianchi Yang each won preservation thesis awards, while Vincent Wilcke received the GSAPP writing prize for his thesis.

The Inquiry: HP lecture series, organized by second-year HP students, hosted a well-attended and remarkable line-up of programs. The lectures varied between topics of conservation, history and theory, for both local and international issues. The series welcomed Demetrios Anglos and Vasiliki Eleftheriou, for a lecture on "The Acropolis Restoration Project & the Use of Laser Technology for Sculpture Cleaning," and Phyllis Lambert who spoke on Building Seagram in the spring.

Studio 1: Reading Buildings
Historic Preservation Studio
Fall 2013
Francoise Bollack, Ward Dennis + Andrew Dolkart, critics, with Erica Mollon + Vincent Wilke

Reading Buildings was the central focus for first semester students in the Historic Preservation Program. The goal of this studio was to give the student the skills to document and analyze buildings – their history, their design, their construction and their context – by using a wide array of tools, from their eyes and other senses to drawing, photography, writing and research. Effective documentation of buildings is important so that we understand their current contributions, evaluate their significance and, where appropriate, argue for their preservation. In order to help students understand buildings not only as single objects but also as part of a larger context, the course focused on a particular area of New York City. This year the focus was the East 80s area in the Yorkville neighborhood of Manhattan. The neighborhood's built environment was influenced by a strong immigrant population and later twentieth-century development based on increased transportation. Though it has many interesting buildings, little research had been done on the history of the neighborhood, and there are few designated landmarks. The first part of the course also used Woodlawn Cemetery in the Bronx as a laboratory for field documentation and visual analysis.

Alexander Corey **A**
Corinne Englebart **B**
Olimpia Lira **C**

A

Design

Entrance detail   Mechanical penthouse

Material highlight   Irregular fenestration

B

Siedenburg Mausoleum Approach

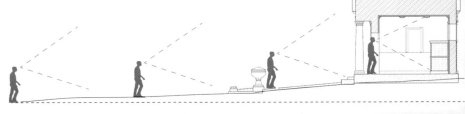

view from road   view from halfway along cemetery path   view from edge of family plot   interpretation of interior space

C

YORKVILLE PRESERVATION PLAN
RECOMMENDATIONS

East 86th and Third Avenue, 1914

East 86th and Third Avenue, 2012

Yorkville Preservation Plan
Historic Preservation Studio
Spring 2014
*Ward Dennis, critic, with
Chelsea Brandt*

The goal of the Yorkville Preservation Plan studio was to examine the past, present and future of the Yorkville neighborhood and to create a comprehensive preservation plan for the area, taking into account such issues as cultural significance, zoning, community outreach and material conservation. For the purposes of this studio, the study area was defined as East 70th Street to East 90th Street, and from Third Avenue to the East River. The blocks south of East 79th and east of York Avenue were excluded from the study due to the significant presence of hospitals and a built fabric different from Yorkville. The studio recommended this area be documented at a later date as part of an East River waterfront study. The Yorkville Preservation Plan attempted to identify the unique historic aspects of Yorkville and provide methods for how the neighborhood can best retain its character defining features in the face of change. In particular, the studio recommended three local landmark districts, over seventy individual local landmarks, material treatment manuals for building owners and educational programming. The studio believed these recommendations would protect the area's unique heritage.

Alex Corey, Elizabeth Fagan, Catherine Fischer, Sara Gershenhorn, Hee Joo Kim, Sloane Taliaferro, Sarah Vonesh + Hugh Ward **A/B/C**

Roosevelt Island Preservation Studio

Historic Preservation Studio
Spring 2014
*Elizabeth McEnaney, critic,
with Chelsea Brandt*

The goal of this studio was to produce an in-depth analysis of Roosevelt Island's historic and social fabric, identify its assets and historic resources and recommend ways to protect these resources in light of pending development pressure. In addition to presenting a depth of new knowledge about the neighborhood, the goal of the report was to identify specific issues that affect the community's historic fabric, most notably the new Cornell NYC Tech campus plan, and to propose solutions that respect and complement the existing social conditions and historic fabric of an area with vital housing and transportation needs. While preservation professionals, municipal authorities and potential developers were among the intended audiences of this plan, it was also, most importantly, addressed to the residents themselves. For this reason, our plan proposed new signage and an updated website to help local residents and visitors learn more about the value of the island's historic resources. This study aimed to provide a framework for responsible growth and suggested the enormous potential of historic preservation practices within any future community revitalization initiative of Roosevelt Island.

Manqing Cao, Lindsay Dobrovolny, Corinne Engelbert, Kat Gardner, Courtney Manchenton, Angela Wheeler, Marena Wisniewski + Dona Marie Yu **A/B/C**

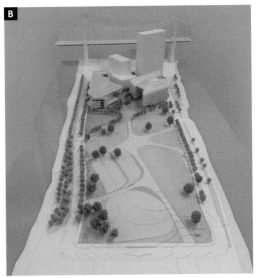

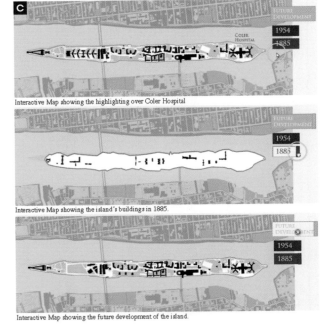

Interactive Map showing the highlighting over Coler Hospital

Interactive Map showing the island's buildings in 1885.

Interactive Map showing the future development of the island.

Red Hook Grain Terminal: An Adaptive Reuse Study
Historic Preservation Studio
Spring 2014
*Belmont Freeman, critic,
with Chelsea Brandt*

Located along the Gowanus Canal in Brooklyn, the Red Hook Grain Elevator was constructed in 1922 and worked to connect New York City to the Great Lake port cities in order to distribute and receive grain. However, decline in maritime trade resulted in the building becoming obsolete. By 1965 it was completely empty and abandoned, standing as a relic of a once prosperous past. The building later became a hotbed for drug use and violent crime, until the building and surrounding land was bought by the current owner, John Quadrozzi Jr., in 1997 in order to house an industrial park known as Gowanus Bay Terminal. Concerning the structure itself, the Red Hook Grain Elevator is a large building of twelve stories, measuring seventy feet wide and four hundred-thirty feet long, with its bulk composed of fifty four, twenty feet in diameter, cement silos that sit atop a long, hypo-style hall. Above the silos sits a corrugated steel rooftop cupola, which held hopper equipment historically used to sort grain. This studio researched the site and developed individual design proposals for adaptive reuse projects. The following points were driving influences in the proposals: attention to materials conservation, response to the site in a contextually appropriate and historically sensitive manner, encouragement of economic growth in the Red Hook neighborhood and addressing issues of ecological sustainability and storm resilience.

Diana Araujo, Angel Castillo, Nick Kazmierski, Olimpia Lira, Michael Middleton, Michael Munro, Andre Stiles + Santiago Zarate **A/B**

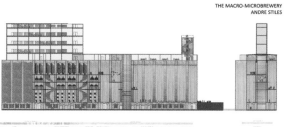

THE MACRO-MICROBREWERY
ANDRE STILES

Translucent concrete is used as an homage to the raw industrial concrete form of the grain elevator. In the contemporary adaptation of historic structures I find it important not only to show expression through architectural form but also through material intervention. The translucent concrete allows the light to come into the newly carved spaces while keeping the historic texture and look of the poured in place concrete. The material gives a new life to the building especially at night when the vertical repetition on the facade is emphasized with fun and distinctive illumination.

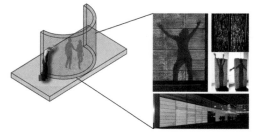

Historic Preservation Colloquium
Historic Preservation
Fall 2013
Paul Bentel + Chris Neville, instructors

This course considered issues within the field of Historic Preservation with relevance to the way it is carried out in the world today. We began by distinguishing between its global presence as a popular movement and the growing ideological discourse among its professional practitioners. We examined these historical manifestations of Historic Preservation critically, seeking a theoretical foundation for our study that is neither determined by the professional discourse nor influenced by prevailing economic and political circumstances. As a baseline, we focused on contemporary subjects pertinent to the curatorial management of cultural heritage such as Significance and Cultural Value; Authenticity and Integrity; Vernacular Culture; Interpretation of Heritage; Place and Context; and Heritage. Special emphasis was given to the relationship between buildings as physical objects and their historical persona; and to the role of Historic Preservation as a field of environmental design. Students were required to present arguments on polemical issues relevant to their own independent research, to express a commitment to a particular point of view and defend it against challenges from their class members. The course was intended to aid students in forming their own professional identities within the field of Historic Preservation by reinforcing their understanding of its intellectual content and encourage them to participate actively in the discursive process by which it unfolds in theory and practice.

Sustainability + Preservation
Historic Preservation
Spring 2014
Erica Avrami, instructor

Preservation can play an important role in creating and managing a sustainable built environment, but significant changes in the policies and practices of the preservation field are required. This course examined the positive and negative effects of heritage conservation vis à vis sustainability and explored tools and strategies for enhancing preservation's contributions toward a more livable planet and society.

The built environment is one of the most egregious culprits with regard to energy and resource consumption, waste generation, landscape destruction and climate change. The evolving sustainability discourse has given rise to greater environmental awareness in architecture, preservation, planning and real estate development. In the face of growing populations, demographic shifts and diminishing resources, sustainability concerns compel drastic changes in the way we develop, design, construct and manage the built environment, particularly in urban regions where market pressures and complex regulatory structures compound decision-making.

Balancing an examination of theory with issues of policy and practice, this course approached sustainability through a tripartite model: environmental, economic and social. It covered fundamental concepts of sustainable land use planning and green building and the role preservation plays.

Cultural Landscapes, Design + Historic Preservation
Historic Preservation
Fall 2013
Charles Birnbaum, instructor

This seminar revealed both the opportunities and constraints in the rapidly emerging discipline of cultural landscape preservation. Although the basics were covered, in an effort to elevate the discourse, special emphasis was placed on the segmented divide between design and historic preservation and nature and culture. In sum, this seminar promoted and advanced an ethic of holistic resource stewardship through the lens of cultural landscapes. Specifically, the seminar addressed the issues, tools and strategies surrounding the planning treatment and management of cultural landscapes. This included historic research and the documentation of existing conditions, methodologies for evaluation and analysis - including the generation of period plans - and the myriad and interrelated issues surrounding treatment, management and interpretation.

Drawing heavily on case studies, supplemented with a small number of local site visits, and required student presentations, this seminar provided an in-depth understanding of both preservation planning tools and how to apply the Secretary of the Interior's Standards to cultural landscapes. Finally, within the context such myriad planning, design and historic preservation challenges as: the physical and financial limitations of available research; how we assess and assign significance; the quest for authenticity; placing a value of antiquity (or weathering); the need to determine a landscape's carrying capacity; and, the recognition of a cultural landscape's palimpsest (historic layers) were also explored.

Old Buildings, New Forms
Historic Preservation
Spring 2014
Francoise Bollack, instructor

This seminar focused on recent, cutting edge architecture transforming old buildings to produce new forms in the United States and world-wide. These projects were examined not as unfortunate hybrids but as provocative works of modern architecture made possible by contemporary ideas of sustainability, by new attitudes to buildings as transmitters of cultural and architectural meanings and by twentieth century artistic developments. The seminar included site visits of projects in New York City with the architects, individual work by each student on specific buildings and lectures on the subject by Françoise Bollack.

Wood: Its Properties, Use + Conservation
Historic Preservation
Spring 2014
John Childs, instructor

Students examined the structure of wood and its physical characteristics, learning to identify specific wood species commonly used in historic architecture. The history of woodworking, joinery, wood products and fasteners in architecture was reviewed, along with the mechanisms of physical and biological deterioration, including fungal and insect attack. Finally, students explored historical and contemporary techniques used in the conservation and restoration of architectural wood.

Preservation Planning
Historic Preservation
Fall 2013
*Carol Clark + Kate
Wood, instructors*

This course was a compre-
hensive introduction to the
field of preservation planning
in the United States. Federal
preservation protections were
examined, as were other preservation planning tools, including local individual and historic
district designations and conservation easements. Financial
incentives for rehabilitation,
including the use of federal
and state investment tax credit
programs and property tax
mechanisms, were explored.

The constitutional un-
derpinnings of landmarks
regulation were emphasized,
as were the means of regulating real estate through land
use planning and zoning.

Guest speakers described
preservation efforts in Chicago
and Pittsburgh, illustrating
similarities and differences in
preservation planning practice.

**Neighborhood
Preservation + Zoning**
Historic Preservation
Spring 2014
Carol Clark, instructor

This course provided an
introduction to neighborhood
preservation issues both in
New York City and in other municipalities across the United
States. It included an examination of New York City's current
approach to rezoning neighborhoods or significant portions
of them, applying contextual
zoning and relying on inclusion-
ary housing to create affordable
housing. Students studied the
recent proliferation of neighborhood conservation district
ordinances nationwide, along
with how their administration
coordinates with the work
of local landmarks, commis-
sions and planning agencies.
Through case studies, students
explored current neighborhood preservation techniques
and examined cutting edge
approaches to using zoning as
a preservation planning tool.

Digital Visualization
Historic Preservation
Fall 2013
Brigitte Cook, instructor

This workshop was about developing dexterity in architectural representation in order to
conceptualize and materialize
the environmental, spatial and
social aspects of an individual
piece of architecture. We built
a three dimensional computer
massing model, which could
be effectively manipulated and
reproduced. A set of graphic
images were produced to
address a series of questions
with shifting scales and topics.
These images were examined
critically for their ability to
foster an understanding of
the meaning of the building.

Stained + Leaded Glass
Historic Preservation
Spring 2014
Drew Anderson, instructor

This course was intended to
give a basic understanding of
the craft of leaded glass. While
familiarizing themselves with
the various tools, materials
and techniques of the craft,
students learned glass cutting
and the assembling of a panel.
During the course students
gained familiarity with the
conservation issues involved
with leaded and stained glass.

Law for Preservationists
Historic Preservation
Fall 2013
William Cook, instructor

This course was designed
to provide students with
answers to the ten questions
all preservationists need
to know about the law:
1. Where does govern-
ment get the authority to
regulate private property for
preservation purposes?
2. What are the appropriate
limits to government regulation of private property?
3. From a legal perspective,
what are historic resources?
4. What regulatory tools exist
to protect historic resources
from private actions?
5. What regulatory tools exist
to protect historic resources
from government actions?
6. What are special legal
considerations regarding
the protection of religiously
owned properties?
7. What laws address the
protection of other spe-
cific historic resources?
8. What legal tools encourage the voluntary protection
of historic resources?
9. What other legal strategies can be employed to
save historic resources?
10. What are the latest
trends and developments
in preservation law?
In the process of learning the
answers to these questions
students developed an understanding of preservation law,
its application, the legal system
and the interface between
preservationists and lawyers.

American Architecture 1
Historic Preservation
Fall 2013
Andrew Dolkart, instructor

This course examined the development of American architecture from the earliest European settlements to the centennial in 1876. Beginning with the earliest Spanish, French, Dutch and English colonial architecture, we explored the American adaptation of European forms and ideas and the development of a distinctly American architecture. The course lectures and readings examined high style and vernacular architecture in rural and urban environments throughout the settled parts of the United States. The course was supplemented with tours and the examination of original drawings and early architectural publications in Avery Library.

American Architecture 2
Historic Preservation
Spring 2014
Jorge Otero-Pailos, instructor

This course surveyed architecture built in the United States, starting with the modernism of the Chicago School and ending with the postmodernism of Deconstructivist architecture. It was designed to provide an understanding of the major protagonists, schools of thought and events shaping the development of American architecture. It was also intended to develop competence in identifying, understanding and analyzing historic buildings, their significance, types and styles. Students built proficiency in the use of the historiographical, visual and intellectual tools necessary to grasp fully the meanings of historic buildings in their various historical, cultural and political contexts.

National Register of Historic Places: Completing National Register Nominations
Historic Preservation
Spring 2014
Andrew Dolkart, instructor

The National Register of Historic Places is the federal listing of buildings, districts, sites, etc. of historic significance. Professionals in the field of Historic Preservation are frequently called upon to complete National Register nominations as part of advocacy for the preservation of a building, in order for an owner to take advantage of historic preservation tax credits or for other reasons. This mini-course examined the criteria for National Register listing and each student completed a minimum of one National Register nomination for a building that the New York State Office of Historic Preservation is interested in seeing listed on the register.

Architecture + the Development of New York
Historic Preservation
Spring 2014
Andrew Dolkart, instructor

This course traced the development of New York City through its architecture and examined the history of architecture as it is reflected in the buildings of the city. We looked at the architectural development of New York from the time the city was a minor colonial settlement, to its development as a great commercial and institutional center in the nineteenth century, through the twentieth century when New York became one of the great cities of the world. We discussed why various architectural developments became popular in New York; how these developments reflected the complex social history of the city; and explored what these developments mean to New York's history. We examined the major architectural monuments of New York's five boroughs, but also looked at the more vernacular buildings that reflect the needs and aspirations of the city's middle- and working-class residents. The class focused on the evolution of residential architecture, the central role commercial architecture has played in the city's history and how New York became the American center for the construction of great cultural and philanthropic buildings. The class lectures were supplemented by several walking tours, including one given by students.

Advanced Research/ Independent Study
Historic Preservation
Fall 2013 + Spring 2014
Andrew Dolkart, instructor

Each semester there is the possibility of registering for "Advanced Research," or independent study within the Historic Preservation Program. Students in the Spring planned a course of self-study and inquiry and sought an advisor to review and grade the work. Advanced Research involved library research, lab work, fieldwork and other research methods, and the final product was a paper, digital design map or something else alternative to a standard paper—whatever the student and advisor agreed was the best format to illuminate the results of the research.

Documentation for Architectural Conservation
Historic Preservation
Spring 2014
David Flory, instructor

This mini–course served as an introduction to graphic tools and conventions for communicating the project scope for which the conservator is responsible. The course was an introduction to how conservators make the best use of existing resources and varied technologies – both low and high tech – for their work, yet still produce information in a format compatible with standard architectural documentation. The course was organized around familiarizing students with Construction Documents (CD's), the architecture industry standard for graphic and written documentation. We explored how these ideas can be unified such that the conservator's needs are met to the greatest extent possible while producing information in formats that can be seamlessly integrated into traditional working documents. Professionals in practice joined the class periodically to advance discussion and present actual projects and the solutions developed to meet specific challenges.

Conservation Workshop
Historic Preservation
Fall 2013
Mary Jablonski, instructor

This course built upon the techniques learned in earlier coursework and applied newly acquired knowledge of building materials to a historic building. The goal of this course was to train the student to look and learn how to investigate a historic building using an actual site. There was also a hands-on component for conservation treatments incorporated into this coursework. Exercises included documentation, sampling, materials analysis, synthesis of information, recommendations for conservation and, for the final project, conservation treatments.

Architectural Finishes in America
Historic Preservation
Spring 2014
Mary Jablonski, instructor

This course explored the decoration, ornamentation and protection of buildings with a wide variety of finishes. Buildings and preservation should not merely be about the outer shell of the building, but how people see themselves and express themselves in the finishes of their homes and public buildings. The course was a mix of lectures, demonstrations, site visits and some hands-on work in the form of conservation treatments. As part of this course, the class worked on a field conservation project performing trial conservation treatments. The site of the project changes each year. Several sessions involved travel time to sites for investigative and conservation work. The remaining sessions were held in the Conservation Laboratory in Schermerhorn Hall.

International Cultural Site Management
Historic Preservation
Fall 2013
Pamela Jerome, instructor

Impetus for the preservation of cultural heritage has developed through the recognition of sites as non-renewable resources. Training is readily available in the specific tasks required to implement preservation, such as documentation and conservation. However, with the exception of sporadic seminars, conferences, short courses or on-the-job training, far less attention has been paid to the larger, more complex and comprehensive issues of management, the process by which the individual components of preservation are fit together and either succeed or fail. This course utilized the conservation process in the Burra Charter as the basis for a rational approach to managing cultural sites. The course had an international focus and reviewed case studies from both historic and archaeological sites. It was divided into three parts: the first focused on the compilation of background information and identification of the key interested parties; then progress to the analysis of the site significance and assessment of existing conditions and management constraints; and finally, the development of the management policy and strategies for its implementation was reviewed. The delicate balancing act between cultural enhancement and exploitation was explored, as well as the need to periodically monitor and reassess management policy.

Conservation of Earthen Architectural Heritage
Historic Preservation
Spring 2014
Pamela Jerome, instructor

From ancient to modern times, building with soil has been one of the oldest and most widely used construction methods next to stone and wood. Earthen construction materials are considered sustainable because of their local availability, insulative properties and low carbon footprint. Approximately 50% of the world's population lives in some form of earthen architecture. Earthen architectural heritage is also recognized in over one quarter of the World Heritage Sites that are cultural or mixed sites.

Construction technologies vary from place to place depending on the quality of the local soil. From the dugouts of Tunisia to the high-rises of Yemen, earthen architecture comes in many shapes and forms. Students learned about the major construction technologies, including hand-shaped or molded sun-baked bricks (adobe), rammed earth (pisé de terre) and puddled earth (cob). Students learned about the different types of clays and their effect on the long-term stability of earthen structures. Some laboratory analyses were reviewed. The class looked at a multitude of case studies from around the world, from archaeological to living heritage and various methods of conservation.

In addition to the lecture readings, the course required each student to pick a site and explore issues confronted by the site's team in terms of preservation of earthen architectural heritage.

Architecture or Revolution: Strategies of Preservation
Historic Preservation
Spring 2014
Xenia Vytuleva + Jennifer Gray, instructors

The idea that architecture could operate politically and help to transform society informed the modern avant-garde across multiple disciplines, from social housing and urban planning to graphic design and cinematography. Dealing with such ideologically charged practices the field of Historic Preservation is forced to reconsider the complexity of the subject and strategic approach. Just as modern architects expanded their activity beyond the traditional domain to work across various artistic mediums, Historic Preservation professionals should formulate their parallel narrative.

This seminar investigated socially conscious, modern design experience from 1900 to the present with special emphasis on the preservation issues. It allowed students to explore the shifting relationships between social change and modern architecture, studying archival materials at The Museum of Modern Art and Columbia University, and provided students with the experience of working directly with primary documents and objects, including blueprints, plans, sketches, models, private correspondences, video, photographs and diaries.

Heritage + Social Justice in a Changing World
Historic Preservation
Spring 2014
Ned Kaufman, instructor

Historic preservation has always expressed a vision of social progress. Sometimes this has focused on instilling patriotism, at other times on conserving resources, beautifying the landscape, protecting local values, encouraging entrepreneurship or promoting economic justice. Today, after a turbulent period of social and environmental activism (1960s–1970s), followed by an equally conflictive move towards market liberalism (1980s–1990s), American society is once again in transition. And, perhaps not coincidentally, new questions are being raised about preservation's relevance. What are the critically important trends re-shaping American society? The social movements that could offer meaningful new roles for heritage conservation? The opportunities for innovative and relevant conservation work?

The course opened with an introduction to fundamental concepts such as justice, fairness, rights, development and inclusion. Next, a review of key issues in American society including poverty, inequality, racism, urban disinvestment and global warming. Third, the core question: how does heritage work contribute – how could it contribute – to social justice?

The course was organized around weekly readings and discussions. In addition, students presented a seminar paper on a topic related to the final theme. Paper topics were chosen to encourage students not only to learn about existing conservation work but also to develop proposals for innovative approaches.

Professional Practice + Project Management
Historic Preservation
Spring 2014
Claudia Kavenagh, instructor

This course was designed to introduce students to professional practice in the discipline of historic preservation. Students learned how the technical knowledge gained throughout their academic studies becomes an integrated part of the larger whole that is professional life. We explored the different career paths within the field of historic preservation; students also gained an understanding of the roles of the various other types of professionals with whom preservationists and conservators typically have interaction. We studied the typical progression of a project through the design and construction phases, with a focus on the role of the preservation professional. Students learned how a project manager develops an approach for a project and then uses that approach to develop a work plan. To accomplish this, the syllabus followed a 'real world' sequence of activities that a preservation/restoration project might follow. Beginning with the writing of a proposal and the development of a work plan, the class looked at practical and logistical matters related to how and when we address various components of a project. We discussed the production of technical drawings and specifications and how that work product translates into bid phase and construction phase activities. Using examples of real projects and two site visits, the course aimed to always include practical discussions of issues that arise during the course of a preservation project and in the work life of the preservation professional.

Classical Language of Architecture
Historic Preservation
Fall 2013
Harry Kendall, instructor

Through a series of lectures, group discussions, informal hand sketches and field trips, this course acquainted students with the basic grammar of the classical language of architecture, the history of its practice and the influential architectural treatises, which generations of architects have referenced as source material for their work.

We focused on developing a working knowledge of the canonical building designs through which we traced the evolution of architectural classicism and the "rules" of composition that characterize successive eras and distinct regional interpretations of classical design. We also explored some of the theoretical underpinnings for classical composition, and the evolution of prevailing theories, through a review of architectural treatises that articulate compositional rationale.

This knowledge enabled the students to describe clearly and with correct terminology, any building in the classical tradition—a key tool for any preservationist in the process of preserving and restoring historic architecture. Such knowledge was also vital in understanding the individual creativity and artistic interpretation that supports this tradition, and its continued relevance within the field of architecture.

GIS for Preservation
Historic Preservation
Spring 2014
Jennifer Most, instructor

A geographic information system (GIS) allows us to visualize and interpret data about places. The creation of maps using GIS can help us answer geographic questions in ways that are quickly understood and easily shared. For this reason, GIS has become a central tool in many fields, including historic preservation, where it has been used successfully in a variety of ways including documenting threats to historic resources and telling the stories of communities and places. This course covered the basics of the popular software ArcMap with a focus on ways GIS can be integrated into the practice of historic preservation.

Historic Preservation Theory + Practice
Historic Preservation
Fall 2013
Jorge Otero-Pailos, instructor

This course looked at historic preservation as a development strategy that has evolved in response to competing forms of development and rapid change. Students were asked to consider the foundations of the profession–its shifting relationship to connoisseurship, narrative, aesthetics, nationalism and collective identity–with an informed and critical eye. They were expected to debate and revise their findings. Supported by readings, lectures and class discussions, students were encouraged to explore the rationales and incentives that have allowed the preservation field to extend its influence, with special attention to the liberalization and expansion of preservation's scope over the last forty years. The western, professionalized approach to the historic built fabric was compared to the ways non-western cultures have addressed permanence and memory within the built environment.

Architectural Metals
Historic Preservation
Fall 2013
Richard Pieper, instructor

This course reviewed the structural and decorative uses of metals in buildings and monuments. The metals covered included iron and steel; copper and copper alloys including bronze and brass; lead; tin; zinc; aluminum; nickel and chromium. The seminar examined the history of manufacture and use; mechanisms of deterioration and corrosion; and cleaning, repair and conservation.

Preserving Modernism
Historic Preservation
Fall 2013
Theo Prudon, instructor

The buildings and sites of the twentieth century have become our cultural heritage. These sites present preservation professionals with unprecedented challenges of both scale and complexity that were not foreseen when heritage policies and practices were initially formulated in the nineteenth century. To achieve meaningful preservation it is not enough to understand the philosophical and aesthetic considerations embedded in this architecture but it is also necessary to fully understand the functional, practical and physical factors that may have influenced their creation and construction. Considering design for new or continued use needs to take into account ubiquity versus significance, historic building typology versus current functionality, design intent, newness and material durability versus the importance of the authenticity of the original fabric, all of which is to be placed in the context of current code, life safety and sustainability requirements. A general discussion of issues was supplemented with examples and case studies from the United States and abroad.

Introduction to Historic Structures + Systems
Historic Preservation
Spring 2014
Theo Prudon, instructor

Structures, Systems and Materials II built upon information introduced in Part I and brought this material up to the present in terms of understanding modern building systems and materials. It addressed how steel frame and concrete buildings are made and how they often fail. The organization of the course relied upon not only the study of the chronological development of the building arts and sciences, but also, as each building system was introduced, the discussion of the pathology modes and conservation approaches followed within the same week.

Historic Replicas: Replacement Materials Workshop
Historic Preservation
Spring 2014
Matthew Reiley, instructor

This course paired a discussion on the suitability of replacement materials in restoration and conservation projects with a practical workshop component. Students were instructed in common restoration techniques such as mold making, lost wax casting and composite mortar patching.

Students gained an understanding of the challenges of replacement materials compatibility with original historic fabric and developed essential manual skills. Hands-on participation included creating decorative replicas for use in the restoration of a NYC landmark.

Stained Glass Conservation
Historic Preservation
Fall 2013
Julie Sloan, instructor

This 4-week intensive seminar prepared students to do condition reports on nineteenth and twentieth stained-glass windows. The first two weeks, we met at Columbia. The first week was a show-and-tell lecture on the materials and tools used in making stained glass and a Powerpoint lecture on the history of the medium from the Middle Ages to the mid-twentieth century. The second week we had a Powerpoint lecture on the deterioration and conservation of the various materials in a window: glass, glass paint, lead, copper, steel and window frames. We also discussed protective glazing. The third and fourth weeks were held at Woodlawn Cemetery in the Bronx. The first half of the first session was a tour of some of the windows in the mausolea. Students were assigned a window in a mausoleum on which to write a condition study. The condition study required historical background and an assessment of the window's condition, deterioration mechanisms and recommendations for restoration. Students were expected to do the historical research between weeks 3 and 4. Week 4 we returned to the cemetery to spend more time looking at the windows and discussing their issues in preparation for writing the study.

Making Preservation Happen
Historic Preservation
Fall 2013
*Anne Van Ingen +
Ed Mohylowski, instructors*

The nonprofit sector is the cornerstone of the historic preservation world. Public programs, policy, advocacy, technical services and financial incentives have all sprung out of the many nonprofit organizations that push the preservation movement forward in this country. Who are these groups? What do they do? And, importantly, how do they operate? This course offered a nuts and bolts, practical introduction to the mechanics of the nonprofit sector: programming, finance, budgeting, fundraising, strategic planning and governance. Leaders in the preservation world in New York also spoke, sharing best practices and thoughts on how they, specifically, achieve their goals.

Soviet Avant-Garde Architecture 1917-1933: How to Preserve an Experiment
Historic Preservation
Fall 2013
Xenia Vytuleva, instructor

This lecture course considered the phenomenon of the Soviet Architectural Avant-Garde as part of a broader cultural history. The response of architectural thought to the machine, as well as the intersection of political and social propaganda, literature, art and cinematography were examined. Special attention was paid to the problems of preserving the fading heritage of experimental practices, such as paper architecture, oral history, temporary projects for International Exhibitions, Stage Design and the projects for National Soviet Competitions.

Concrete, Cast Stone + Mortar
Historic Preservation
Fall 2013
*Joan Berkowitz +
Norman Weiss, instructors*

The format of this course was lecture, laboratory exercises and field trips. It was one of a series of core courses on architectural materials recommended to the students focusing on conservation issues.

Introduction to Architectural Materials
Historic Preservation
Fall 2013
George Wheeler, instructor

The course familiarized students with the structures and materials of traditional building, beginning with wood framing and load-bearing masonry walls. The course also introduced students to how buildings are made, how they often fail and what can be done about it. The organization of the course relied upon not only the study of the chronological development of the building arts and sciences, but also, as each building system was introduced, the discussion of the pathology modes and conservation approaches followed within the same week. Field trips to see the situations discussed in class were integral to the course and occurred weekly during the first half of the semester.

Conservation Science
Historic Preservation
Spring 2014
George Wheeler +
Norman Weiss, instructors

This course was required for
students planning to focus
on materials conservation in
their second year. This course
was a foundational course
for students interested in
architecture conservation. The
course included laboratory
basics of sampling, testing
and procedure; basic properties of building materials; and
the physical and theoretical
considerations involved in
building "conservation."

Brick, Terracotta + Stone
Historic Preservation
Spring 2014
Dan Allen, George Wheeler +
Norman Weiss, instructors

This course explored the
group of traditional masonry
materials: brick, terra cotta
and stone. The format included
lectures, demonstrations and
field trips. The goals of the
course were to provide: a
historical overview of material
manufacturing and sourcing
as architectural materials with
a focus on the 18th century to
the present; an understanding
of their fundamental material
properties in relation to their
use and deterioration in a
range of masonry construction
systems; and an exploration
of the state-of-the-art means
and methods of their repair,
maintenance and conservation.

Interpretation + Architecture
Historic Preservation
Fall 2013
Jessica Williams, instructor

This course was designed to introduce students to the theory
and practice of interpretation, a
process of communicating the
meanings of a cultural resource
to an audience. Through readings, class discussion and case
studies, students explored
such topics as philosophies of
interpretation, methods of interpretation and current issues
and challenges in interpretation. The course drew upon
literature from historic preservation, museum studies, public
history and related disciplines.
As interpretation is based on
sound scholarship, this course
stressed the importance of link-
ing research and analysis to the
site in question and examined
methods of presenting the
resulting of this scholarship to
the public in informative, provocative and engaging ways.

Historic Preservation
Advocacy
Historic Preservation
Spring 2014
Tony Wood, instructor

The preservation of many of
our most important individual
landmarks and historic districts
has depended on success-
ful advocacy campaigns.
Whether seeking landmark
protection, trying to derail
an ill–considered proposal to
alter a protected resource or
advancing pro–preservation
public policy, preservationists need to have sharply
honed advocacy skills and
instincts in order to succeed.

Making the case for preservation, developing and energiz-
ing a constituency, mastering
the policy decision–making
processes, creating political
will, using media and designing
and implementing effective
strategies, were among the
essential components of a
successful advocacy effort explored in this course. Drawing
from preservation's history, the
key principles of advocacy were
discerned, their application
analyzed and their strengths
and weaknesses assessed.

Whether the 1940s con-
frontation with Robert Moses
over the future of Manhattan's
Battery, the multi–year effort in
the late 1950s and early 1960s
to protect Brooklyn Heights,
the 1980s campaign for City
and Suburban Homes or this
decade's battle over Edward
Durrell Stone's 2 Columbus
Circle, preservation's past and
present offer us a wealth of
advocacy examples from which
to extract and analyze both the
fundamentals and finer points
of preservation advocacy.
Preservation advocacy case
studies provide a rich vein of
intellectual capital to mine for
insights and lessons that can
benefit preservation advocacy efforts in all settings.

Thesis 2
Historic Preservation Thesis
Fall 2013 + Spring 2014
Advisors from the Faculty

The thesis was a clear, well-researched substantial argument in support of a position on a question of general interest in the field of historic preservation. Students began work on their theses in the fall without registering for a course. There were two group meetings for all students and faculty in the fall semester to give students a chance to articulate and refine their thesis topic, decide on a faculty advisor and begin research to answer their thesis question. In the spring semester students registered for Thesis 2 and presented again to all members of the faculty to assess progress on their thesis. In April, the students met for an hour with a jury of their advisor and readers to defend their thesis and hone their thoughts on the topic.

Cities on the Edge: Significance + Preservation of Hillside Squatter Settlements in Korea
Historic Preservation Thesis
Fall 2013 + Spring 2014
Jee Eun Ahn
Pamela Jerome, advisor

Hillside squatter settlements in Seoul and other major cities in Korea were formed on the mountains and hillsides as a result of exponential population growth during the rapid urbanization following the Korean War. A large number of refugees and urban migrants were displaced from urban centers and relocated to the outskirts of cities, as modernization and urban development expanded outward from the city centers in the 1960s and 70s. Commonly known as Dal-dong-ne's, these settlements were stigmatized as blighted areas with substandard housing conditions and low-income households. Over the past few decades, these areas have been eradicated by urban renewal and replaced with clusters of high-rise apartment buildings. The intimate scale and intricate networks of streets of these towns are the foundation for

the strong sense of community that is characteristic of these settlements. Therefore, the destruction of these areas not only erases a significant fragment of South Korea's historic urban landscape, but also weakens the socio-cultural identity of these neighborhoods.

Recent movements attempt to rejuvenate these neighborhoods, while maintaining the existing fabric of the towns. This thesis first analyzed the significance of the physical townscape of the hillside squatter settlements, then identified the role of preservation in the future development schemes that strive to save the existing structures, as the foundation for reclaiming a sense of community. Integrating preservation measures into sustainable town-regeneration plans can improve and protect physical resources and strengthen positive aspects of local identity, as well as provide social benefits for marginalized communities. For the sustainable management of historic resources and for the sustainable future of preservation practice itself, preservationists should proactively engage in the process of heritage work to help people enhance their quality of life.

Pressing Issues: In-Kind Terra Cotta Replacement in the Twenty-First Century
Historic Preservation Thesis
Fall 2013 + Spring 2014
Emily Barr
Theodore Prudon, advisor

Architectural terra cotta was the most popular building material in America between 1890 and 1930. As an era of innovation, the characteristics of terra cotta and appropriate construction methods were not fully understood. With building construction halted during the Great Depression and changing architectural styles, demand for terra cotta dropped to a low, and the industry fell into decline, nearly disappearing completely. As terra cotta buildings began to age and deteriorate, the industry no longer existed to provide material replacement as needed. Various alternative materials were explored and used for reasons of availability and cost. However, performance and appearance of some of these materials was deemed unsatisfactory and the continued need for more appropriate replacement materials led to a recent revitalization of the terra cotta industry.

Modern terra cotta production has incorporated new technology to: improve the quality of the product, reduce time necessary for production, lower cost and thus increase the feasibility of replacing terra cotta in-kind. With better quality control of the production process, a more predictable and dimensionally stable terra cotta product is achieved raising the important question: while preservation encourages the use of in-kind replacement, is it actually still the same material? This paper sought, through a review of current production processes in comparison to historic methods, a material analysis to examine the characteristics of current material and the effects of modern fabrication processes. In addition it intended to review traditional installation techniques to ensure replacement interventions better accommodate the characteristics and capabilities of the material.

The Historic American Buildings Survey + Interpretive Drawing: Using Digital Tools to Facilitate Comprehensive Heritage Documentation
Historic Preservation Thesis
Fall 2013 + Spring 2014
Susan Bopp
Belmont Freeman, advisor

The Historic American Building Survey (HABS), a federal New Deal program largely unchanged since its inception in 1933, is the nation's largest archive of historic architectural documentation. Surveys include three sections that describe a historical building or site: written historical research, measured drawings and black and white photography. This thesis focused on the drawing portion of a HABS survey, specifically investigating the nature and usefulness of the types of drawings allowed by the current drawing guidelines and standards as well as how contemporary digital tools can facilitate drawing production and analysis. While current HABS standards call for a strict method of researched and measured documentation, within that methodology exists a diverse range of drawing types that accurately express the desired information but are not all necessarily utilized in practice. In an attempt to reconcile contemporary practice of architectural drawing within the limits of the Drawing Guidelines for HABS, there was extensive investigation of the Interpretive Drawing clause within the Guidelines and how these interpretive drawings could reunite a new generation of architects with the federal program for documenting historic structures. Analysis of HABS's history and its sister programs of the Historic American Engineering Record and the Historic American Landscape Survey as well as critique of current practices in drawing were ultimately synthesized by putting to practice different techniques for producing interpretive drawings in the form of case studies.

Discarded Treasures of an Infelicitous Past
Historic Preservation Thesis
Fall 2013 + Spring 2014
Chelsea Brandt
Belmont Freeman, advisor

This thesis project generated a set of standards for the preservation and adaptive reuse of Progressive Era Jails–roughly 1880s through 1930s–in the United States. A brief look at the history of penal reforms formed a background of basic knowledge of the penal system in order to better understand the findings and recommendations presented. The focus was adaptive reuse cases of jails, followed by a detailed look at Progressive Era jails and their character-defining features, program layout, circulation and supervision components and structural integrity. Based on these four basic principles, preservation recommendations were given and implemented into a design for the adaptive reuse of the 1906 York County Jail in York County, Pennsylvania.

What's on the Surface Does Matter: The Conservation of Applied Surface Decoration of Historic Stained Glass Windows
Historic Preservation Thesis
Fall 2013 + Spring 2014
Alyssa Grieco
George Wheeler, advisor

A stained glass window is both an architectural building element and an individual work of art. A stained glass window is composed of a variety of materials, mainly glass, lead and surface decoration, each of which has its own conservation issues. Surface decoration, which includes vitreous glass paint, silver stain and enamels, is an under appreciated component of stained glass windows. Though it does not pose a major threat to the physical stability or safety of the window, surface decoration defines these windows as works of art, with imagery that holds the window's history, including a direct view into the traditions, ideals and beliefs of the people of their time.

The conservation of the surface decoration of stained glass windows has never been fully analyzed, and both glazing and conservation professionals seek information regarding the history of the materials and techniques used in order to create or restore a stained glass window. The methods and techniques used to maintain and conserve the decoration vary depending on a number of circumstances, including the location of the window, the history and traditions of the people involved and the tools available to the conservators. Ethical considerations need addressing in order to be sure that the authenticity of each work is maintained.

In God We Trust? Preserving Historic Church Interiors
Historic Preservation Thesis
Fall 2013 + Spring 2014
Leah Lanier
Richard Piper, advisor

Research reports from preservation professionals suggest that providing current preservation tools with practical knowledge of traditions and beliefs associated with historic houses of worship can facilitate a more comprehensive understanding and approaches for preserving the overall integrity of such sites. Using redundant historic Christian churches as an example, the study investigated this suggestion using mixed methodology to evaluate the efficacy of multi-family residential adaptive-reuse conversions as a preservation approach. In order to create a conceptual model for this evaluation, this methodology combined a Comparative Religion and Religious Studies methods model with current historic preservation tools for assessing the significance and integrity of historic properties. The model was applied to a series of multi-family residential conversion case studies with the following goals: to interpret and identify the church's interior components and to ascertain the strengths and weaknesses of the adaptive-reuse approach.

Measuring the Impact of Historic District Designation on Real Estate in New York City
Historic Preservation Thesis
Fall 2013 + Spring 2014
Julia Barksdale Lewis
Anthony Wood, Erica Avrami + Jesse Keenan, advisors

Though carried out in practice for centuries, historic preservation, as a professional field, is relatively young and has not yet fully harnessed data to support the theories of the field. This thesis researched new ways to analyze historic districts using data and recommended methods for future analysis that evaluate how historic districts function in New York City. While the designation of historic districts was always somewhat controversial, recently, historic district designation came to the forefront of discussion in New York City. The real estate community has begun to use data to generate studies in opposition to historic district designations.

This thesis evaluated and critiqued the methodology developed and recommended ways in which it can be improved, setting up a framework for future research and data collection. As the accessibility and quantity of data usage increases, some of this information could potentially be applied to the study of historic preservation. The reasoning behind the arguments for and against historic district designation in New York City was dissected by focusing on specific arguments that were raised prior to designation and generated a methodology for the evaluation of historic districts through existing data sets. A framework for future studies that could be conducted was provided in case the data became available to further this research.

Adapting the Architectural Avant-Garde: A Design Proposal for Paul Rudolph's Orange County Government Center

Historic Preservation Thesis
Fall 2013 + Spring 2014
Beth Miller
Theodore Prudon, advisor

As culture and technology evolve, how will modern architecture fare? The thoughtful and deliberate adaptation of and addition to a work of modern architecture can salvage it from the grips of obsolescence by creating a radical new work. This thesis explored the history of obsolescence in architecture through the twentieth-century and its entanglement with the avant-garde. It addressed the difficulty of adapting modern architecture of the recent past, since it has yet to accrue age value or appreciation by the general public and is still in the process of being understood within the field of architecture itself. In particular, the focus was on the complexities of working with the architecture of Paul Rudolph that has waned in functionality and popularity, especially the controversial case of the Orange County Government Center, which posed a great challenge to preservation efforts.

While modern architecture continues to hold value and meaning for society, myriad forces work against its durability. As architecture becomes increasingly entwined with and dependent upon technologies, systems and materials that have shorter life spans, buildings themselves are threatened with obsolescence. We must, therefore, carry modern architecture into the future, not as a relic but with renewed functionality and significance, so an entirely new architecture can be created that is richer in meaning and succeeds in meeting the increasing complexity and accelerating flux of contemporary life. The avant-garde is inherently bound to obsolescence, championing innovation and progress while declaring all that preceded obsolete; the avant-garde leaves obsolescence in its wake. In this sense, it is the avant-garde that has become mainstream; the truly radical work of architecture eschews obsolescence, preserving works of architecture by declaring them infinitely adaptable.

A Seismic Retrofit to Rehabilitate the Long Beach Civic Center

Historic Preservation Thesis
Fall 2013 + Spring 2014
Talene Montgomery
Jorge Otero-Pailos, advisor

At the core of this thesis was a challenge to expand preservation criteria to include the integrity of the urban design concept. The ever-greater scales and complex assemblages of modern and contemporary architecture have implications not only for surface quality and streetfront appearance, but also for massing and urban relationships. The thesis made a case for the preservation of urban design intent through investigation of the American civic center complex. In order to test a strategy of preservation-by-design for the rehabilitation of the urban civic center complex, this thesis took the now-threatened Long Beach Civic Center as a case study. The city of Long Beach, California is moving forward with a plan to raze its 1977 Civic Center complex, designed by a consortium of local firms. City officials cite seismic deficiency and an inflated retrofit budget as grounds for the appropriateness of a total rebuild of the complex today. This thesis argued for the preservation of the existing City Hall and Main Library buildings by way of a retrofit. Built at a moment when Long Beach's downtown was itself in dire need of a retrofit, the City Hall and Main Library complex represent a civic effort to revitalize the city. This preservation design proposal attempted to make the case that it is possible to preserve the urban design features of the civic complex using creative design solutions to address both the city's expanded programmatic requirements and the potential seismic vulnerability of its structures, while maintaining the character-defining urban features of the original 1977 complex.

William Sumner Appleton + the Society for the Preservation of New England Antiquities

Historic Preservation Thesis
Fall 2013 + Spring 2014
William Morache
Jorge Otero-Pailos, advisor

This thesis project sought to explore professionalization in the history of preservation through the work of the Society for the Preservation of New England Antiquities and its founder, William Sumner Appleton. Appleton is credited with advancing preservation toward a professional system of organization and a more scientific method in the treatment of resources. While SPNEA's efforts successfully documented, managed and preserved old New England houses, this system also created a division of labor between the preservation professional and the restoration laborer. Through SPNEA's development of a professional approach to historic structures, Appleton separated labor from craft at a time when labor was a prominent issue in the Boston social and political landscape.

Through case studies of several early restoration projects, this project showed how Appleton specifically alienated the product of restoration from the restoration work itself. In these restoration projects it is clear that Appleton did not seek to develop any system of preservation education or technical training. Through contract bidding, the utilization of multiple general contractors and general lack of interest in the workmen involved in various house restoration projects, Appleton and SPNEA separated the tradespeople of restoration projects from the professional actions of preservation.

Considering the longstanding credit to SPNEA in the development of a professional approach to the field of preservation, this social isolationism and alienation of labor in the restoration process explains why the connection between the Arts & Crafts and preservation movements did not coalesce in the same way as in nineteenth-century Britain. This scientific, object-oriented approach also contributed to the persisting view of preservation as elitist and isolated from social issues.

The Comparative Analysis of Biological Growth + Common Cleaners Based on Organism Identification + Biological Mechanisms

Historic Preservation Thesis
Fall 2013 + Spring 2014
Jennifer Pont
Helen Thomas-Haney, advisor

Biological growth on stone monuments and buildings is a common concern in architectural conservation. It is usually removed through the use of commercial biological growth cleaners. There are a number of these products on the market whose efficacy varies by growth type and substrate. With years of experience a conservator gains a sense of what products work best based on the type of biological growth present, however most of this knowledge is based on trial and error in the field.

This thesis took a more systematic approach to cleaning biological growth. Popular commercial products owe their efficacy to the susceptibility of different biological organisms to the active ingredients present in the cleaner. Past studies on the subject of biodeterioration have taken two approaches: looking at the DNA identification growth found on stone and testing the responses of different forms of biological growth to commercially available biocides. These commercially available biocides are not the same as commercially available cleaners that work through biocidal mechanisms, with cleaners generally having lower toxicity and subject to less strict government regulation.

This thesis compared and analyzed the alterations caused by each chemical agent on specific forms of biological growth, through the collection and propagation of samples of biological growth and laboratory testing. The samples were monitored before, during and after treatment. The effects of the cleaners were analyzed and compared to understand any differences between the reactions of cleaners and growths, and to what each growth was most and least vulnerable.

Fire-Damaged Stone: The Effects of Heat, Flame + Quenching

Historic Preservation Thesis
Fall 2013 + Spring 2014
Beata Sasińska
George Wheeler, advisor

Stone is often perceived as an enduring material; however, many forces act on stone to cause its destruction. Of these forces, fire causes sudden and often irreversible damage on a large scale and is a risk to every building. Both the immediate and long-term effects of fire damage on stone are only partially understood, since it is such an uncontrollable phenomenon. Through both oven heating and direct flame testing, this thesis explored the effects of fire damage on four common stone types: Cold Spring granite, Indiana limestone, Vermont marble and Portland sandstone. In addition, the potential damage caused by "shocking" the stone with cold water and, thereby, creating a temperature differential was tested through the quenching of a portion of both oven and flame-heated samples. The immediate effects, such as color change and structural instability, were evaluated while simultaneously exploring the relationship among temperature, flame, quenching and long-term durability.

The Performance of Two Alkoxysilane Consolidants on Three Berea Sandstones through Controlled Environmental Stress Cycling

Historic Preservation Thesis
Fall 2013 + Spring 2014
Melissa Joanne Swanson
Chris Gembinski, advisor

This thesis contributed to the body of knowledge about the performance of sandstone consolidants in North America. A sandstone consolidant in use in Europe was tested alongside a consolidant in use in North America. Based on laboratory testing of sample stone treated with the two consolidants, this thesis analyzed the performance of the consolidants in comparison to one another. Establishing the important performance characteristics of a successful sandstone consolidant and identifying the characteristics of the three Berea sandstones, and the two consolidants being tested, allowed for an analytical performance of these materials. Controlled environmental stress cycling in the laboratory exposed the consolidated stone to conditions approximating those in the field. Comparing the maximum biaxial flexural strength of the stone samples revealed comparable performance the two consolidants, in consolidating each of the three sandstones.

A Case Study to Determine Significance + Establish Evaluative Criteria for the Adaptive Reuse of the Seamen's YMCA House

Historic Preservation Thesis
Fall 2013 + Spring 2014
Yojana Vazquez
Paul Bentel, advisor

The Seamen's YMCA House in West Chelsea was built in 1931 for the seamen entering the New York Harbor during the Great Depression. The purpose of the building was to provide services to young men and boys from the sea. These services included religious life, educational programming, social activities and ample housing. By 1967, there was no longer a need for merchant seamen in West Chelsea, so the building was converted to a Narcotic Addiction Control Commission rehabilitation center. It remained such until 1973 when it was converted into the Bayview Correctional Facility. The Department of Corrections remained in the building until it was officially closed in March 2013, leaving the building for sale and its future in West Chelsea undetermined.

The goal of this thesis was to determine a way to adapt the interior of an existing building and integrate new programming by developing a three-tier system to analyze the significance of the interior spaces. The three-tier system determined which spaces or architectural elements should be preserved and which could be sacrificed to accommodate the new programming without losing significance. The Seamen's YMCA House was analyzed, and an adaptive reuse was proposed to show that utilizing the three-tier system allows one to effectively determine how to best integrate new programming into an existing building without losing the historical significance.

The California Coastal Act + Historic Preservation

Historic Preservation Thesis
Fall 2013 + Spring 2014
Jessica Vermillion
Liz McEnaney, advisor

In 1972, the California Coastal Commission was established by voter initiative via Proposition 20. The passing of Proposition 20 gave the Coastal Commission authority over the distribution of coastal development permits for four years. The passing of the California Coastal Act in 1976 gave the Commission this authority indefinitely. Under the Coastal Act, the Commission was tasked with protection of coastal resources including: shoreline public access and recreation, terrestrial and marine habitat, visual resources, landform alteration, agricultural lands, commercial fisheries, industrial uses, water quality, offshore oil and gas development, transportation and development design, among various others. Also under the California Coast Act, coastal cities and counties were asked to develop Local Coastal Programs (LCPs) that must be approved by the Coastal Commission. After the Coastal Commission approves the LCPs, a local agency is then made responsible for issuing coastal development permits. Under these LCPs, communities are able to implement policies that address historic preservation issues. While some communities do not specifically mention historic preservation as one of the goals of their LCP, others do. Through examination of various Local Coastal Programs, including those that both do and do not address historic preservation, recommendations for how other coastal communities can incorporate historic preservation into their LCPs were made. California provides an important lesson for other states because the Coastal Act shows how historic preservation can and should be a part of larger policy conversations.

Extracting the Exhibited Interior: Historic Preservation + the American Period Room

Historic Preservation Thesis
Fall 2013 + Spring 2014
Vincent Wilcke
Andrew Dolkart, advisor

This thesis examined the history of preservation advocacy in relation to the collecting of American interiors conducted by the Metropolitan Museum of Art, the Brooklyn Museum, the Museum of Fine Arts in Boston and the Philadelphia Museum of Art in the early twentieth century. The American interiors these institutions collected were installed as period room displays where furniture, paintings and small decorative objects were exhibited as unified compositions. Underwritten by the progressive idea that aesthetics and morality were connected, museum reformers saw the American period room as a way to combat Victorian excess while attempting to assimilate the thousands of eastern and southern European immigrants who had come to the United States in the 1880s to a defined set of American values. Museum period rooms, however, were critiqued by preservation groups, which were determined to keep historic buildings preserved in situ. Arguing that they were rescuing the nation's great interiors from dilapidated obscurity, museum leaders insisted that the rooms they purchased were not valued locally. Museum period rooms did shift attention toward the architectural heritage of the United States, but they did so by dismantling important buildings that were often in no impending danger of demolition. Fearing the loss of local landmarks, preservation advocacy groups formed in reaction to the consumption of architectural fragments. American period rooms generated a contentious discussion between museums and advocacy groups over the cultural management of architectural heritage. Separated from their original purpose, American period rooms are currently being reevaluated by curators and museum professionals who are working to make them relevant to modern audiences.

Perceiving the Spirit of Manhattan's Chinatown: A Study of the Evolution + Preservation of the Signage Designed for Historic Chinese Association Buildings

Historic Preservation Thesis
Fall 2013 + Spring 2014
Tianchi Yang
Andrew Dolkart, advisor

It is a common experience to be caught by the overwhelming signs when walking through the streets of Manhattan's Chinatown. However, lying among the normal, modern commercial signage are some traditional signs, most of which are for historic family, district and merchant associations. Traditional signage plays an important role in Chinese architecture in identifying a building or a place, and communicating the spirit of the place through calligraphy. In the early years of Chinese arrival to the East Coast of the United States, these kinds of association were founded for the purpose of allowing members to support each other, and the signage for them came into being as a tradition from China. If an analogy is drawn between the stores and restaurants of Manhattan's Chinatown and leaves of a tree, then the associations will be the roots of that tree. Some of the surviving signs date back to the turn of the twentieth century, and some are newer replacements in traditional or evolutionary forms. Yet hanging on the facades or the interior halls, they are rarely recognized with respect for their values to the association headquarters and Manhattan's Chinatown.

The intent of this thesis was to uncover and interpret the signage for associations in Manhattan's Chinatown so as to inspire the appreciation of this signage, which is closely tied up with the spirit of Manhattan's Chinatown, by Chinese and people from other cultures. To critically study the histories of evolution and preservation of this signage, including the changing ways of how the signage and buildings are related, this thesis focused on four case studies: Lin Sing Association, On Leong Chinese Merchants Association, Chinese Consolidated Benevolent Association and Lee's Family Association.

Neighborhood Conservation Districts: An Assessment of Typologies, Effectiveness + Community Response

Historic Preservation Thesis
Fall 2013 + Spring 2014
Max Abraham Yeston
Carol Clark + Clara Irazábal, advisors

Neighborhood Conservation Districts (NCDs), are preservation planning tools with valuable approaches to neighborhood preservation. The strategy gives communities the opportunity to have a more active say in how their neighborhoods are shaped without having the physical identity of their surroundings be determined by market-based, Euclidean zoning and without the sometimes more onerous rules of historic districts. From a preservation standpoint, an NCD is appropriate for neighborhoods that might not merit traditional historic designation, either because the building stock is not old enough, or the original built fabric has been compromised by extensive alterations. Building upon previous studies that have taken a comprehensive look at the wide range of NCDs, this thesis focused on three cities: Cambridge, Massachusetts; Raleigh, North Carolina; and Philadelphia, Pennsylvania. Each city brought forth different criteria and design regulations. In this assessment of how specific NCDs are performing now, the basic questions were: are some NCDs meeting their self-expressed and explicit goals better than others? How do different standards of design review perform in different NCDs, and how do various community stakeholders view the effects of regulations? Examining the views of stakeholders on the ordinances against the language and intent of the laws themselves revealed whether NCDs could be viewed as an effective preservation tool for areas that might not fit full historic designation requirements. By taking into account the demographic and economic data for these particular neighborhoods, along with participants' views, the study assessed unintentional impacts of the different ordinances and ascertained whether there could be room for improvement.

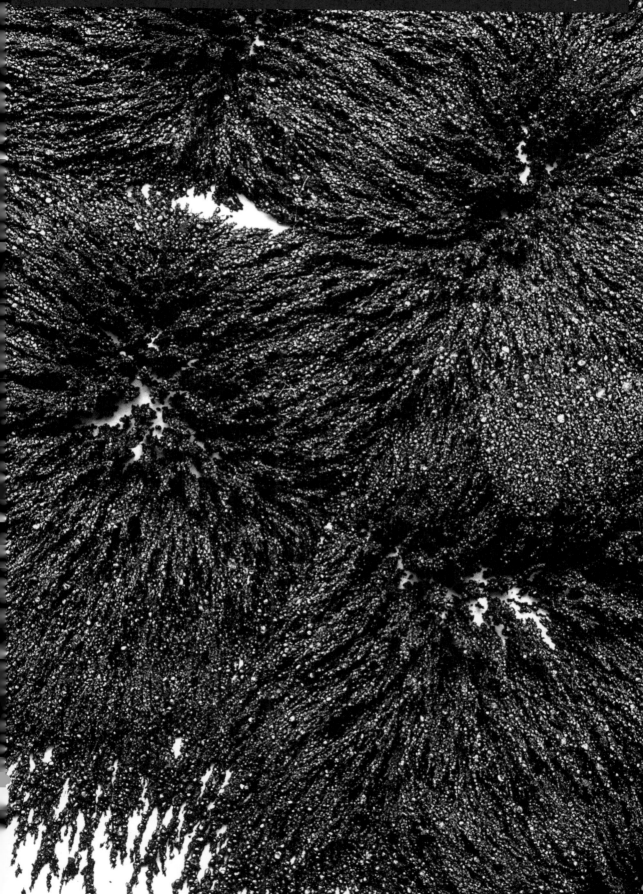

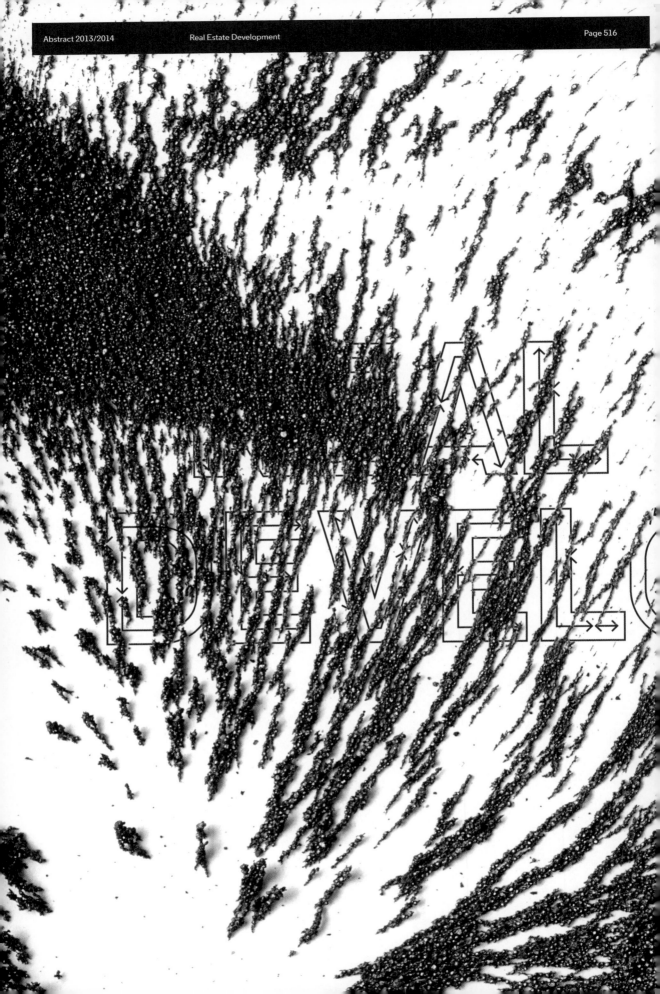

Real Estate Development Program
Vishaan Chakrabarti, director

Development is at the epicenter of the forces shaping our world today, be it the economy, the environment or the planet's inexorable march towards urbanization. Columbia's rigorous Masters of Science in Real Estate Development program—structured in the context of the world's most innovative laboratory for architecture, planning and preservation—provides an unrivaled platform to tackle these pressing issues. Building off the extraordinary resources of Columbia University and the City of New York, students learn from both industry leaders who provide current real world knowledge and outstanding faculty who provide a lifelong theoretical underpinning.

The core mission of the RED Program is to create visionary builders of the global urban environment. The program focuses intensely on the three pillars of the field, namely the financial, the physical and the legal. We teach development as a creative act in which issues of program, sustainability, building technology and construction are taught alongside intensive financial and transactional coursework. This holistic curriculum directly engages the future of entrepreneurial, "ground up" development, which in turn allows our students to recognize and create value where others cannot.

The students are required to synthetically apply their studies in both domestic and international case studies and are increasingly traveling – with a particular focus on the cities of the emerging "BRIC" economies—in response to the globalization of the industry and the densification of the planet. As the world has become more urban than rural—with issues of development, infrastructure, environment and competitiveness at the forefront – we stand at the cusp of the transformation of our field into an endeavor that is global in scope, entrepreneurial at heart and creative in practice.

Real Estate Development Practicum

Real Estate Development
Summer 2013
Abby Hamlin + Douglas Gauthier, coordinators, Morris Adjmi, Christopher Cooper, Michael Kirchmann, Robert Garneau, Rosa Chang, Jennifer Leung, Eric Liftin, Brian Loughlin + Frank Lupo, critics, with Yoojin Jang, Courtney Hunt, Dolores O'Connor, Bo Liu, Michael Schissel, Christine Nasir, Allison Schwarz + Sam Alison-Mayne

Real estate development is a dynamic, multi-disciplinary field that requires solid knowledge of the business of real estate and a full understanding of the art of building design and development. The Development Practicum was a interdisciplinary course that combined formal classroom training in real estate development practice with hands-on studio experience in the fundamentals of site and building design. The course was organized around the analysis of two development sites in New York City. These case studies were the framework for students to acquire knowledge about the integration of physical and financial thinking that is the essence of development practice. In addition, they served as a focal point for students to acquire the skill set necessary to conduct physical and financial evaluation of development opportunities.

The two components of the Practicum were a lecture series and the development studios. A developer led the weekly Practicum lectures. Their purpose was to introduce students to the various methods and measures developers use to analyze the risk and reward of prospective projects. Required readings and assignments supplemented the lectures. The lectures covered a broad array of topics and sectors, providing students with a comprehensive understanding of the issues they must address and the techniques they must use in order to make successful development decisions.

For the development studios the class was divided into smaller sections. The studio director, a trained architect, led each section. In studio, students worked specifically on the physical considerations of development, by creating basic design schemes for the two case study sites. They completed site observations, zoning analyses and massing studies, and they devised a typical floor plan and building program for each site. Through studio, students learned the spatial norms of building design and their effect on the functionality and marketability of different building types. This experience prepared students to make more confident and creative development decisions and to become better, more informed clients for the architects and other design consultants who they will later retain. The culmination of the Practicum was a recommended development scheme for each site that showed a full analysis of the site's physical and financial issues. Students prepared this scheme individually so that each one gained the full benefit of devising an approach to development decision-making.

Pathom Karnchanapimolkul **A**
Say Park **B**
Eng Ng **C**
Andy Golubitsky **D**
Will Weber **E/F/G**

B   5. BAM cultural district

NOW
upcoming competition

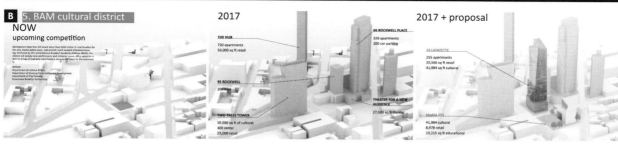

2017

2017 + proposal

E

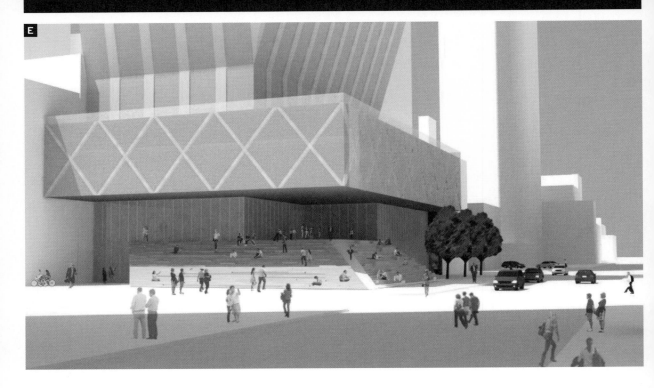

F

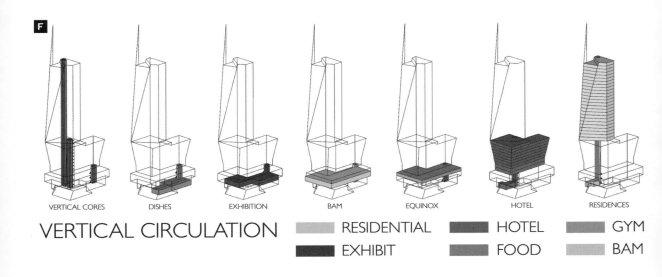

VERTICAL CORES   DISHES   EXHIBITION   BAM   EQUINOX   HOTEL   RESIDENCES

VERTICAL CIRCULATION

RESIDENTIAL	HOTEL	GYM
EXHIBIT	FOOD	BAM

G

The Transaction Process: Debt, Equity + the Art of Negotiation
Real Estate Development
Summer 2013
Mitchell Adelstein, instructor

This elective taught practical methods and techniques used by investors, lenders and equity investors: how to underwrite value-add opportunistic income-producing real estate; finance positions in real estate using various debt facilities and/or equity vehicles; and understand the transaction process through group participation in a mock transaction case study. The class was split up into "Deal Teams" that were responsible for underwriting and negotiating a deal to purchase, finance and close the transaction. Each group presented their analysis and discussed the transaction process during the final session. Upon completion of this elective, students were able to demonstrate capabilities and knowledge through case study and understand the roles of each key player in the transaction process. Students learned best practices in sourcing debt and equity capital, constructed various debt and equity underwriting models and learned the art of negotiation by participating in a mock transaction.

History of Real Estate Development in New York City
Real Estate Development
Summer 2013
Kate Ascher, instructor

The History of New York City Real Estate Development offered a historical survey of the last four centuries of real estate development in NYC. It relied not only on existing sources, widely available and held by Columbia libraries, but also on material from the collection of Seymour Durst—a patriarch of one of New York City's foremost real estate families and a passionate collector of New York City historical memorabilia. The course covered the period from the original Dutch settlement of New Amsterdam in the early 1600s through the present time. However, each presentation also contained thematic elements, using real estate developments to examine social and economic forces of the period. The topics ranged from the earliest systems of landholding and the evolution of the Manhattan street grid through the development of the nation's first public housing projects and the construction of the world's tallest skyscrapers. The latter part of the course touched specifically on modern themes that continue to shape the real estate environment of the city today. These included the continued regeneration of a once-industrial waterfront, the ever-evolving nature of public-private partnerships in development and the seminal connection between transportation hubs and real estate.

Skyscrapers: Cities in the Sky
Real Estate Development
Fall 2013
Kate Ascher, instructor

Urban development in the twenty-first century takes many forms, but none quite so interesting as the skyscraper. With swelling cities and growing concerns about the environment, vertical living has become the preferred way of life for millions of people around the world. But just how these tall buildings are designed, constructed and operated remains a mystery to many–even to those who live in them. This course looked at every aspect of life at great height–from the origins of tall buildings in New York and Chicago, to the economics of skyscraper design, to the technologies that lie behind skyscraper construction and operation, to the sociological and urban design implications of this popular urban form, to the shape and nature of the skyscrapers of the future. Supported by a variety of readings on the subjects of tall buildings, it drew on case studies relating to skyscrapers around the world and featured occasional guest speakers involved in development or construction.

The Works: Infrastructure Challenges + Opportunities
Real Estate Development
Spring 2014
Kate Ascher, instructor

As seamlessly as they have expanded to accommodate demands far beyond those envisioned in the nineteenth century, infrastructure networks around the world are struggling to adapt to the challenges of the twenty-first century. Once the driving force behind the rise of towns and cities across America and elsewhere, the development of adequate energy, water and transportation networks today lags behind real estate development in many parts of the world. This course looked at the connections between infrastructure and real estate in economic development – both over time and today – to understand the challenges and opportunities that these largely invisible systems present to developers today. It took the New York region as its laboratory, but also incorporated case studies from other American and foreign cities – focusing particularly on those who have best used infrastructure to their advantage in promoting successful development. It also grappled with the questions of infrastructure financing, and examines the role that the development community can play in mitigating the impact of shortfalls in public sector infrastructure spending in cities around the world.

International Real Estate Core
Real Estate Development
Spring 2014
Daniela Atwell +
Trevor Atwell, instructors

The International Real Estate
Development Core course introduced students to the macro
growth trends that are central
to the changing opportunities
within the global commercial
real estate world, as well as the
drivers, challenges and risks
associated with the opportunities in the emerging world, and
how to value the risk against
the reward when entering a
new and developing market.
The course broadly addressed
the ways in which to evaluate
one market against another, as
well as the variety of possibilities of taking advantage of the
benefits of international real
estate strategies, from portfolio
diversification, distribution
of specific sector expertise in
new markets with demand, to
the identification of unique opportunities in frontier markets
experiencing a dislocating
positive inflection in economic
or geopolitical conditions.

**International Real
Estate Regional Electives:
Brazil, India + Turkey**
Real Estate Development
Spring 2014
Selected RED Faculty

The purpose of the regional
electives was for students to
research and to develop market
specific knowledge and investment strategies. The course culminated with students presenting their portfolio allocations to
an investment committee panel
made up of industry executives from the institutional and
investment banking industry.
Each regional team was initially allocated a specific dollar
amount by the industry investment committee. Students
and professors returned at the
end of the regional elective
to argue for more or for less,
and did so by presenting a nuanced, fact-based assessment
of their region. This real-time
evaluation required students
to develop market specific
expertise through applied
portfolio management. Over
winter break, selected members from each team traveled to
the specific regions with their
professors to actively engage in
testing the methods and strategies which they had articulated
over the course of the semester.

**Developing a High-
Performance Building**
Real Estate Development
Fall 2013
*Charlotte Matthews + Steven
Baumgartner, instructors*

This course applied the
technical know-how of high
performance building to the
real world scenario of a building
project. Students, organized
into development teams, promoted green design, construction and operation strategies
within the constraints of a fixed
budget, competing devel-
oper and investor priorities,
policy drivers and inhabitants and contrasting views
of market demand. Students
developed pay-back scenarios,
explored financing strategies,
undertook informal market
analysis and learned to seek
out and apply precedents and
lessons learned from other
green building projects.

**Real Estate Entrepreneurial-
ism for Architects, Builders,
Developers, Buyers + Sellers**
Real Estate Development
Fall 2013
Hank Bell, instructor

This course was led by one of
the first practitioner academics to define the independent
discipline of development.
The lectures were designed to
fill in the gaps with practical
knowledge and hard lessons
learned from generations of
practitioners. Students were
provided with the know-hows
of materializing their visions
at the entrepreneurial scale.

**Hyperdensity + the
Future of the City**
Real Estate Development
Fall 2013
Vishaan Chakrabarti, instructor

This course, based on Professor
Chakrabarti's forthcoming
book A Country of Cities:
A Manifesto for an Urban
America, hypothesizes that hyperdensity—defined as density
above 30 units/acre—paired
with robust transit infrastructure is a potential "silver
bullet" for addressing many
of the economic and social ills
confronting the United States
today. Structured as an analysis
of urban policies that have led
to America's profligate use of
land, and as a proposition on
how to correct course with new
policy initiatives for creating an
"infrastructure of opportunity,"
the book envisions a county of
towers, trains and trees as the
best path to keep our nation
and our developing planet
economically, environmentally
and socially sustainable. Given
the nation's role as a global
purveyor of culture, America's
embrace of a far denser land-
use pattern is imagined to influence the development pattern
of countries with emerging
economies, where billions are
moving from poverty to middle
class affluence worldwide.

Internship + Individual Research
Real Estate Development
Spring 2014
Jessica Stockton King, instructor

Structured as an internship research class, students had the opportunity to select from a group of public agencies, financial institutions, private developers and non-profit organizations actively involved in real estate. The course was designed to provide participants with hands-on experience working with real estate and real estate related issues. Independent research efforts included development feasibility, financial analysis, market research, asset management, policy review and industry studies.

Thesis
Real Estate Development
Spring 2014
Vishaan Chakrabarti + Jessica Stockton King, instructorsr

The thesis is an important part of the real estate development curriculum. It was an individual investigation of the student's own choice that was supervised by a faculty member and intended to demonstrate the student's ability to structure an argument about an issue or problem significant or clearly relevant to real estate development practice or the development profession. The thesis was the culmination of the three-semester course of study and demonstrated a synthetic understanding of the research and professional skills and substantive knowledge bases, which form the content of the curriculum of the Real Estate Development Program.

Thesis I: Research
Real Estate Development
Fall 2013
Jesse Keenan, instructor

This course examined the leading qualitative and quantitative research methods in the built environment professions. Concentration was placed on the methods of architecture, urban economics, construction management and applied real estate finance. With an eye for the development of a thesis, students worked independently to develop a framework for undertaking the completion and defense of a thesis in the Spring semester. Whether empirical, applied or observational, students gained the opportunity to develop critical analytical skill sets, which allowed them to construct an operational research design and then test the hypothesis and methods underlying such efforts.

Private Equity + Capital Raising
Real Estate Development
Fall 2013
Mark Weidner + Michael Clark, instructors

This course exposed students to the fundamentals of real estate private equity, basic terms, players in the industry, various roles of professionals, legal and financial aspects of real estate private equity in today's environment and taught a broad base of understanding in private equity real estate to prepare students in the concepts, terms and fundamentals that govern the real estate private equity markets. The course was taught from the perspective of the General Partner in managing funds and the Limited Partner in investing in funds. Additionally, outside industry experts guest spoke on their real estate private equity experience. These leading industry professionals included intermediaries and prominent LPs and GPs. The class focused in particular on current fundraising issues as well as on the structuring of private equity transactions. The course was of particular interest to students who wanted exposure to real estate private equity in the future, either as a General Partner, Limited Partner or Local Operating Partner domestically or internationally.

Hotel Development + Investment Analysis
Real Estate Development
Fall 2013
Adam Feil, instructor

The course covered the complete financial cycle of hotel investment analysis including development, lending, operations, investment analysis, renovation decisions and acquisition or disposition. Real estate valuation principles and procedures were explored with emphasis on the replacement cost, sales comparison and income capitalization approaches. Additionally, the role and function of the asset manager were discussed with emphasis on investment underwriting, operations analysis, portfolio management, strategic investment analysis, market strategy, management contracts, franchises and involvement with the property management team.

Retail Real Estate + Development
Real Estate Development
Spring 2014
Gary Fogg + Dan Mandelbaum, instructors

The success of the shopping center is driven by a combination of the strength of the real estate and the retailer. In the case of retail real estate, the success of the retailer is arguably more correlated to the fundamentals of the underlying real estate than the tenants of other asset classes such as office and industrial. This course discussed retail real estate from the perspective of both the retailer and the landlord/developer. A thorough understanding of the retailer's business model will increase the likelihood of success for retail real estate investors and developers. At the same time, the class reviewed the primary considerations of the retail developer and owner, including tenant mix, shopping center design, leasing and valuation. A strong emphasis was placed on leasing and financial valuation. The lease not only outlined the economics of rent and expenses; it also established various rights and restrictions of both the landlord and that tenant.

Real Estate Finance 3: Capital Markets
Real Estate Development
Spring 2014
Merrie Frankel, instructor

This course focused on the debt and equity markets that are linked to real estate assets. Both the public and private markets were examined in detail. Topics include the history of real estate cycles, the US mortgage finance system, the agency mortgage-backed securities (MBS) market, the non-agency MBS market (subprime, Alt-A and jumbo), commercial mortgages and mortgage-backed securities (CMBS), structured products such as CMOs and CDOs, MBS valuation, real estate investment trusts (REITs), commingled real estate funds (CREFs), real estate limited partnerships (RELPs) and master limited partnerships (MLPs), derivative products, and asset allocation and real estate portfolio theory.

Affordable Housing Finance Techniques
Real Estate Development
Fall 2013
Richard Froehlich + Chuck Brass, instructors

This course presented a detailed review of the techniques for financing affordable housing. In combination with the focus on financing techniques, the course also looked at the development issues associated with this complex area and the policy focus of governmental programs. Incentives, public-private partnerships, the use of tax exempt bonds and the securitization of debt are all techniques initially developed for use in residential finance and in the financing of affordable housing. The crisis in credit and mortgage markets is impacting every segment of the real estate finance industry, including affordable housing. The residential finance system that has evolved in the US over the past 50 years is in the process of breaking down and being remade. Housing policy and the federal role in making residential mortgage markets function, as well as serving the affordable housing needs of the country, is in flux. Although the course focused on finance and financing techniques, it considered the role of the public sector in regulating and creating incentives for the development and financing of housing in particular. The public sector's role ranges from the establishment and regulation of the capital markets, to the creation of tax incentives and specialized treatment for real estate enterprises and to the offering of particular subsidies for the development of affordable housing. An understanding of the public sector's financial and regulatory role is essential for understanding real estate financial markets in general and housing markets in particular. Every real estate project, and especially affordable housing projects, has a hidden partner: the federal government. The course was primarily taught through the case method. Each class had a case, finance problem and reading assignment.

Real Estate Investment Analysis
Real Estate Development
Summer 2013
Frank Gallinelli, instructor

This course was intended to benefit those students with a somewhat limited background in finance by offering an "applied finance" approach to mastering key real estate investment concepts. Using several different property types as examples, we evaluated various scenarios of potential acquisition, cash flow, financing, resale, development and partnership.

In our analyses we looked at specific metrics to identify what appeared to be favorable about each investment, what was problematic and what might be missing from the scenario as presented. We looked for factors that might optimize each real estate investment transaction and for those that might cause it to fail. As necessary, we reconstructed each transaction and sought alternatives that could yield more favorable or more reasonable results.

The objective was for students to learn to recognize and understand key concepts and metrics through an inductive approach. An additional objective was for students to develop a sense of how one can "read" the financial work-up of a property like a story: to look behind the numbers to apprehend not only what they reveal but also what they might be warning us to dig deeper to uncover.

Commercial Leasing
Real Estate Development
Spring 2014
Marty Gold + Mitchell Nelson, instructors

This course looked at commercial leasing from both a landlord and tenant perspective, and contained both legal and business analysis of the most important provisions and issues in leasing today. It provided a firm basis for understanding space leases as the revenue stream behind building operations, financing and profits. Allocation of risks related to the provision of space in a building was a consistent thread in the conversation. The readings included clauses from standard leases and articles about the subject matter, as well as some court decisions that illuminated the complexities and conflicts.

Launching a Real Estate Venture
Real Estate Development
Fall 2013
Abby Hamlin, instructor

In this course we discussed the challenges and rewards of real estate entrepreneurship and explored alternative strategies for launching an entrepreneurial real estate venture. After learning about the role and structure of a business plan, students focused on creating and presenting individual plans for their future real estate development businesses. In this combination lecture and lab course, the professor provided guidance and counsel, but each student researched their business idea and built a supportable case for their future business plan.

Capstone - Development Case Studies
Real Estate Development
Spring 2014
Abby Hamlin, Genghis Hadi + Shawn Amsler, instructors

The class utilized various real estate development and investment case studies, in conjunction with outside real estate developers and investors within the industry. The cases reached across a broad array of product types, situational decision-making and business styles. Students developed rapid development decision-making and management skills while working in a team-based process where all aspects of the real estate business proved to be critical success factors. Training used real world case studies of actual development sites, in real time, that required defining new development and repositioning plans and focusing on essential feasibility. This class was the synthesis and implementation of the skills learned throughout the student's immersions in development curriculum. A series of four intensive team charrettes involved programming and design for selected sites. The final work product was a presentation to a committee of real estate professionals and faculty which included the following deliverables: Zoning and Regulatory Approval Analysis; Financial Feasibility Models; Return on Investment Analysis; Market Analysis Report; Product Design Plans; Marketing and Implementation Schedule and Budget; and Investment and Exit Strategy Report.

Property in Common: the Nexus between Architecture + Real Estate
Real Estate Development
Spring 2014
Catherine Ingraham, instructor

Architecture's relation to real property has been, to date, almost fully defined by the limited, yet significant, role architecture has played in real estate valuation. Real property adds a wildly speculative dimension to what is already a projective practice, and both architecture and real estate are now in the business, to some degree, of monetizing psychological life. There are persuasive contemporary reasons for undertaking this subject matter: the puzzling undervaluation of design both in the marketplace and in the public imagination; the difficulty in designing credible public space in American cities; a housing crisis that has revived political debates over fundamental entitlements; and multi-tiered conflicts between property, infrastructure and ecological systems that global development encounters at every turn.

This course looked at systemic and theoretical issues that underlie these contemporary dilemmas in architectural design and real estate development. Its goal was to examine points of confluence/nexus between property, real estate systems and architecture that are significant not only for specific buildings or development projects but also for systems of sovereignty, finance, design, law, justice and nature that such a nexus advances or inhibits. Property —in general and as manifested in contemporary real estate development—and architecture together form matrices that are simultaneously concrete, paradigmatic and transcendental. These matrices give deeply consequential form, rule and norm to our physical and conceptual environments.

Institutional Real Estate Investment
Real Estate Development
Summer 2013
Andre Kuzmicki, instructor

The course examined institutional real estate investment strategy and decision-making. Topics included portfolio theory and the role of real estate in an institutional portfolio; investment styles; manager and vehicle selection; and risk assessment. Cases were extensively used in this course. The objectives of the course were to establish a context for institutional approaches to real estate; expose the students to a variety of investment vehicles and structures, some of which they had to examine in greater depth in subsequent courses; and to further their investment evaluation skills, emphasizing both qualitative and quantitative analysis.

New Directions for Development: Rethinking Workplaces, Buildings + the City
Real Estate Development
Spring 2014
Andrew M. Laing, instructor

This seminar class explored emerging trends that impact the shape of future development. Trends that were explored included the impact of new technologies on how we work, live and use space and how this will affect the design and development of workplaces, buildings and the city. We identified innovations in work, technology and space which the developer will need to be familiar with to provide cutting edge products given rapidly changing corporate and end user expectations. Through a combination of selected readings, case studies, discussions and presentations, students gained an understanding of: the future of the workplace and the office building, the impact of information technology on how and where work takes place, how this is affecting building types and urban developments, the emerging demands of corporate organizations for new ways of using space, suggesting new requirements for building types and cities, and how developers, designers and city governments should think differently about development in the future.

Real Estate Law Fundamentals
Real Estate Development
Fall 2013
Richard Leland + Fried Frank, instructors

This course examined development and investment issues as they interfaced with property, zoning, contract, securities and tax law. The course provided students the opportunity to actively engage legal professionals in mitigating and resolving contractual and regulatory risk.

Market Analysis for Development
Real Estate Development
Summer 2013
Ryan LeVasseur + Shuprotim Bhaumik, instructors

This course examined critical factors in national, regional and urban real estate markets that determine development opportunities. Course topics included business and construction cycles, regional and urban economic trending, restructuring of urban space dynamics, hotel and retail feasibility and demand analysis, commercial and industrial location theories and demographic analysis and projection techniques.

Being the Client
Real Estate Development
Summer 2013 + Spring 2014
Brooks Mcdaniel, instructor

The real estate development process is rife with potential complications and pitfalls. By understanding the distinct phases of the process and the decisions that are required in each phase, a developer can minimize risk and increase the potential value of a development. Additionally, a developer orchestrates the efforts of a team of consultants and city agencies to move a project towards completion, so an understanding of the roles and responsibilities of the various members of the project team will contribute to the efficiency of the decision making process.

This course explored the development process with respect to site selection, design, construction, value and risk. The objective of The Architecture of Development was to gain an understanding of the role of the full development team, expose the students to a variety of case studies and provide a framework for decision making during the development process.

Finance Modeling 2
Real Estate Development
Summer 2013
Min Suh, instructor

This was the second level financial modeling course meant to further develop the fundamental skills and higher level modeling techniques required to create real estate specific financial models utilizing the Microsoft Excel spreadsheet software. Topics included core real estate form construction, asset specific modeling components, flexible model construction, leverage integration, analysis techniques and best practices.

Post-Storm Development: Opportunities for Rebuilding + Innovation
Real Estate Development
Spring 2014
Brandon Mitchell + Neil Chambers, instructors

This course examined fundamental questions and realities about threats to coastal communities throughout New York City from increased storm events such as hurricanes, superstorms, extensive rainfall, storm surge and intense winds. Some of the questions the class addressed include: What kind of leadership (political, economic and design) and opportunities (structural and non-structural) for innovation is the public sector capable of providing to the post-Sandy rebuilding effort, as well as emergency preparedness? Is the private sector and are homeowners able or willing to innovate on water management, energy and materials? Do parts of the City need to be re-planned, re-designed, rezoned or returned to open space? Are the various New York City action plans and reports being implemented and, if so, to what effect? What is the cost to the public and private sector of rebuilding and protecting against future extreme storm events?

Underwriting
Real Estate Development
Fall 2013
Roger Nussenblatt, instructor

This course covered all major facets of underwriting income-producing commercial real estate from a lending perspective. Students learned how to effectively underwrite stabilized office, retail, industrial, multifamily and hotel properties. Emphasis was placed on credit evaluation, cash flow analysis, break-even analysis, market analysis, sponsorship and loan structure. Exit strategies including securitization and loan sales were also examined.

Underwriting 2
Real Estate Development
Spring 2014
Roger Nussenblatt, instructor

The course covered all major facets of underwriting the repositioning of income-producing commercial real estate from a lending perspective. Students learned how to effectively underwrite transitional office, retail, industrial, multifamily and hotel properties. Loan structure, interest reserve analysis, LIBOR caps, reposition timing, credit evaluation, market analysis and sponsorships were major focuses of the course. Exit strategies including permanent takeout financing and loan were also discussed.

Residential Marketing
Real Estate Development
Summer 2013
Elisa Orlanski Ours, instructor

This course reviewed case studies and lessons learned from programming residential Master Plans to Micro Units. The focus of the course was on public programming—outdoors spaces, lobbies, amenities, hotel services and mixed use components—and private planning—new construction versus conversion, relationship of multiple towers, view studies, unit mix, residential guidelines for cores and back of house/front of house circulation.

Tax Issues in Acquisitions + Developments
Real Estate Development
Spring 2014
Richard O'Toole, instructor

This course was an overview of federal income tax and local tax issues that affect the planning and execution of urban real estate developments. Topics addressed included income tax treatment for sellers as well as alternatives to cash acquisitions, transfer and mortgage recording tax concerns, issues with equity partners and distinctions between condominium and rental developments.

Public-Private Partnerships in Real Estate Development
Real Estate Development
Fall 2013
Robert Paley, instructor

This course explored public sector involvement in real estate development and was designed to impart a set of skills necessary to manage the complex medley of governmental actors with conflicting goals and agendas in public/private development. Case studies were drawn from a variety of projects, primarily in the New York City metropolitan region. These case studies provided an opportunity to examine the motivations, powers and constraints of public agencies, as well as the approaches to planning projects, soliciting support, sustaining momentum and structuring public/private partnerships.

Affordable Housing, Development + Policy
Real Estate Development
Spring 2014
Ed Poteat, instructor

This course used the affordable housing techniques discussed in previous semesters to design and plan an actual affordable housing development. Besides utilizing affordable housing techniques such as tax credit and tax exempt bond financing, the course also looked at the other aspects of affordable housing development such as design and constructability elements, community involvement and political considerations. Developers must be a "jack of all trades" to successfully execute a new project. Although a keen understanding of affordable housing finance is a necessity for any successful developer, development requires an understanding of several disciplines. Political considerations have stymied many feasible affordable housing developments. Design and constructability issues have severely delayed or bankrupted a financially feasible project. This course discussed the role of intermediaries and government agencies in the creation of affordable housing.

Asset Management + Ownership
Real Estate Development
Spring 2014
Sara Queen, instructor

This course studied the issues that impact an asset from initial investment through disposition, with a particular focus on leasing, repositioning strategies, hold-sell analysis and operations. The focus was to demonstrate how effective asset management works with property management, leasing, construction/development and accounting to maximize financial performance. Overall, the class emphasized real-world issues and examples through the life cycle of an asset.

Urban Economics
Real Estate Development
Summer 2013
Ryan Severino, instructor

This course focused on the introduction of space and location to microeconomics. It intended to give students of real estate development an understanding of the underlying economic principles related to real estate. Economic theory enables the understanding of the existence of cities, their size and how they grow. It can also be utilized to understand land rents and uses, the economics of housing and the economics of commercial real estate.

Alternative + Distressed Investment Strategies
Real Estate Development
Fall 2013
Donald Sheets, instructor

This course was designed to introduce the framework of commercial real estate alternative investment strategies, primarily from a principal-based approach. Legal, strategic and valuation techniques were explored using a case study method. Relative value, subordination principals, catalysts and trade mechanics also were explored throughout the course. Public and private fixed-income and equity markets were explored, as well as emerging and derivative-based strategies.

Construction Management + Technology
Real Estate Development
Fall 2013
Joel Silverman, instructor

This course bridged the physical disciplines with the regulation and financial complexities of modern development. The course provided an overview of construction technologies, the construction process and construction management. Course topics included cost estimating; value engineering; scheduling and management methods; contract documentation and administration; RFP/bidding; insurance; labor relations; civil and mechanical engineering; and, delivery systems design and implementation.

Real Estate Finance 1
Real Estate Development
Summer 2013
Manish Srivastava, instructor

This course was an introduction to the methods of financial analysis for real estate investments. Topics included methods of valuation, cash flow forecasting, computer modeling, debt, leverage and deal structures. Emphasis was placed on the financing of individual projects. This course required greater than average preparation time. It was heavily oriented toward numerical analysis and made use of case studies and computer spreadsheet analyses.

Real Estate Finance 2: Case Studies + Development Modeling
Real Estate Development
Fall 2013
Min Suh, instructor

This course covered real estate financial modeling applications utilizing Microsoft Excel and ARGUS. Topics explored include model structures and advanced techniques, development project financial modeling, third party software integration, REIT modeling, asset level GAAP modeling, real estate portfolio modeling, waterfall models and optimization. Students demonstrated capabilities and knowledge through a combination of assignments and in class discussion.

Global Property Investments in Emerging Markets
Real Estate Development
Summer 2013
John Tsui, instructor

This course provided very practical case studies coupled with lectures from senior executives focused on investment in real estate assets and entities in global developed and emerging markets. Cases focused on bottom up valuation approach versus the widely used top down valuation approach. As an alternative to land residual technique reconciliation, cases illustrated partitioning of cash flow and residual value. The curriculum encompassed case studies ranging from an overview of emerging market property investments and their risks, restructuring of a busted convertible loans of a Chinese property company, sale lease back and "built to suit" logistics warehouses in Brazil, acquisition of distressed empty office buildings in Berlin, investing in high yield and special situation in China and India, structured debt and hybrid equity and quasi debt securities investments in Chinese listed property entities.

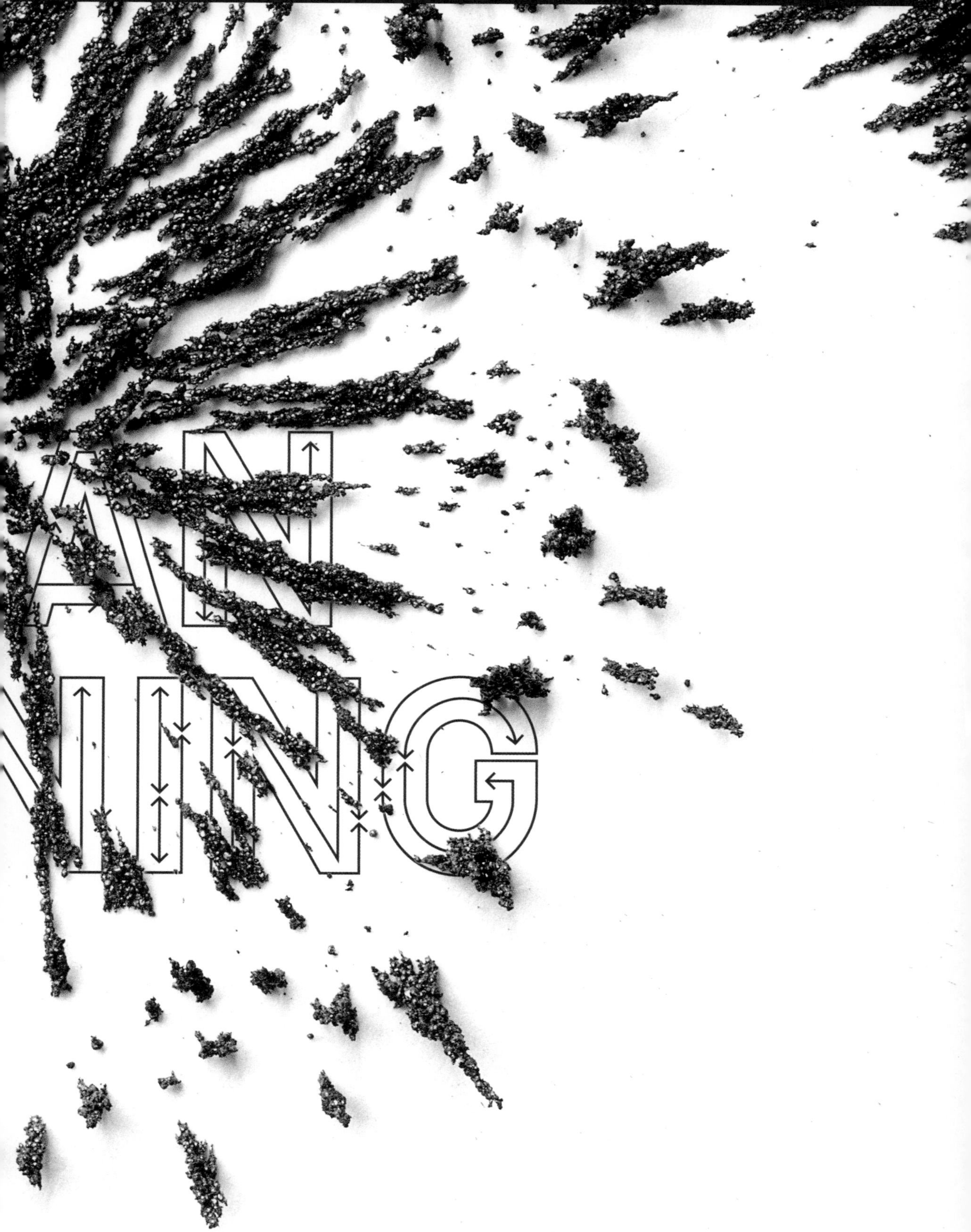

Urban Planning Program
Lance Freeman, director

The Urban Planning program had an exciting and productive academic year. We successfully completed the reaccreditation process with the Planning Accreditation Board. The reaccreditation is important for at least two reasons. First, reaccreditation certifies the quality of our academic offerings and serves as a "good-housekeeping" seal of approval from the premier professional planning organization in the United States. Reaccreditation serves to reassure students and alumni that they have a well-respected professional credential and consequently enhances the professional opportunities of current and former students. The reaccreditation process also required a self-study and the development of a strategic plan. This was important because the required self-study provided for us the opportunity to take stock of where we are as a program and to set objectives for what we would like to accomplish. The program remains committed to educating a diverse group of planning professionals to be technically competent, ethically engaged and politically committed to fostering the betterment of peoples and sustainable places.

We continued the trend of having an exceptionally diverse student body including a large number of Chinese students. We have also turned to addressing the question of Chinese urbanization hosting several lectures on the topic and hosting Professor Xin Li as a visiting professor for the 2014-2015 academic year. Xin Li earned her Ph.D. in Urban Planning from the Massachusetts Institute of Technology. Professor Li will advise students on their Master's theses and teach courses Environmental Planning in China and Land Use and Housing Policy in China.

We offered a number of exciting studios this year including international studios in Tokyo, Japan; Port of Spain, Trinidad and Tobago; and, Rio de Janeiro, Brazil. Closer to home, planning studios addressed an array of challenging problems including bus rapid transit in Rockland and Westchester counties, privatelydeveloped in-fill housing on New York City Housing Authority properties, the reuse and redevelopment of the former Post Office site into Moynihan Station and planning for economic development around Gowanus Bay in Brooklyn. These studios give students the opportunity to hone their planning skills while working with a client to address a planning problem.

We are proud of the continued involvement of several alumni including Gary Roth who taught the Moynihan Studio course, and Eldad Gothelf who taught a course on zoning in New York City, in our program. Their professional experience strengthens our curriculum and their continued involvement helps connect current students with alumni.

Finally, we would like to congratulate the forty-five students who graduated from the Urban Planning program this year. We are confident they will be successful and hope they remain active members of the Urban Planning program.

Advanced Urban Planning Studio: After Sandy
Urban Planning
Fall 2013
Ethel Sheffer, critic, with Matthew Mueller

During the Fall 2013 semester at Columbia University's GSAPP, the advanced urban planning studio was tasked with studying post-Sandy recovery and developing a set of recommendations for Manhattan Community District 1. The studio worked on ways to improve resilience to future disasters in Lower Manhattan. We delivered nine recommendations for Community Board 1 to better address the needs of the District's vulnerable populations. The report also summarizes three months of data compilation, interviews, observations and analysis. The recommendations were as follows: designate one or more facilities in the District to house resilience planning activities, called Disaster Orientation Logistics Locations; educate residents with the knowledge and tools to assess their own risks; encourage residents to self-identify and communicate their own needs and vulnerabilities; utilize a sign-out sheet as a practical exercise that reinforces communication and disaster response; rethink communications by encouraging bottom-up processes and low-tech solutions; incorporate larger, institutional and organizational networks; coordinate information sharing within existing community and business groups; create opportunities for collaboration through community roundtables; and incorporate resiliency into the existing school-building agenda.

Heidi Brake Smith, Peter Chung, Benjamin Engle, Justine Shapiro-Kline + Julie Sophonpanich **A/B/C**

Gowanus Bay Terminal: Planning Red Hook's Resilient Industrial Ecosystem
Urban Planning
Spring 2014
Michael Fishman, critic, with Peter Chung

The Gowanus Bay Terminal (GBX), a multi-user industrial site, sits on Red Hook's waterfront in Brooklyn, New York. It is home to the retired Port Authority Grain Terminal built in 1922, the retired Ellis Island Ferryboat Yankee and the soon to be retired cement bulk carrier Loujaine. The site is made up of thirteen upland acres and thirty-three acres of underwater development rights. Our studio explored resilient industrial expansion within the context of the opportunities and challenges facing the Red Hook community. Through resident interviews, community meetings and an online survey, we identified the following issues facing the neighborhood: poor transportation access; limited public waterfront access; residential development pressure based on the predicted increase in population over the next twenty years; resiliency and flooding issues; failure to retain industrial businesses; and high unemployment rates. Based on these issues, we recommended the following site programming to enhance both the private and the public components of GBX: expand the park space, land and retrofit the Loujaine to provide a community programming space, expand the industrial site to include pre-cast concrete production, enhance the local ecology, promote resiliency and educate the public through green infrastructure and programming.

Philip Betheil, Yuheng Cai, Wei Guo, Daniel Hewes, Olivia Jovine, Sharon Moskovits, Kellie Radnis + Houman Saberi **A/B**

Guiding Sustainable Development in East Port-of-Spain
Urban Planning
Spring 2014
Clara Irazabal, critic, with Natalie Quinn

This studio created a plan for sustainable development in Port of Spain, Trinidad and Tobago, for the Inter-American Development Bank (IDB) in conjunction with the Ministry of Planning. The project evaluated the context of and community support for three major physical interventions proposed for the city: river revitalization through parks, an aerial cable car transit system and preservation of cultural heritage, which together aim to improve the environmental, economic and social sustainability of Port of Spain. These proposals resulted from an analysis of environmental and economic challenges to a sustainable Port of Spain undertaken by the IDB, who would finance the projects through loans to the government. The three projects are to be implemented in East Port of Spain, a disenfranchised but culturally rich area of the city characterized by informal settlement in the mountainous city margins. The mission of the studio was to guide the progression of the three proposals such that the residents of East Port of Spain were included in the development of these plans. In each of the project areas, the studio recommended a process rather than specific design recommendations, because they felt it is critical that the community members drive these interventions.

Meagan Aaron, Alexandria Fiorini, Franziska Grimm, Jihyeon Jeong, Rachel Levy, Erica Mollon, Yesmin Vega + Xuzheng Wang **A/B/C**

Tappan Zee Bridge: Promoting Transit Options
Urban Planning Studio
Spring 2014
*Floyd Lapp, critic, with
Benjamin S. Engle*

Our studio's mission was to provide land use, transit and financing recommendations to Rockland and Westchester Counties for the Tappan Zee Bridge and I-287 corridor. As of now, a series of bus rapid transit ("BRT") proposals are slated to be implemented along the corridor by 2018. Our analysis built upon the State's Mass Transit Task Force ("MTTF") Final Report on BRT planning, published in February, 2014. Constructing and operating BRT in a primarily low-density, suburban environment is a significant undertaking and consequently must be evaluated prudently. First, we analyzed commuting patterns and relevant demographics in the I-287 corridor. We then provided an in-depth analysis of the suitability of BRT stations that the MTTF proposed, using an outcomes matrix that assembled a variety of transportation, land use and demographic criteria. We provided a similar matrix for a series of transit-oriented development sites along the corridor. We also assessed whether a substantial improvement to existing transit services could be achieved by upgrading existing bus routes, as opposed to a full BRT implementation. Finally, we explored additional measures of congestion pricing, variable tolling and transportation demand management that may offer additional promise in reducing congestion along the greater I-287 corridor.

Eric Blair, Junda Chen,
Yung Chun, Qihan Li,
David Perlmutter, Yinan Tong +
Crystal Wang **A/B/C**

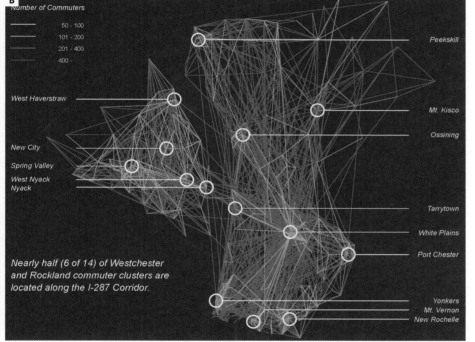

Number of Commuters

50 - 100
101 - 200
201 - 400
400 -

Peekskill

West Haverstraw

Mt. Kisco

Ossining

New City

Spring Valley

West Nyack
Nyack

Tarrytown

White Plains

Port Chester

Nearly half (6 of 14) of Westchester and Rockland commuter clusters are located along the I-287 Corridor.

Yonkers
Mt. Vernon
New Rochelle

Tokyo: Reimaging Aoyama Street

Urban Planning
Spring 2014
Naka Matsumoto, critic,
with Emily Gordon

The Tokyo studio was tasked with developing recommendations for Tokyo-based real estate corporation Hulic Co., Ltd. on the future identity of Tokyo's Aoyama Street. The developers saw Aoyama as a microcosm for future development of Tokyo. In formulating recommendations for Hulic, the studio undertook two phases of research: before the site visit and during the site visit. Before visiting the site, the studio researched Japan and Tokyo, in particular, through various sources ranging from statistics from Japanese government agencies to interviews with Japanese academics. While on site, street surveys, pedestrian and bicycle counts, building typology observations and various conferences with local government officials and Japanese experts were also done to supplement our prior research. Taking the issues of Japan's aging population, the 2020 Olympics, occurrence of natural disasters, our client's interest and the overall well-being of the Japanese public, the Tokyo studio came up with recommendations that we felt would address these three main issues, along with the needs of our client and the Japanese public. Presented here in this exhibit were the findings and final set of recommendations we proposed to our client.

Ariana Branchini, Ola El Hariri, Kyle Innes, Patrick Jelasco, Jordanna Lacoste, Ying Li, Chunxiao Xu + Yidan Xu **A/B**

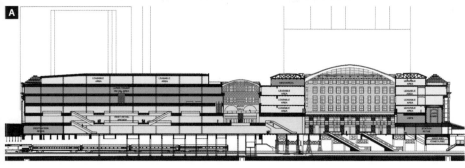

Moynihan Station: Planning for a New Midtown Destination
Urban Planning
Spring 2014
Gary Roth, critic, with Taylor Miller

The James A. Farley building, also known as the future home of Moynihan Station was first built in 1912 and formed a scenic boulevard echoing Pennsylvania Station. This former post office will be retrofitted into a world-class train station and a new destination in Midtown West. This studio was tasked with solving a number of challenges presented by the Moynihan Station redevelopment project, specifically creating a programming plan for the one million square feet of space unused by the future train station plan. Challenges with the space include connectivity, as the building is surrounded by moats, the large floor plate vestiges from the building's operation as a post office and the need for substantial new infrastructure. The studio concluded that Moynihan Station's train station component could not solve the current and future congestion problems of Penn Station mostly for physical reasons; therefore, it should act as overflow space for Penn Station until a new Penn Station is constructed. For potential tenants, the studio recommended a research lab and co-work office type space, as well as an exhibition hall, would adapt easily to the existing space.

Shuran Chen, Olga Chernomorets, Bingruo Duan, Kirk Logan, Jawaher Al Sudiary, Ushma Thakrar, Qihao Wang + Juting Xu **A/B/C**

Planning for Infill: Preserving Public Housing in East Harlem
Urban Planning
Spring 2014
Ethel Sheffer, critic,
with Anna Oursler

Investors and city leaders have recognized that public housing estates collectively represent the last large-scale stock of publicly controlled land in New York City – lending themselves to affordable housing development – but these sites are burdened by intense conflict between the New York City Housing Authority and housing residents. Last year, NYCHA released a proposal to create market rate housing at both Washington Houses and Carver Houses in East Harlem by leasing specific sites to private developers. The plan would ostensibly help resolve a major funding gap for NYCHA and allow for backdated repairs to occur to the residential buildings and grounds. However, the plan would also bring rapid demographic and economic change to East Harlem. Our studio recommended alternatives to NYCHA's infill development proposal that reflect the Community Board's vision for East Harlem, promote an appropriate mix of affordable and market rate housing and improve the existing quality of life for the residents of Washington and Carver Houses. This task led us to propose new zoning conditions, define residential building specifications, imagine new grade-level uses and design creative public spaces within the two sites. Our research and ideas directly related to the future of public housing in New York City.

Elizabeth Cohn Martin, Matthew Do, Sarah Ellmore, Peter Erwin, Mengxun Han, Maxwell Holdhusen, Xiaomin Qian + Xin Tan **A/B/C**

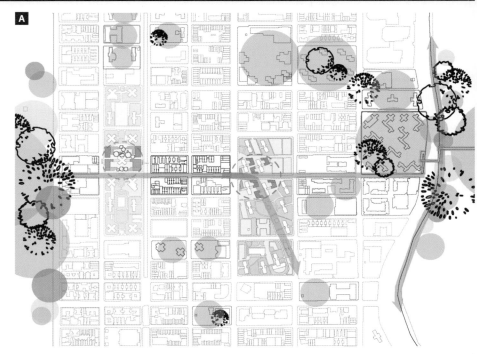

Possible building massings at Carver Houses under the stipulations of NYCHA's Pre-RFP. (source: George Janes and Associates)

A

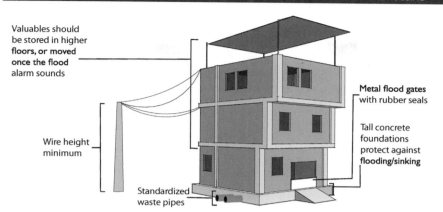

DESIGN GUIDELINES
CREATING FLEXIBLE STANDARDS TO ENCOURAGE HIGH QUALITY INCREMENTAL HOUSING

Valuables should be stored in higher floors, or moved once the flood alarm sounds

Metal flood gates with rubber seals

Wire height minimum

Tall concrete foundations protect against **flooding/sinking**

Standardized waste pipes

B

Social asset: community square

Physical asset: private recycling center

Physical asset: Open air cafe

Physical asset: Sushi restaurant

Physical asset: Residences

Social asset: Public-use soccer field

C

Asset: Open space in the Parque Nacional da Tijuca

Asset: Businesses along Avenida das EngenheiroSouza Filho

Asset: Famous Castelo das Pedras Nightclub

Problem: Flood-prone marshland

Potential: Employment in Barra da Tijuca

Problem: Pollution in Lagoa da Tijuca

Rio das Pedras: A Community Based Approach to Neighborhood Integration
Urban Planning
Spring 2014
Alejandro de Castro Mazarro + Marcela Tovar-Restrepo, critics, with Anne Krassner

Rio das Pedras is one of over one thousand favelas, or informal settlements, in Rio de Janeiro, Brazil. Contrary to popular conception of these communities, Rio das Pedras is home to a vibrant economy and tight knit community. With Studio X and the Mayor's office as our client, we provided a 'toolbox' of potential interventions, which capitalize on the assets and ameliorate some challenges that face the community of Rio das Pedras. These suggested upgrades would empower the community, enabling the residents of Rio das Pedras to choose which tools would best address their needs based on the problems they face every day. This assessment served two functions: to act as a guidance tool to analyze proposals and work put forth by the community and the Rio das Pedras initiative, to create a long-term, informed dialogue about the direction of the community; and to prioritize upgrading goals in the neighborhood as put forth by its community members and suggestions from Studio initiatives. Ultimately this work was intended to re-frame of Rio das Pedras, and the favelas of Rio de Janeiro, as legitimate, vital and positive elements of the entire city's fabric and vitality.

Alexander Altskan, Rebecca Book, Hannah Fleisher, Jessica George, Laura Groves, Chang Liu, Da'Quallon Smith + Xiaotian Sun **A/B/C**

Economics for Planners
Urban Planning
Fall 2013
Moshe Adler, instructor

Cities are run by city governments. These governments are providers of infrastructure and goods themselves and regulate the provision of goods by private firms; they promote health and welfare through land use and environmental regulation, and they are charged with ensuring that political power and economic resources are distributed equitably. Yet governments operate in societies where resource allocation is governed primarily by markets. This course explored how economics provides tools, frequently controversial, to guide decisions about when and how government should be involved in providing or subsidizing services and in shaping market activity.

Private Partnerships, Privatization + the New City Government
Urban Planning
Fall 2013
Moshe Adler, instructor

The current budget deficits that local governments face gave new life to the call to "reinvent government." Public/private partnerships and privatization posed questions both about the proper role of government, on the one hand, and about who governs on the other. They also brought up the practical question of how best to manage them, given that the criteria for "best" must involve considerations not only of financial costs but also of access and control. The integration of private contractors and not-for-profit organizations into the government reached such a level that managing them became a requirement of the practice of urban planning. To some, the relationship between the government and its private partners evolved to such a degree that it was no longer hierarchical but co-dependent, best viewed as the relationship between nodes in a network. The course examined when public/private partnerships and privatization make sense, as well as the structure of the new government and the tools available for its governance.

Techniques of Project Evaluation
Urban Planning
Spring 2014
Moshe Adler, instructor

Governments engage in two types of activities. They provide goods and services and they engage in economic development projects that create jobs and a tax base for their communities. The course covered the mains tools for analyzing these two types of government activities.

The tool for determining whether the government should deliver a particular good or service is cost/benefit analysis. This is a method for placing a monetary value on goods such as museums, reduced pollution or saving endangered specie, which are typically not traded in the private market and therefore have no market price that can be used to measure their benefits. Cost/benefit analysis also shows how to sum streams of costs and benefits that accrue over different time periods and how to evaluate projects that will yield uncertain benefits, such as a dam that would be useless unless there is a storm. Cost/benefit analysis analyzes the consequences of a project to all members of society. The tools for assessing the value of an economic development project are location quotients, shift-share and input/output analysis. All methods require statistical analysis of data. The course covered the use and analysis of both government and opinion survey data.

Introduction to Geographic Information Systems
Urban Planning
Fall 2013
Jessica Braden, instructor

This course provided instruction in GIS techniques for land use analysis using ArcGIS. Students enrolled in the course used real world scenarios to learn the spatial visualization techniques necessary for effective communication in the planning field. The course was held in the School's GIS Laboratory, a computer facility dedicated to the instruction of computer applications.

Civic Hacking
Urban Planning
Fall 2013
Georgia Bullen, instructor

"Civic" – (adj) of, or pertaining to a city, citizens, citizenship; e.g. civic engagement
    "Hacking" – (v) activity done by "hackers," usually meaning computer related, but generalized to people who reuse, repurpose or bend processes, tools, etc to be used for other means; e.g. hacking the system
    Technology is changing how people interact with the environment and how we understand the environment itself. Social Media, cell phones, social networking, crowdsourcing, apps and other Web tools all provide a window into how people move, interact, feel and even see spaces. These tools, plus the Open Data Movement, have started to bridge the worlds of civic engagement and technology with cities and city agencies hosting "hackathons" and "app competitions." Fundamentally technology of this type changes the relationship between citizen and city, reinvigorating conversations about power, access and democracy.
    This workshop class explored the tools available for civic hacking in real life applications, focusing on using the human-centered design process to change the future of participatory planning.

Developing Urban Informality
Urban Planning
Fall 2013
Alejandro de Castro Mazarro, instructor

This course drew from the experience of the seminar "Formalism and Informality in Latin American Architecture," taught at GSAPP during the Fall semester of 2012. It aimed to strengthen the International Development curriculum of GSAPP's Urban Planning program and to relate Urban Planning, Urban Design and Architectural disciplines that focus on the urban poor.
    Poverty and inequality are too often perceived as problems attained to their present condition, so little effort is made to analyze the historical sequence of urban planning programs and design practices that emerged in the nineteenth-century. This lack of emphasis in historical precedents – in their success and failures – has weakened the consistency of some contemporary programs and practices dealing with informality such as "urban acupuncture", "slum upgrading", "sites and services", "progressive housing", and "social housing".
    This seminar exposed, explored and questioned contemporary, acknowledged urban planning programs and urban design strategies dealing with informality. To this purpose, it showcased related texts and projects that could be understood as historical paradigms and paradoxes of current programs developing urban informality. These international case studies included, among others, examples from Indonesia, Hong-Kong, Thailand, Kenya, Peru, Brazil, Chile, Colombia, Mexico, Nicaragua, India, United Kingdom and Argentina.

Fundamentals of Urban Digital Designy
Urban Planning
Spring 2014
Alejandro de Castro Mazarro, instructor

The Fundamentals of Urban Digital Design (FuDD) course provided conceptual and practical tools to enhance the visual literacy of urban planners. Departing from the premise that images are act as a language, students developed a visual tale describing life in cities. The course particularly explored how to provide efficient visual evidence that supports students' own narration, and how to use rhetorical strategies that emphasize aspects of their tale. During FuDD's course, students chose an urban area and composed a tale describing a) the physical and social context where a family lives, b) the activities that their members perform during a regular week, and c) the expectations that they have for their future at this area. From a technical point of view, FuDD's seminar taught students how to produce digital presentations, books, and exhibitions. Students learned to edit photographs, figures, maps, diagrams, and renderings, with software such as Autocad; Adobe Indesign, Photoshop, and Illustrator; and Microsoft Excel.

Introduction to Housing
Urban Planning
Fall 2013
Lance Freeman, instructor

This course addressed many of the housing issues that have vexed planners and policy makers for decades. Examples of such questions included: Why is there a shortage of affordable housing? Should everyone be guaranteed a right to decent housing? When, if ever, should the government intervene in the provision of housing? This course provided students with the analytical skills to address the questions previously listed. In addition, students learned to take advantage of the plethora of housing data available, so as to be able to assess housing market conditions in a particular locality. With these skills students became better prepared to formulate effective housing policies.

Quantitative Methods
Urban Planning
Fall 2013
Lance Freeman, instructor

The purpose of this class was to introduce students to the concepts, techniques and reasoning skills necessary to understand and undertake quantitative research. By the end of the semester students were able to: design a quantitative research proposal, conceptualize a quantitative statistical model, estimate a quantitative statistical model and interpret the results of descriptive analyses, t-tests, chi-square and multivariate regression analyses. Students learned to hone their skills through a combination of attending weekly class meetings, participating in weekly labs, completing written assignments and writing a research paper that tests a hypothesis using quantitative techniques.

Public Financing of Urban Development
Urban Planning
Spring 2014
Richard M. Froehlich, instructor

Public Financing of Urban Development was an introduction to how public entities finance urban development on a pay as you go budget basis and by issuing public securities. We examined how public entities leverage limited capital resources through the issuance of debt, including a review of limitations put on such debt. We discussed current economic conditions, debates about Federal programs/debt and current issues in funding governmental activities. We explored the limitations of tax exempt financing. By examining different financial tools we reviewed how investment is made in mass transit, health care facilities, schools, public utilities and housing. The class also delved into rating agency requirements, security disclosure rules, current market dynamics and the mechanics of offering bonds for public sale. Students had an opportunity to discuss criticism of public financing as well as failures and bond defaults. Students were expected to review financial information for actual finance transactions being marketed in the public markets. The course consisted of a mix of lectures, class discussion and group presentations. Students were evaluated on a short paper delivered prior to mid-term, a group presentation to the class on a topic that relates to public finance, a final paper and class participation.

NYC Land Use Approvals
Urban Planning
Fall 2013
Eldad Gothelf, instructor

The course took a real-world approach in examining the various land use approval processes in New York City. Students reviewed the ULURP public review process, the Board of Standards and Appeals variance process, the Landmarks Preservation Commission procedures and other elements of governmental approval processes. Students attended public hearings, reviewed past cases and critically analyzed what got approved, what did not and why. By following current and past development projects through these processes, students gained an understanding of the interplay between planning and politics.

Sustainable Urban Development: International Perspectives
Urban Planning
Spring 2014
Jyoti Hosagrahar, instructor

Today, for the first time in human history, more than half of the world's population lives in cities. With increasing urbanization, uneven economic development, and depleting resources, cities in the twenty-first century demand serious consideration in order to manage them appropriately. The idea of minimizing our impact on the natural environment is now a generally accepted goal. At the same time, exploiting resources, both natural and cultural, is accepted as necessary to achieve the goals of economic development. While consensus is possible on the broad objectives of urban sustainability, the approaches, and efforts at accomplishing them vary widely. This course explored the diversity of contemporary debates around sustainability and the city, and investigates the management of change in the urban environment to nurture positive and enduring relationships amongst the natural and social worlds, and the built environment. Culturally embedded processes in diverse settings play a significant role in sustainable improvement efforts. While balancing the sensibilities of a globalized and interconnected world, we emphasized local context and the historicized cultural particularities of a place in achieving sustainability. Our objective was to work towards a framework for making cities sustainable.

History + Theory of Planning
Urban Planning
Fall 2013
Clara Irazabal, instructor

This course addressed the history of the planning profession in the United States with its intellectual evolution, while focusing on planning functions and planning roles. The course considered multiple rationales and alternative means of understanding and practicing planning. Particular attention was paid to the interplay of power and knowledge, ethics and social responsibility and issues of race, gender, class and identity. Consideration to some aspects of history and theory of planning in other parts of the world was included in comparative perspective.

Presentations as Strategic Planning Tools
Urban Planning
Fall 2013
Andrea Kahn, instructor

Public presentations provide powerful tools to focus attention and influence the outcomes of urban planning and design processes. When planning professionals stand up in front of community groups to explain a neighborhood up-zoning proposal or leading designers address review boards about creative urban and architectural schemes, speakers must clearly communicate the merits of their visions to see their initiatives realized. Compelling presenters invite even the most doubtful listeners to become planning and design advocates. Conversely, great ideas, poorly communicated, rarely get materialized.

This seminar approached presentation as a strategic element of planning and design practice. It engaged the presentation process critically, exploring it as a means of argumentation, an education tool and a form of public advocacy. Today, diverse tools exist to help planners and designers deliver their messages; nonetheless, the ability to craft and deliver a strong presentation remains an elusive goal for many. By emphasizing how to effectively integrate visual and verbal content in relation to messaging goals, the seminar examined challenges associated with conveying complex planning and design ideas to non-professional audiences. Readings, discussion and hands-on presentation opportunities provided participants with concepts, analytic tools and practical techniques necessary for developing strong presentation skill sets.

Real Estate Finance for Non-Real Estate Students
Urban Planning
Spring 2014
Joshua Kahr, instructor

The course was intended for planners and other students in GSAPP interested in real estate development and financing, but in need of an introductory explanation of concepts and valuation techniques. Topics within the course included: introduction to real estate markets and cycles; real estate cash flows and valuations; financing income-producing real estate properties; financing real estate development construction; liquidity risk and the benefits of diversification; important entities in the real estate industry; and evaluating the financial performance and strength of real estate entities.

Planning Methods
Urban Planning
Fall 2013
David King, instructor

This was an introductory course designed to help prepare students for common analysis methods used in planning practice. Common methods of analysis were covered using publicly available data sets and data collected through assignments. Through weekly readings, lectures and lab sessions students gained a basic understanding of the tools and skills required in planning practice. Students also attended one of three lab sections each week.

Transportation + Land Use Planning
Urban Planning
Spring 2014
David King, instructor

Urban sprawl, smart growth, traffic congestion and green cities are ideas that share a common policy linkage: integrated transportation and land use planning. This course was an overview of land use and transportation policy and planning drawing primarily on the United States experience with autos and transit. By introducing principles of urban planning, civil engineering, economics and public policy, students learned how to use planning tools, polices and other infrastructure investments to help develop effective places and networks. By the end of this course students were able to think critically about the transportation and land use implications of accessibility, environmental and urban design policies. In addition, students understood the mutually reinforcing incentives of transportation and land use systems at local, regional and national scales.

New Patterns of Metropolitan + Regional Development
Urban Planning
Fall 2013
Floyd Lapp, instructor

Across the United States and around the world, metropolitan regions have been experiencing explosive growth and change. Central cities are gaining population once again; however, many affluent residents of these cities have moved further out because of geographical, technological and cultural changes. We are also witnessing a trend in the opposite direction, as residents and economic activities from suburban and rural areas gravitate toward metropolitan regions. Between the "inside-out" expansion of the core and the "outside-in" growth from rural and small towns, metropolitan regions have been rapidly expanding.

Metropolitan regions face a range of challenges including the need to bring growing numbers of immigrants and minorities into the economic mainstream; to deal with traffic congestion and reconfigure metropolitan transportation systems; to preserve the green infrastructure of public water supplies, farmland and wildlife habitat; and to manage growth in ways that protect each region's cultural heritage and sense of place. In large metropolitan regions, planners are struggling to create new institutions and effective strategies to deal with these challenges. Terms such as Sustainable Development, New Urbanism and Smart Growth have entered the popular lexicon as communities look for ways to come to grips with metropolitan and regional forces and promote "green" plans. This course provided students with an overview of these challenges and the emerging strategies for management and change. Though the principal focus was on regions of North America, the techniques and institutions that we examined related to those concerned with metropolitan planning throughout the world.

Introduction to Transportation Planning
Urban Planning
Fall 2013
Floyd Lapp, instructor

Although many urban planners see this subject as formulas, models and attempts to predict travel behavior, it is more understandable by relating land use and the potential transportation connection. The hierarchy of transportation modes begins with the shortest distances between two points – walking, usually up to a distance of a mile or twenty minutes and biking, which takes one a bit further. The automobile and various modes of transit, such as the bus and rail, are much more regional and are part of a network. In dense urban areas, where space is at a premium, transit is the way to travel because more persons are moved more rapidly. However, America's love affair with the automobile, furthered by major funding for highways across a mostly low-density environment, does not always relate the most appropriate mode of travel to land development. This course contrasted the rise, fall and the latest attempts at knitting together transit into the metropolitan fabric while trying to improve the dilemma of too many people taking to the road for the convenience of being stuck in traffic.

Planning for Emerging Economies
Urban Planning
Fall 2013
Xin Li, instructor

This course focused on contemporary urban challenges that emerging economies are facing as part of the interconnected world economy and society. These challenges ranged from increasing competition for economic growth, to environmental protection versus economic development, housing reform and slum upgrading in the process of urban renewal, rising conflicts over land use and property rights, urban-rural migration and the rising power of social media. Students had the opportunity to take a comparative perspective on how countries with different institutional settings deal with similar urban planning problems. Cases covered in the course were drawn from countries in Asia, Latin America and Africa.

Environmental Policy + Planning in China
Urban Planning
Spring 2014
Xin Li, instructor

This course explored the environmental ramifications of economic development in China after the country's first environmental protection law was enacted in 1989. Over the past twenty–some years, although both national and local Chinese governments have passed numerous environment–related policies and regulations, residents in China have experienced a deterioration of their living environment concerning air and water quality, food safety and brownfields. As conflicts over these problems and related news reports escalated in recent years, the Chinese government confronted an extremely pressing request to tackle them, both from its citizens and the international community. But how could it accomplish this task when the damage was done and the consequences seemingly so un–reversible?

This course exclusively focused on environmental management that targets urban China. Using major environmental programs as case studies, students learned to understand the rationale and theories behind each program and to evaluate the effectiveness and weaknesses of the program. In the light of the burgeoning use of the Internet and social networks, students also learned strategies for engaging civil society in sustainable development. Topics covered include air and water pollution, brownfields, green energy and climate change.

Land + Housing Policy in Asia
Urban Planning
Spring 2014
Xin Li, instructor

Over the last three decades, as a result of the fast rate of urbanization, a number of Asian economies experienced an astonishing rise of low–income urban population. Accompanying this phenomenon was the demand of these low–income households for affordable housing and land. Governments in countries like China, India, Indonesia and Vietnam faced the challenge of designing housing and land policies that were economically, politically and socially feasible. Although having long been implemented in advanced economies like the United States, such policies were still at an early stage in less–developed economies.

Land and housing are closely intertwined in the design of any affordable housing policy for both urban–rural migrants and the existing urban poor. This course focused on the important relationship between land and housing in Asia. In particular, it explored how local and national governments have used land control mechanisms and planning tools to promote affordable housing programs. We first reviewed the distinctive characteristics of property rights exclusively associated with land and housing. Then we extended our analysis to specific land and housing reforms adopted by both the advanced–Singapore, South Korea, and Hong Kong–and less–advanced economies in Asia. By juxtaposing these economies in similar institutional settings, students applied the analytical tools they learned in this course to the current challenges of land and housing reforms in Asia.

Advanced Research 1 + 2
Urban Planning
Fall 2013 + Spring 2014
Trisha Logan, instructor

Each semester, there is the possibility of registering for "Advanced Research" within the Urban Planning Program. This is what you may know as "Independent Study". The student plans a course of self–study and inquiry, and seeks an advisor who reviews and grades the work. Students must submit to the Urban Planning office a one–page description of the project, including methodology, goals and final product, as well as the advisor's name and the number of credits before the end of the add–drop period. Although students did the research on their own, the advisor reviewed the final work against the description and goals of the proposal.

Introduction to Environmental Planning
Urban Planning
Fall 2013
Peter Marcotullio, instructor

This course provided an introduction to the background and practice of environmental planning through a review of the history of urban environmental planning thought and an investigation into the impacts of urbanization at different scales. Students were also introduced to the tools of environmental planning in order to evaluate issues in both developed and developing countries.

Planning for Climate Change in Urban Ecosystems
Urban Planning
Spring 2014
Peter Marcotullio, instructor

This course provided background to debates on urban planning for climate change. The questions the course addressed included: What is an urban ecosystem? How do we analyze the opportunities and challenges to climate change for urban ecosystems? What are the GHG emission concentrations and sources from urban ecosystems? What are the GHG sinks within urban ecosystems? What are some effective mitigation strategies to reduce GHG emissions from urban ecosystems? How can urban ecosystems adapt to climate change?

The course was divided into four sections: introduction to the issues; urban ecosystem analyses: urban areas as sources and sinks for GHGs; mitigation; and adaptation strategies.

Sustainable Zoning + Land Use Regulation
Urban Planning
Fall 2013
Jonathan Martin, instructor

Sustainable Zoning and Land Use Regulations introduced the basic techniques of land use control as practiced in the United States today with an emphasis on regulations that support green building practices and promote sustainable development patterns. Attention was given to the history, development and incidence of a variety of land use regulations, from the general–or comprehensive–plan to the advanced, including growth management and recent sustainable zoning practices. Of interest to the students was a focus on the practical questions of what works, what does not and why. Guided by readings from a wide range of sources, including adopted and proposed sustainable ordinances, the course was structured as both a seminar and lecture format incorporating the following: General Land Use Regulations, Sustainable Land Use Regulations, Growth Management, Residential Regulations / Development Fees and Regulation of Aesthetics.

Land Use Planning
Urban Planning
Spring 2014
Jonathan Martin, instructor

This course presented the nuts and bolts of land use planning as practiced in the US today and gave students the opportunity to develop/ design a land use plan for a small hypothetical city. Through lectures and readings students were exposed to contemporary land use planning issues, including urbanization and urban growth trends, ethics, quality of life indicators, ecological land use planning and inner-city revitalization.

Negotiations for Planners
Urban Planning
Spring 2014
Lee E. Miller, instructor

This course introduced students to the art of negotiating and influencing. Planners spend much of their time negotiating and seeking to influence others, yet generally devote little time thinking about how to effectively negotiate and exert influence. They tend to focus only on the outcomes achieved, and fail to explore how the processes or tactics on which they relied could have been varied to attain even better results. The goal of this course was to explore both the theoretical and practical aspects of negotiating and influencing. In this seminar, we reviewed the literature dealing with negotiating and influencing, engaged in influencing and negotiating in a variety of settings and studied the negotiating and influencing process.

Urban Design for Planners
Urban Planning
Spring 2014
Justin Moore, instructor

This course was an introduction to urban design through weekly discussions and design workshops. The discussions focused on the history, theory and analysis of urban forms, spaces, landscapes and systems through presentations and case studies. The workshops developed a project-based exchange and application of the interdisciplinary ideas and techniques - from art and architecture to landscape architecture and environmental engineering - that designers use in developing projects in the urban context. This work used a site in New York City as a context for exploring the complex interactions between users, program, buildings, public spaces, infrastructure, and environmental systems in the definition and performance of urban spaces and landscapes.

Advanced GIS
Urban Planning
Spring 2014
*Juan Francisco
Saldarriaga, instructor*

Advanced GIS was a research seminar aimed at covering a variety of advanced techniques in geographic information systems analysis, for both practice and research. As a skills–based seminar, the course operated with a two–fold mission: to critically discuss the theories, concepts and research methods involved in spatial analysis and to learn the techniques necessary for engaging those theories and deploying those methods. Further, the class worked to meet this mission with a dedicated focus on the urban environment and the spatial particularities and relationships that arise from the urban context.

Planning Law
Urban Planning
Fall 2013 + Spring 2014
Andrew Scherer, instructor

This was a core course exploring the legal foundations of planning in the United States. Case studies and legal readings provided the foundations of understanding zoning, environmental law, aesthetic regulations and housing policies.

Territorial Imperative: Twentieth Century New Towns
Urban Planning
Fall 2013
David Smiley, instructor

Central to the logic of New Towns during the twentieth-century was the precise delineation of territory. Modern land use, planning and urban design practices were based on the rationalization of parcels of land, which could thereby be exchanged, regulated and controlled. The seemingly unknowable morass of nineteenth-century European industrial metropolis, fueled by an Enlightenment belief in rational progress, generated an epistemological shift based on the total control of action and space, a *territorial imperative*. Garden City and CIAM devotees alike, capitalist or communist, for homeland or colony, the New Town was rooted in a belief that regions with specified patterns containing settlements of fixed size and stipulated uses would create well-functioning *communities*. That this authoritarian control of space and human activity–which optimistically yoked together the formal methods of the Ideal City to the social content of Utopia–could be represented as socially progressive is a paradox of twentieth-century design.

   This paradox was the entry point for the research of this class. We investigated the theories and histories of New Towns in their Euro-American context and in their colonial dispersal, among their protagonists and critics, and through their trajectory in the overlapping disciplines required by implementation: urban planning, urban design, policy and architecture.

   The class also undertook the documentation of a number of New Towns because further interpretation, comparisons, analysis, comprehension and evaluation are precluded in the absence of such data. The study of plans and sections, occupants and programs, scale and size, infrastructure and siting and policy and planning frameworks allowed us to understand more precisely the methods and means of the territorial imperative. With

their dramatic rise in Asia as well as the active renovation of many extant examples, historic New Towns may yet offer new possibilities.

Physical Structures of Cities
Urban Planning
Spring 2014
David Smiley, instructor

This lecture course focused on the historic emergence of contemporary urban form. The course reviewed the complex social, political and economic dynamics that shape contemporary cities. Beginning with the birth of the industrial city in the nineteenth century, the course took its subject matter from early planning attempts such as tenement house regulation and garden cities up to recent concerns with postmodernism, new urbanism and sustainable development. The course focused principally upon the American experience but also drew from Western Europe and contemporary trends in global urbanization in Africa and Asia.

Political Economy of Development Planning
Urban Planning
Spring 2014
Smita Srinivas, instructor

Political economy studied institutions and modes of governance. It attempted to capture different models of how society's politics and economy are intertwined. The course was also a discerning look at the language, models and actual history of social change. There are many 'schools' within the field of political economy attempting to describe issues such as the role of the state, the optimal path to development and the most equitable forms of redistribution. These also comprise strong behavioral and institutional assumptions about locality and nationality and how to run urban and other development projects. This course was essential for the international development planning specialization. It provided skills to analyze any development approach and an understanding of the limitations and opportunities in project planning.

Development Strategy for Technology + Industry
Urban Planning
Spring 2014
Smita Srinivas, instructor

This course was about economic development strategy and focused on how to build industry as a core element of a viable economic planning process and how to plan for technology capabilities. This was a case–based and discussion course with attention to planning strategy and planning outcomes. In order to critically approach strategy, we drew on planning sensibilities such as concern for the long–term economy, political astuteness, minimizing externalities, promoting employment and concern for the environment. This course drew on examples of more or less successful economic strategies, as well as contention about data, analysis and political context. Industry studies can be analyzed at several different units and scales, and one of our tasks together was to assess 'success'.

Students analyzed and debated several cases at urban, regional and national levels of economic plans. They delved deep into technology and sector details such as semi–conductors in Taiwan, automotive clusters in Detroit and the health industry clusters in India and the United States. We studied dominant debates about why some light manufacturing strategies are successful, which technological capabilities have flourished in certain cities and why special economic zones are so popular in some countries. Fundamental to this, we actively debated the economic and planning arguments that drive certain strategies.

Local Economic Development Planning
Urban Planning
Fall 2013
Stacey Sutton, instructor

Urban planning is charged with attending to the myriad dynamics that make places attractive for living, working, investing and visiting, as well as with weighing the politically palatable, socially acceptable and financially feasible dimensions of social actions. Economic development is an essential component of urban planning that is primarily concerned with the "economic" health of urban dwellers and urban spaces. Therefore, economic development focuses on questions of economic growth, capital investment, local competitiveness, in addition to poverty reduction, equitable opportunity structures, employment, wages, human capital development and labor market practices. This seminar demanded reflection on ways that assumptions about the 'public good,' equitable development, 'public' and 'private' interests, social stratification, the market, racialization of space, costs and benefits, equality and geographic scale–neighborhood, city, region, global–affect the ways LED planning and decisionmaking are carried out. This course questioned whether these assumptions influence the types of outcomes we accept as "Fair and Just." Students came away from this seminar ready to examine economic development dilemmas with both technical acumen and essential, yet underemphasized, critical thinking skills.

Neighborhood Change
Urban Planning
Spring 2014
Stacey Sutton, instructor

This course engaged with extant debates within planning, policy and sociology about neighborhood dynamics. We started with theories of change, revitalization, gentrification, community planning and segregation. While some neighborhood shifts result from intentional actions and concerted planning efforts, much of what we observed and experienced as neighborhood change had deep historical, structural and local contextual roots. We examined dynamics in New York City neighborhoods, learned about neighborhood stakeholders, examined how benefits and burdens are distributed and raised fundamental questions regarding the direction of urban development. In other words, we used the neighborhood lens to illuminate urban concerns pertaining to access, equity, civic capacity, opportunity, rights and responsibility.

The three primary objectives that this course addressed included: developing a common conceptual framework and language for understanding why neighborhood change is often hotly contentious and how spatial identities are framed; sharpening methodological and analytical skills for neighborhood-level research; and learning how to apply conceptual tools and research techniques to better analyze and communicate place-based policies, programs and planning decisions.

Planning for Retail
Urban Planning
Spring 2014
Stacey Sutton, instructor

In cities across the United States, banal and uninviting commercial corridors have been transformed into alluring shopping destinations. Previously "under–retailed" neighborhoods have experienced the emergence of alluring shops and eateries, and neighborhoods long celebrated for distinctive shopping and dining options are increasingly populated by national and regional chain stores and suburban–style retail establishments. This graduate seminar focused on the processes, practices and effects of urban retail restructuring. It examined the physical and economic infrastructure of downtown shopping districts and neighborhood Main Street corridors. It considered the changing form and function of retail landscapes and commercial life since the mid to late–twentieth century. This course guided students in integrating place–based historical facts and theories of urban decline and revival, with industry and firm data to formulate new plans for urban retail districts. This course covered four broad areas: (1) An overview of the causes for urban business district decline and strategies for revitalization; (2) Market analysis tools and techniques; (3) Commercial revitalization policies, community intervention strategies, conventional and alternative investment options; and (4) The formulation of a place–based or retail sector–based plan.

Environment, Climate Change + Vulnerability of Urban Cities: Our New "Normal"
Urban Planning
Fall 2013
Marcela Tovar-Restrepo, instructor

Climate change constitutes one of the most urgent issues of our time. It has worldwide implications from the exacerbation of poverty, to the loss of environmental, political, economic and social security. Climate change threatens both industrialized and less industrialized world regions. Vulnerable social groups in precarious positions bear the burden of phenomenon including displacement, interethnic and social conflicts, alteration of food production patterns and livelihoods and spread of diseases among others. This course explored the vulnerability of urban populations with an emphasis on context specific impacts in low and middle-income nations. Using case studies, we analyzed how climate change impacts different social groups in our cities and identified adaptation and mitigation strategies being currently implemented. Tools to draw on climate change scientific data and the uncertainty inherent in future projections, were provided. Students had the opportunity to study and engage with climate change and development international processes including the United Nations Framework Convention on Climate Change, Rio+20, Post 2015 agendas such as the Sustainable Development Goals, COP-19 and the United Nations Convention to Combat Desertification. They participated directly in some of these processes while visiting the Women's Environmental and Development Organization (WEDO). Students were assigned specific responsibilities and tasks to present at the end of the fall semester, such as analyzing the papers submitted by countries and civil society organizations to COP-19, participating in preparing WEDO's workshop for COP-19 with national authorities from different countries attending the meeting and preparing the post-2015 papers coming out of COP-19.

Transnational Planning
Urban Planning
Fall 2013
Marcela Tovar-Restrepo, instructor

Planning in our interrelated world often transcends the boundaries of particular localities within nation states. Transnational planning is planning that occurs through societal relations spanning pluri-locally, between and above the traditional container spaces of national societies without a clear 'headquarters' or 'motherland.'

This course explored the production and transformation of new and conventional types of spaces and planning engagements in a transnational arena. Through contemporary case studies, we explored different agents that engaged in transnational planning including international organizations, national and local public and private agencies, transnational NGOs and transnational community organizations. We aimed to understand the different subfields of transnational planning in which they engage–related, for instance, to border planning, environmental planning, labor management, infrastructure building, institution building, gender equity, housing, transportation, health, cross-sectoral governance and participation–and performed SWOT analysis to assess their institutional and socio-spatial effectiveness. We also paid attention to the way in which subjected populations resist, adapt or coproduce the planning deployed upon their communities, and, in the process, transnational subjects are (re)shaped.

Politics of International Placemaking
Urban Planning
Spring 2014
Marcela Tovar-Restrepo, instructor

The creation and recreation of urban places is an essential component of planning practice across the world. Planners are agents that mediate global political and economic pressures, on the one hand, and local socio-cultural and institutional conditions, on the other. Within these multifaceted contexts and interacting with communities, they facilitate an ongoing process of glocal placemaking. This course explored the practices and politics of placemaking and how they impact and are impacted by the (re)production and (de/re)territorialization of cultural practices, institutional arrangements, and spatial traits/trends in multiple and varied localities across the globe at the turn of the twenty-first century. The students were expected to critically analyze and compare the nuanced differences across planning contexts, assess the level of effectiveness of planning approaches used in addressing such conditions and their resulting place-based effects, and envision better planning practices to make progress in the attainment of more just cities.

Site Planning + Support Systems for Development
Urban Planning
Fall 2013
Graham Trelstad, instructor

This course introduced students to the specific techniques employed by planners and developers to achieve a livable and healthful urban environment through effective and efficient site design.

Environmental Impact Assessment
Urban Planning
Spring 2014
Graham Trelstad, instructor

This course explored the key procedural elements of NEPA, SEQRA and CEQR—the key analytic techniques used in impact assessment—and investigated how application of environmental impact assessment affects project outcome. Lectures introduced students to the statutory requirements of the laws, important judicial decisions interpreting the laws and standard methodologies for conducting environmental assessments. Case studies were used to illustrate the effect of the environmental impact assessment on design and implementation of projects or governmental actions. Practical assignments gave students an introduction to the state of practice and the range of analytic techniques used in environmental impact assessment.

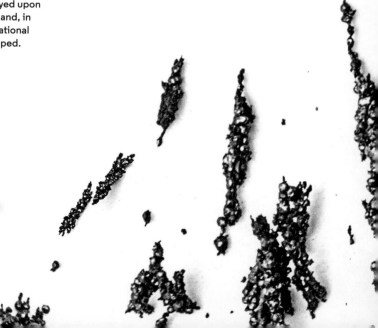

Introduction to GIS
Urban Planning
Spring 2014
Jeremy White, instructor

This course introduced spatial concepts and GIS technical skills using ESRI's ArcGIS software. Students learned spatial analysis and visualization techniques as well as data acquisition and management approaches through a combination of lecture and lab sessions. The course focused on GIS for the planning field and was held in a classroom dedicated to the instruction of computer applications.

Thesis 1 + 2
Urban Planning Thesis
Fall 2013 + Spring 2014
David King, instructor

A six-credit, two-semester thesis is an essential part of the planning curriculum. It is an individual study or investigation of the student's own choice, but it is closely supervised by a full-time faculty member of the Urban Planning Program. The thesis demonstrates the student's ability to structure an argument surrounding an issue or problem significant to planning practice, planning theory and/or the profession itself.

The second semester of a six-credit two-semester thesis is an essential part of the planning curriculum. It is an individual study or investigation of the student's own choice, but it is closely supervised by a full– time faculty member of the Urban Planning Program. This course is an individual research project of the student's own choice which is closely supervised by a full-time faculty member of the Urban Planning Program. Students write and defend their thesis research during the term and submit a digital copy of their final thesis to the urban planning program.

The Effects of Urban Conflict + the Role of Community-Based Initiatives in Baghdad
Urban Planning Thesis
Fall 2013 + Spring 2014
Sarah Almukhtar
Clara Irazábal, advisor

The invasion of Iraq by America and its allies in 2003 represented a transformation for the country's capital city, Baghdad. This conflict was particularly urban, maintained a neo-liberal agenda to change the political and economic structures and resulted in strong divisive security measures being implemented throughout the city, thus altering the urban environment. The changes to the city created significant challenges for Baghdad's residents – they became isolated, segregated and often immobile. Consequently, many of their social and economic networks were severed. While governmental plans for redevelopment have been mired in corruption and stalled implementation, several community-based initiatives have emerged which seem to transcend and/or address the urban challenges that Baghdadis face. These initiatives were explored through case studies in terms of their network structures, successes, limitations and potential to contribute to the redevelopment of Baghdad. Planners have an important role in identifying these initiatives, analyzing them to illuminate successful paths for both sustainability and growth, and understanding the stakeholders who are part of the universe the initiatives operate in for beneficial partnerships and stronger networks.

The Implications of Planning Failure: Evaluating the Impacts of Land Reclamation Policies on Fishermen Communities in Bahrain
Urban Planning Thesis
Fall 2013 + Spring 2014
Fatema Alzeera
Clara Irazabal, advisor

The critical relationship of state and civil society is observed globally, such as in the case of public strife in the Kingdom of Bahrain. The uprisings that took place throughout the Arab Spring have continued to the present day, begging the question: what conditions produced the current relationship between state and society? This study investigated this question through the lens of state-led land reclamation. As the case study suggests, while reclamation plans have ensured both economic and industrial growth for the state, they inevitably caused detrimental economic and social losses to an already disadvantaged community within society. The failure in planning, however, portrays a bleaker image of the government's inability and unwillingness to respond to civic complaints regarding public planning projects. Using the research as a microcosm of state planning provided a framework for understanding the reciprocal between the polity and its citizens. The failure of planning in Bahrain, from process to practice, explains the current weakening of the state.

The 2009 Health Care Reform + Insurance Coverage for Migrant Construction Workers in Beijing, China
Urban Planning Thesis
Fall 2013 + Spring 2014
Amy Yang
Xin Li, advisor

By the year 2020, China aims to achieve universal health care coverage. The most recent health care reform was passed in 2009. With three major health care insurance schemes already in place, the Central Government has had success in insuring urban residents, urban employees and rural residents. However, one of the most vulnerable populations remains inadequately insured and unseen: the migrant construction worker. This worker is either a rural – urban migrant who cannot access many urban health care resources because of rural hukou, or the severely disenfranchised temporary laborer at the lowest–rung of the construction industry. Standing at the intersection of two highly vulnerable and invisible populations, migrant construction workers are at compounded risk of entirely slipping past any formal health care infrastructure. Thus, this thesis sought to investigate how the most recent 2009 health care reform attempted to capture this doubly vulnerable population within the formal health care system. Interviews were conducted with migrant construction workers in Beijing and with scholars, which were

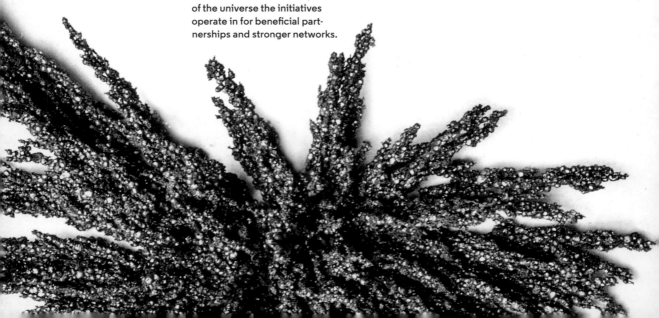

complimented with data extracted from the China Health and Nutrition Survey. Migrant construction workers tended not to be aware of the services they could access or the benefits to which they have a right, nor were they highly interested in obtaining them; there were more pressing issues to worry about such as financial security. However, these findings are compounded by a highly complex social, economic and political context. Although legal tools do exist to reinforce labor laws, it often requires time, knowledge of the convoluted legal system and political savvy to successfully use them, none of which a migrant construction worker is likely to have. Thus, construction migrant workers lie at the intersection of two disenfranchised groups making them especially invisible to the political eye.

Planning with Character: Gotouchi Kyara + Place Branding in Japan
Urban Planning Thesis
Fall 2013 + Spring 2014
Lissa Barrows
Lance Freeman, advisor

As part of urban planning, local governments in Japan have developed a unique type of city branding that uses gotouchi kyara ご当地キャラ, which are community character mascots representing cities, towns, or villages that highlight significant aspects of the area, such as famous foods or tourist attractions. The character mascots tap into the already present character goods and kawaii culture of Japan, are cost effective and sustainable, are a means for bringing the community residents together, and easily lend themselves to local economic development. Thus, the character mascots are a major strategy for place branding. A geographical information system cluster analysis suggests that the origin of gotouchi kyara in Japan was dispersed in the early 1980s, became random in the 1990s and began to cluster in the mid-2000s. Clusters that are far apart from each other can be found throughout Japan, and hot spots of multiple gotouchi kyara are found in the smaller cities, towns and villages in the south of Japan and cold spots are found near Tokyo. The proliferation of gotouchi kyara is most dense around the major metropolitan areas. Criticism exists for the mascots, but "character power" is undeniable in contemporary Japanese society.

The Impact of the Congestion Charging Scheme on Greenhouse Gas + Air Pollutants Emissions in London
Urban Planning Thesis
Fall 2013 + Spring 2014
Lingjun Bu
Lance Freeman, advisor

On February 17, 2003, a Congestion Charging Scheme (CCS) along with traffic management measures were introduced in central London, operating Monday to Friday, 7:00 A.M. to 6:00 P.M. On February 19, 2007, the Congestion Charging Zone was extended westward, covering additional 2.6 percent of the Greater London area. Transport for London claimed that the CCS helped to reduce 18 percent of the traffic volume and 30 percent of the traffic congestion in its first year operation. The purpose of this paper was to examine the impact of the Congestion Charging Scheme on greenhouse gas and air pollutants emissions. In order to examine such impacts, the research compared the emission volume changes of greenhouse gas and air pollutants before and after the CCS.

Exploring the Impact Factors on the Frequency of Applications for Zoning Amendment in the City of New York
Urban Planning Thesis
Fall 2013 + Spring 2014
Tiancheng Cai
Lance Freeman, advisor

The socio-economic impact of zoning and its amendments have long been core planning issues, while there is little research about the zoning amendment behavior itself. This study aimed to realize the impact factors on the frequency of zoning amendment applications under Uniform Land Use Review Procedure in New York City. Based on the zoning records from 1976 to 2012 and census data, the Poisson Regression and Negative Binomial Regression model was used to compare the fifty-nine community districts, discovering that the larger area, the higher income level, the larger proportion of non-Hispanic white population and the lower owner-occupied rate a community had, the higher the frequency of applications.

Small Scale/Global Ambition: Strategies of Architectural Production + Global Urban Competitiveness in Medellín, Colombia
Urban Planning Thesis
Fall 2013 + Spring 2014
Ellis Calvin
Stacey Sutton, advisor

Globalization and the hegemony of neoliberalism created a situation in which cities compete with other cities for business, wealthy residents and tourism. This global urban competition spans national borders and has exacerbated levels of inequality. Cities often employ strategies of architectural production, typically monumental, highly symbolic urban design projects to create a city image and brand that is attractive to global capital. Medellin, Colombia focused instead on building small scale, yet iconic, urban design projects in marginalized communities, primarily to reduce poverty, crime and inequality under Mayor Sergio Fajardo, 2004 through 2007. These projects, known as Integral Urban Projects, raised the international profile of Medellin as a city reinventing its image using innovative strategies to raise the quality of living for its most disadvantaged citizens. Over the last ten years, however, the city's priorities began to shift as it received more international media attention and recognition. Does Medellin's ability to leverage small-scale, peripheral strategy of architectural production represent a more egalitarian approach to attracting capital, inviting tourism and generating influence, or do the pressures of global capitalism nullify the city's efforts to reduce inequality?

Beijing Parking Issue - A Case Study in Lama Temple Area
Urban Planning Thesis
Fall 2013 + Spring 2014
Long Chen
David Andrew King, advisor

Beijing Old City was built hundreds of years ago. The structure of Beijing Old City was not designed for automobiles, which is why it is currently unable to meet the needs of current traffic conditions. With the rise in car ownership in Beijing, parking became a serious problem for the city, especially for the Old City. The government established a number of policies and solutions for parking in Beijing Old City, but the results were not satisfactory as the government might not fundamentally understand the cause of the parking problem. Through case study of a historical preservation district in Beijing Old City, this thesis sought to determine the major problem of parking in the area and discover the root of the problem in the studied area. By calculating the usage rate of parking facilities and analyzing parking prices, a comprehensive conclusion of parking problems in the study area emerged. The paper also includes data collection methodologies and discussion on current and future policies of parking regulations in Beijing, which in the end, lead to possible solutions for parking in the study area.

Real-name Registration System as a Way to Improve Social Service Security: A Case Study of Migrant Construction Workers in Nanjing
Urban Planning Thesis
Fall 2013 + Spring 2014
Yiwen Chen
Xin Li, advisor

Currently in China, the universal social service system has strict geographical boundaries, which specify the service boundaries as well. All citizens can enjoy universal service in the cities where their Hukou – China's household registration – is registered. However, when people begin to migrate, social services delivery becomes a problem. In 2012, population of migration reached 236 million, which was about one-sixth of total population in China. In the absence of formal organization such as trade unions, improving the well-being of temporary workers in informal sectors is a major concern. These people are also characterized as informal citizens and are not covered by the basic social protection scheme granted to citizens. This thesis researched how local municipal government can deliver service to migrants. Through the case demonstration of the recent implementation of the Real-name registration system for migrant construction workers in Nanjing, where obtaining Hukou is not easy for migrants, research determined that the Real-name registration could be an effective approach toward improving the social service security of migrant construction workers.

Living Globally: Exploring the Need for Foreign Enclaves in Shanghai
Urban Planning Thesis
Fall 2013 + Spring 2014
Peter Chung
Stacey Sutton, advisor

More often than not, the principles of ethnic integration trump segregation in today's post-modern, cosmopolitan cities. However, in different urban contexts segregation may actually induce economic benefits. Foreign urban enclaves in emerging economies can function as residences for highly skilled foreign workers who collectively contribute toward a municipality's economic output. This study examined the need for foreign transnational enclave communities in Shanghai. The hypothesis was that the planning of foreign enclaves is necessary because such environments provide a socially and culturally familiar space for expatriates allowing them to establish a lifestyle in an otherwise unfamiliar urban setting. The findings suggested that although this was a strategy that Shanghai implemented in the past to retain the skills of foreign workers, the circumstances have changed. Western expatriates are more integrated than they are segregated, and their locational decisions are based on factors other than maintaining a sense of cultural and social familiarity. The thesis argues that in the context of Shanghai, planned foreign enclaves are not necessary due to the city's historical trajectory, current economic state and a gradual economic independence through improving domestic capabilities.

Sustaining Art Ecosystem: Social Diversity + NGO — Government Cooperation in Song Zhuang Art Village
Urban Planning Thesis
Fall 2013 + Spring 2014
Yan Chu
Xin Li, advisor

In recent decades, many cities in China have encouraged the cultural and art sector as a pathway for urban development. With this trend, many art districts and clusters rose and failed and, in Beijing and Song Zhuang, became the largest original artists cluster in the whole country. While prevailing voices interpret this phenomenon as the result of "rent" changes, this paper argues that "art ecosystem diversity" in Song Zhuang has greater impact on attracting artists. Borrowing the concept from natural ecosystem diversity, "art ecosystem diversity" refers to the dynamic interactions and relations among civil society, government, non-governmental organization, artists and villagers. Art ecosystem diversity is strengthened and also leads to a diversified pattern of social stakeholders in the system as well as a mixed-use pattern of land use. While Song Zhuang gains popularity, it is also facing potential impedances, such as loss of diversity and over-commercialization. The analysis conclusion suggests that non-governmental organizations, as representative of public bodies, and its cooperation with governments and artists can anchor the diversity of Song Zhuang and sustain its art ecosystem.

The Changing Values of Planning: Comprehensive Planning in White Plains + Westchester County, NY
Urban Planning Thesis
Fall 2013 + Spring 2014
Benjamin Engle
David King, advisor

Municipalities create comprehensive plans to provide a long-term vision for growth and development and to determine the strengths and opportunities that will assist them in instituting ordinances and making future planning decisions. The New York Department of State indicates that comprehensive planning at the municipal level should provide a variety of goals that include both the intermediate and long-range time period. New York State law requires local zoning to be "in accordance with comprehensive plans" but does not mandate their implementation. The State legislature's encouragement to prepare and adopt comprehensive plans has been effective; 70 percent of municipalities with planning boards in New York State have adopted a plan. County governments and non-for-profits are also developing comprehensive regional plans that are designed to guide decisions at both the municipal and regional levels. With so many plans and policies guiding an area, do the values of a local municipality match those at the county and regional levels? The methodology for approaching this question was a qualitative review of comprehensive plans created during the second half of the twentieth century. The City of White Plains provides an opportunity to evaluate how the values of a small suburban city that has undertaken multiple comprehensive plan initiatives relate to the planning values of Westchester County. Through an investigation of the past three comprehensive plans by the City of White Plains and the Westchester County Planning Board, this thesis determines how values and initiatives are represented between the corresponding plans and whether comprehensive planning successfully addresses perennial planning initiatives and concerns.

The Impact of Syrian Refugees on Jordan's Water Resources + Water Management Planning
Urban Planning Thesis
Fall 2013 + Spring 2014
Aleena Farishta
Clara Irazabal + Tess Russo, advisors

With the ongoing physical violence in Syria, refugees from this country have been fleeing to neighboring countries to seek refuge. Since 2011, Jordan opened its borders to approximately 600,000 Syrian refugees who have either attempted living in the urban areas of Jordan or have adjusted to refugee camps in the northern part of the country. This number is expected to rise to 1.2 million refugees by 2014 according to Jordan's Ministry of Water and Irrigation. As the Jordanian government has not acknowledged the refugee capacity problem, this thesis questioned how a water resourcescarce country plans sustainably for its future. Focusing on Jordan's water resources, this thesis evaluated what kind of impact the influx of Syrian refugees will have on the water sector. Groundwater depletion was found to be a major concern for Jordan's water resources prior to the refugee influx, since the total water extraction rates exceeded the renewable water amount. The overall water usage of 600,000 refugees was estimated to be about 2.3 percent of the total water consumption in Jordan. This consumption rate could increase by at least 2.2 percent if the number of refugees increases to the expected 1.2 million by 2014. By analyzing literature on water management planning in Jordan and case studies of refugee planning, conducting a water budget analysis prior to the refugee influx and after the influx and carrying out interviews with water and refugee planners in Jordan, this thesis discussed recommendations to plan for the refugees in a manner which would reduce the stress on Jordan's water resources.

Pittsburgh School Closures: The Impact on Physical + Social Neighborhood Dynamics
Urban Planning Thesis
Fall 2013 + Spring 2014
Emily Gordon
Clara Irazabal, advisor

School closures can have enormous effects on students and families living in a neighborhood. School districts in many urban areas in the United States were recently faced with the challenge of how to deal with a shrinking school-aged population, budget crises, aging facilities and poor academic performance. This led some districts to close large numbers of school buildings. A prime example occurred in Pittsburgh, Pennsylvania in 2006. This research examined changes in population count, racial composition and housing characteristics in three affected neighborhoods of Pittsburgh following the decision by the Pittsburgh Board of Education to close twenty-two schools that year. The research examined how large vacant facilities affect the neighborhood's physical and social dynamics. Data analysis, interviews and site analysis helped to answer the research questions. The findings suggest that school vacancies have a negative effect on neighborhoods to varying degrees, and the neighborhood's ability to cope with this loss is determined by a number of factors such as desirability of the area and community resources. Recommendations can help other cities to better plan for closures in the future to ensure the most equitable outcomes.

Governance + Gentrification in Creative Industry Clusters - A Case Study of Three Creative Clusters in Beijing

Urban Planning Thesis
Fall 2013 + Spring 2014
Peiqin Gu
Xin Li, advisor

The thesis aims to reveal the relationship between the government's cultural creative industry development policy and the response from the creative class. The thesis mainly assumes that the policy plays an important role in guiding the formation of creative clusters but fails to facilitate creative businesses in the long run. Through interview and second hand data collection in three creative industry clusters, 798 Art Zone, No.46 Fangjia Hutong and Nanluoguxiang in Beijing, the thesis mainly finds that the existing governance strategy can't protect the identity of 798 Art Zone and No.46 Fangjia Hutong, the roles of creative class were marginalized in redevelopment process and the government should learn from Nanluoguxiang's case in constructing platform to promote the participation of creative class to balance the interests of different stakeholders in clusters.

Evaluating the Effect Urban Rail Expansion on Regional Density Distribution in Portland, OR

Urban Planning Thesis
Fall 2013 + Spring 2014
Emily Heard
David King, advisor

Over time, American cities significantly decentralized and this development pattern, dubbed 'sprawl', became seen as a costly and inefficient development pattern that should be limited. In urban planning literature, sprawl is seen as inherently connected to a car centric physical environment. This puts improving accessibility via alternative transportation modes at the forefront of many solutions to sprawl. Transit availability and likewise transit success is seen as inherently connected to sufficient urban density. Sprawl is a regional problem because spatial dispersion goes beyond the current limits of jurisdictional regulations. As regions attempt to design effective strategies to navigate the problems created by urban sprawl, they frequently consider expanding their transit systems as an incentive for more concentrated development. This thesis examines the effectiveness of investing in new transit infrastructure, particularly fixed rail transit such as light rail and commuter rail, as a regional strategy to increase urban density by exploring the changes that have occurred in Portland, Oregon over the course of twenty years as they have rapidly expanded their transit system.

Demolition + the Shrinking City: Philadelphia + Camden

Urban Planning Thesis
Fall 2013 + Spring 2014
Jean Heo
Stacey Sutton, advisor

This research compared the demolition policies and practices of two shrinking cities within one metropolitan statistical area—Philadelphia, Pennsylvania and Camden, New Jersey. Both cities experienced major population losses due to deindustrialization and outmigration, and, despite their physical proximity, the current states of the two cities are vastly different with Philadelphia having somewhat stabilized and showing recent upticks in population, while Camden continues to struggle. Both cities have an abundance of abandoned buildings, where demolition is not uncommon. This research, therefore, aimed to understand how each city's demolition and vacancy policies have affected the current landscape, spatially, socially, economically and how prominent, if at all, a "smart decline"-oriented framework has been in the implementation of such planning tools.

Where does demolition occur—within what social, economic and spatial contexts? To what extent do demolitions happen there? The data analyses were restricted to 2008-2012, to correspond to the U.S. Census' American Community Survey. These questions were central to understanding how actual demolition work and policy discourse stack up against each other, even within this short timeframe. The hope was that officials, researchers and other scholars would see the importance of knowing both the short- and long-term impacts of demolition in shrinking cities, and how policies have shaped demolition practices, or how policies should be reworked to better reflect a city's goals.

The Impact of Informal Network on Rural-Based Creative Sectors in China

Urban Planning Thesis
Fall 2013 + Spring 2014
Hui Jiang
Xin Li, advisor

This thesis highlights the significance of the informal network and industry performance of rural based creative sectors in China. The rural based creative class is characterized by small and medium enterprises and relies on tacit knowledge exchange and information transfer. Facing the rural economic development challenges in China, the formal network, like official and governmental organized platforms, has its limitations. In contrast, the informal network is more flexible to connect different individuals in the sector, generating a greater knowledge spillover effect for the rural creative class. A traditional crafts sector, the Hunan Embroidery sector, was studied as an example of Chinese rural based creative class. A thorough study of different types of networks by interviewing stakeholders in the sector revealed the significance of informal networking to the rural-based creative class.

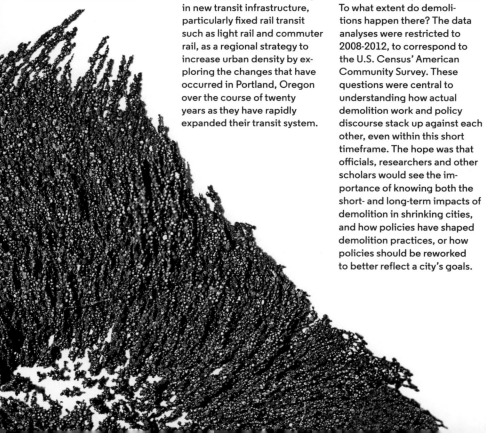

Where Do Political Will + Community Needs Meet? The Case of the Aerial Cable Cars in Rio de Janeiro, Brazil

Urban Planning Thesis
Fall 2013 + Spring 2014
Anne Krassner
David King, advisor

In the last decade, aerial cable cars were popularized as the leading remedy for the mobility hurdles faced by informal settlements in Latin America. Academics credit aerial cable-car systems around the world with helping to change the perception of informal settlements and help integrate them, both physically and socially, into the formal city. However, the community of Complexo do Alemão, where the city of Rio de Janeiro inaugurated its first aerial cable-car system in 2011, is unsatisfied with the government's choice to build a cable car in their community, and proposals for cable-car systems in other favelas around the city have been met with heavy protest. This thesis explores the disconnect between the government's effort to increase mobility and accessibility by building the cable car, and the community's negative response to this "innovative" technology. This thesis unpacks the process of planning the cable cars in Complexo do Alemão, as the community experienced it and as it was framed by the state of Rio de Janeiro. The lack of transparency throughout the planning process and integration of the project with the most pressing needs of the community, as well as absence of accountability of the government to the residents of Complexo do Alemão, resulted in a missed opportunity to truly improve the life of the people living in the neighborhood. As the Brazilian government continues to invest heavily in large infrastructure projects such as the Teleférico, it is imperative that these projects be in touch with the needs in the communities, which they affect so that government funds can be utilized and optimized to truly improve the quality of life in Brazilian cities.

Vacant Space + Temporary Use: Understanding Development Cycles in Berlin's Neighborhoods of Friedrichshain + Kreuzberg

Urban Planning Thesis
Fall 2013 + Spring 2014
Taylor Miller
Lance Freeman + Jonathan Martin, advisors

Due to its complex history, Berlin is prone to a large amount of vacant space particularly in comparison to other European cities. This thesis sought to understand the nature, promotion, support and shedding of vacant and temporary use in cities as part of a larger development cycle through the case study of Berlin's neighborhoods of Friedrichshain and Kreuzberg. A review of plans, interviews, site visits and the updating of the city's database on vacant space contributed to a better understanding of the process at play. These sites were then analyzed through the development cycles of J.R. Whitehand and Ernest Burgess to see if the process of construction and change in the city of Berlin could be explained by these models.

Equity of Transit in the Twin Cities: A Benefit-Based Study of the Racial Equity of Access to Transit

Urban Planning Thesis
Fall 2013 + Spring 2014
Matthew Mueller
David King, advisor

As many cities in the United States build new transit lines and expand existing transit services, there is no clear understanding of whom the new transit is being built to serve, whether the new services will be equitable to all racial and ethnic groups, and the impact it will have on potentially transit dependent populations. Through an analysis of the residential proximity to transit, the differences in the racial demographics served and the frequency of transit service at each transit stop, this study focused on understanding the unequal distribution of travel opportunity in the Twin Cities while reframing the debate on transportation planning and the creation of new transit lines beyond an analysis of service areas and economic benefits into understanding benefit-based claims of racial and ethnic inequality.

This study looked at the Twin Cities of Minneapolis and St. Paul, Minnesota where a significant investment in new transit services has occurred over the last several decades, as they built a new light rail and streetcar system, which is currently in the planning and construction phases for expansion. How equitable are the existing services towards all racial groups in the region, and do the currently planned transit improvements represent a move towards equity? By analyzing the unequal distribution of travel opportunity in the Twin Cities, we were able to expand our understanding of the issues and formulate specific recommendations to reduce both the benefit-based inequity as well as the procedural-based inequity found in the Twin Cities.

Planning for Resource-Rich Communities: Learning through Comparisons of Energy Booms + Busts in the American West

Urban Planning Thesis
Fall 2013 + Spring 2014
Callie New
Stacey Sutton, advisor

Through investigating four resource-rich localities through case studies, this research first sought to describe how short-term resource extraction projects yielded from technological innovations within the industry have shaped the physical, economic and social landscapes throughout the cycle of boom and bust. Findings suggested that without efforts for long-term job creation, investments made in physical infrastructure, community facilities and housing are without purpose. Holding these realities in mind, the situation of present-day Pinedale, Wyoming and Watford City, North Dakota was explored, as these cases represent the newest wave of energy extraction due to the development of hydraulic fracturing. The research then sought to answer under what condition these resource-rich areas employ mitigation strategies.

The outcome of these strategies was evaluated in order to conceptualize how small boomtowns might follow a trajectory unlike predecessors. Understanding that diversification is the key to these boomtowns' survival, this research lastly questioned to which strategies and at which point in the cycle public officials should channel efforts. Finally, recommendations were made as to how comparable resource-rich communities may begin to re-strategize local authority to ensure environmental protection. Economic development suggestions were made to seek to retain key stakeholders within the oil and gas sector while leveraging the ability to use the industry to create efforts for the promotion of long-term public good in this most recent energy landscape.

The Effects of Land Use Right Transaction Approaches on Residential Property Price – A Case Study of Beijing, China
Urban Planning Thesis
Fall 2013 + Spring 2014
Wenting Pang
Xin Li, advisor

Ever since China carried out the Land Use Right Tendering, Auction and Listing Policy in 2002, controversies on whether competitions introduced by the new policy would lead to rapid increase in land transaction price have not stopped, with concerns that higher land price would in turn be an incentive of increasing housing price. In this paper, the effects of land use right transaction approaches are tested through the Hedonic Pricing model based on residential land use right price, property price and other influential factors such as accessibility, environment and location of main urban areas in Beijing. Results showed a slight correlation between transaction approaches and residential land use right price, but a more significant relationship between previous residential housing price and land use right price.

From Rhetoric to Reality: A Look at the Implementation of Transit-Oriented Development Plans along the Gold Line in Los Angeles County
Urban Planning Thesis
Fall 2013 + Spring 2014
Natalie Quinn
David King, advisor

The City of Los Angeles, known for its car dependency, has been making strides to revive public transportation in the city. In addition to transit system expansion and improvement, transit-oriented development (TOD) policy was enacted throughout the city and county in comprehensive plans, community plans, special zoning ordinances and the Metro Joint Development Program. TOD in this research is defined as high-density mixed-use development in close proximity to one or more forms of public transportation. The social, economic and environmental benefits of TOD justify its use as an alternative to traditional auto-oriented development. Although the benefits of TOD are well understood, less research has been done to assess the success of implementation in achieving truly mixed and economically accessible transit neighborhoods. This study examined the implementation of TOD policies surrounding phase one of the Metro Gold Line in Los Angeles County, a light-rail line completed July 2003. Analysis focused on density, mix of land use and economic accessibility within a quarter-mile radius of eleven light rail stations.

Investigating the Impact of Smart Growth Policies on Floodplain Development
Urban Planning Thesis
Fall 2013 + Spring 2014
Shraddha Ramani
Stacey Sutton, advisor

The effects of climate change are a growing threat to communities around the world. Coastal areas are especially vulnerable to flooding due to rising sea levels and extreme storm events. Long term planning efforts include adaptation to these changes and mitigation to address the root causes of climate change. However, sometimes these efforts counteract each other. Smart growth is a strategy that addresses many of the root causes of climate change by creating denser communities that are less reliant on automobiles. However, creating denser communities on coastal floodplains goes against adaptation measures by putting an increased number of people at risk. Controlling external factors such as community size, land use and housing types, this study compared floodplain development in New Jersey, which has a smart growth plan, to Long Island, which does not have a regional growth plan.

Are Resiliency Plans Addressing Climate Change in an Equitable Way?
Urban Planning Thesis
Fall 2013 + Spring 2014
Sarah Shannon
Clara Irazabal, advisor

This paper explores equity issues within climate change and resiliency plans in developed cities by evaluating New York City's Special Initiative for Rebuilding and Recovery through the use of two case studies: Lower Manhattan and the South Bronx. In order to evaluate in terms of equity, this report assessed the level of vulnerability facing Lower Manhattan and the South Bronx by using Caroline Moser's asset adaptation framework. This approach first looks at the types of socio-economic vulnerabilities of the groups most affected by climate change related disasters. It then seeks to identify a range of "bottom-up" climate change strategies at the individual, household and community levels, while also assessing "top-down" interventions of external actors at city and national levels. Understanding the connection between vulnerabilities, assets and the various adaptation or resilience strategies allows for the development of recommendations to support the urban poor.

The Impact of the Public Process in Rebuild by Design

Urban Planning Thesis
Fall 2013 + Spring 2014
Justine Shapiro-Kline
Lance Freeman, advisor

From June 2013 to April 2014, the United States Department of Housing and Urban Development sponsored an interdisciplinary design competition, Rebuild by Design, to cultivate innovative proposals for Hurricane Sandy recovery and to increase the region's long-term resilience. Ten teams worked with specific municipalities in New York, New Jersey and Connecticut. This thesis examines the competition process, and asks what impacts the stakeholder engagement process had on the design proposals. Using a comparison of the proposals before and after the engagement phase, as well as observation at public events and interviews with team members, I found that the public process shaped the proposals in distinct ways for each of the teams, and, at the same time, the competition attracted and sustained the attention of members of the affected communities. The public process did not generally yield new ideas, but refined those already extant in the early-stage proposals. These findings have implications for future public design competitions, participatory planning processes and disaster recovery efforts.

Changing Retail Composition in Greenwich, CT 2000 - 2013

Urban Planning Thesis
Fall 2013 + Spring 2014
Heidi Brake Smith
Stacey Ann Sutton + Graham Trelstad, advisors

This study is an examination of retail composition on Greenwich Avenue, the "Main Street" corridor in the Town of Greenwich, Connecticut between 2000 and 2013. Retail composition is affected largely by demographic and economic activity, but it is also influenced by a community's history, culture and image. Commercial corridors are where neighborhood change becomes visible and can be measured by observing store openings and closings as well as change in type. The study focused on changing retail composition, density and patterning in an affluent community to understand the underlying changing consumer demands, cultural and socio-economic dynamics at work. The thesis attempts to understand the components affecting a shopping corridor and whether there is an underlying relationship amongst the shopping classifications over time.

Patient Accessibility to Primary Healthcare in Brooklyn, New York

Urban Planning Thesis
Fall 2013 + Spring 2014
Gillian Barlow Sollenberger
Stacey Ann Sutton, advisor

The primary concern for patients in healthcare shortage areas is accessibility, which in turn can reduce the long-term costs necessitated by treating initially undiagnosed illnesses. This thesis examines primary healthcare resources in Brooklyn, New York, revealing the barriers that prevent doctors from providing care and patients from receiving care, as well as areas with low accessibility to primary care. The key to accessibility is the provision of primary healthcare during business hours as well as nights and weekends, in addition to the ability to accept walk-ins.

Urban planners and public health professionals have worked closely together to provide buildings and services to serve these needs, although in the recent past this cooperation has not been present in New York State. This thesis stands as the first part of the research required for the integration of primary care resources in Brooklyn communities, as well as recommendations that begin to retie the urban planning and public health professions. Research consisted of the following: policy research, surveying existing primary care providers in Brooklyn, mapping of existing resources and demographic conditions, cluster analysis and interviews with healthcare provider professionals.

Embracing Water: A Study on How Cities Have Planned for Floods in the Past

Urban Planning Thesis
Fall 2013 + Spring 2014
Julie Sophonpanich
Lance Freeman, advisor

Every year, floods affect over 100 million people. Flooding comes in many different shapes and forms, such as storm surges, heavy rainfall, high tidal levels and river floods. There are numerous scientific researches on flooding and the different ways that cities and city agencies have approached flooding, but little ties together accounts of floods and urban planning. This thesis investigates the various ways cities have planned for flood-prone disasters in the past.

Three case studies were chosen to represent vulnerable flood-prone cities – Rotterdam, New York City and Bangkok – for their long history of dealing with flood-related issues and their current flood planning initiatives. Although these case studies do not represent all types of floods in every city around the world, they gave an example of how cities vulnerable to floods have planned for disasters in the past. The lessons learned from these three case studies provided takeaways of good planning processes that can be studied and implemented in any country that is also facing flood-prone disasters.

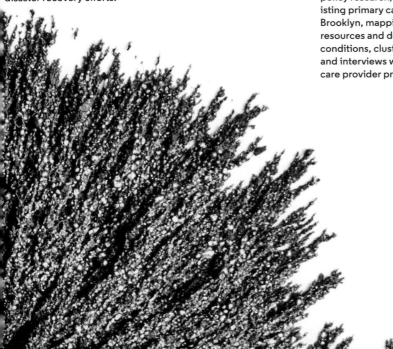

Business Composition Change in the 798 Art District of Beijing + Reasons Behind It
Urban Planning Thesis
Fall 2013 + Spring 2014
Yifu Sun
Stacey Sutton, advisor

This study begins with an analysis of the 798 Art District as it has existed since 2002, using historical art district maps as its primary data source. Counting and cataloging the properties on the yearly guide map revealed that a major business composition change occurred within this short period of time of 2007-2013. Since the oldest version of the historical map is that of 2007, this study's quantitative analysis began in 2007 and ended in 2013. As a complementary resource, this study conducted archival research so as to fill in the gap between 2002 and 2007. The above-mentioned approaches sought to answer the research questions in a complex, comprehensive way. The emergence of 798 was a remarkable cultural phenomenon, changing Beijing's inner-city fabric in a profound and probably long-lasting way. By basing itself on data drawn from historical maps, and by extending the research and analysis to embrace scholarly documents, media coverage and observations, the study probes the underlying causes of the gentrification process happening within 798.

Teens + Improvised Spaces: A Study of Appropriation of Outdoor Places
Urban Planning Thesis
Fall 2013 + Spring 2014
Ella Ver
Clara Irazabal, advisor

In contemporary cities, teenagers have been excluded from public open spaces through design and policy. This study examines design as a form of control that induces users' behavior in space through formal and informal rules that limit acceptable actions that can be conducted in spaces. What can we learn from teens' use of open space? How can we facilitate creativity and freedom within the realm of designed space? This thesis explores behavior through observations, interviews and site drawings in three appropriated spaces in the Bay Area of California: a stairwell, a public plaza and a convenience store parking lot. The study hypothesizes that teens' reasons for appropriating these places include a combination of exclusion from open spaces by socially dominant groups and the users' need to express independence. This hypothesis was only partially supported by findings. Teenage users expressed feelings of belonging and ownership in these places and exhibited creative ways of using the built environment. This study demonstrates that the fields of design, planning and policy can better serve this population by relaxing their control of users and of the built environment to allow for more creativity, freedom and active appropriation.

Positive Youth + Community Development in Brownsville, Brooklyn
Urban Planning Thesis
Fall 2013 + Spring 2014
Sherrie Waller
Clara Irazabal + Stacey Sutton, advisors

To address the power imbalance in the planning of poor neighborhoods, city planning and community development have started to incorporate participatory practices. However, rarely do participatory practices give power to residents by allowing them to be decision makers in the planning of community development strategies. How can planning become transformative and consider capacity building, community empowerment and true redistribution of power from professionals to community members?

This thesis considers how community-based organizations have acted as transformative planners by creating spaces for residents to participate in the decision-making and implementation of community improvement projects. It considered the work of the Brownsville Community Justice Center and its partners in facilitating resident involvement, specifically for youth of color engaged in the juvenile or criminal justice system, in the improvement of a disenfranchised community. This thesis sought to understand the value of involving youth, who are at a critical stage in their development, in community improvement efforts. Furthermore, this research speaks to the need for planners to create processes that introduce, engage, and incorporate residents in community development approaches so that they can be in positions to make informed decisions for their community.

State vs. Local Management of Groundwater: The Cases of California + Nevada
Urban Planning Thesis
Fall 2013 + Spring 2014
Christine Wen
Lance Freeman, advisor

Groundwater has unique properties that make it a valuable case study in management and social cost. Local agencies usually lack the resources to adequately monitor and supervise groundwater withdrawal. However, groundwater properties vary widely among locations, rendering centralized state one-plan-for-all management difficult. Groundwater is public since connected to other parts of the ecosystem, and any tampering percolates throughout the system, but it is simultaneously private because of relations to land tenure and property rights. This paper looks at groundwater policies in California, where state laws are absent and rule of capture applies, and Nevada, where there is no private ownership of groundwater and the state is responsible for its allocation. Patchwork management produces a more spatially uneven trend as well as data collection frequency, as is the case of California. While cities, counties and local agencies have the capacity to manage groundwater, they should be held accountable for regular data collection and contribute to a unified database. The California Database of Groundwater Levels that was started in 2012 was a step in the right direction toward a more comprehensive state oversight.

To What Type of Neighborhoods Do the Chinese Tend to Move: A Study of Chinese Americans in the City of New York, 1970-2010
Urban Planning Thesis
Fall 2013 + Spring 2014
Chuanxi Xiong
Lance Freeman, advisor

The Chinese American is a major part of the fast growing Asian population in the City of New York. This thesis focuses on the change in the spatial distribution of Chinese Americans in the city during 1970-2010, whether Chinese Americans are assimilating with other ethnic groups in this period and what kind of neighborhoods they tend to concentrate in. Using Census and PUMS data, I found that the cultural and ethnic ties may trump other factors in Chinese Americans' location choices, and they are not largely assimilated into the major population.

Neighborhood Conservation Districts: An Assessment of Typologies, Effectiveness + Community Response
Urban Planning Thesis
Fall 2013 + Spring 2014
Max Abraham Yeston
Carol Clark + Clara Irazábal, advisors

Neighborhood Conservation Districts (NCDs), are preservation planning tools with valuable approaches to neighborhood preservation. The strategy gives communities the opportunity to have a more active say in how their neighborhoods are shaped without having the physical identity of their surroundings be determined by market-based, Euclidean zoning and without the sometimes more onerous rules of historic districts. From a preservation standpoint, an NCD is appropriate for neighborhoods that might not merit traditional historic designation, either because the building stock is not old enough, or the original built fabric has been compromised by extensive alterations. Building upon previous studies that have taken a comprehensive look at the wide range of NCDs, this thesis focused on three cities: Cambridge, Massachusetts; Raleigh, North Carolina; and Philadelphia, Pennsylvania. Each city brought forth different criteria and design regulations. In this assessment of how specific NCDs are performing now, the basic questions were: are some NCDs meeting their self-expressed and explicit goals better than others? How do different standards of design review perform in different NCDs, and how do various community stakeholders view the effects of regulations? Examining the views of stakeholders on the ordinances against the language and intent of the laws themselves revealed whether NCDs could be viewed as an effective preservation tool for areas that might not fit full historic designation requirements. By taking into account the demographic and economic data for these particular neighborhoods, along with participants' views, the study assessed unintentional impacts of the different ordinances and ascertained whether there could be room for improvement.

Carbon Finance Opportunities in Transportation + Clean Development Mechanism in Developing Countries – Examining the Interplay of Investment, Emission Reduction + Carbon Credit Revenue: Bogota Trans-Milenio + Chongqing BRT
Urban Planning Thesis
Fall 2013 + Spring 2014
Ji Yeun Yu
David King, advisor

The Clean Development Mechanism (CDM), established under the 1997 Kyoto Protocol and overseen by the United Nations Framework Convention on Climate Change, provides a funding mechanism for Greenhouse Gas (GHG) reduction projects in developing countries. Despite the logical relationship with GHG, the transport sector represents a small percentage of projects approved for CDM financing, possibly because of its complex and lengthy implementation process as well as the general large scale cost. In an attempt to examine CDM's practical applicability as a financing tool for the transport sector, this study focuses on CDM's financial contributions to select BRT projects: Bogota's (Colombia) TransMilenio and Chongqing (China) BRT. The study concludes that CDM financing has limited and marginal impact for the project completion and direct costs. However, its practical applicability rests in mitigating the project's financial risk. CDM's limitation remains in the market-driven nature of the Certified Emission Reduction price and other fundamental issues in the mechanism itself.

The Making of Public Open Space Accessible to Underserved Populations in Urban Villages
Urban Planning Thesis
Fall 2013 + Spring 2014
Xiaowan Zhang
Xin Li, advisor

Urban villages, a unique form of slum in China developed from rural settlements, represent an existing conflict in allocation of public resources to different social groups. Public resources, such as public infrastructure and social services, have been poorly provided in these areas. The majority of residents in urban villages are low-income, migrant workers. Unfortunately, the needs of these migrant tenants for a fine living environment have not been sufficiently incorporated in cities' urban planning policies. This study explored the usage of Public Open Space by urban village residents, using a case study of Baishizhou Village, the largest urban village in Shenzhen, China. The results of surveying POS visitors and interviewing public officials, residents and related design professionals suggest that, in the planning process of POS, policymakers considered only the needs of the landlords, while neglecting the fact that most users of the POS are migrant tenants. Thus, incremental planning of urban villages that incorporates the need of urban migrants is necessary during the process of urbanization. "Incremental upgrading" rather than "comprehensive redevelopment" should be better understood and pursued by Chinese planners, and citizenization of residents in urban villages should be the pioneering transformation approach.

Social Capital, Entrepreneur Network + Small City Development in Central + Western China: A Case Study of Xixia City

Urban Planning Thesis
Fall 2013 + Spring 2014
Chi Zhang
Xin Li, advisor

Reducing the regional economic gap and better developing the currently underdeveloped small cities in Central and Western China are two challenges confronting Chinese and international scholars. This thesis chose Xixia City, a small mountainous city in the Central China region, as a successful case in economic development to explore whether and how local entrepreneur networks function as social capital stocks to help these small cities overcome their common disadvantages and catalyze local economic development. By interviewing members of the Xixia local entrepreneur network and officials, this thesis seeks to understand the history and structure of the Xixia local entrepreneur network and identify the social capital stocks in Xixia City. Based on these data, this thesis summarizes the benefits of the local entrepreneur network and uncovers the positive lessons we learn from the Xixia's local network in order to encourage this local economic development and industry innovation throughout China's underdeveloped small cities.

Location Analysis of 3D Printer Manufacturing Industry

Urban Planning Thesis
Fall 2013 + Spring 2014
Shichen Zhang
David King, advisor

Advanced manufacturing has been well addressed in American policies, especially since 2010 when America wanted to revitalize the economy and create jobs by taking advantage of its competitive sectors. 3D printing is a typical advanced manufacturing industry that is high value added, driven by technological innovation, highly skilled labor, cutting edge materials and production process. This industry emerged in America in the 1980s and surged ahead in the recent decade. The distribution of 3D printer companies is not bound within California where 3D printing was invented, but has spread out to the Southeast, Mid-Atlantic and the Great Lakes. This thesis looks into two questions: what are the location factors of 3D printer manufacturing industry; why can some cities that are not noted for high-tech clusters attract 3D printer manufacturers. In this thesis, two case studies of 3D printer producers are presented. The first was the biggest 3D printer firm 3D Systems Corp's relocation from California to Rock Hill, South Carolina in 2005, and the second was a promising firm MakerBot Industries' establishment and development in Brooklyn, New York City since 2009. My hypothesis was that highly skilled labor, knowledge sharing and business networks are important factors affecting location decisions.

Correlation Between Land Use + Metro Rail Ridership in Los Angeles

Urban Planning Thesis
Fall 2013 + Spring 2014
Zhewu Zhuang
David King, advisor

As oil prices continue to rise and traffic jams make daily travel harder than ever, public transportation is widely considered a preferred option for major metropolitans worldwide. Los Angeles County, facing the worst congestion in the nation, has several Metro rail extensions on the way. As rail stations are expected to grow, there are a great number of Transit Oriented Development projects involving the existing and new stations that aim to increase transit ridership. This paper studies the correlation between rail station ridership and land uses around the station in Los Angeles County. The findings suggest that different land use around different stations have different results.

After Losing Land: Reemployment Opportunity for Landless Peasants in China: A Case Study of Yangguanzhai Village

Urban Planning Thesis
Fall 2013 + Spring 2014
Biying Zhu
Xin Li, advisor

This thesis provides an analysis of factors that influence the reemployment opportunities for landless peasants after their lands are acquired by the State due to fast urbanization. This thesis aims to determine these factors by observing the difference between the peasants who can find reemployment easily and others who cannot. I collected data through interviews and surveys that were conducted in Yangguanzhai Village.

**Addressing Declining
Bicycle Use in China:
Factors Associated with
Bicycle Ownership + Use**
Urban Planning Thesis
Fall 2013 + Spring 2014
Linghong Zou
David King, advisor

China is experiencing a drastic
decline in bicycle use and
substantial increase in auto
travel. This major mode shift
has significant social as well
as environmental implications.
In addressing the diminishing
cyclist population, the Chinese
government issued policy
guidelines featuring benchmarks to sustain bicycle use,
but such guidelines were based
on limited understanding of
who chooses to bike and why.
This study aimed to provide
a better understanding of
factors associated with bicycle
ownership and use as a basis
for developing measures and
incentives to promote the bicycle use in China. A nation–wide
online survey was conducted to
understand the characteristics
of bicycle users and public
attitudes towards bicycling. Logistic regression models were
used to test the importance of
bicycle infrastructure and other
physical environment factors
relative to socio-demographic
factors and personal attitudes.
The results showed strong
correlations of higher bicycle
ownership and use with lower
household income, shorter
commute distance, leveraged
bicycle infrastructure, positive
attitudes towards cycling and
negative attitudes towards
automobiles. Similar regression analysis was also used
to explore the influence of
various factors on propensities
for future bicycle use. Further,
the study revealed substantial geographic variance of
bicycle use within the country.

Urban Planning Ph.D. Program
Lance Freeman, director

The goal of the Ph.D. Program in Urban Planning is to educate and train scholars and researchers in the general field of urban and regional planning. Substantive areas of study include: affordable housing, regional transportation planning, urban economic development and international development, among others. These substantive concerns are approached both theoretically and methodologically. In the former instance, students draw, for example, from neo-classical economics, participatory democracy and law. In the latter, they utilize key informant interviews, statistical analysis of secondary data, mixed methods and case study design among other research designs. Emphasis within the program is given to the role of space and of collective action on the part of governments and civic organizations. Of particular concern are issues of social justice and democracy.

Doctoral Colloquium 1 + 3
Urban Planning Ph.D.
Fall 2013
David King, instructor

The primary purpose of this doctoral colloquium was to reflect on the role of research design in social science scholarship. We focused on general approaches to research as well as more specific methodologies such as case study design, comparative analysis, mixed methods and historical research. As part of this discussion, we investigated the issue of representation.

Doctoral Colloquium 2 + 4
Urban Planning Ph.D.
Spring 2014
Lance Freeman, instructor

The purpose of this course was to equip students with skills to conceptualize, write and critique empirical research. Such research is a staple of professional journals such as the *Journal of the American Planning Association* and the *Journal of Planning Education and Research*. This course accomplished this objective by introducing students to the dominant paradigms that shape much empirical social science research, asking students to critique scholarly research, propose alternatives and to produce a draft of an empirical journal article.

The course used examples of research debates from urban planning to illustrate different research strategies. Typically, the readings included examples of empirical studies accompanied by readings that explain in more detail the particular research strategy used in the examples. Students also had the opportunity to propose alternative strategies for addressing the research questions examined in the examples. Through practice, students honed their research design skills. In the final part of the course students presented and critiqued each other's research designs.

Advanced Planning Theory - Exploring the State: Institutions, Organizations + Rule Making
Urban Planning Ph.D.
Spring 2014
Smita Srinivas, instructor, with Amanda Bradshaw

There can be no planning or policy outcome without the involvement of the state in some form. This advanced seminar was for Ph.D. students in the Urban Planning program. It presented approaches to the State and public plans drawn from across disciplines that inform different types of planning. The readings for the seminar drew on seminal development discourses on different types of plans and policies across the world. The readings also served to place in context the Anglo-American tradition of urban and regional planning and its theories. In this seminar, we studied the state's component organizations, institutional underpinning, norms, rule making and processes of administration. Each week some sections of important books and associated articles were read and discussed in detail. The readings covered diverse topics such as the state as policy arena, democracy and governance, organizational theory, questions of bureaucracy, rationality and planning; the emergence of informal and formal institutions and rule making, behavioral or cognitive frameworks for state action and response, state sanction and legitimacy and public sector reform. There were important differences in the theoretical underpinnings of the readings, but they shared some common strands as well. Across the disciplines and professional approaches, were also readings on symbolism and power, organizational learning, coercion, communication and rule interpretation.

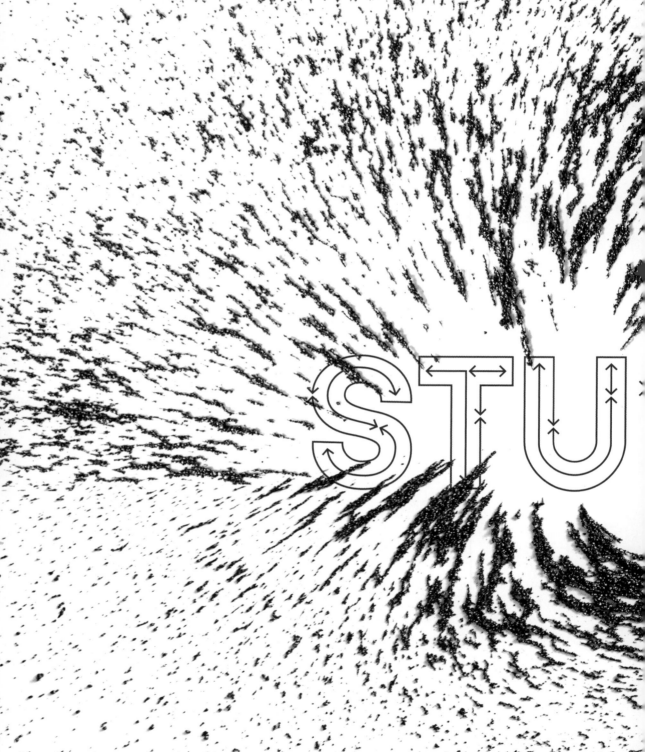

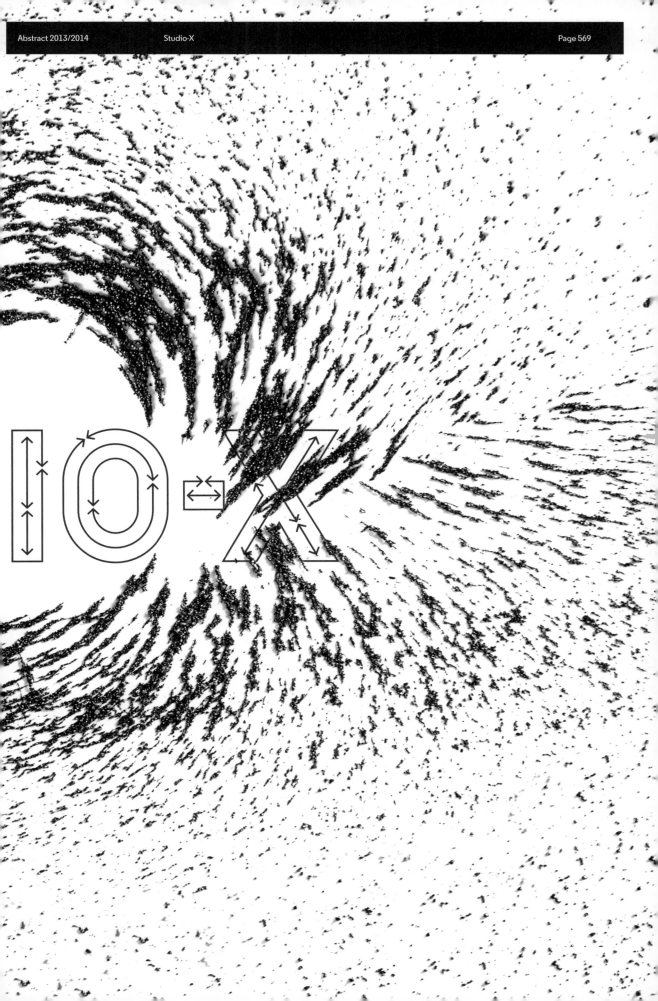

Studio-X Global Introduction
Mark Wigley, dean
Marina Otero Verzier, director,
Global Network, Programming

It started as an experiment, with a pilot project in downtown New York City in 2008. Today, the Studio-X global network spans the globe with eight high impact laboratories for exploring the future of the built environment.

With locations in the downtown cores of Amman, Beijing, Istanbul, Johannesburg, New York, Mumbai, Rio de Janeiro and Tokyo, Studio-X enables the best minds from Columbia University to think together with the best minds in Latin America, the Middle East, Africa, Eastern Europe and Asia. It brings together scholars, professionals, students and decision makers, from different backgrounds and cultures, to foster research collaboration by organizing academic activities and public programs.

The 2013-2014 academic year was a key period in the establishment of Studio-X as one of the most valuable resources in the Graduate School of Architecture, Planning and Preservation. Its global network has continued to evolve as the exchanges between Avery Hall and the Studio-X locations have triggered new conversations and projects, in which every program in the school has become an active participant in the global network.

With the launch of Studio-X Istanbul in November 2013 and Studio-X Johannesburg in March 2014, Columbia University further deepened its longstanding relationship with Turkey and with South Africa, fostering new collaborations with partners from across Europe and the African continent.

With the completion of the global network came incredible experimentation. Conceived for the Bi-City Biennale of Urbanism\Architecture (UABB) 2013 and curated by Marisa Yiu, the first installment of the POP-UP Studio-X Shenzhen/Hong Kong generated new modes of thinking within the context of the Pearl River Delta. From December 2013 to February 2014, Studio-X directors shared research materials that reflected upon the concept of "urban border" across national and international spaces, and a host of events examined questions of cross-border education, Chinese contemporary identity and the role of cultural preservation in the context of rapid development. Despite its temporary nature, POP-UP Studio-X Shenzhen/Hong Kong left a permanent legacy of collaboration among the global Studio-X locations, Avery Hall and local partners such as Asia Art Archive, Parasite, Ink Society and the Chinese University of Hong Kong.

2013 also marked the launch of the Rio das Pedras Initiative, a flagship project that brings Columbia University and the Studio-X global network together with the School of Engineering, the School of Public Health, and international and Brazilian experts to think about future scenarios for informal communities and new mixed-use inclusive housing in Rio. For the first time this initiative included participants from multiple disciplines within GSAPP–Real Estate Development, Urban Design, Architecture and Urban Planning–who came together through shared research focusing on the 80,000 people in Rio das Pedras, and exploring key strategies for a more sustainable and equitable development in the region.

The recently launched research series on Security Regimes—critically examining global spaces of exception—and on Architectures of Sharing—focused on resilient networks for dissemination, translation and knowledge-sharing—continue to evolve as the Studio-X fellowship program and other major research projects—on mobility and transport, preservation or urban health—develop under the leadership of GSAPP faculty members and Studio-X directors.

All these collaborative modes of education, research and action were only possible through a continuous flow of exciting ideas and people. Traveling, therefore, continues to be at the heart of the Studio-X project and one of the core values of the global university. In 2013-2014 all architecture students traveled to a Studio-X location around the world as part of their spring trips, also known as X-Week. CCCP, Urban Planning, Urban Design and Real Estate Development programs also conducted international fieldwork from Studio-X hubs. Students shared their experiences as travelers and global researchers through 1,000 photographs from more than 20 cities around the world, which were cataloged in the X-GRAM book given to all graduating students at GSAPP's May 2014 commencement. During the Summer of 2014 faculty members continued the global exploration leading student summer workshops in Brazil, China, Japan, Jordan, South Africa, Switzerland and Turkey.

The creation of the Studio-X Jam Sessions and the Studio-X Research Guide—curated by the Studio-X directors together with Columbia University Librarians from Avery Architectural & Fine Arts Library and Global Studies—support and supplement these educational experiences by providing research materials and platforms for sparking conversations around contemporary challenges in global cities.

With the relationship between Avery Hall and its global network solidified as a crucial pedagogical dynamic, the university of the future is becoming a reality.

Global Network Directors **A**
Pop Up Studio-X Shenzhen **B**

Notes:
For other images or links:

**POP-UP STUDIO-X
SHENZHEN AND
HONG KONG:**
Press releases:
http://eepurl.com/J2OoH
http://eepurl.com/OTZUH

Microsite:
www.popup.studio-x.org
Images: www.flickr.com/
photos/studio_x_new_
york_columbia_gsapp/
sets/72157638609680555/

www.flickr.com/photos/
studio_x_new_york_co-
lumbia_gsapp/
sets/72157641877011893/

XGRAM
Forthcoming book: http://
issuu.com/gsapponline/
docs/2014_0522_xgram_issuu
Flickr group: https://www.
flickr.com/groups/xgram2014
https://www.flickr.com/
photos/studio_x_new_
york_columbia_gsapp/
sets/72157642125547533/

RESEACH GUIDE:
http://library.columbia.
edu/subject-guides/
avery/StudioX.html

JAM SESSION:
Images: https://www.flickr.
com/photos/studio_x_new_
york_columbia_gsapp/
sets/72157644783914582/

ISTANBUL OPENING:
Press Release:
http://eepurl.com/IsAQD
Images: https://www.flickr.
com/photos/studio_x_new_
york_columbia_gsapp/
sets/72157637602685124/

JOHANNESBURG OPENING:
Press Releases:
http://eepurl.com/PWO4v
http://eepurl.com/QIK8b
Images: https://www.flickr.
com/photos/studio_x_new_
york_columbia_gsapp/
sets/72157643364389145/

STUDIO-X GLOBAL NETWORK:
Mark Wigley
(Dean, Columbia University GSAPP)
Nora Akawi (Director, Amman Lab)
Gregory Bugel (Exhibition Coordinator,
Global Network Programming)
Magu Bueno (Director, São Paulo Lab)
Selva Gürdogan (Director,
Studio-X Istanbul)
Daisuke Hirose (Director, Tokyo Lab)
Li Hu (Director, Studio-X Beijing)
Malwina E. Łys-Dobradin
(Director, Global Network Special
Projects)
Mpho Matsipa (Director, Stu-
dio-X Johannesburg)
Pedro Rivera (Director, Studio-X
Rio de Janeiro)
Rajeev Thakker (Director, Studio-X
Mumbai) Nicola Twilley (Director,
Studio-X New York City)
Marina Otero Verzier (Director,
Global Network Programming)
Marisa Yiu (Curator, POP-UP
Studio-X Shenzhen/Hong Kong)

STUDIO-X STEERING COMMITTEE:
Mabel Wilson (Chair)
Amale Andraos
Vishaan Chakrabarti
Clara Irazabal
Reinhold Martin
Jorge Otero-Pailos
Hilary Sample
Smita Srinivas
Enrique Walker

www.arch.columbia.edu/studio-x-global

Amman Lab
Studio-X
Fall 2013 + Spring 2014
Nora Akawi, director

Questions on citizenship, representation, access and memory were central to the discussions at Studio-X Amman Lab this past year. In recent years, the evolving landscape of Amman has reflected the intensity of the changes transforming the region. Throughout the history of Amman, population growth, residential expansion and fast densification, even sudden bursts of investment, are largely the result of neighboring conflict. Migration, uprisings and continuous renegotiations of the notion of citizenship are reshaping cities in the Arab region at a speed that makes a generation of architects and planners work in a state of constant transition and uncertainty. In this context, uncertainty becomes not an obstacle, but a driving force towards a collective making of a sustainable and equitable city.

The Amman Lab became a point of reference in the region for experimental design, programming and research dedicated to investigating the future of cities. Amman Lab activities -- lectures, symposia, screenings, workshops and roundtables -- are today recognized occasions for architects and designers in Amman and the region to get together to exchange knowledge and ideas with GSAPP faculty and students.

The Collecting Architecture Territories project (CAT) expanded to the region this past year through a summer workshop organized in collaboration with the Amman Lab in June 2013 led by Mark Wasiuta and Craig Buckley with Adam Bandler and Jordan Carver. In Spring 2014, GSAPP students traveled to Amman, Beirut and Doha as part of the Kinne travel program, and attended the CAT Amman Minutes event held on March 9th, 2014, where fourteen curators, artists, architects, critics and writers gathered from GSAPP and around the region for a full-day symposium co-curated with Darat al Funun.

During the 5th Public Space Workshop, GSAPP students joined forces with students and expert hackers from Jordan, Turkey and India to collaboratively develop proposals and prototypes for responsive designs in public spaces in the city.

In Fall 2013, Amale Andraos traveled to Amman with students for the studio "Architecture and Representation: the Lens of Diplomacy" and Karla Rothstein and the students in the studio "Death Lab: Transience" traveled to Amman for field research and met with various experts, religious leaders, planners and thinkers investigating the relationships between death, the city and memory.

In January 2014, the Amman Lab launched the X-Talk series, following the format developed by Studio-X Beijing. Inaugurated by artist Rayyane Tabet, who shared a seven-year long research, design and art project focusing on the trans-Arabian pipeline (TAPLine).

Through the Amman Lab, a new research topic was introduced at GSAPP focused on the politics of preservation and memory in the context of Israel/Palestine. The studio course "Jerusalem and the Occupation of Memory" was taught by Craig Konyk and Nina Kolowratnik, and travelled to Amman, Jerusalem, Tel Aviv and Ramallah to analyze the site and meet with the various Palestinian and Israeli stakeholders and academics involved in the preservation of Lifta, a Palestinian village in ruins located on the Western edge of Jerusalem.

Additional film screenings, lectures, roundtables, field visits and workshops at Studio-X Amman are curated to aggregate and share knowledge, build on existing research, and promote a continuity of critical feedback, communication and collaboration between GSAPP and scholars, architects, artists, designers and other active citizens and stakeholders in Amman and neighboring cities.

X-Talk by Professor George Katodrytis (American University of Sharjah) at Al-Balad Theater in Amman, "Emergent Materials and Performative Urbanism" A
Rahel Aima, co-Founder The State magazine, at Collecting Architecture Territories: Amman Minutes at Darat al Funun B
Public Talk by Moataz Faissal Farid + Karla Rothstein, "Extraordinary Existence: Cairo's City of the Dead" in downtown Amman C
5th Public Space Workshop Final Presentation at the German Jordanian University in Amman D
Collecting Architecture Territories Summer Workshop: Meeting with Zeina Arida at the Arab Image Foundation in Beirut, Mark Wasiuta + Craig Buckley E

Studio-X Beijing
Studio-X
Fall 2013 + Spring 2014
Li Hu, director

After nearly five years in Beijing, Studio-X continues to expand its influence in the region by hosting diverse programming in architecture and urban planning, and developing research on finding and implementing effective solutions for China's urbanization challenge. Studio-X Beijing successfully functions as a platform for exchanging ideas and knowledge.

Facilitated by GSAPP, intense projects were produced by Studio-X Beijing this past year, such as the joint international workshop: "REFRAME: Public Space Proposals for New Gonghua City" by the China Megacities Lab of Columbia University, CAFA and Urbanus; "The Future of the Museum in China" directed by Jeffrey Johnson and Zoe Florence with Studio Pei Zhu; a lecture by Prof. David Grahame Shane; the exhibition CRITICAL COPYING (II); an Open House event for newly-admitted and prospective students; and as an active member of The Studio-X Global Network, Studio-X Beijing joined in POP-UP Studio-X Shenzhen as part of Bi-City Biennale of Urbanism/Architecture.

In close collaboration with Columbia University's Center for Sustainable Urban Development, Studio-X Beijing participated in the traveling exhibition People Building Better Cities (PBBC) from September 28 to October 20 in 2013. PBBC has since been shown in Bangkok, Rio de Janeiro, Sydney, Johannesburg, Nairobi, Mumbai, Delhi and Chennai.

The X-Talk Series, initiated with the lecture "Journey of Discovery" by Huang Juzheng, chief director of Architect Magazine, continued to include speakers from related design fields, such as the presentation "Social Design" by Zang Feng from People's Industrial Design Office, "Sheng Jing Ji He" by Li Xinggang, "A Little Big World/ Redefining Prefab for Rural and Nature" by Zhu Jingxiang, and "On the Immediacy of Objecthood and Situatedness of Architecture" by Liu Yichun.

As one of the X-Series events, X-Agenda Micro-Exhibition Series was initiated by Studio-X Beijing in September of 2012 intended to advance the awareness and self-reflection of a new generation of Chinese architects and designers' practices, and by which a better understanding of current urban and architectural issues can be attained. Three Chinese architecture studios were invited to participate in X-Agenda Series, including Atelier Li Xinggang, Atelier Deshaus and Architect Zhu Jingxiang. At the end of 2013, X-Conference series-02 was organized as a critical reflection and discussion on the works of these three offices and the issues generated from the works. Studio-X Beijing continues to collaborate with local schools and institutions, such as the Asia Design Forum held by Architectural Record and supported by Studio-X Beijing and other firms, China-Eu Metropolis Think Tank Summit, Culture Diversity of International Metropolis, hosted by Beijing Contemporary Art Foundation.

Aimed at exploring the top issues of urbanization and architecture through practical practices, Post Bubble Urbanism research was initiated by Studio-X Beijing to study urgent urban issues address the dramatic urban transformations of the last twenty years, and generate provocative and informative propositions for the future of the cities. This long-term research continues to welcome the participation of GSAPP students and faculty, as well as the Columbia Global Centers and other Studio-X nodes.

Reframe: Public Space
Proposals **A**
X-Agenda Micro
Exhibition Series **B/C/D**

C

X-Agenda 系列微展 /
A Micro-Exhibition Series

置身于一个高速变化的社会中，当下中国
年轻一代建筑师的天职面临着重挑战，我
也祖幸运地有着形形色色的机遇。我们去
为何做？如何做？在沉没于空间、形式、
材料等基本建筑命题的问时，我们不得不
去思考建筑这件租苦工作的原始动机。希
希望以此来不断校正前行的方向。

X-Agenda 系列微展由 Studio-X 哥伦比亚大
学北京建筑中心发起举办，旨在推进和反
思当下年轻一代中国建筑师。设计师的实
践。X-Agenda 看重关注对设计和建造实践
的思考与探索，立场与方向。希望在浮躁
的建设现象下，为思想开辟一块土壤，从
不同的角度来探讨一个青年群体的未来的
方向。单个展览是微型的，整体的影响可
以是广大的。X-Agenda 热情邀请大家的参
与与批评。

Situated in a society that is going through
unprecedented changes, the new generation
of architects in China today is faced with
multi-faceted challenges, while at the same
time blessed with abundant opportunities.
What should we take on? Why do we do it?
How to do it? Besides indulging ourselves
in the daily practices through space, form,
material and so on, we must constantly
reflect on the very motivation behind our
endeavors in this tough profession, with the
hope to constantly realign the focus of our
practices.

Columbia University GSAPP's Studio-X
Beijing initiates and supports a series of
micro-exhibition titled X-Agenda
which aims to advance the awareness and
self-reflection of a new generation of Chinese
architects and designers practices,
X-Agenda will focus on the state of thought
and ideas, statements and directions, under
the current circumstances.

D

Studio-X Istanbul
Studio-X
Fall 2013 + Spring 2014
Selva Gürdoğan, director

Istanbul is a generous city. Any time you dig a hole in the streets of Istanbul you discover yet another civilization. In this remarkable multi-layered place generating new modes of thinking and new ways of sharing ideas about the built environment with colleagues around the world is not only an opportunity but an act of responsibility. It is a great honor to be here.
Mark Wigley

On November 5, 2013, the Studio-X global network of research laboratories opened a new location in downtown Istanbul. Studio-X Istanbul celebrated in its launch as the only cultural space in the city dedicated to discussions of architecture and urbanism. Directed by Selva Gürdoğan, Studio-X Istanbul stimulates, inspires and energizes local, regional and global communities.

Studio X hosted several exhibitions and programs to inaugurate its permanent home and become a center for architecture in the city:

Collecting Architectural Territories
November 5, 2013 –
January 4, 2014
Curated by Mark Wasiuta, Adam Bandler + Jordan Carver

One of the most significant developments reshaping the intersection of art and architectural practice over the last three decades is the veritable explosion of institutions and foundations that have emerged out of private art collections. Collecting Architecture Territories is a research and teaching project that attempts to assess the breadth and diversity of such institutions – they range from experimental new museums to renovated industrial, commercial or military buildings – and to map the effects of these institutions on conventional museological practices and forms of collecting.

Cemetery of Architects
Tayfun Serttaş
January 31 – March 28, 2014

The exhibition was an archive of architectural inscriptions witnessed on buildings in Istanbul, dated from the 1870s to 1930s, a period that corresponds to the modernization period within the Ottoman Empire.

Trilogy of the Deserted City
Tayfun Serttaş

Trilogy of the Deserted City was an experiment dedicated to problematizing the consequences of the loss of populations through periodic emigrations from Istanbul. In the three consecutive layers of fake investigation and misdirection, the "desertedness" that was sought, followed, watched, evidenced, researched and interrogated was internalized. Thus the exaggerated urban metaphor became a game through a one-person search against the city and collective memory by the individual.

'Compressed: Guantánamos'
March 25, 2014 – May 9, 2014

What makes Guantánamo and its equivalents around the world distinct from other prisons? 'Compressed: Guantánamos' presented Guantánamo as a starting point to reflect on states of exception and the ambiguities when the rule of law is suspended. Additionally, the 'Guantánamo Public Memory Project' displayed the interactive effort of students from eleven different universities in the United States who examined both historical and contemporary aspects of Guantánamo. Thirteen core topics were investigated and presented for discussion. Contributors included the Columbia Global Centers in Turkey and the Columbia University Institute for the Study of Human Rights Truth Justice Memory Center Civil Society in the Penal System Association.

'Children's Istanbul' Workshops and 'Growing up in a Growing Metropolis'
May 23 – June 7, 2014

Studio-X Istanbul hosted workshops for children every Saturday for three months in collaboration with Informal Education – çocukistanbul. The workshops encouraged the children to visualize and talk about their experiences of Istanbul.

'Growing Up In A Growing Metropolis' curated by Sinan Logie includes works of artists that focus on Istanbul, such as Ceren Oykut, Ali Taptık, Serkan Taycan, and Sıla Yalazan, along with those of the children.

Growing up in a Growing Metropolis A
Children's Istanbul B
Compressed Guanatanamos C
Cemetery of Architects D/E

Studio-X Johannesburg
Studio-X
Fall 2013 + Spring 2014
Mpho Matsipa, director

Columbia University's Graduate School of Architecture, Planning and Preservation launched Studio-X Johannesburg in March 2014 in a three day program of events. The opening events took place at Studio-X Johannesburg, from March 14 – 16, 2014 and included A Reception and Exhibition Opening for Taking it to the Streets: The Art of Public Life, curated by Tanya Gershon. This exhibition explored the role of the street performer in the construction of a vibrant public sphere in Johannesburg. Gershon, a student of the CCCP Program and graduate of the M.Arch Program at GSAPP, developed this research on the spatial politics of the informal network of street performers in Johannesburg as part of her Masters thesis. The exhibition included a street art installation by Nolan O. Dennis and Fuzzy Slipperz as well as music performed by Hlasko and BLK JKS sndsystm DJ – Mpumi Mcata of the critically acclaimed South African rock band – BLK JKS.

Directed by Mpho Matsipa, Studio-X Johannesburg seeks to support and sustain local and global exchange in the future of cities as well as to serve as a platform for innovation and experimentation in design, research and the production of urban knowledge. In the face of the official narratives of apocalyptic urbanization and crisis within African cities, Studio-X Johannesburg aims to craft a creative public platform that explores alternative imaginaries of the city. Its particular focus on different forms of global connection, productive collaboration and exchange will nurture encounters amongst researchers, urbanists, theorists, filmmakers, artists, activists, architects and policy makers, while simultaneously being attentive to power asymmetries and the ethics of engagement within relations of global exchange. As such, Studio-X Johannesburg offers a new site for critical transdisciplinary engagements within a rapidly transforming African metropolis.

Other themes explored in the three day launch included discussions on Mapping, Justice and Sustainability between Global Africa Lab and a multi-disciplinary South African panel of experts; What it Is, an experimental video installation and performance by Studio-X Johannesburg award-winning resident artist, Noluthando Lobese in collaboration with Mello Moropa, Lindiwe Matshikiza and Vishanthe Kali; a film screening of Jonah by Sundance Film Award nominee, Kibwe Tavares (Factory Fifteen); a public lecture and one day student exchange led by GSAPP faculty and co-founders of LOT-EK Ada Tolla and Giuseppe Lignano; and a panel discussion by young creative practitioners on Tactical Urbanism led by Liz Ogbu. The launch event ended with a public lecture and exhibition by GSAPP adjunct associate professor and founder of MoDILA, Mokena Makeka.

GSAPP faculty and students have been active in South Africa for many years, most recently through Global Africa Lab, a research lab that explores urban topologies of the African continent and its diaspora. Studio-X Johannesburg has received considerable media coverage such as national and international newspapers: The Mail and Guardian; International Business News; forthcoming publications on Swedish Public Broadcaster and online culture magazines and blogs such as Okay Africa and Soul Providers. The overwhelming response from media, the creative community, researchers and activists suggests a promising future for Studio-X Johannesburg as a site for creatively re-thinking – and re-making – cities at a global scale. With the launch of Studio-X Johannesburg, Columbia University will further deepen its longstanding relationship with South Africa and foster new collaborations with partners from across the African continent.

Acknowledgements:
Professor Safwan M. Masri, Executive Vice President for Global Centers and Global Development

Dean Mark Wigley Graduate School of Architecture Planning and Preservation

Dr. Mpho Matsipa, Studio X Johannesburg Director

Professor Mario Gooden, co-Director Global Africa Lab

Mabel Wilson, Nancy and George E. Rupp Professor at GSAPP, Chair of the Studio-X Steering Committee, and co-Director Global Africa Lab

Giuseppe Lignano, Adjunct Assistant Professor and co-founder of the architectural design studio LOT-EK

Ada Tolla, Adjunct Assistant Professor and co-founder of the architectural design studio LOT-EK

Malwina Lys-Dobradin, Director Global Network Special Projects

Mokena Makeka, Adjunct Assistant Professor, founder and principal of Makeka Design Lab and founder of MoDILA

Marina Otero, Director, Global Network Programming

Jacqueline Sitterle, Chief of Staff, Office of Global Initiatives, Columbia University

Wits Students **A**
Global Africa Lab **B**
Kibwe Tavares Screening **C**
Kibwe Lot-ek **D**

A

B

C

D

Studio-X Mumbai
Studio-X
Fall 2013 + Spring 2014
Rajeev Thakker, director

Since its inception in 2011, Studio-X Mumbai has tested its role within the region of cross-cultural and interdisciplinary exchange of knowledge and information by participating in an increasingly diverse set of programs ranging from talks and lectures, exhibitions, conferences, workshops and public installations.

In 2013, Studio-X Mumbai continued with the monthly series, 'Tall Tales,' providing individuals a chance to share real life conditions through storytelling. We renewed our interest in collaborating with the ARChive of Contemporary Music in NYC, and for Indian Music Week 2013 we created a project called 'Synth City', which aimed to create, discover and explore synths and their ability to express spaces or connect with localities within the city like Chor Bazaar 'Thieves Market' and Haji Ali 'The Mosque on the Sea.'

Once again, EMBARQIndia and Columbia Alumni coordinated events such as 'Re-Thinking Parking' by Dr. Paul Barter, renowned expert on parking and transportation planning, and transportation expert Amit Bhatt to speak about 'Raahagiri' or 'Car Free Days' in cities like Delhi. Working with Dr. Jyoti Hosagrahar of the Sustainable Urbanism Lab at GSAPP, 'Innovating Public Space in Urban India' in January 2014 questioned how we could re-think public spaces in Indian cities today. In contrast, a lecture by Siddharth Menon on 'Rural Building Practices' shed light on how local craft and knowledge play important roles in the production of rural architecture in India.

Politics, law and policy have always played a crucial role in the formations and usage of our urban environments and our program through the group 'We, the People' presented the Civic Action Toolkit, a step-by-step guide containing tools and tips for citizens in taking up civic issues in their respective localities. In January 2014, Vishaan Chakrabarti, Director of the MSRED program at GSAPP, spoke on his book 'A Country of Cities' arguing that well-designed cities are the key to solving America's great national challenges: environmental degradation, unsustainable consumption, economic stagnation, rising public health costs and decreasing social mobility. Barnard College's Anupama Rao conducted several workshops dealing with her notions on Subaltern Urbanism and most recently, in collaboration with Columbia Law School Professor Katarina Pistor, hosted 'Land between the Formal and the Informal.'

Our events related to design and the environment ranged from a presentation by graduating students of Industrial Design Center entitled 'Design as a catalyst for change' and the MARS Architects unveiling of the Water Bench, an urban furniture prototype capable of rainwater harvesting. Water as a crucial resource was further explored by Anne Camilla in her talk, 'The Waterline - harvesting rainwater in Urban India,' which attempted to enhance the existing water pipeline infrastructure of the city. We invited critical professionals and academics to speak on a host of design related ideas which included a book launch, 'Architecture of Rafiq Azam,' who's work in Bangladesh has forged a path of critical resistance to global homogenous architectural language and an intimate connection to nature itself, and Professor Valerio Olgiati from ETH Zurich and his lecture on his recent works intimately linked with global contexts. Professor Yehuda Safran from GSAPP also enlightened Mumbai's architectural historians with his fascinating lecture on the Brutalists of modern architecture, and Juan Herreros lectured on his recent array of critical work in the framework of contemporary practice.

Studio-X exhibitions engaged a wide variety of subjects ranging from the 'Collaborative Bridges' workshop looking at cross-cultural collaborations to the annual GSAPP Public Bit (PSW5) workshop led by Jenny Broutin and Kamal Farah, which involved travel to Amman, Istanbul and finally Mumbai exploring public space as the primary interface for meaningful exchanges in cities done in collaboration with students from KRVIA. GSAPP fielded a second workshop entitled 'Knowledge City' where Professors Frederic Levrat and Phillip Anzalone conducted an intense seven-day production, in collaboration with local students from the BSSA School of Architecture, which resulted in a phenomenal public installation and event along the waterfront. 'Dharavi: Places & Identities,' organized by Martina M. Spies, 'PEOPLE BUILDING BETTER CITIES' conducted by Anna Rubbo of the Earth Institute and Global Studio, a popup exhibit 'Mumbai Anthropocene: Housing, Culture and New Imaginaries of the City's Industrial Core' by University of Michigan's Mitch McEwen, took up integrative approaches to urban problems. 'Paradise Lodge', a collaborative arts project, brought alumni from Goldsmiths in London to India for a concentrated period of artistic creation, interaction and dialogue on urban life and Studio-X Mumbai's 'Architecture as an Open Process,' with the support of the Swiss Consulate, brought a collection of the studio's architectural and creative works to Studio-X, recreating the atmosphere of their workshop in Alibaug.

The agenda for 2014-15 brings the beginning of research projects through an established fellowship program helping Studio-X to develop stronger connections to local and international knowledge on urban issues.

Collaborative Bridges **A**
Innovating Public Space **B**
Knowledge City **C**
Mumbai Interface **D**

A

B

C

D

Studio-X New York
Studio-X
Fall 2013 + Spring 2014
Nicola Twilley, director,
Carlos Solis, program
coordinator

Summer 2013 brought the final travels in Studio-X NYC's flagship sixteen-month survey of the built environment and augmented landscapes of the United States, Venue. In collaboration with the Nevada Museum of Art's Center for Art + Environment, Venue concluded its exploration of America's urban hinterlands in a cross-country trajectory that encompassed underground health mines, neutrino detectors and the world's largest organism: a honey fungus in eastern Oregon. In addition to documenting its travels at v-e-n-u-e.com as well as on media partner The Atlantic's website, Venue's work was on display at the Nevada Museum of Art beginning June 13, 2014.

Back home on Varick Street, Studio-X NYC continued with its usual busy schedule of talks, workshops and events. Among the highlights were an exhibition and accompanying series of programs exploring aeriality, from the NYC air rights market to wind-engineering skyscrapers, and from air defense planning to the "Aerial Arts" of Robert Smithson and Walter de Maria. We also took a sustained look at topics as diverse as urban health, drone warfare and the architecture of abortion clinics.

Finally, we end with the good but still sad news that Studio-X NYC closed its doors at the end of the semester.

Studio-X NYC was founded by Dean Mark Wigley in 2008 as the test-site for what became the Studio-X Global Network: an off-campus space in which GSAPP could experiment with what an urban futures laboratory that was outside the school could be, think and do.

Over the years, first under the direction of Gavin Browning and then in the hands of Geoff Manaugh and Nicola Twilley, and thanks to an army of innovative collaborators, both from among the GSAPP faculty, student body and elsewhere, Studio-X NYC prototyped a series of spatial and intellectual formats to promote productive exchange: exchange between the school and the city, interdisciplinary exchange and, more recently, global exchange.

The experiment succeeded: today, as you can see documented in these pages, the Studio-X Global Network has expanded to include dynamic nodes in Rio, Istanbul, Mumbai, Johannesburg and Beijing, as well as lab outposts in Tokyo and Amman.

Thanks to shared research and programs coordinated by Marina Otero, Director of Studio-X Global Network Programming, the network now offers a unique global platform from which to consider the most pressing challenges and opportunities facing the world's cities—and one that is more and more integrated into the school's curriculum and training. Meanwhile, Studio-X NYC Director Nicola Twilley used the network as a launching pad for an innovative new Regional Foodshed Resilience practicum, to be taught concurrently at GSAPP and in Mumbai starting in September 2014.

Thank you for making this crazy experiment such a success!

Make it Happen Workshop, Don't Go Back to School **A**
Very Large Organizations: Exhibition **B**
Roundtable conversation, "A Total Reset" for Public Housing **C**
Interpretations: Critical Shifts, Marina Otero, Mark Wigley, Mark Wasiuta + Adam Bandler **D**

Studio-X Rio de Janeiro
Studio-X
Fall 2013 + Spring 2014
Pedro Rivera, director

Over the past three years, Studio-X Rio has explored and experimented with a broad spectrum of questions related to the future of cities through different sets and formats of activities. Since the opening of the space at Praça Tiradentes in the core of Rio de Janeiro, there have been over a hundred events both within its walls and spread all over the city. More than two hundred faculty and students have visited Studio-X, researched and developed proposals for Rio. Such intensity of exchange reflects the collective effort embraced by so many faculty, staff and students, as well as the other Studio-X peers and the growing network of people and institutions it has cultivated.

Today we can say that Studio-X Rio is consolidated as the most active space for architecture and urban related content events in the city. Its recognition both as a global – as a Columbia University initiative – and a local institution was the result of a strong commitment towards the challenges and aspirations of Rio de Janeiro today, carried through sincere and respectful dialogue and cooperation among people from all over.

During 2013, Studio-X Rio conducted a joint effort with ITDP Brasil and Transporte Ativo, dedicated to proposing a network of bike lanes for the downtown of Rio. The proposal was carried in a collaborative process with bicycle users, which included a series of workshops and site surveys that culminated in an exhibition and report offered to the municipality. The first kilometers of the network were already implemented, highlighting the synergistic nature of Studio-X.

Studio-X Rio also launched a series of lectures, called New Carioca Architecture, dedicated to revealing the young and talented architects working in the city today. So far there have been over twenty documented lectures, with the intention to organize exhibitions of the work.

In 2014, different programs at GSAPP were invited to join a two year flagship initiative focused on Rio das Pedras, a major favela in Rio that defies all the stereotypes about favelas. This was the first time that Urban Planning (Mazzarro and Restrepo), Architecture (Kaseman and Correa-Smith) and a joint studio by Real Estate and Architecture (Chakrabarti and Sample) engaged on the same project, with special contributions from Columbia University's School of Engineering as well as the Mailman School for Public Health. The initiative also included a whole week of lectures and activities during the Kinne trip and engaged with an array of local experts and community members.

The next chapter in the Rio das Pedras Initiative will include a summer workshop dedicated to compiling previous work, add new ideas and prepare the ground for the spring 2015 studios; a publication and a book for the same year; and conferences in Rio and New York with contributions from other Studio-X cities.

The Rio das Pedras Initiative exhibited one of the ways in which Studio-X has the potential to contribute to the academic core of the school, by identifying key opportunities for investigation and a consistent network of local collaborators, as well as benefiting Rio by engaging Columbia University in the most pressing challenges of the city.

Kinne Week Rio das Pedras Lecture Series **A**
New Carioca Architecture Series, Pedro Rivera, Jean Pierre-Martin, Célio Diniz, Duarte Vaz + Pedro Évora **B**
New Carioca Architecture Series **C**
Bicycle Urbanism, Mikael Colville-Andersen, Ciclo Rotas Lecture Series **D**
Studio Sangue Bom Mixer at Rio das Pedras CAIC High School **E**

D

E

Studio-X Tokyo
Studio-X
Fall 2013 + Spring 2014
Daisuke Hirose, director

River flows timelessly, but water never be the same. Bubbles gone and come over standing water, never being sustained long." Kamo-no-Chomei

What was has always been. What is has always been. What will be has always been." Louis I. Kahn

The world is changing. So is knowledge. The change of change – acceleration – is exponential. The University can no longer be the only place of production and dissemination of knowledge today. The University must positively open the door to be a dynamic agent to catalyze knowledge. That is the basic instinct of Studio-X Tokyo Lab.

Tokyo Lab initially started when a small group of GSAPP grads in Tokyo gathered at a Breakfast Meeting at the Hill Top Hotel with Dean Mark Wigley, who attended and provoked the International Architectural Education Summit at Tokyo University in 2009. His assertion, "We don't know what Architecture is, but still sincerely pursue after it," was outstanding, sounding like Kahn's paradox: Architecture Does Not Exist.

In Japan, it is easy for a designer to make any kind of building, as they are backed up by "Never Say No" formidable general contractors who are ready to challenge any forms, any technology limit, any material for designers. So why has Architecture become so serious an issue? Sincere dedication to darkness is the answer. James Polshek, the first Modernist Dean of Columbia, once said, "You don't need Architectural education in Japan, because you have tradition."

Studio-X Tokyo Lab's mission is bridging the gap between Certainty and Uncertainty in the twenty first century and becoming the place to pursue certainty in uncertainty as Japanese tradition suggests. All We-Xs pursue Xs; anything, anytime, anyplace, in nothing, no when and nowhere.

Code Dojo **A**
In Search of Lost Time **B**
RISE Japanese Industry **C/D**
Solomonoff + Chakrabarti
Studio Mid Review **E**
Think Big Sendai **F**

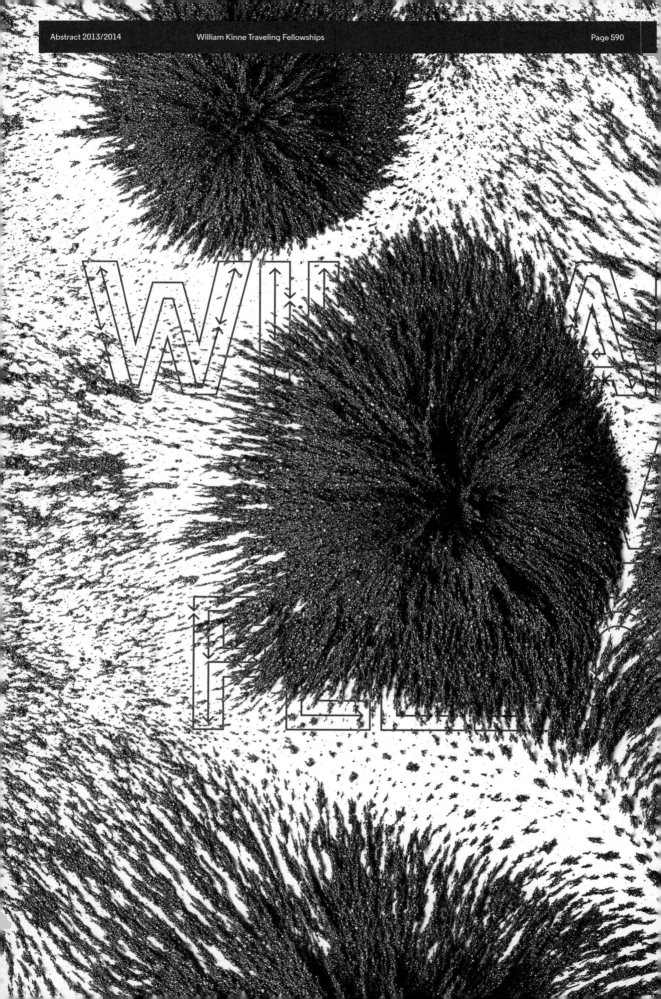

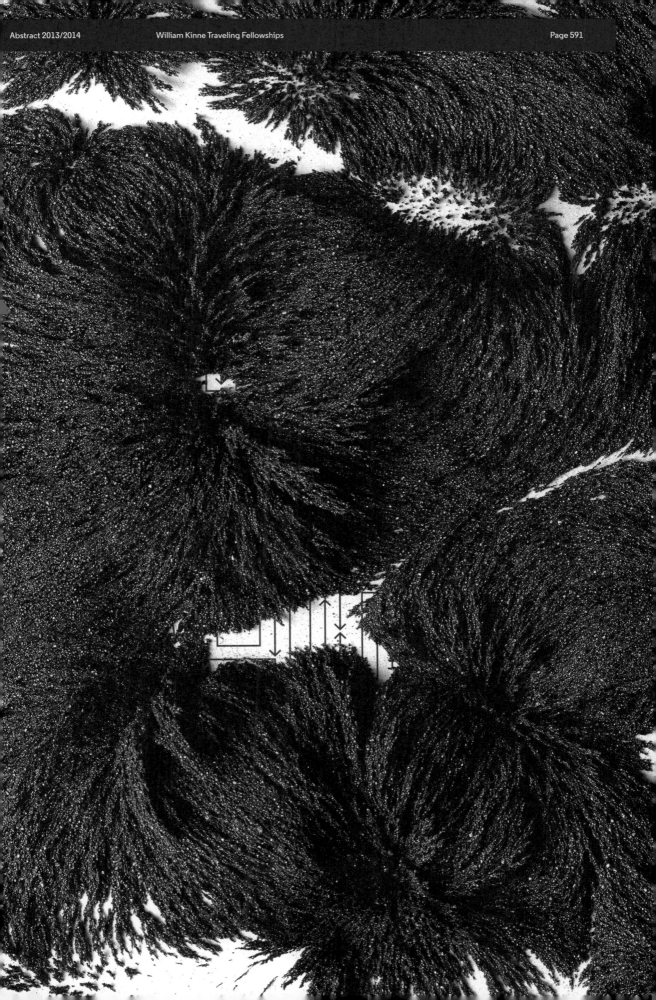

William Kinne Traveling Fellowships
Mark Wigley, dean

Traveling is one of the cores of the global university. A continuous flow of exciting ideas and people is at the heart of any radical experiment in collaborative modes of education, research and action.

The School is the beneficiary of a considerable bequest from the late William Kinne and has at its purpose the enrichment of student's education through travel. The GSAPP Committee on Fellowships and Awards decides each year how to disburse the annual interest of the William Kinne Fellows Trust, according to the following procedure: Available funds are divided among the programs in the school, proportionate to the length of each program and the number of students enrolled. This year, students completing their Masters of Architecture Degree, Advanced Architectural Design Degree, Master of Science in Urban Planning, Master of Science in Historic Preservation, Master of Science in Real Estate Development, Master of Science in Urban Design and Master of Science in Critical, Curatorial and Conceptual Practices in Architecture traveled to over 20 cities around the world, visiting all of the Studio-X locations, becoming part of the greater GSAPP global network initiative.

2013—2014 Kinne Trips

Fall 2013 Studio 5 Travel Locations (M.Arch/AAD):
Moscow, Russia [Markus Dochantschi, Phu Hoang]; Baku, Azerbaijan [Markus Dochantschi]; Amman, Jordan [Amale Andraos, Karla Rothstein]; Medellín, Colombia [Cristina Goberna]; San José, California [Michael Bell]; Tokyo, Japan [Lynne Breslin + Kunio Kudo]; Johannesburg, South Africa [Mabel Wilson]; Oslo, Norway [Craig Konyk + Jorge Otero-Pailos]; Bangkok, Thailand [François Roche]; Istanbul, Turkey [Phu Hoang]

Fall 2013 M.S. Urban Planning Travel Locations:
Kansas City, Kansas; San Francisco, California; Raleigh, North Carolina; Bear Run, Pennsylvania; Shandong, China; Tokyo, Japan; Beijing, China; Shenzhen, China; Xi'an, China; Singapore, Republic of Singapore; Henan, China; Oslo, Norway; Munich, Germany; Berlin, Germany; Stockholm, Sweden; Edinburgh, Scotland. [Trisha Logan, Andrew Dolkart + Pamela Jerome]

Spring 2014 Studio 4 Travel Locations (M.Arch):
Hong Kong, China [Kazys Varnelis + Jochen Hartmann]; Tokyo, Japan [Toru Hasegawa + Mark Collins]; Long Island, New York [Bob Marino]; Zürich, Switzerland [Scott Marble + Laura Kurgan]; Stuttgart, Germany [Scott Marble + Laura Kurgan]; Houston, Texas [Michael Morris]

Spring 2014 Studio 6 Travel Locations (M.Arch/AAD):
Rio de Janeiro, Brazil [Hilary Sample + Vishaan Chakrabarti; Keith Kaseman + Noah Levy; Galia Solomonoff + Amy Maresko; Markus Dochantschi + Caroline Ihle]; Brasilia, Brazil [Markus Dochantschi + Caroline Ihle]; Bogotá, Colombia [Steven Holl + Dimitra Tsachrelia]; Beirut, Lebanon [Mark Wasiuta]; Amman, Jordan [Mark Wasiuta; Craig Konyk + Nina Kolowratnik]; Doha, Qatar [Mark Wasiuta]; Johannesburg, South Africa [Mario Gooden, Carson Smuts + Mokena Makeka; Ada Tolla, Giuseppe Lignano + Thomas de Monchaux]; Tokyo, Japan [Leslie Gill + Mike Jacobs; Jeffrey Inaba + Benedict Clouette]; Istanbul, Turkey [Lise Anne Couture, Jessica Ngan + Rob Eleazar; David Smiley + Kyle Hovenkotter; Shahira Fahmy + Emanuel Admassu]; Beijing, China [Jeffrey Johnson + Pei Zhu]; Cairo, Egypt [Shahira Fahmy + Emanuel Admassu]; Mumbai, India [Juan Herreros, Diana Cristóbal + Maria Esnaola; Frederic Levrat, Phillip Anzalone + Angie Heo]; Zürich, Switzerland [David Benjamin]; Stuttgart, Germany [David Benjamin]; Paris, France [Michael Bell + Zachary Kostura; Enrique Walker]; Marseille, France [Michael Bell + Zachary Kostura]; Lausanne, Switzerland [Enrique Walker]; Jerusalem, Israel [Craig Konyk + Nina Kolowratnik]

Spring 2014 M.S. Urban Planning Travel Locations:
Port of Spain, Trinidad and Tobago [Clara Irazábal + Natalie Quinn]; Tokyo, Japan [Emily Matsumoto + Emily Gordon]; Rio de Janeiro, Brazil [Alejandro de Castro Mazarro, Marcela Tovar, Anne Krassner + Daniela Atwell]; Mumbai, India [Trevor Atwell] Portland, Oregon [Trisha Logan]; Miami, Florida [Trisha Logan]

Real Estate Development Travel Locations:
Beijing, China [Chuck Laven]

M.S. Urban Design Travel Locations:
Delhi, India; Kisumu, Kenya; Medellín, Colombia

M.S. Historic Preservation Travel Locations:
Indianapolis, Indiana; Bear Run, Pennsylvania; Chicago, Illinois; Boston, Massachusetts; Philadelphia, Pennsylvania; Santa Cruz, California; Nashville, Tennessee; Seoul, Korea; Rome, Italy; Darwen, England; London, England, York; New Delhi, India. [Trisha Logan, George Wheeler, Andrew Dolkart + Pamela Jerome]

CCCP Thesis Travel:
Texas, United States [Caitlin Blanchfield]; Mexico City, Mexico [Elis Mendoza]; San Salvador, El Salvador [Sabrina Wirth]; Cairo, Egypt [Ashraf Abdalla]; Istanbul, Turkey [Javaira, Shahid]; Madrid, Spain [Javier Anton]; Johannesburg, South Africa [Tanya Gershon]; India [Devina, Kirloskar]

Hasegawa + Collins Studio, Tokyo, Japan **A/E**
Konyk + Kolowratnik Studio, Amman, Jordan **B/C**
Johnson + Zhu Studio, Beijing, China **D/F**
Konyk + Kolowratnik Studio, Jerusalem, Israel **G/H**
Sao Paulo, Brazil **I/J**
Brasilia, Brazil **K**
Dochantschi + Ihle Studio, Brasilia, Brazil **L**
Gill + Jacobs Studio, Tokyo, Japan **M**
Dochantschi + Ihle Studio, Rio de Janeiro, Brazil **N**

G

H

I

J